VOCATIONS OF POLITICAL THEORY

Jason A. Frank and John Tambornino, Editors

VOCATIONS *of*

POLITICAL THEORY

University of

Minnesota Press

Minneapolis London

The University of Minnesota Press gratefully acknowledges permission to reprint material from chapter 1, which contains an excerpt from the article "A New Credo: Make Money, Not War," by Barbara Crossette, *New York Times* (24 August 1997): section 4, p. 1. Copyright The New York Times Company; reprinted by permission.

Published by the University of Minnesota Press
111 Third Avenue South, Suite 290
Minneapolis, MN 55401-2520
http://www.upress.umn.edu

Printed in the United States of America on acid-free paper

Library of Congress Cataloging-in-Publication Data
Vocations of political theory/Jason A. Frank and John Tambornino, editors.
   p. cm.
  Includes index.
  ISBN 0-8166-3537-4 (hc)—ISBN 0-8166-3538-2 (pbk.)
  1. Political science. I. Frank, Jason A. II. Tambornino, John, 1968–
JA71 .V63 2000
320'.023—dc21   00-008267

11 10 09 08 07 06 05 04 03 02 01 00   10 9 8 7 6 5 4 3 2 1

CONTENTS

ACKNOWLEDGMENTS

This volume grew out of the conference "Vocations of Political Theory" held at The Johns Hopkins University, February 27–28, 1998. We thank the University for its generous financial and institutional support; William Connolly, Matthew Crenson, Richard Flathman, Kirstie McClure, and Sheldon Wolin for their encouragement, advice, and assistance; Marge Collignon, Evelyn Stoller, and Lisa Williams for their administrative support; and the many graduate students in the Department of Political Science who helped, especially Jacqueline Best, Vicki Hsueh, Michelle McLaurin, Davide Panagia, Paul Saurette, Nicholas Tampio, Kathryn Trevenen, and Paul Winke. For helping to make the volume a reality we thank (in some cases, a second time) Mark Brown, Lisa Disch, Tom Dumm, Peter Euben, William Connolly, Matthew Crenson, Richard Flathman, Kirstie McClure, Melissa Orlie, Morton Schoolman, and Sandy Thatcher. Finally, we thank Carrie Mullen and Robin A. Moir at the University of Minnesota Press for their interest and patience.

JASON A. FRANK AND JOHN TAMBORNINO

INTRODUCTION

Calling in Question

*The calling is not a call that has gone by, but one that has gone out and
as such is still calling and inviting; it calls even if it makes no sound.*[1]
—Martin Heidegger, *What Is Called Thinking?*

I

A paradox of postwar political theory is that periodic assessments of its current state, often expressing disappointment, anguish, and lament, are so vig-
orous and provocative as to belie the assessments.[2] Moreover, the answers
these assessments offer to the question "What should political theory be?" or
"What is the 'nature' of political theory?" are seldom conclusive. This is as it
should be. As Sheldon Wolin wrote in the opening pages of *Politics and Vision*
(1960), such demands for final definition or resolution cannot be met in the
case of political theory or political philosophy. This mode of thinking does
not have "an essence with an eternal nature. . . . No single philosopher and
no one historical age can be said to have defined it conclusively, any more
than any one painter or school of painting has practiced all that we mean by
painting."[3]

There are, of course, numerous postwar theorists who have offered timeless definitions of political philosophy; those, such as Leo Strauss, who have
understood it as the perennial concern to "replace *opinion* about the nature
of political things by *knowledge* of the nature of political things."[4] Such
ahistorical definitions of political philosophy seek to establish clear boundaries for thinking, thereby excluding serious consideration of work outside
of those boundaries. Thus Mark Lilla, in a recent article on Jacques Derrida,
describes postwar French thought (with the exception of Raymond Aron) as
symptomatic of the general decline of twentieth-century political philosophy,
as it has failed to provide "disciplined and informed reflection about a recog-

nizable domain called politics."[5] Yet this demand that political philosophy focus on an immediately "recognizable domain" is too confining. It limits political philosophy to preconceived and seemingly unchanging conceptual boundaries—what counts as "political" is assumed rather than explored and argued for. Rather than assuming that the domain of politics is settled and fixed, political theory should include ongoing consideration of what counts as politics, of what is to be included in the domain of the political.

The concerns animating this volume—the character and status of contemporary political theory, its place in the academy and its role in public life—do not presuppose such clear lines of inclusion and exclusion. Rather, like Wolin, the contributors treat political theory as a situated mode of thinking, one that changes over time in response to changes in political, intellectual, and cultural contexts. Nevertheless, political theories and theorists do bear an important relation to one another, possessing a family resemblance (for Wolin, a "continuity of preoccupations")[6] as they address not only the novelty of their particular context, but also political problems and concerns that appear, in some form, in various contexts.

Unlike some historians of political thought, the contributors to this volume do not believe that political theory is exhausted by the context of its production, that it is of little use in the face of present perplexities, that "we must learn to do our thinking for ourselves."[7] Working between the Scylla of philosophical universalism and the Charybdis of historicism, the contributors revisit major past thinkers in order to return to the question of political theory's vocation—a question poignantly posed by Wolin thirty years ago—in light of the dizzying changes that have ensued since then. In doing so, contributors attend to both "continuity" and "innovation" in political thinking.

Before John Rawls's *A Theory of Justice* (1971), a work often credited with the revival of political theory in postwar America, and amid widespread declarations of the end of ideology and the death of political theory,[8] Wolin inaugurated a probing reassessment and redeployment of political theory, exploring its relation to the academy in which it resided and to the public it addressed. In his influential essay "Political Theory as a Vocation" (1969), Wolin argued that theory (and the *bios theoretikos*), far more than method (and the *vita methodi*), is attuned to the fluctuating circumstances and vicissitudes of politics, it appreciates the subtleties of tacit political knowledge, and it enlarges and sharpens political vision.[9] Against the then reigning

behavioralism and methodism of American social science, with its reductionist accounts of the political and its complicity with the status quo, Wolin
argued that the vocation of political theory lay not only in its concern for the
res publica and the sense that contemporary political arrangements are "systematically mistaken." It lay also in the ability of theory to sharpen judgment and to attend to the complexities of political life. Political theorists do
not offer salvational "gifts to the demos"—philosophical foundations, rules,
codes, or institutional designs that spare the polity the difficulties of actual
political engagement.[10] Nor should theorists engage in self-absorbed intellectual activity, concerned only with the work of other theorists, completely
removed from the world of politics.[11] Rather, political theorists offer a political education in the "subtle, complex interplay between political experience
and thought," facilitating nuanced, nonformulaic political judgment.[12] As
such, Wolin outlined a vocation for political theory that did not suppress,
displace, or overcome politics, but that attended to the ongoing challenges of
thoughtful political action.[13]

What has become of this vocation? As Wolin's essay for this volume attests,
the contemporary political context has transformed the answers that might
be provided to this question and, more fundamentally, challenges our ability to speak of a "vocation" at all.[14] Wolin's earlier reflections resonate with
Weber's influential discussions of the "vocations" of science and politics, and
distinguish political theory's "vocation" from the narrow economism of the
"professions."[15] Yet Wolin no doubt meant for the term to resonate more
widely than this. According to the *Oxford English Dictionary,* "vocation" origi-
nates in a Latin noun of action, *vocare,* meaning to call or to summon. Its
oldest and predominant English usage signified the Pauline conception of a
divine calling, but during the fifteenth and sixteenth centuries the term increasingly referred also to the activities of everyday life. As Weber noted in
The Protestant Ethic and the Spirit of Capitalism, the Reformation's devaluation
of monastic asceticism and its emphasis on the sanctity of worldly acts (what
Charles Taylor has aptly characterized as its "affirmation of ordinary life") led
to an intensive commingling of the secular and the sacred.[16]

"Vocation" came to mean any position ordained by God, and eventually to
mean any social station or function (e.g., soldier or craftsman) underwritten
by divine order. Even in its relatively secularized later usage, "vocation" implied the existence of an established and integrated social order: one's vocation is a position to which one is called by the social order of which one is

a part. This fusion of the divine and the ordinary lurks within the solemnity and piety still conveyed by the term.

In *Politics and Vision* Wolin discusses vocation when emphasizing the values of unity and cohesion in Calvin's conception of the church and of the political community, and the way in which stability and order required civil law, political institutions, and a "system of vocations."[17] Vocations, involving distinctions of status and eminence, and of office and obligation, would prevent individuals

> from wallowing in "universal confusion." They outfitted the individual with a sort of social map, a sense of direction "that he might not wander about in uncertainty the rest of his days."[18]

Few political theorists today have not, at some point, wallowed in confusion or wandered in uncertainty. This is in part because social orders of the sort Calvin had in mind are hard to identify. Indeed, the very existence of integrated social orders has been challenged by recent political theorists. What Ernesto Laclau describes as the "impossibility of society"—the impossibility of a clearly bounded and integrated sociopolitical order—seems to undermine the ability to speak of a vocation, properly understood, including that of political theory.[19] Wolin himself, returning to the question of political theory's vocation in his essay in this volume, contends that in the present era of rapid technological and economic change, political theorists have difficulty knowing whom or what to address, leaving them bereft of a sense of calling, vertiginous in their lack of direction.

The leisurely pace assumed by most theorists to be necessary for political reflection also seems to be under assault, as what Paul Virilio terms the "violence of speed" has come to pervade everyday experience.[20] Accelerating tempos (and such recent governmental manifestations as "fast-track" negotiations) outpace the slower temporalities of political deliberation, and reduce our capacity for effective intervention and thoughtful action. As Wolin recently put it, today "political time is out of synch with the temporalities, rhythms, and pace governing economy and culture. Political time, especially in societies with pretensions to democracy, requires an element of leisure."[21] In our era of high speed and constant change, Wolin argues below, theory's attempt to keep up, to be equally fast-moving and productive, may lead it to mimic the very forces that endanger it. It may also lead political theory away from its long-standing presumptions regarding the connection of politics to place. The promise of a democratic politics freed of spatial limits has found both defenders and detractors among contemporary political theorists (including contributors to this volume), dividing those who seek new political possibilities within these transformations from those who lament the disappearance of common public space.[22]

Further conditions impinging on contemporary political theory are familiar to today's theorists: the collapse of socialism; the institutionalization of neoconservative thought and the apotheosis of "the economy"; the decline of state sovereignty and of the institutions of democratic accountability; increased capital, population, and information flows; ecological destruction; the resurgence of ethnic conflict and religious fundamentalism; and the proliferation of micropolitical movements too easily reduced to the category "identity politics." How these conditions, and their impact on the academy and on public life, might be assessed and critically engaged by political theorists is a theme in the essays to follow, one addressed at varying degrees of specificity and abstraction.

It is, needless to say, impossible in the space of this introduction to trace the impact of these conditions on contemporary political theory, and on the academy and public life in general. Nevertheless, two developments should be noted, both of which relate to questions of the parameters of the political mentioned above. The first might be characterized as the *proliferation of the political* in recent critical writing, academic and otherwise. Most closely associated with the flourishing of Cultural Studies in the United States, this proliferation emerges not only from feminists' compelling claim that the "personal is political," but also from Michel Foucault's portrait of social relations saturated with power. On these accounts, the political is located not only on the macropolitical level of state institutions, but throughout the micropolitical level as well, in various cultural formations and subject positions.

The proliferation of the political has led to a second theoretical development, what Chantal Mouffe characterizes as the *return of the political.* By this she means the primacy of politics itself to recent theoretical work—the open, ongoing public contestation of an array of issues—rather than its containment within the coded realm of the ethical.[23] Although this "return" has often been debated in terms of the (re)emergence of antifoundational political thought, the essays that follow presume, for the most part, an antifoundational position, pursuing questions that lie beyond the foundation/

antifoundation debates of the 1980s. These two developments have contributed to the flourishing of political theory over the past two decades, but they have also posed a number of difficulties for theorists. Indeed, they are precisely the developments criticized by Wolin in his lead essay. Stated simply, if everything is political then the term loses its meaning. Moreover, what becomes of political theory when there is a plethora of theory in the academy, nearly all of which is presented as in some way "political"?

The constitution, clarification, and renewal of "the political" are paramount in Wolin's work, and are presented as fundamental concerns of both political theory and political action. Crucially, for Wolin the political concerns matters that are *public* and *common,* matters of general, shared concern to a community or collectivity.[24] The extent to which political theorists can speak meaningfully and coherently of the political, while loosening its distinctiveness and assumptions of publicity and commonality, is treated (without consensus) by a number of the contributors.

The decline of positivism and behavioralism, which has coincided suggestively with these developments in the academy, has also contributed to political theory's sense of uncertainty, since political theory has often defined itself in opposition to these positions. As Mark Reinhardt recently wrote, the "tacit settlement" established between political theorists and political scientists during the 1970s, wherein theorists were to serve as custodians of the "old texts," leaving "'the real world'" to their empirical colleagues, has been undone.[25] This has resulted from both the increasingly theoretical work of political scientists (especially rational choice and game theory) and the empirical turn of much contemporary theory (particularly studies in political culture, which see "texts" in all spheres of social life).[26] The proliferation of the political, and the accompanying loosening of disciplinary and subdisciplinary boundaries, has surely enlivened political theory. But it also poses questions as to the identity of political theory, and challenges us to discern anew its above-noted "continuity of preoccupations."

One such continuity may be discerned in the troubled interaction between political theory and politics itself. Self-criticism among political theorists (not to mention criticism presented by nontheorists) frequently concerns itself with contemporary political theory's remove from "real" politics, with what appears to be its increased abstraction and limited relevance. Jeffrey Isaac has thematized this as political theory's "strange silence" in the face of recent political events, especially the epoch-defining fall of the Soviet Bloc.

Although the force of this challenge must be acknowledged (and is acknowledged by a number of the contributors), we question the assumption that political theory should avoid straying from direct engagement with current events, that it had best concern itself with immediate, practical matters and restrict itself to familiar political vocabularies. Certainly a good deal of political theory can and should do this, but restricting political theory to immediate, practical matters prevents it from achieving the distance often needed to gain purchase on our present situation, and to suggest unfamiliar terms and unforeseen possibilities.[27]

Indeed, the events of 1989, which Isaac suggests might serve to orient political theorists, have also contributed to the disorientation and uncertainty we wish to emphasize. Changes in the thinking of Vaclav Havel—who is often presented as the exemplary political intellectual and actor, and contrasted with North American political theorists—are revealing on this point. Havel's earlier writings commend "living within the truth," "politics and conscience," and "total dedication," and often convey moral clarity, indignation, and precise attributions of responsibility. Yet his postrevolutionary writings increasingly emphasize the "'postmodern'" condition, the dangers of "arrogant rationality" and the "cult of objectivity," "'otherness'" and "difference," and the "mysterious complexity of Being."[28] Far from a simple realism or pragmatism, or from preoccupation with immediate, practical matters, politics is conceived as a searching, uncertain "art of the *impossible*." Thoughtful, humane politics, for Havel, must never become deaf to the call of Being.

Attention to the continual emergence of unforeseen possibilities may reconfigure the "calling" of political theory—a calling no longer dependent on the sanction of divine command or on an integrated social order. Such a calling may no longer be a "vocation," in its earlier sense. In *What Is Called Thinking?* Heidegger gestures toward a calling that has neither a point of origin nor a manifest destination, and toward a mode of thinking that *responds* to the calling without asserting a final answer. This mode of thinking is a questioning, but one that loosens the imperative of resolution; unlike Cartesian doubt, this mode of thinking involves, crucially, "questioning the questioner." If the calling of political theory no longer provides a map or sense of direction to keep us from wandering about in uncertainty, our conversation about and around this elusive calling may nevertheless offer provisional orientation. Our responses to the calling of political theory may illuminate and extend its continuity of preoccupations, thereby keeping the calling alive.

The essays in this volume, written by both emerging political theorists and those well-established, respond to this calling. They possess connections and tensions so numerous as to make summary difficult. Nevertheless, in what follows we trace the contours of these discussions and explain the order in which we have arranged the essays. Although the volume is not a Festschrift for Wolin, all of the essays bear some relation (in places, highly critical) to his work, and most refer and respond to his lead essay for the volume. The dialogues between Wolin and the other contributors not only set the framework for the volume, but also challenge some of Wolin's less optimistic conclusions. They do so by demonstrating that political theory is very much alive today, and that significant political possibilities remain to be explored and theorized.

Revisiting the arguments he made thirty years ago in "Political Theory as a Vocation," Wolin concludes that political theory today should concern itself less with vocation than with *invocation*. While vocation suggests a calling to practice or action, invocation suggests *recalling* memories and losses. As such, invocation calls us to reflect on political theory's inauguration in loss. Such concern with loss, with the defeated and the disappeared, is necessary in a world in which, paradoxically, the single constant is change, in which innovation itself has been routinized and normalized. Wolin argues that the social sciences and humanities have themselves contributed to this dramatic development since his initial essay. Whereas "Political Theory as a Vocation" was a call to theorize in a discipline defined by unreflective positivism and conservatism, Wolin now warns us of our tendency to "overtheorize," to produce theory in quantities and varieties analogous to the rapid, flexible production of consumer goods. Such overproduction of theory contributes to the overproduction of politics, to what we have described as its proliferation.

Once innovation, and the production, marketing, and distribution of theory and politics, become constant, we seem to be in a situation that lies beyond anomalies, crises, and turning points. The transcendence of crisis, while often described (and celebrated by Frances Fukuyama and others) in terms of the "end of history," is better described, Wolin suggests, as an impoverished, dangerously "postpolitical" age. Consequently, the task of political theory may be to invoke that which has been defeated but has not wholly disappeared, to recall the traditions, practices, and beliefs that have not survived the triumphs of modernity, and that provide critical counterpoints to it.

This task is further evaluated in the second section, "Theorizing Loss." Concern with the defeated that has not wholly disappeared, with forgotten wrongs and injustices, with the ghosts "haunting" modern progress, is also central to Wendy Brown's "Specters and Angels at the End of History." Drawing on Derrida and Benjamin, Brown reflects on how, like the Angelus Novus, the "storm of progress" blows us into the future, leaving us incapable of knowing our point of destination or of directing the storm to fit our chosen ends. In such a predicament, our relations to past and future are ones of bewilderment and anxiety, narratives of progress are no longer convincing, and the future no longer promises to be a site of justice. Given this, political theorists must reconsider how different forms of historical consciousness enable or constrain present political thinking, and how they may provide new avenues for political action. In particular, Brown argues against a "Left melancholia" still attached to history and its attendant "ideal of revolutionary possibility." The melancholiac seeks to recover losses but is blind to how, in Benjamin's words, every historical moment, including one defined by the uncertainty of increased temporality, "has its own revolutionary chance." Brown urges us to respond to this condition by "cultivat[ing] memory while we foster a means of 'gaily parting with the past.'"

In "The Politics of Nostalgia and Theories of Loss," J. Peter Euben continues with the themes of the theoretical and political dimensions of loss. He strives to articulate a conception of political nostalgia that is, in Brown's terms, nonmelancholic, and that is free of *ressentiment* and the longing for lost purity. Euben observes that whereas philosophy begins with a sense of wonder, political theory begins with a sense of loss. In Western political theory there have been various responses to constitutive loss. Euben elaborates four of these responses (terming them synchronic, philosophic, perspectival, and diachronic) and carefully reveals their connections. In contrast to Brown's turn to Derrida's "haunting" and Benjamin's "dialectical image," Euben suggests that the most promising response to loss may be found in Machiavelli's political perspectivism. The longing for political renewal evident in Machiavelli's republicanism should not be reduced to a longing for pure origin untainted by political conflict. Rather, it is a longing invigorated by the promise of renewed agonistic contestation over the moment of political founding, by the democratic promise of fashioning and refashioning the political world.

Brown's and Euben's reflections on the temporal complexities of political theory, and the significance of historical consciousness for political action, lead to the section "Thinking in Time." Russell Arben Fox's "Can Theorists Make Time for Belief?" probes the temporal dimensions of contemporary political theory and politics with attention to religious belief—the "other" in narratives of progress and secularization. Modern, secular politics is largely a "disbelieving discourse," Fox argues, and is most deeply disbelieving in its constitution of time. Though seldom criticized, presumptions of disbelief marginalize believers in political discourse, and make fundamental religious belief a difference beyond negotiation, one that cannot be assimilated to even the most "neutral" procedures and deliberations. Moreover, secular temporal presumptions insulate fundamental features of modernity—of human life conceived as management without end—from some of the most radical theoretical and political challenges. Considering how religious beliefs, and their alternative temporalities, might be incorporated into political theory need not entail rejection of secular temporality, but it helps us think about and negotiate the costs of being put on "modernity's clock."

In "The History of Political Thought as a 'Vocation': A Pragmatist Defense," David Paul Mandell also considers how political theorists might enter into dialogue with the past in order to better understand the present and identify future possibilities. Observing the inadequacies of Quentin Skinner's historicism, in which the past is categorically separated from the present and thus is of no use as a resource, and Richard Rorty's pragmatism, in which past and present are only casually distinguished, Mandell turns to John Dewey's historical pragmatism. In Dewey's pragmatism, exemplified in his reconstructions of classical liberalism, problem-solving involves understanding the past in order to determine which aspects of it are best preserved and which are best overcome. In such efforts, the historically minded political theorist is something of an "intellectual coalition-builder," sifting through that which has been preserved and that which has been forgotten, assembling elements so as to equip us in our present predicament. In contrast to Wolin, Mandell urges political theorists to reconsider their objections to "methodism," and to be more concerned with solving the practical problems of everyday life than with offering "epic" political visions. Moreover, in contrast to the authors of many of the surrounding essays, Mandell remains optimistic regarding the possibilities for reconstructing and reinvigorating liberalism, especially its notions of progress.

Mandell's concern—the relation of the past to the everyday, often mundane problems in the present—leads into the fourth section, "Politics and the

Ordinary." Thomas L. Dumm's "Political Theory for Losers" resonates with the concerns of Wolin, Brown, and Euben, as he considers how democratic theorists might negotiate the irreducibility of loss. Rather than longing for heroic acts of recovery, Dumm pursues these concerns through a distinctly Cavellian politics of "the ordinary." Drawing on Ralph Waldo Emerson's and W. E. B. Du Bois's accounts of tragic personal loss (of their sons), Dumm considers how losses and unexpected turns of fortune, especially those occurring on the cusp of public and private life, chasten theoretical hubris while also revealing politics to be part of everyday experience. Everyday experience—the often uncanny realm of the ordinary—can itself provide resources for democratic politics. Consequently, political thinking is not only about collective crises, which Dumm takes to be Wolin's primary concern, but equally about ordinary living and the everyday challenges of continuing in the face of loss. Dumm warns that "to cast off the everyday so as to engage in the epochal is a step that democratic thinkers cannot afford to take."

In a similar vein, Linda M. G. Zerilli's "Feminism's Flight from the Ordinary" attempts to make sense of the widespread criticism that feminist theory—with its abstract concepts and occasionally arcane debates—fails to comprehend the ordinary life of women. Drawing on Wittgenstein, Zerilli considers how the "'craving for generality'" involves a "'contemptuous attitude towards the particular case,'" and how even theorists she would largely endorse, such as Judith Butler, do not always attend to the limitations of theory for feminist politics. Instead of calling for further clarification of concepts, or for a more thorough account of the social construction of gender, Zerilli questions the imperative that feminist theory explain why the world is as it is and what must be done to change it. More generally, Zerilli comes to stress, as did Arendt, that politics is more about *acting* than about knowing.

Zerilli's considerations of the tenuous relationships between epistemology and politics, and between theory and practice, are further elaborated in the essays comprising the fifth section, "Political Knowledge." Mark Brown's "Conceptions of Science in Political Theory: A Tale of Cloaks and Daggers" is an effort—long overdue—to rethink the relationship of political theory to natural science. Focusing on the work of Wolin, particularly his appropriation of Thomas Kuhn, Brown details the extent to which political theorists have defined themselves in opposition to natural scientists, but have done so in contradictory ways. On the one hand, theorists have insulated themselves from the methodological imperialism of science with the Aristotelian claim that questions of politics are essentially different from those of science. On the other hand, theorists have drawn on postpositivist philosophies of science to argue that science is no less perspectival and constructed than political theory. Each of these strategies has led political theorists to ignore the specificities of scientific practice and its effects on politics. Turning to the work of Bruno Latour, especially his notions of "hybrid artifacts" and "actor networks," Brown considers possibilities for integrating scientific findings and the study of scientific practice into political theory. Doing so would reconfigure the boundaries between academic disciplines and allow us to view science as a potential site of politics.

A complementary effort to loosen the distinction between political theory and political practice, and its attendant disciplinary distinction between theoretical and empirical knowledge, is found in Lon Troyer's "Political Theory as a Provocation: An Ethos of Political Theory." Through an examination and criticism of Wolin's distinction between theory and method, and his reading of Foucault, Troyer argues that political theory should be defined less by its form or content than by its *stance*—as a restless provocation within an often conservative discipline.

By examining the relation of the academy to popular culture and social struggle, a position parallel to that of Troyer is advanced by Shane Gunster in "Gramsci, Organic Intellectuals, and Cultural Studies: Lessons for Political Theorists." Gunster begins with Stuart Hall's hope that British cultural studies "find an institutional practice . . . that might produce an organic intellectual," in order to consider how the theoretical frameworks and intellectual practices of cultural studies might help connect academic political theory to social movements. Echoing Wolin at points, Gunster argues that if political theory wishes to be critical it must become more "organic," as its current remove from emancipatory social struggles—the result in part of its specialized vocabularies and inward-looking tendencies—amounts to a crisis in thinking and politics. In such a crisis the organic intellectual is a compelling ideal, as it recognizes both the importance of developing theory in the academy and the need for relevance to social movements outside the academy.

The essays by Brown, Troyer, and Gunster lead into the final section, "Practicing Political Theory." This section presents noteworthy examples of *doing* political theory—in a manner that crosses disciplinary boundaries and employs canonical thinkers to illuminate political issues resonating far beyond the academy. Samantha Frost's "Reading the Body: Hobbes, Body Politics, and the Vocation of Political Theory" returns to an endlessly interpreted thinker (a thinker, she argues, revealingly *mis*interpreted), drawing our attention to Hobbes's notion of "thinking-bodies" in order to shed light on contemporary questions of corporeality, materiality, subjectivity, and difference. Not only does returning to Hobbes enrich and sharpen our thinking on these matters, but it demonstrates the extent to which "familiar" thinkers remain unsettling and provocative.

Jill Locke's "Work, Shame, and the Chain Gang: The New Civic Education" relies on the insights of contemporary political theory to illuminate recent developments in public policy in the United States. In particular, Locke examines the growing concern with "shamelessness," embodied in policies that aim to order and educate a public bereft of a common ground by subjecting "shameless" citizens to public vision and censure. This is seen most dramatically in the resurgence of chain-gang labor to punish prisoners and admonish the public, as laborers function as objects through which Americans of disparate persuasions patch together some notion of the common. Questioning this imperative of commonality, Locke examines how it is secured by the state and how, unlike some of its earlier manifestations, it resists resignification.

Finally, in "The Nobility of Democracy" William E. Connolly returns to a now "canonical" figure, Nietzsche, who is at the center of heated interpretive disputes. Connolly explores the respects in which Nietzsche's treatments of inequality and difference, of the significance of corporeality in political thinking and ethics, and of a pathos of connection across cultural distance and difference, may provide inspiration for democrats. Connolly also returns to the opening theme of temporality, considering the respects in which the increased speed in many domains of life may be, in sharp contrast to Wolin's conclusions, *conducive* to equality and democracy. It may be so in that it alerts us to the contingency of identities and hierarchies that otherwise would be seen as natural. "When the pace of life accelerates, nature ceases and becomes art." In exploring these possibilities, Connolly advances recent efforts to fashion a post-Nietzschean conception of democracy sufficient to late modern conditions.

This introduction is not meant to confine or delimit the essays to follow; it should soon become clear to the reader that their connections and tensions are even more numerous than suggested here. And our brief portrait of the current intellectual and political terrain is done in necessarily broad strokes.

We have attempted only to stage some of the discussions and disagreements that follow, ones that we hope will continue beyond the parameters of this volume. Together, these essays envision new avenues for theorizing politics in the face of contemporary uncertainties. The orientation they provide, though provisional, may help us to respond to the challenges these uncertainties pose.

NOTES

1. Martin Heidegger, *What Is Called Thinking?* trans. J. G. Gray (New York: Harper & Row, 1968), 124.

2. Such assessments include Arnold S. Kaufman, "The Nature and Function of Political Theory," *Journal of Politics* 5 (1954); Leo Strauss, *What Is Political Philosophy and Other Studies* (New York: Free Press, 1959); Sheldon S. Wolin, *Politics and Vision: Continuity and Innovation in Western Political Thought* (Boston: Little, Brown and Company, 1960); Isaiah Berlin, "Does Political Theory Still Exist?" *Concepts and Categories: Philosophical Essays,* ed. Henry Hardy (London: Hogarth Press, 1978), 143–72; George Kateb, *Political Theory: Its Nature and Uses* (New York: St. Martin's Press, 1968); Sheldon S. Wolin, "Political Theory as a Vocation," *American Political Science Review* 63 (1969): 1062–82; Glenn Tinder, *Political Thinking: The Perennial Questions* (Boston: Little, Brown and Company, 1979); Brian Barry, "The Strange Death of Political Philosophy," *Democracy, Power and Justice: Essays in Political Theory* (Oxford: Clarendon Press, 1989 [written in 1979]), 11–23; Melvin Richter, ed., *Political Theory and Political Education* (Princeton: Princeton University Press, 1980); John S. Nelson, ed., *What Should Political Theory Be Now?* (Albany: State University of New York Press, 1983); David Miller and Larry Siedentop, eds., *The Nature of Political Theory* (Oxford: Clarendon Press, 1983); Terence Ball, "Introduction," *Idioms of Inquiry: Critique and Renewal in Political Science,* ed. Terence Ball (Albany: State University of New York Press, 1987), 1–10; Benjamin Barber, *The Conquest of Politics: Liberal Philosophy in Democratic Times* (Princeton: Princeton University Press, 1988); Tracy B. Strong, *The Idea of Political Theory: Reflections on the Self in Political Time and Space* (Notre Dame: University of Notre Dame Press, 1990); Terence Ball, "Whither Political Theory?" *Political Science: Looking to the Future,* vol. 1, ed. William Crotty (Evanston: Northwestern University Press, 1991), 57–76; David Held, ed., *Political Theory Today* (Stanford: Stanford University Press, 1991); John G. Gunnell, *The Descent of Political Theory: The Genealogy of an American Vocation* (Chicago: University of Chicago Press, 1993); and Jeffrey C. Isaac, "The Strange Silence of Political Theory," *Political Theory* 23, no. 4 (1995): 636–52. Also see the responses to Isaac's essay in the same issue.

3. Wolin, *Politics and Vision*, 1–2. Or, as Nietzsche contends, "all concepts in which an entire process is semiotically concentrated elude definition; only that which has no history is definable." Friedrich Nietzsche, *On the Genealogy of Morals*, trans. Walter Kaufmann (New York: Vintage Books, 1989), 80.

4. Leo Strauss, "What Is Political Philosophy?" in Hilail Gildin, ed., *An Introduction to Political Philosophy: Ten Essays by Leo Strauss* (Detroit: Wayne State University Press, 1989), 3–58, 5 (italics added). By using the terms "political philosophy" and "political theory" interchangeably we reject Strauss's distinction between them. Hannah Arendt emphasizes that political thought, in contrast to political philosophy, is guided by "living experience" and faces the vicissitudes of political action. See "The Gap between Past and Future," in *Between Past and Future* (New York: Penguin, 1977), 3–15; and *The Human Condition* (Chicago: University of Chicago Press, 1958), 220–30.

5. Mark Lilla, "The Politics of Jacques Derrida," *New York Review of Books* 45 (June 25, 1998), 36–41, 36.

6. Wolin, *Politics and Vision*, 3.

7. Quentin Skinner, "Meaning and Understanding in the History of Ideas," in James Tully, ed., *Meaning & Context: Quentin Skinner and His Critics* (Princeton: Princeton University Press, 1988), 29–67, 66. A number of Skinner's writings subsequent to his methodological arguments, however, have returned to the lessons of past thinkers for present guidance. See, for example, Quentin Skinner, "The Republican Ideal of Political Liberty," in *Machiavelli and Republicanism,* ed. Gisela Bock, Quentin Skinner, and Maurizio Viroli (Cambridge: Cambridge University Press, 1990), 293–309.

8. The "end of ideology" argument is most closely associated with Daniel Bell's *The End of Ideology* (Cambridge, Mass.: Harvard University Press, 1988 [1st ed. 1962]). Peter Laslett infamously declared: "For the moment, anyway, political philosophy is dead" in his *Philosophy, Politics and Society* (Oxford: Blackwell Publishers, 1956), vii.

9. Wolin, "Political Theory as a Vocation," 45, 51, 53, 59.

10. In a review of Rawls's *Political Liberalism* Wolin writes: "Democracy should not depend on elites making a one-time gift to the demos of a predesigned framework of equal rights. This does not mean that rights do not matter a great deal, but rights in a democracy depend on the demos winning them, extending them substantively, and, in the process, acquiring experience of the political, that is, of participating in power, reflecting on the consequences of its exercise, and struggling to sort out the common well-being amid cultural differences and socioeconomic disparities." Sheldon S. Wolin, "The Liberal/Democratic Divide: On Rawls' *Political Liberalism,*" *Political Theory* 24, no. 1 (February 1996): 97–119, 98.

11. Isaac, in "The Strange Silence of Political Theory," fears that the preponderance of contemporary academic political theory is wholly removed from contemporary politics. Stanley Fish, on the other hand, argues forcefully that theory *cannot* contribute to politics in any significant way. See "Mission Impossible: Settling the Just Bounds between Church and State," *Columbia Law Review* 97, no. 8 (December

1997): 2255–2333. A nuanced discussion, drawing on Wittgenstein and Oakeshott, of the relations (and *nonrelations*) of theory to practice is found in Richard E. Flathman, "Theory and Practice, Skepticism and Liberalism," in *Toward a Liberalism* (Ithaca: Cornell University Press, 1989), 14–47.

12. Wolin, "Political Theory as a Vocation," 60, 62.

13. See also Bonnie Honig's criticism of the assumption that "the task of political theory is to resolve institutional questions, to get politics right, over, and done with, to free modern subjects and their sets of arrangements of political conflict and instability." Bonnie Honig, *Political Theory and the Displacement of Politics* (Ithaca: Cornell University Press, 1993), 2.

14. The earlier context may already have been uncongenial for vocation. Indeed, Wolin's essay was inspired in part by a questionnaire distributed by the American Political Science Association in the 1960s, instructing members to indicate "the vocation of the political theorist" by checking one of the boxes in a list of classifications to be used for organizational purposes. Wolin, "Political Theory as a Vocation," 24.

15. See Max Weber, "Science as a Vocation" and "Politics as a Vocation," in *From Max Weber: Essays in Sociology,* ed. H. H. Gerth and C. Wright Mills (New York: Oxford University Press, 1959), 129–56, 212–25. For an illuminating discussion of the vexed relationship between "vocation" and "profession" as it pertains to public intellectuals see Bruce Robbins, *Secular Vocations: Intellectuals, Professionalism, Culture* (New York: Verso, 1993).

16. Max Weber, *The Protestant Ethic and the Spirit of Capitalism,* trans. T. Parsons (London: Unwin Hyman, 1930), 79–92; Charles Taylor, *Sources of the Self: The Making of Modern Identity* (Cambridge, Mass.: Harvard University Press, 1989), 211–304.

17. Wolin, *Politics and Vision,* 183.

18. Ibid. Wolin is quoting Calvin's *The Institutes of the Christian Religion.*

19. Drawing on Derrida, Laclau argues that political theorists of late modernity must come to terms with "the *infinitude of the social,* that is, the fact that any structural system is limited, that it is always surrounded by an 'excess of meaning' which it is unable to master and that, consequently, 'society' as a unitary and intelligible object which grounds its own partial processes is an impossibility." Ernesto Laclau, *New Reflections on the Revolution of Our Time* (New York: Verso, 1990), 90.

20. Paul Virilio, *Speed & Politics: An Essay on Dromology,* trans. M. Polizott (New York: Semiotext(e), 1986). Similar concerns are expressed by Michael Walzer in "The Last Page," *Dissent* (Summer 1994): 432.

21. Sheldon Wolin, "What Time Is It?" *Theory & Event* 1, no. 1 (1997): 1–10, 4.

22. For a defense of post-territorial democratic politics see William E. Connolly, *Identity\Difference: Democratic Negotiations of Political Paradox* (Ithaca: Cornell University Press, 1991), 198–222; on a more metaphorical plateau see Gilles Deleuze and Félix Guattari, *Nomadology* (New York: Semiotext(e), 1986). In addition to classic treatments of the subject by thinkers such as Montesquieu, Rousseau, and Tocqueville, arguments for the necessary connection between democratic politics and place

can be found in Daniel Kemmis, *Community and the Politics of Place* (Norman: University of Oklahoma Press, 1990). See also Sheldon S. Wolin, "Rethinking Democracy and Counterrevolution," *Nation* (April 22, 1996): 22–24.

23. Chantal Mouffe, *The Return of the Political* (New York: Verso, 1993). Mouffe draws heavily, as have many other current thinkers emphasizing the primacy of the political, on Carl Schmitt's *The Concept of the Political,* trans. George Schwab (Chicago: University of Chicago Press, 1996). Some of these thinkers are more true to Schmitt's authoritarianism, viewing his political decisionism as a means to reconstitute a more stable, integrated, clearly bounded social order, and to clarify present political uncertainties. Others, particularly those associated with the journal *Telos,* have drawn a democratic populism from Schmitt's thoroughgoing critique of liberal proceduralism.

24. See especially *Politics and Vision,* 3–11; Sheldon S. Wolin, "Hannah Arendt: Democracy and the Political," *Salmagundi* 60 (1983): 3–19; Sheldon S. Wolin, "Fugitive Democracy," *Democracy and Difference: Contesting the Boundaries of the Political,* ed. Seyla Benhabib (Princeton: Princeton University Press, 1996), 31–45; Sheldon S. Wolin, "Norm and Form: The Constitutionalizing of Democracy," *Athenian Political Thought and the Reconstruction of American Democracy,* ed. J. P. Euben, J. R. Wallach, and J. Ober (Ithaca, N.Y.: Cornell University Press, 1994), 29–58; and Wolin, "What Time Is It?" 1–4. Wolin's delineations of politics, the political, and democracy are too complex to be covered here. He often emphasizes the distinction between politics (characterized as an institutional, ceaseless, often mundane activity) and the political (as creative, episodic, intense). Democracy, then, is a mode of political action that seeks such creative, revolutionary moments of commonality, interrupting and challenging existing political arrangements.

25. Mark Reinhardt, "Look Who's Talking: Political Subjects, Political Objects, and Political Discourse in Contemporary Theory," *Political Theory,* vol. 23, no. 4 (November 1995): 689–719, 694. For earlier arguments that political scientists must attend to the interpretive and theoretical dimensions of their research, which they most wish to deny, see Charles Taylor, "Interpretation and the Sciences of Man," *Philosophy and the Human Sciences: Philosophical Papers, 2* (Cambridge: Cambridge University Press, 1985), 15–57; and Terence Ball, "Deadly Hermeneutics; or *Sinn* and the Social Scientist," *Idioms of Inquiry,* 95–112. Our treatment of the relationship between political theory and political science is, as is Wolin's, primarily theoretical and meta-theoretical. The essays to follow by Mark Brown and Shane Gunster treat the relationship more empirically, as does Gunnell, *The Descent of Political Theory.* See also the essays by Thomas Bender, Ira Katznelson, and Rogers M. Smith in the symposium "American Academic Culture in Transformation: Fifty Years, Four Disciplines" in *Daedalus* 126, Number 1 (Winter 1997).

26. For one of many examples of political theorists pursuing "empirical" matters see Frederick M. Dolan and Thomas L. Dumm, eds., *Rhetorical Republic: Governing Representations in American Politics* (Amherst: University of Massachusetts Press, 1993).

27. Wendy Brown similarly cautions political theorists against limiting them-selves to the given and the present, and against conflating theory and action, in "The Time of the Political," *Theory & Event* 1, no. 1 (1997): 1–8. Isaac does not claim that all political theory should be practical and present-minded, but that this should be its center of gravity.

28. Compare Vaclav Havel, *Vaclav Havel, or, Living in Truth,* ed. Jan Vladislav (London: Faber and Faber, 1986), 36–122 and 136–57, to *The Art of the Impossible: Politics as Morality in Practice,* trans. Paul Wilson (New York: Fromm International, 1997), 55–65, 87–102, 115–23, 236–43. For a thoughtful, deeply personal discussion of the extent to which, since 1989, "the political landscape has been transformed beyond recognition" (10), see Ira Katznelson, *Liberalism's Crooked Circle: Letters to Adam Michnik* (Princeton: Princeton University Press, 1996). See also Sheldon Wolin, "Beyond Marxism and Monetarism," *Nation,* March 19, 1990, 372–74.

PART I

INVOKING POLITICAL THEORY

I // POLITICAL THEORY

From Vocation to Invocation

I

The occasion for the following essay was a conference devoted to the future—to future political theorists and their future and to the future of political theory. No millennial justifications were needed for those choices. A perennial uncertainty and controversy have accompanied political theory: about its relationship to political and social science, to philosophy, and to history, as well as its relationship, if any, to the "real" political world. In my case any invitation to contribute to a volume concerning the future is no simple matter. If that is not sufficient warning about the temporal divide between us, be prepared for a confessional note.

My formative experiences are: a child during the Great Depression, a flier in World War II, a Jew during the era of the Holocaust, and an activist during the sixties—all, except the last, experiences dominated by loss. Although cultural conservatives might count the sixties as a disaster, it was, instead, the loss of liberal innocence. I have asked myself many times how to think about loss—perhaps as the attempts of ordinary men and women to gain a modest purchase on the world, to make a living, only to find it all gone smash by forces over which they have no control? or as the fate of ordinary youths, barely out of high school, their lives suddenly over in the twisting, helpless spiral of a plane out of control, its black smoke tracing a blasphemous trail against a brilliant Pacific sky, most of the doomed having little idea of making a living, only of outwitting death? In a culture that measures life by notions such as progress, development, innovation, and modernization, loss tends to be an experience we are advised to "get past." Loss belongs to history, while politics and life are about what is still to be done. But maybe loss is related to power and powerlessness and hence has a claim upon theory. . . .

How to memorialize loss theoretically? Shall we memorialize it as contingency, the ill-luck of the draw, as mis(sed)fortune, a mere shortening of our

allotted span, another footnote to the Book of Job? Among conservative political theorists of the past—Burke, Tocqueville, and Hegel, for example—
loss figured importantly in their responses to the French Revolution, and it is
no exaggeration to count political loss as what qualifies them as moderate
counterrevolutionaries rather than as reactionaries. Let me try to place the
stakes in a more contemporary context by quoting from Adorno:

> [K]nowledge must indeed present the fatally rectilinear succession of victory
> and defeat, but should also address itself to those things which were not em-
> braced by this dynamic, which fell by the wayside—what might be called
> the waste products and blind spots that have escaped the dialectic. It is in
> the nature of the defeated to appear, in their impotence, irrelevant, eccen-
> tric, derisory. What transcends the ruling society is not only the potentiality
> which it develops but also that which did not fit properly into the laws of
> historical movement. Theory must needs deal with cross-grained, opaque, un-
> assimilated material, which as such admittedly has from the start an anachro-
> nistic quality, but is not wholly obsolete since it has outwitted the historical
> dynamic.[1]

I have chosen that text because it dramatizes a familiar theme in the history
of political theory—and in much else—about triumph and defeat. It pictures
the triumphant movement as shoving aside, ignoring, the "defeated"—the
defeated as that which even the "dialectic" has refused to appropriate, that
which is not merely superseded, but surpassed, "anachronistic." What sur-
vives of the defeated, the indigestible, the unassimilated, the "cross-grained,"
the "not wholly obsolete" is what should interest the theorist.

I propose a gloss on that passage of Adorno's: Supposing the thesis has
defeated but not obliterated the antithesis, even though potentially it could;
the thesis does not choose to destroy the antithesis nor to ingest it, because,
paradoxically, the peculiarity of this particular thesis is the condition attached to its perpetuation: if it is to continue as the triumphant thesis, it
cannot eliminate, though it has neutralized, the antithesis; indeed, it must see
to it that the antithesis remains just healthy enough, even though anachronistic or cross-grained and oppositional. The relationship is symbiotic in the
biological sense rather than the dialectical: Symbiosis exists when two different organisms live attached to each other, or one as a tenant of the other, and
contribute to each other's support. The antithesis is not lost but subsidized;

or perhaps its representatives do not know whether they are lost or even subsidized; they may believe the symbiosis represents just deserts.

I want to pursue these glosses with reference to my original essay, "Political Theory as a Vocation," but now complemented by the notion of invocation.

II

Vocation and invocation produce contrasting resonances. While vocation is associated with "calling" and—thanks to Max Weber and Martin Luther—is freighted with a rich genealogy, invocation is associated with "recalling," and its genealogy or theoretical relevance seems, at first glance, unpromising, since it is apt to be associated with defect, as in the recall of faulty cars. But defect suggests that something is missing, and invocation does have that association. In ancient Rome an invocation was an appeal to a departed deity. While vocation implies action, a practice, invocation may be said to imply memory and to enjoin recovery. Vocation predicates a certain commitment, "ideal" though not disinterested, to the particular practice in question. Invocation is a response to a certain kind of loss.

A few centuries ago there was a ready answer to the obvious question raised by referring to a practice as a calling, "Who does the calling?" Who authorizes it? Secularism has long since rendered the old answer quaint, but it may not follow that the question itself is irrelevant or necessarily obscurantist.

Consider, for example, the formulation "X is a democratic theorist" or "Y does democratic theory." Are X and Y "called" to "do" democratic theory? By whom? And should theory then become institutionalized, programmatic, and the theorist someone who is certified as a qualified democratic theorist? Or is being a democratic theorist simply a matter of self-selection, a contingent choice of a specialty? Or is the idea of a democratic theorist or of democratic theory an oxymoron and the idea of a calling superfluous in that context? Or is the concept of a calling still plausible, even urgent, in the context of pseudo-democracy, not as a personal choice or as institutional certification but as a public commitment for a time when the idea of publics has pretty much been superseded by that of constituencies or dissolved into various identities based on race, gender, or sexual preference?

For Weber it was precisely the threat to calling in an age of disenchantment that prompted him to distinguish the person called both from the merely technically accomplished and from the enthusiast and to assert at the same time that a person with a true sense of vocation was a rarity because of the demanding combination of exceptional intellectual talents and a moral commitment to the standards prevailing in a particular intellectual "discipline."

Something else is set in motion by the concept of an intellectual calling. The substance of what it is the committed practitioner intends to practice, what he or she is called to, is elevated because deemed worthy of dedication and selflessness, thereby justifying the aura of authority claimed by the practitioner. The paradox that Weber begins to explore is that at the same time that the modern practice of knowledge was attaining unequaled rigor such that the phrase "the search for truth" could be uttered without embarrassment, and the idea of authority taken for granted, that conception of practice was being threatened by two equally modern, well-entrenched subversions, one the cultivation of subjective individualism and the other of objective or rational self-interest. The one causes vocation to lapse into dilettantism, the other to harden into professionalism. To survive, the idea of vocation might have to be revoked and replaced by the sobrieties of method or invoked: Invocation as vocation's conscience recalling it to the cross-grained.

In Luther's formulation there was an aspect of vocation that got lost when Weber attempted to adapt *Beruf* to the age of bureaucratization, the nation-state, and capitalism. For Luther a calling presupposed a certain structure to the community, including a "place" into which the practice fit. In extending hospitality to the holder of a vocational office, the community, in turn, presumed that in pursuing his/her calling the practitioner would, ipso facto, be acting in the interests of the community, and that the community stood in need, not merely in want, of what the practitioner provided. The identity of the community was not problematic: the community was a "historical settlement," either local or provincial, but not yet nationalized. Not "the" community but a noncommunity of communities and of communities within communities. Significantly, for Weber the master theorist of organizational rationalism, vocation rested on an inner decision of the individual, with the inner signifying the passion, devotion, and conviction denied by the structures among which the called had to find a place. Vocation was thus historically out of place and necessarily cross-grained.

III

But what of invocation, of that which signified that something irreplaceable has gone, perhaps fled or been rendered ineffectual, with the result that the world has been diminished? What is at stake is not mere recognition of loss but how one works through it. To invoke presupposes that one has a grasp of how things have been, perhaps how something came to be, how some practice, expectation, or value became sufficiently powerful to gain a foothold and become established in the world. Certainly earlier centuries were no strangers to loss. Thucydides declared that one of the aims of his *History* was to prevent the actions and events of a great war from being forgotten. Loss as the result of a lapse of memory was thus understood to be a historical rather than a theoretical problem. The historian's task was one of recovery and the reconstruction of "true" memory, especially the memory of extraordinary actions, rather than assessment of the effects on the political of the passing or demise of some practice, expectation, or value. The historian's invocation is properly addressed to Mnemosyne, the goddess of memory and Muse of history. Appropriately, Thucydides leaves his *History* unfinished at the point where the contemporary political consequences of the Peloponnesian War press for consideration.[2] Wars have always been among the major instigators of change; yet wars are "over," even though their consequences may not be evident until long afterward. The distinctiveness of modern forms of power is captured by the phrase "the process of modernization," the institutionalization of continuous change so that everything—how, where, and even whether we live, how we relate and communicate—assumes the character of an advance toward incompleteness. But the advance of modernization is made possible by the *displacement* and *replacement* that accompany it. Loss is as often a prerequisite as a side effect. When the casualties involved have figured importantly not only in personal lives but in the fabric of common concerns and, at the same time, the rate at which casualties are produced radically exceeds the limits of ordinary expectancy, with the result that there is not enough time to mourn, to absorb the loss and make sense of it, then there is the political equivalent of blocked grief. For example, the loss may be acted out by erecting a memorial—to the Confederate dead, to the Holocaust, to those who died in the Vietnam War—yet the resentments remain and the questions are unresolved. Blocked grief can take many political forms, some of them twisted: the politics of religious fundamentalism, the religion of patriotic fundamentalism (invoking a mythical common law or original constitution).

In response, a postmodern sensibility might interject that when change is normal, then there are only two constants, appearance and disappearance, both of which reduce to one, change. So why invoke? Why grieve, especially when functional equivalents can be designed? That solution, however, need not foreclose some questions. Who or what has departed? To focus on our present concerns, Is it theory that has departed? Or the theorist? To suggest that theory or theorists are absent and require invocation because they have ceased to be a presence seems only slightly less perverse than the implicit suggestion that they were once objects of veneration. So, what sort of presence are they now? And are they being welcomed into a community, a *Gemeinschaft*, or, instead, into a *Gesellschaft*? Are they a vocation or a profession or dilettantism?

IV

To begin with the most obvious: the number of theorists is, depending on one's view of quantities, impressive or alarming. Although there may be comparatively fewer academic positions in political theory, there are, undeniably, more academics with incomparably more diverse identities claiming to be theorists, more journals devoted to theory, and more theoretical books and articles than in the entire previous history of the world. And the number is not appreciably diminished if one restricts theory to mean "political" theory. Perhaps the strongest testimony to the attraction of theory is that even political scientists, who used to pride themselves on being a collective of hard-nosed empiricists and quantifiers poised to pounce at the slightest scent of theory, now invest their hopes for survival in rational choice, the in-house version of theory. One is tempted to say that the choice of rational choice itself may qualify as rational because there exist hospitable communities with well-defined hierarchical structures that respond to that same language, the business corporation and the public bureaucracy. Does this signify that the supremely practical world has become theory-dependent, and that as a consequence theory-power has become a social or political reality? What kind of world might it be that would welcome not only rational, economics-inspired theories but also theories that rational theorists view as irrational, Adorno's cross-grained representatives? Has, then, an imagined unity of vocation dissolved into various professional forms with different constituencies? And are these multiple possibilities reflective of a new condition in which politics is finally freed of the constraints of an overarching political and becomes a politics of multiplicity?

Certainly it is new politics when, in a constitutional democracy, politics is widely presumed to be merely a synonym for power relationships[3] and at the same time is alleged to be so ubiquitous that one is hard-pressed to identify what is nonpolitics. Moreover, the proliferation of politics is not a simple quantitative phenomenon involving more and more of the same elements but instead is hailed as the discovery or invention of diverse forms of politics, of heterogeneity.

The profusion of politics created by academics is paralleled by the "real world" industry that produces politics similar to the way that conventional industries produce material goods. The production of politics is made possible by think tanks, pollsters and survey researchers, and pundits. Who owns the means of political production? And is the heavily subsidized research university merely a way of describing a division of labor and a different plant location? What can it mean that a society that produces unparalleled material abundance also produces more politics than any previous society?

Let us call this situation, where no one is called but virtually anyone can come, and where an invocation seems superfluous, "overtheoretization," and let us describe the objects of theories as composing a world profuse with politics, a world of political plenty where the supply of manufactured politics is sufficient to allow political action and power to be perceived in virtually every relationship, presumably no monopolies. In this world both theory and politics are ubiquitous and indeterminate. It might seem then that invocation is in a condition worse than anachronistic; it is emeritus, senile. The conception of political theory as vocationless practice is threatened by incoherence or, alternatively, it is enjoying a healthy disjointedness—which is the literal synonym for incoherence. But if we have a situation of disjointed theorists, overtheoretization, and a surplus of politics—that is, a large amount of political activity that goes nowhere—and possibly even an abundance of power, why haven't the laws of supply and demand driven down the price of politics, power, and theorists instead of making them more expensive? Why, if not a monopoly, at least a political oligopoly? Perhaps because of a disconnection. . . . Which brings me to the next question:

What of the political, of that conception of commonality and shared fate? One could say that it is a casualty of the essentialism of antiessentialism and let the matter drop. Instead think of its departure as marking the crumbling of the language of commonality. What remains of commonality is the experience of feeling embarrassed by references to "the common good" or even to its corrupt form, "the public interest." Politics takes advantage and promotes privatization, attacking what has been left exposed by a weakened commonality, erasing affirmative action, affirming a punitive welfarism, loosening the connection between public education and democracy while strengthening the influence of business interests over educational policy. Thus the answer to an earlier question of how to memorialize loss is: as a voucher; how to theorize it: as the privatization of commonalities, as reversing what had been achieved only after intense *political* struggles.

The sentence of archaism that has been passed on the language of commonality is reflective of something more serious than a move in a Lyotardian language game. Consider the profound change in the nature and status of public administration. It used to be described as "public service" to distinguish it from business practices and to demarcate the difference between serving the common good and working for private profit. Now government work is publicly stigmatized as bureaucracy, privately sneered at as the last refuge for minority preferences, and practiced as managerialism and as a prep school for admission to the private sector. Perhaps diversity, with its simultaneous advocacy of hyperpluralism and its demands for inclusiveness, has placed too great a strain on the political, causing it to lose whatever coherence it may have had.

Despite or rather because of disenchantments, Weber balked at embracing reflexivity and clung to the notion of vocation. Was this because he did not doubt that in the practices of the natural sciences the ideal form of true knowledge was now realized, and that in the process the idea of vocation had been preserved? And this even though Weber recognized that science was subverting the communal structures and belief systems that originally had made the idea of vocation meaningful—so much so that when Weber tried to defend "politics as a vocation" he appealed not to truth but to conviction, citing Luther's "Ich kann nichts anders" as the appropriate motto of political man.

For a post-Weberian generation—and I include myself—that found inspiration in alternative, antipositivist philosophies of science, the theoretic primacy of science remained largely unchallenged. On the contrary. The work of Kuhn and others in the history and philosophy of science was invigorating not only because it offered a counterparadigm of science to the positivist paradigm popular among political and social scientists but because it seemed to locate science in a context much like that being traced by some political theorists: a context charged with political contingencies and elements of subjectivity, presided over by an obtuse scientific establishment reluctant to recognize a growing gap between a regnant theory and the purported reality it explained.

v

Yesterday's animosities, as well its areas of mutual concern, are today's indifferences. Assuming that indifference on matters of importance ought not necessarily be viewed indifferently, allow some reflections on that dramatic change and the contrast that it presents to the situation three decades ago, when theory seemed older because its critics categorized it as "traditional" or "normative" and political science seemed younger thanks to the rejuvenating effects of the alleged revolution of behavioralism. My original essay was in part a protest against what might be termed the "undertheoretization of the world" by political scientists and behavioralists, and in part an attempt to indicate the *political* consequences of undertheoretization. Undertheoretization characterizes an uncritical *mentalité* of which many variations are possible. One was described in my original essay: the obsession with perfecting methods of inquiry and relying upon empirical analysis to yield testable propositions and, ultimately, valid laws covering the phenomena under investigation. In general this variation—call it positivism—was driven by a need to find out how the world works and sustained by the faith that there was "a" way to find out, the way of scientific method. It was also driven by a fear that a world left underexplained would fall victim to a riotous subjectivism of which academic political theory was one ideological expression.

And so, instead of theory, the search was for "laws" and "regularities," in part because the investigators were suspicious of deviance and in part because they feared chaos. The actual consequence of undertheoretization was not chaos but conformism. What were—and are—the theoretical implications and political consequences of "undertheoretization"? I shall return to that question shortly. First its opposite.

Why "overtheoretization"? And what, if any, are its consequences? If it is being subsidized, what social or political function or contribution is being performed? And whence the urge to theorize even though the idea of theory is ridiculed and condemned by some of the most influential "theorists" of postmodernism? Is it related to the change in the status of politics?

Among the populace politics used to be, and still is, redolent of corruption; now among the cognoscenti it is associated with domination, even though a plausible case might be made for corruption being as prevalent as domination and its necessary condition. Yet the very generality of corruption, the lack of a focused victim, seems to disqualify it as a theoretical object, a casualty of the declining importance of the language of commonality. Domination and its variants (oppression, subjugation, rape, patriarchy, etc.), on the other hand, are the subjects of highly sophisticated theorizing, sensitive to gradations of wrong, to the variety of contexts, different victims, insistent that their subject be theorized. Perhaps overtheoretization is representative of a new and refined theoretic sensibility that has come into being, expressed in the normalization of "heavy" terms, such as domination, violence, oppression, terror—terms that once were reserved for the exceptional or abnormal. Is overtheoretization a response to rampant wrong, and hence fully warranted as a description of both private worlds and the official world, and not at all superfluous or hyperbolic? Or is it trapped in a symbiotic relationship, and if so, to what?

But if overtheoretization is the response to rampant wrong, how to explain a housing situation in which the most notorious theorists of wrong are not only extended hospitality by a certain community, the academy, and even honored as they are being "called"? Where, despite the rage of self-styled "cultural conservatives" for cultural wars to purge the academy of alleged radicalisms, the most subversive, dangerous, and deliberately outrageous among them find that, despite their best efforts, their market value rises in synch with the Dow Jones Index as the most affluent institutions, those most integrated into the same power structures responsible for the wrongs exposed by critics and ever hospitable to the powerful elites that man them, bid for the most celebrated subversives? And how is it that subversion flourishes alongside class divisions within the academy—between "regular" appointees and "gypsies" or contract laborers, not to mention union-busted teaching assistants?

How might we try to understand this peculiar condition where under-theoretization has mutated into overtheoretization, where academic discourse is overloaded with discourses speaking on behalf of those whose lives have been deeply damaged by the official structures of power? In a fragmented academy, where the plane of generality, once represented by ideals of a liberal or humanistic education, has been displaced by particularities, to whom are the theoretical discourses being addressed, and what is the theoretical status of the addressee? Is it as hapless as that of the "citizen" in the public rhetoric? How to characterize and account for an ongoing system of wrongs and for the various discourses specializing in wrongs? I want the emphasis here to fall on "ongoing."

An insight into the "ongoing" is provided by a recent story in the *New York Times*. It described the emergence and popularity of publications that deal solely with the reporting of "the juicy inside stuff" of politics, the tactics, intrigues, and strategies, but not the substantive issues, much less the stakes for those affected by the outcomes and decisions. It depicted a politics deprived of substance, a hermetic politics without a public, the political as pure tactics. Inside politics with no "outside." The story also reported how politicians and their staffs were such avid consumers that work stopped when the periodicals appeared. As an afterthought the story mentioned that the subscription price of these publications was well over two hundred dollars, and that profit margins ran as high as 40 percent, thanks to corporate advertising.[4]

One question suggested by the account might be, what sort of condition, other than narcissism, has been created by accepting as politics actions and actors severed from the concerns that traditionally were their raison d'être? How is it possible for a society to sustain this disembodied, supremely tactical version of politics? Would it be analogous to having *The Prince* unqualified by *The Discourses*? Perhaps a contrast might illuminate what is striking, even unique, about this condition.

Whatever the shortcomings of my original essay, its reference point was plainly to a widely acknowledged crisis in American politics centered in the Vietnam War. Although at the time the war was understood to be connected to other conflicts, such as those over civil rights and racism, and to the revolts taking place in the inner cities, the fact that there was a center lent an intensity to politics as well as to theorizing. The essay accused political science of complicity by its uncritical, accommodative relationship to power, and of being so focused on methodological applications as to be unaware that it was merely producing a simulacrum of the existing political order. Like that of classical paradigm-workers, the ordinary reflex of political scientists was to dismiss any anomalies that might imply that the system was violating its own norms or falling seriously short of them. In the eyes of critics, anomalies were symptomatic of crisis, and crises seemed to be everywhere, not only in the political and constitutional crisis associated with the war, with race relationships, and later with Watergate, but also in the emerging concerns about ecology, the status of the family, sexual mores, and the claims of women. While domestically the political seemed too narrow, too inelastic, in terms of the license it granted to presidential power and to the reach of the national security state, the political was too elastic, too expansive, too inclusive.

In this setting the idea of crisis was pointed and deeply invested with its etymology from the ancient Greek, where *krisis* referred to a condition so grave as to force a turning point. Crisis signified a pathological condition with three essential aspects. First, it represented a decisive moment, either recovery (that is, political renewal) or death (that is, the continuing transfiguration of the state into a megapower justified in demanding the unlimited sacrifices celebrated in John Kennedy's inaugural address and, necessarily, requiring new political and economic structures appropriate to that scale). Second, it was a general condition of politics involving serious constitutional questions as well as questions that transcended the law: about the effects of imperial ambitions upon free institutions at home, and about whether democracy was possible within the present political framework, and about the connections between injustices being visited on a weak minority and what Marx called "wrong in general." And third, it was a moment of suspense and urgency in which things could go one way or the other: Kennedy might attack Cuba; the war might be extended to Cambodia; the police violence against nonviolent African-Americans might also be turned against antiwar demonstrators. Theory had, therefore, to adopt a broadly conceived form of intervention sufficient to encompass the scope of the problem yet sufficiently concrete and pointed so as to be able to interpret swiftly changing events to a broad but deeply divided public.

Now in that context "critical" meant something very different from what it tends to mean today, when it is related more to "critic" than to "crisis"—that is, it carries a more contemplative, Kantian, spectatorial connotation of a "judgment" in search of distance rather than an intervention driven by urgency. It is theoretic theory rather than political theory. And even though it makes references to real-world controversies, its engagement is with the conditions, or the politics, of the theoretical that it seeks to settle rather than with the political that is being contested over who gets what and who gets included. It is postpolitical.

But what if society, like theory, is in retreat from general norms and is converging instead toward theory by preferring to be decentered? To whom or what is the claim of wrong being addressed? How can one dissolve the public into differences, that is, privatize the public as the personal, and then launch an appeal that seems to presuppose a public of shared values traditionally represented by the idea of the citizen? Conservatives and post-modernists alike are antistatist, except that conservatives know what some postmodernists have forgotten, that multiple centers mean multiple masters: witness feudalism, the great Western experience of decentered societies, and then consider the baronial claims of Ted Turner (with or without Lady Jane) or of George Soros or of Bill Gates.

If the plane of generality is proscribed to the contemporary theoretical vocabulary and, as a consequence, no paradigmatic theory is possible, nor any concept of anomalies, at least not in the sense previously understood, then the paradox: critical theorists are normal scientists for a society without a paradigm; the new paradigm is the nonparadigmatic, and critical theory is the revolt of the normal scientists, or is normal theory for a world that has apparently transcended anomalies, crises, and turning points.

Perhaps, however, there is something paradigmatic left: the domination of the world by change, by changes that are, to a significant degree, premeditated, however imperfect the grasp of unintended consequences. Change as the euphemism for the systematic gain and loss of power,[5] which is helped along as the prevalence of change undercuts the fact/norm distinction: the fact of change, the particular form that it assumes in a technology-driven culture (say, a computer or genetic cloning), is simultaneously an assertion of power-as-value, as the embodiment of a demonstrable superiority. That means, among other things, that the standpoint of criticism is undercut: power erases the disjunction between fact and value; fact has become value and value inseparable from the fact of its embodiment. The connecting element is power made possible by the loss, by that power which has been eliminated or cast off to allow full rein to fact.

To say that critical theory is normal suggests that it has taken or usurped the place of description and that this accounts for why, in the absence of crisis, criticism flourishes, and why it has assumed the forms that it has—that is, forms that are adapted to a world without crises, anomalies, or turning points.

V I

What is the shape of the present political world such that it is either immune to crisis or capable of postponing it indefinitely, but at the same time acknowledges that misfortune, intolerance, inequalities, and injustice are present, yet is so self-assured as to be broadly tolerant to theories that proclaim themselves to be subversive, transgressive, even outrageous—and that are viewed as such by conservative commentators? Here is a not unrepresentative pronouncement about the condition of the world:

> Has there ever been a moment quite like this? In the United States high yield retirement accounts are making near-millionaires of thousands of salaried workers and hourly wage earners. In India resort towns are crammed. . . . No major international wars are being fought. The world has its ugly regional conflicts . . . but no Stalin, no Hitler, no Mao. . . . Democracies flourish. The end of the cold war has removed ideological chains and with them distortions of economies rooted in big-power rivalries. . . .[6]

Or as a writer put it in the *Wall Street Journal*, the present state of the nation's economy is "utopia." Or as an economic advisor to the president put it, "This is the best of all possible worlds."

The importance of such pronouncements is not that their authors make no allowance for the possibility of, say, a lapse into a recession; or that no one seems upset by the hyperbole. Rather what is significant is that there is no notion of a turning point. A setback perhaps, even a downturn. Instead a system seemingly crisis-proof. It is as though the sole motor of change is the one embodied in the dynamics of the system itself; that the system sets the terms or limits of change so that setbacks do not disrupt the perpetual motion machine. The appropriation of change means control over the definition of acceptable risks or consequences, injuries, damages: e.g., downsizing, worker obsolescence, safety standards in the workplace, income gaps, health care, etc. I shall call this the "systematization of loss." In the official rhetoric, how-ever, loss is integrated into a system that is represented as too complex, too universal and interconnected—in short, so overpowering (literally) yet ex-quisitely sensitive as to forbid actions any more challenging than those en-veloped in the Delphic soporifics of the chairman of the Federal Reserve Board. Certainly the conviction that we live in utopia is not wholly ground-less, given the opportunities of the educated or trained for achieving wealth and status, the low levels of unemployment (leaving aside the quality of the jobs), scientific progress, technological innovations, and the unchallenged status of the world's only super- and potentially interstellar power.

Yet there is the dark and seemingly inseparable side: the horrendously harsh system of criminal justice, the persistent racism, the hostility toward the aspirations of women, the widening chasms between classes, the epic levels of political and corporate corruption, the reluctance of political and corporate leaders to confront ecological dangers except by proposing a sys-tem whereby industrialists who pollute less than their assigned quota may sell that differential to those who pollute more: which provokes the question, which is the nightmare, the problem or the solution? But the answer is "both and simultaneously." Or, stated differently, the answer is that we live in a utopia in which loss has been systematized, a utopia whose existence de-pends symbiotically on the perpetuation of dystopia.

Perhaps, then, it is the combination of utopia and dystopia that is the peculiarity of our time. To be sure, every epoch embodies some elements of that combination, and Dickens did characterize a certain epoch as "the best of times" and "the worst of times." To cite such examples, however, only obscures the peculiar relationship between the contemporary utopia and its dystopia. Dystopia is not the name for a political condition where injustice is frequent, or officials act arbitrarily, or the populace is systematically misled—although these actions may, in fact, recur regularly. Rather, dystopia repre-sents a political condition in which injustice, arbitrariness, and deception literally contradict the core principles that form the identity of the utopia. Racism is dystopia's antithesis to utopia's equal protection of the laws. Thus the two, though antithetical, are connected: we might think of utopia as the positive pole, dystopia as the negative.

For the most part, although not always, past theories of utopia were unambiguous: their realization did not depend upon the misery, insecurity, and dependency of many but was supposed to preclude those evils. So the peculiarity of this utopia is that unlike previous utopias, where the blessed land was depicted as the antithesis of the wicked and unjust world "outside," the realized utopia incorporates dystopia. Its opposite is "inside" because this particular utopia cannot be realized without dystopia, without reproducing it; hence utopia never promises to eliminate dystopia, merely to be allowed to recruit from its meritocratic escapees. The very language used, "the *persistence* of racism," "*generations* of those on welfare," is not meant to call the utopia into question but to state some of its conditions while offering object lessons. Similarly the periodic calls for cleaning up political and corporate corruption. A few sacrificial bulls may be offered up but, as every Poli Sci 1 student learns, the system could not work without corruption or with republican civic virtue. Since the eighteenth century, it has promoted, instead, the policy sciences for containing and, if necessary, ameliorating dystopic manifestations, though never eliminating them altogether.

The inherency of dystopia within utopia was understood early on when the ideological representation of the utopia, of its allegedly lawlike character, was first adumbrated by Adam Smith and then confirmed by the so-called "gloomy science" of the Manchester School of economics.

What does the persistence of dystopia signify? If it does not represent a crisis because of its inherency, then where, if anywhere, is crisis located? If crisis has lost its salience in the "real" world because the real has annexed the symptoms of crisis to the "ideal," made evil integral to the process, that would suggest either that the concept of crisis should simply be abandoned or, alternatively, that it should be sought in a different location.

The first alternative is a counsel of surrender to precisely that form of technological determinism advocated daily by the pundits, but perhaps at least one concession has to be entered into the classical conception of crisis: the notion of a crucial turning point may have to be discarded, defeated by the combination of utopian and dystopian elements.

A historian of an earlier generation once remarked that "1848 was the turning-point of the 19th century on which the century forgot to turn." One hundred and fifty years after that revolutionary moment went uncelebrated, one is tempted to say that ours is a century unable to turn, except linguistically. This would confirm Marx's worst fear, conceived in the *Grundrisse*, of a capitalism that would experience ups and downs yet be sufficiently crisis-proof to avoid an apocalypse. Marx's gloom would be deepened had he witnessed the institutions developed by later capitalism to ameliorate crises: the IMF, the World Bank, the European Union, and the Federal Reserve system. To which we might also add the political counterpart, the politics of centrism. Thus we are left with the two remaining criteria of crisis: urgency and generality. What in our present condition might satisfy those criteria? It would not be difficult to show that social, economic, political, and cultural inequalities—all those dystopian phenomena—are running deep and wide in our society, and that, given the present concentration of power in the society, there is no evidence of a will to reverse them or of the oppositional culture committed to nurturing that will.

Marx's utopia envisioned not only the liberation of productive power, the power that formed the necessary condition of all the other forms of power, but that the material and cultural fruits of power's liberation would be shared as equally as possible and, just as important, shared synchronistically—that is, the benefits would not be confined to some while others would have to postpone their gratifications. To state it differently, Marx might be said to have envisioned a society in which every member was contemporaneous with every other member, dwelling in the same material and cultural temporality and enjoying its advantages.

But what if our utopia is peculiar, not only because it depends on dystopic elements, or because it systematically excludes many of its members from the advantages of utopia, but because it forces many of its members to remain in a different epoch or epochs than that being experienced or exploited by those who occupy various levels of power and reward in the utopia? The first group remains mired in history—and, parenthetically, makes cultural studies possible—while the second has evolved into some ahistorical stage, that is, a stage in which the traditional idea of history has been transcended. The post-historical stage is characterized by the rapid changes associated with technological innovation—so rapid that while innovation may be temporarily experienced, its relentlessly protean character means that it cannot be *lived*. It cannot be preserved, held in trust, or inherited. The most spectacular form of continuous change is, of course, in communications, especially in computer technology. To illustrate our point that change is the euphemism for a new constitution of power relationships: Consider Silicon Valley; consider further those, mostly of poor Hispanic extraction, who patiently assemble the chips crucial to the technology: one knows for certain that when the workday is over the chip assemblers do not go home and click on Windows 2000.

The difference in epochs also marks contrasts in wealth, power, education, and life-chances. The difference in epochs and the contrasts in power have their political counterpart; that brings me to the second criterion of crisis, the criterion of generality. The political is the most revealing of these differences because it is there that the manipulation of epochs is most evident or blatant. The mass of the population is periodically doused with the rhetoric of democracy and assured that it lives in a democratic society and that democracy is the condition to which all progressive-minded societies should aspire. Yet that democracy is not meant to realize the demos but to constrain and neutralize it by the arts of electoral engineering and opinion management. It is, necessarily, regressive. Democracy is embalmed in public rhetoric precisely in order to memorialize its loss of substance. Substantive democracy— equalizing, participatory, commonalizing—is antithetical to everything that a high-reward, meritocratic society stands for. At the same moment that advanced societies have identified their progressive character with perpetual technological innovation they have defined themselves through policies that are regressive in many of their effects. Democracy is where those effects are registered. By virtually every important official norm—efficiency, incentives to unequal rewards, hierarchical principles of authority, expertise—it appears anachronistic, dysynchronous. The crux of the problem is that high-technology, globalized capitalism is radically incongruent with democracy. Politics, society, and individual modes of existence are being defined in ways that empirically falsify democracy as untrue of the powerful utopian side and therefore suitable for the powerless dystopian side.

But are the surviving forms of democracy sufficiently cross-grained to form the stuff of a continuing opposition to the technological thesis of corporate, global capitalism, or is democracy doomed to become merely an archaic deposit in the archaeology of power? The answer depends importantly on the vocation chosen by a "class" that is, by the standards of technological capitalism, as anachronistic as the idea and practice of democracy.

The crisis of democracy is also a crisis for the intellectual, especially for the academic intellectual in most of the social sciences and humanities. A climate of opinion is being developed in which tenure, academic freedom, and faculty role in university governance are likely to be changed in favor of even more managerial control. At the same time, the idea of the "virtual university" tailored to the needs of a technologically driven society is gaining support, not least because it offers the hope, mainly illusory, that by a severely practical curriculum its students can climb the wall separating the dystopian from the utopian side. When scrutinized according to such measures as cost-effectiveness, the bottom line, and productivity, the ideals of the humanistic liberal arts education cannot survive, except as an appendage to the culture industry or as a Potemkin village where the sons and daughters of the rich and infamous receive a polish unobtainable elsewhere. Otherwise, from the point of view of our utopia managers, there is no justification for the remainder of traditional scholarly and intellectual activities.

It would be nice to end on an uplifting note and invoke political theory to come to the aid of democracy, but besides being fatuous that call may be too late in the day. During the few decades that have elapsed since my original essay the academic intellectual has undergone a dizzying series of intellectual permutations—Marxism, critical theory, poststructuralism, deconstructionism, neopragmatism, etc. The theorist, in other words, has replicated the pace of technological change: he and she are synchronous with the utopia. That means, among other things, that they have aligned themselves with a future that is identified not with the elevation of the brawny, but with the care and feeding of the brainy classes. While the brainy classes live lives of permanent revolution, the masses, who represent the stuff of democracy, live lives of quiet desperation at the opposite end of that revolutionary pole, which Gramsci described as "detached from their traditional ideologies."

Gramsci also defined crisis: "The old is dying and the new cannot be born."[7] Perhaps our invocation might revise this definition to read, "The new is killing us and the old, as yet, is not required to be reborn, but revitalized." Revitalized, that is, as an element in the unborn theory that will recognize democracy as the dystopia of our time and understand that the opposite is condemned to be oppositional.

NOTES

1. *Minima Moralia: Reflections from Damaged Life,* trans. E. F. Jephcott (New York: Verso Books, 1996), 151.

2. For the controversy about whether or not book 8 of Thucydides' *History* is unfinished, see A. W. Gomme, A. Andrewes, and K. J. Dover, eds., *A Historical Commentary on Thucydides,* vol. 5 (Oxford: Clarendon Press, 1981), Introduction and Appendix 1.

3. "What I am attentive to is the fact that every human *relation* is to some degree a power relation. We move in a world of perpetual strategic relations." Michel Fou-

cault in Lawrence D. Kritzman, ed., *Michel Foucault: Politics, Philosophy, Culture* (New York: Routledge, 1988), 168.

4. Melinda Henneberger, "Seeing Politics, and Mirrors, in the Coverage of Capitol Hill," *New York Times,* 6 October 1997, C-1.

5. To be sure, Kuhn's classic account of paradigms emphasized that scientific revolutions were accompanied by alterations in scientific conventions. In its strong version that claim seemed to make insufficient allowance for continuities in scientific conventions. When pressed by critics Kuhn conceded that his original formulation was overstated—thus supplying a personal example of continuity. Lakatos's criticisms and Kuhn's response can be found in Imre Lakatos and Alan Musgrave, eds., *Criticism and the Growth of Knowledge* (Cambridge: Cambridge University Press, 1970), 91–195, 231–78. See also Kuhn's preface.

6. Barbara Crossette, "A New Credo: Make Money, Not War," *New York Times,* 24 August 1997, section 4, p. 1.

7. *Selections from the Prison Notebooks,* trans. Q. Hoare and G. N. Smith (New York: International Publishers, 1971), 275–76.

PART II

THEORIZING LOSS

2 // SPECTERS AND ANGELS
AT THE END OF HISTORY

*A Klee painting named "Angelus Novus" shows an angel looking as though he is
about to move away from something he is fixedly contemplating. His eyes are star-
ing, his mouth is open, his wings are spread. This is how one pictures the angel of
history. His face is turned toward the past. Where we perceive a chain of events, he
sees one single catastrophe which keeps piling wreckage upon wreckage and hurls it
in front of his feet. The angel would like to stay, awaken the dead, and make whole
what has been smashed. But a storm is blowing from Paradise and has got caught
in his wings with such violence that the angel can no longer close them. This storm
irresistibly propels him into the future to which his back is turned, while the pile
of debris before him grows skyward. This storm is what we call progress.*
—Walter Benjamin[1]

*If Benjamin's generation was forced to recognize that "capitalism will not die a
natural death," ours has had to learn the further lesson that capitalism is not, for
the foreseeable future, going to die at all.*
—Irving Wohlfarth[2]

From every corner of contemporary discourse, we know that the pace of contemporary social, cultural, economic, and political change is unprecedented.
Technological obsolescence occurs at the inception of production, deracinated human lives are ubiquitous and normal, divorce rates have almost
caught up with marriage rates, yesterday's deal is history, today's corporate
giant is the material of tomorrow's dissolved or merged identity. If "all that is
solid melted into air" in the last century, economic, social, and technological
transformations now occur so rapidly that their effects often do not even
coalesce as solids before metamorphosing into something else. This much we
know and recount to ourselves regularly. But we do not know much about
the relationship of this pace of change to the history that contours and fills it,
nor to the future that it heralds. On a daily basis we live the paradox that this

most fast-paced epoch in human history harbors a future that is both radically uncertain and profoundly out of the grasp of the inhabitants of the present. Moving this fast without any sense of control or predictability, both past and future have become sites of bewilderment and anxiety. In consequence, we inheritors of a radically disenchanted universe feel our impotence more strenuously than humans may ever have felt it before, even as we occupy a global order more saturated by human power than ever before. Power without purpose, power without lines of determination, power without end in every sense of the word.

Perhaps at no other historical moment has Benjamin's angel been such a poignant signifier of our predicament. We are blown backward, without vision or agency, into the future as debris piles up in the single catastrophe that is history beyond and outside of human invention or intervention, a history of subtle unfreedom. We cannot close our wings against the storm, cannot not be blown—that moment has been extinguished by contemporary history itself. Our capacity to intervene in the trajectory and effects of capital (as the most powerful moving force in modernity), to the extent that it ever existed, appears exhausted. So history surges on, but without promise that past suffering will be redeemed, without promise of eventual worldwide or even local emancipation, well-being, wisdom, or limitations on suffering. Nihilism seems far too thin a term for such circumstances.

How to rectify this condition, which is to say, how to rectify our impotence in the face of a present and future of driven, rushing aimlessness? Part of the answer to this question lies in how we might refigure the relation of the present to the past, how we might articulate the mass and force of the past in the present when that weight and trajectory can no longer be captured by a progressive narrative. The political importance of rethinking the relation of past to present in the context of a ruptured narrative of progress cannot be understated. At stake are both the question of what kind of historical consciousness is possible and appropriate for contemporary political critique and analysis, and the problem of deriving agency for the making of a more just, emancipatory, or felicitous future order. To see how urgently both are needed, we might consider two instances of contemporary anxiety and confusion about historical political thinking, one drawn from the political domain and one from academic debates.

In contemporary political parlance, the present's relation to the past is most often figured in terms of idealizations of particular epochs or individuals on the one hand, and reparations and apologies for past wrongs on the other. What does this figuring cover over, defer, or symptomatize in the present, what might it disavow about the bearing of the past on the present? German repayments to looted European Jewish estates from the 1930s, White House apologies to African Americans for enslaving or mistreating them, state compensation to interned Japanese-Americans in California during World War II, U.S. debates about reparations to Native Americans for stolen lands, China's resentment about Japan's failure to issue a written apology for its atrocities in the 1930s, even litigation by families who have suffered from wrongful findings in murder trials—what is the significance of conceiving historical trauma in terms of guilt, victimization, and above all, reparation and apology? Is the establishment of guilt and the measure of victimization that is secured by an apology or by material compensation presumed to conclude the historical event, to seal it as past, to "heal" it, or to bring it to "closure"? Is this referral to the law and to an economy of debt and payment a way of attempting to designate the past as really past, and to liberate the present from this past? What anxiety about the way these past traumas *live* in the present might be signified by such impulses to resolve them through a structure of wrong, debt, and payment?

Another sign of contemporary anxiety about history's bearing on the present is signified by a particular mode of criticizing poststructuralist challenges to materiality and objectivity. Responding to formulations that challenge brute facticity and, more generally, call into question objectivist or positivist accounts of history, many of these critics proclaim: "But the Holocaust really happened—it involved massive dislocation, human slaughter, obliteration of communities, artifacts, and archives." There are two questions begged in the rejoinder that something "happened" in history: (1) What account of this happening has the most veracity and why? (2) What is the meaning of this historical occurrence for political and cultural life in the present? Of course the Holocaust happened, but an itinerary of its occurrence that itemizes the devastation it wrought does not tell us what it means for those, sixty years later, living in its historical aftermath. Thus, an insistence on the materiality or facticity of the Holocaust is as dodgy about the question of how the Holocaust lives in the present as that insistence believes its putative opposition to be. The historical questions for the political present are not answered by a factually precise accounting of the North American slave trade in the nineteenth century, or by an itinerary of the homosexuals, gypsies, Jews, and Communists killed by European fascists in the 1930s and '40s. Rather, the political questions produced by the current crisis in historiography, and by the breakdown of a progressive historical metanarrative, include these: How do the histories of slavery, colonialism, or Nazism press upon contemporary North American and European political, social, and cultural life? How do these histories contour, constrain, and haunt the present? No empirical or materialist history can answer these questions, yet this very failing would seem to be what invocations of such histories are warring against, both in their claims to truth and in their reproach of those histories that call truth into question. Alas, the complex political problem of the relation of past to present, and of both to future, is resolved neither by facts nor by truth. While scholars of postcolonial orders understand this well, precisely because colonial histories suffuse the postcolonial present in such overtly discursive fashion, it is no small irony that the hegemonic histories of the metropoles still cling to objectivity as historical and political salvation.

If one problem inspiriting this essay concerns the failure of conventional historiographies to provide contemporary political orientation, the second concerns the ground of political motivation in the present, perhaps most succinctly characterized as a crisis in what Arendt termed "love of the world."

Sheldon Wolin has argued that we live in a time chiefly characterized by change.[3] Ours is a present that is hurtled into the future without regard for human attachments, needs, or capacities. A present that dishonors the past by erasing it with unprecedented speed and indifference. A present that equates the recent past with the anachronistic, with insufficient *technē* to survive. A present in which a political man of knowledge is a policy wonk rather than a reader of political histories. A present whose inevitable and rapid eclipse is uppermost in the political consciousness of its inhabitants. How can such a present be loved, and if it cannot be, what would our investments be in addressing its ills? What is there to attach to in a world of such incessant and rapid change? How can one love the world generated by this present sufficiently to want to do right by it? From what depth of feeling, conventionally cultivated through lifelong and generations-old attachments and values, can such a time be simultaneously embraced—providing the basis for love and loyalty—and challenged, fomenting the spirit of political activism? If there are no such depths or sources of continuity to draw upon, from what wellspring do we affirm our time, engage our dilemmas, define our imperatives? What incites our grievances and spurs our hopes?

A time of incessant change, Sheldon Wolin reminds us, is also one satu-rated with loss.[4] In his consideration of "invocation" as a figure for the poten-tial value of political theory and political theorists, he recalls that invocation in ancient Rome "was an appeal to a departed deity," an effort to recover something lost.[5] As a practice, "invocation may be said to imply memory and to enjoin recovery."[6] Walter Benjamin, writing half a century earlier amid another historical time that both confounded the modernist ideal of progress and harbored unfathomable orders of power and loss, invoked an angel to refigure the presence of the past in political thought. The angel signified memory and reparation, as well as despair, hope, and a disguised mean-ing in—and thus partial redemption of—human suffering. More recently, Jacques Derrida has revisited Marx's texts to develop an image of the present as inhabited by specters and ghosts of past and future. Deities, angels, spec-ters, and ghosts . . . what to make of these creatures rising from the pens of radical thinkers in the twentieth century as they attempt to grasp our rela-tion to past and future, and in particular as they attempt to articulate the prospects for a postfoundational formulation of justice? What leads a radical democrat to speak of deities, a Marxist literary critic to invoke angels, and a deconstructive philosopher of language to speak of specters and practice "hauntology"? What must be exhausted in certain strains of secular, progres-sive thought for the quasi-theological elements conventionally opposed to such thought to be conjured as valuable, perhaps even essential?

This chapter explores this question indirectly, through consideration of the reflections of Derrida and Benjamin on the problems of historical con-sciousness, the relation of the past to the present, memory, and loss. Derrida's *Specters of Marx* offers an imaginative—some have said outrageous—reading of selected texts by Marx and, by way of that reading, a critique of conven-tional understandings of Marx's contemporary legacy. However, my interest in *Specters* is less with Derrida's reading of Marx than with his experiment in reconceiving the press of history on the present, an experiment that may break more radically with progressive historiography than does genealogy as formulated by Nietzsche and Foucault. Through a discourse of spectrality that includes ghosts, haunting, and conjuration, Derrida experiments with a mode of historical consciousness that does not recur to discredited narratives of systematicity, periodicity, laws of development, or a bounded, coherent past and present. Derrida's effort is also attentive to the problem of political judgment and political hope, and attempts to establish terrain for both without locating either in a narrative of progress or founding either in meta-physical precepts. Walter Benjamin's "Theses on the Philosophy of History" and other meditations on historical consciousness offer a critique of prog-ress, rework the meaning of historical materialism through that critique, and offer grounds—or at least handholds—for revolutionary political action. Benjamin is the consummate theorist of political despair, yet mines a unique strain of hopefulness from the same ground as the despair. Locating histori-cal understanding "within the cultural work of mourning" allows for the possibility of redeeming historical losses, a redemption that is foreclosed by melancholic attachments to those losses.[7] Achieving this redemption through a certain kind of "activation" of the past seizes and reconfigures the present as well. Together, Derrida's and Benjamin's work on history offer partial strategies for configuring responsible political consciousness and agency in an uncertain time after progress.

DERRIDA'S SPECTERS OF MARX

How do we figure history at the end of (modern) history, when the presump-tion that history progresses has been exposed epistemologically as theologi-cal and experienced practically as a cruel hoax? What is history's postpro-gressive shape, weight, and force, and what language can best express those parameters? What kind of historical discourse is not merely antiprogressive (as genealogy is often said to be "Whig history in reverse") but disrupts a progressive narrative by relocating historical meaning onto some other space and idiom? That is, what discourse of history can provide a way of conceiv-ing the relationship between past, present, and future without setting its com-pass points through or against a discourse of progress? For Derrida, these questions are threaded through a historically specific question about Marx: how do we figure both Marx's thinking and Marx's legacy outside of a pro-gressive historiography, when the history of Marxism in a progressive vein quite literally ended, when Marxism as political possibility and political imperative (and Derrida will tolerate no less politically invested version of Marx's thought) died a decade ago? Derrida's reading of Marx against con-ventional Marxist historiography is thus simultaneously a reading of Marx against Marxism and a reading of Marx against present-day anti-Marxists who celebrate the death of Marxism. Derrida aims to deprive the present of its sense of triumph over Marxism, its sense of being done with Marxism, a sense he believes Marxism has colluded in through its own historiography, its own wager on progress.

We begin with a hypothesis Derrida poses lightly across his text: Are ghosts and spirits what inevitably arise at the end or death of something—an era, desire, attachment, belief, figure, or narrative? When we have arrived at the erstwhile end of history, should it surprise us if history reappears in the form of a haunt? To put it differently, when we cease to figure history in terms of laws, drives, development, or logic, are ghosts what remain? Derrida's question is cast only in part from a psychoanalytic direction in which suppression, repression, and the logic of mourning govern consciousness. It issues as well from his speculative philosophical musings about death, about the effect of death on the living, about the way the dead live among the living, the way the past lives indirectly in the present, inchoately suffusing and shaping rather than determining it. For Derrida, the language of haunting is our confession that dead things live; ghosts contravene the finality of death for the living, they undo the line between death and life.

Derrida's own beginning in this text: "Someone, you or me, comes forward and says: I would like to learn to live finally."[8] Learning to live, Derrida insists, involves first coming to terms with the non-opposition of life and death, a non-opposition conventionally figured by ghosts, the live figures of the dead, one form of life after death. Thus, to learn to live, to embrace the non-opposition of life and death, "it would be necessary to learn spirits," to learn when, how, and why they appear, and how we conjure or invoke them.[9] Affirming this non-opposition also entails living without conceits of foundations, origins, and progress, and especially without clear distinctions between the real and the fictive, the ideal and the material, the past and the present. And learning to live without all of these props in turn means learning to practice ethical conduct and pursue political justice in the context of a world that is contingent, unpredictable, not fully knowable, and directed neither by external forces nor by internal logics. Again, the figure Derrida offers for this orientation and practice is learning to live with haunts or specters with things that shape the present, that render the present as always permeated by an elsewhere, but in an inconstant, ephemeral, and hence not fully mappable fashion. Ghosts thus emblematize a postmetaphysical way of life, a way of life saturated by elements—could we call them "material conditions"?—not under our sway and that also cannot be harnessed to projects of reason, development, progress, or structure. Ghosts figure the impossibility of mastering, with either knowledge or action, the past or the present. They figure the necessity of grasping certain implications of the past for the present only as traces or effects (rather than as structures, axioms, laws, or lines of determination) and of grasping even these as protean. "Learning to live, finally," means learning to live with this unmasterable, uncategorizable, and irreducible character of the past's bearing on the present, and hence with the unmasterable and irreducible character of the present as well. "Learning to live" means living without systematizing, without conceits of coherence, without a consistent and complete picture, and without a clear delineation between past and present. Living with ghosts, permitting and even exploiting their operation as a deconstructive device, means living with the permanent disruption of the usual opposites that render our world coherent between the material and the ideal, the past and the present, the real and the fictive, the true and the false. Ghosts are what rise from materialism, periodicity, and objectivity after each has been slain by the exposure of their untenable predicates. We quarrel with these ghosts and also quarrel with each other about these ghosts—their shape, their meaning, their longevity. Both kinds of quarrels affirm and produce their existence; neither kind stabilizes the meaning of the past for the present.

In asking what it would mean to "learn to live, finally," Derrida intends to ask anew not only about the epistemological orientation or ethical pose of individuals (ethics) but about political orientation, and matters of justice (politics).

The time of the "learning to live," a time without tutelary present, would amount to this . . . : to learn to live with ghosts, in the upkeep, the conversation, the company, or the companionship, in the commerce without commerce of ghosts. To live otherwise and better. No not better, but more justly. But with them. No *being-with* the other, no *socius* without this *with* that makes *being-with* in general more enigmatic than ever for us. And this being-with specters would also be, not only but also, a politics of memory, of inheritance and of generations.

No justice . . . seems possible or thinkable without the principle of some responsibility, beyond all living present, within that which disjoins the living present, before the ghosts of those who are not yet born or who are already dead. . . . Without this non-contemporaneity with itself of the living present, without that which secretly unhinges it, without this responsibility and this respect for justice concerning those who are not there, of those who are no longer or who are not yet present and living, what sense would there be to ask the question "where?" "where tomorrow?" "whither?" [10]

Derrida's formulation of justice in this instance is radically unfamiliar to political theory. It has little relation to a distributional definition, nor is it procedural, tethered to law, or even to measures of participation or shared power. Rather, justice in this text is less institutional or spatial than temporal: it pertains almost entirely to responsible relations between generations. For Derrida, justice concerns not only our debt to the past but the past's legacy in the present; it informs not only our obligation to the future, but responsibility for our (ghostly) presence in that future: "Justice carries life beyond present life or its actual being there. . . ." [11] Justice demands that we locate our political identity between what we have inherited and what is not yet born, between what we can only imagine and the histories that constrain and shape that imagination. This is a notion of political identity quite at odds with identity shaped by fixed social coordinates and especially group affinity. Justice, Derrida argues, is literally incoherent if dehistoricized, detached from futurity, or confined to a self-identical present. But not only must justice have futurity, it is what *makes* futurity insofar as it generates the future's relationship to the present as a "living on" of present efforts and aims. Justice entails the present generation's responsibility for crafting continuity, as well as the limits of that responsibility and that continuity.

How to argue for the imperative of this continuity without reliance on the usual moral and historiographic ruses? This is Derrida's political project with the specter, namely the figuring of a novel mode of temporality as a basis for political responsibility, a mode that honors and redeems the past without recourse to *Geist* (or any other logic of history) and that is also responsive to imagined future generations, even offers them a certain promise and guarantee, without pretending that it can orchestrate their relations. This strange and intangible figure of the specter is what Derrida proffers as a site of renewal for historical consciousness and political agency after all modernist logics of history and political change have given up the ghost.

The present-past relation conceived spectrally recasts not only the weight and force of the past in the present but vital elements of the political present as well. As we shall see, Derrida exploits the specter's quality of "inbetweenness" to disrupt certain modernist formulations of ontology, theology, epistemology, and teleology that underscore conventional forms of political critique and political value tethered to a stable notion of the present. The specter as the "becoming body" challenges ontology as fixity, and challenges as well the distinction between material dimension and concept. The specter as a "carnal form of spirit" both disrupts an otherworldly and idealist formulation of theology and the subject, and at the same time undoes the materiality conventionally associated with the body. "Neither soul nor body, and both one and the other," the specter bypasses materiality and its putative opposite.[12] To elaborate these points, Derrida draws on the paradoxical dimension of Marx's invocation of the specter in the "Communist Manifesto," that most "real and concrete" of Marx's writings that simultaneously issues from a historically specific location and is a world traveler in history. This text that, as a written text, is rivaled only by the Bible as a force in history, also outmoded itself quickly even by Marx and Engels's own account. Written in a specific time and place, and replete with references revealing that specificity, it takes on a transcendent and universal life, yet only through readings that, in various times and locations around the globe, are themselves historically contingent. Moreover, in opening the "Manifesto" with the specter as a figure of power and agency, Derrida argues, Marx invokes "this first paternal character, as powerful as it is unreal, a hallucination or simulacrum more actual than what is blithely called a living presence."[13] The specter, unreal yet potent, operates in the opening paragraph of the Manifesto as the vehicle for the great unifying project of modern Europe. "All the Powers of old Europe have entered into a holy alliance to exorcize this specter: Pope and Czar, Metternich and Guizot, French Radicals and German police-spies."[14] This ghost of the future, this incontestably immaterial figure, has also precipitated one of the mightiest alliances of modern European history. In this way, the paradoxical opening of the "Manifesto" reveals the nonviability of the tangible materialism that will be its leitmotif. This is the tension that Derrida exploits in Marx's work: Marxist materialism is haunted (and undone) by the specter with which he commences, the specter that he himself has conjured but also seeks (fruitlessly) to exorcize.

What Derrida terms the "spectral asymmetry" of the specter, its felt presence without being seen, our incapacity to see what looks at us, disrupts all conventional specularity, and in this way wreaks havoc with the epistemology of empiricism, especially empirical accounts of power.[15] Spectral asymmetry is achieved both through what Derrida calls the "visor effect" of the specter seeing without being seen and through what he terms the "commerce of specters," the multiple and inconstant character of their appearance. This asymmetry interrupts conventional specularity insofar as the power of the specter is not empirically observable but is no less tangible for being invisible. In a spectral relation, Derrida argues, we feel the force of the look. In a historical dimension, this means that the dead and the not yet born intermittently press constraints or demands with an unmistakable but invisible power, a power that also exceeds our conventional formulations of agency in power. This challenge to specularity, to both the tangibility of power and the reciprocity of visibility between actor and acted upon, disrupts empirical and systematic efforts to apprehend both power and history, and especially the power of the historical in the present. While "haunting is historical . . . it is not dated, it is never docilely given a date in the chain of presents. . . . Untimely, it does not come to, it does not happen to, it does not befall, one day, Europe. . . ."[16]

Finally, what Derrida terms a "hauntology," which analyzes the work of the specter in history and history-making, harbors both an eschatology and a teleology, but "incomprehensibly," that is, in a manner that does not add up to a comprehensive account of history's relationship to the present. The specter reverses the usual understanding of history as origin (and the present as the teleological fruit of the origin) by virtue of the fact that the specter is always a *revenant*. The specter begins by coming back, by repeating itself, by recurring in the present. It is not traceable to an origin or to a founding event, it does not have an objective or "comprehensive" history, yet it operates as a *force*. Moreover, Derrida insists, we cannot control the comings and goings of specters because they are by nature "furtive and untimely," they "upset time," just as justice must entail an upsetting of the present, a referral of the present back toward our ancestors and forward toward the unborn. Hence, Derrida characterizes the politics of spectral consciousness as a "being-with" specters that is also an insurgent "politics of memory, inheritance, generations."[17] To have this consciousness is to live actively with—indeed, to activate politically—the spirits of the past and the future, the bearable and unbearable memories of the past and weight of obligation toward the unborn. Derrida has rendered impossible (as will Benjamin) any pure categories in the attempt to separate history from memory by insisting on the political face of history as a persistent question of the way the past is remembered or disavowed. We inherit not "what really happened" to the dead but what lives on from that happening, what is conjured from it, the way that past generations and events occupy the force fields of the present, how they claim us, how they haunt, plague, and inspirit our imaginations and visions for the future.

Thus far, I have emphasized Derrida's engagement of the specter to recast the relation of past, present, and future, a recasting that disrupts linear time, progressive time, causal time, predictable time, and hence disrupts the very periodicity required by a division into past, present, and future. Yet this disruption is not to be equated with abolition of this division. Rather, the figure of the specter underscores the weightiness of the relation between the three terms. It signals the unbidden imposition of parts of the past on the present, and the way in which the future is always already populated with certain possibilities derived from the past, the way in which the future is constrained, circumscribed, inscribed by the past, the way in which it is haunted before we make and enter it. This formulation of the past's heavy yet indeterminate appearance in present and future time does not simply give us a new historical determinism, potent without being mappable or predictable. Rather, it enables a novel kind of agency with regard to the place of history in the present, an agency signaled by the notion of "conjuration."

If ghosts are "furtive and untimely," if they come and go as they please, they can also be conjured and exorcized—solicited, beckoned, invoked, dismissed—and thus made to live in the present or leave the present in a manner that shapes present and future possibilities and constraints. Conjuring, always a mixture of conscious and unconscious activity, is also precise and deliberate activity paradoxically combined with pure hope. We conjure the not-yet-true (whether the dead as alive, or an imagined triumph) in an effort to make it true. Conjuration is the term through which Derrida reads not only Marx's own rendering of French revolutionaries in Roman garb, but Marx's formulation (drawn in part from Shakespeare's *Timon of Athens*) in *The Economic and Philosophic Manuscripts* of the transmutation of paper into gold and of gold into personal, social, and political power.[18] Conjuring is also what political actors do with specters they must defeat: we conjure *away* certain historical haunts just as we conjure *forth* others. Historiography as hauntology is thus not only a new mode of figuring the presence of the past, the ineffable and unconquerable force of the past, it also opens the stage for battling with the past over possibilities of the future. In figuring the past as "alive" in the present, conjuring supplies the capacity to invoke and diminish it, to demand its presence on stage or to attempt to banish it to the wings. Of course, conjuration is never only or fully in our hands, but neither is it in the hands of God, historical facticity, or metaphysical axioms.

A characterization of the past as haunting the present and as conjurable in the present challenges not simply linear but progressive history. In Derrida's reformulation, history emerges as that which shadows and constrains, incites or thwarts, rather than as that which moves, directs, or unfolds. History as a ghostly phenomenon does not march forward in a progressive manner—it doesn't even march. Rather, it comes and goes, appears and recedes, makes and loosens its claim. And it changes shape, that is, the same event or formation does not haunt in the same way across time and space. The notion of progress as that which unfolds the future is also undone by Derrida's image of political life as a stage in which specters of past and future at times appear unbidden and at other times are conjured by those vying for particular futures vis-à-vis particular interpretations of the past or particular claims of homage to the past.

But Derrida's work with the specter is not only intended, and perhaps not intended at all, as a general historiography. Rather, it is a historically specific and historically remedial move. Recall that Derrida's beginning in this work affirms the specter as something that arises at the end of something, at the moment of death or loss. The specter as a figure for history thus pertains to Derrida's diagnosis of our time both as haunted by the end of history and as a time itself "out of joint," struggling with some way in which it is at odds with itself, some way in which it is internally asunder. Each of these postulations is considered separately below.

"After the end of history, the spirit comes by *coming back* [*revenant*], it figures both a dead man who comes back and a ghost whose expected return repeats itself, again and again."[19] The moment when history ends is also the moment when we are ghosted by history, by that which we no longer believe in, because what has really ended is a certain concept of history, a concept by which we continue to be haunted.[20] The inevitability of a ghosted return of a fundamental concept following its exhaustion is part of what Derrida calls the logic of haunting, in which the present is haunted not simply by what transpired in the past but by what was confused or misnamed in the past, what remains unclear in meaning. To be haunted by something is at once to experience the profundity or significance of something from the past and at the same time not to know what that something was. When we say, "I'm not sure why but I am haunted by what she said to me yesterday," we affirm that haunting occurs at the point of uncertainty about the meaning of an event, an utterance, a gesture. The phenomenon remains alive, refuses to recede into the past, precisely to the extent that its meaning is unsettled and open-ended, to the extent that it remains interpreted and contested by the present. But this haunting of the present also disturbs settled meanings in the present. To be haunted by something is to recognize that we are unsettled by it, disoriented by it, even if we cannot name or conquer that challenge. The logic of haunting is thus a logic in which the permanent open-endedness of meaning and the permanent limits of mastery are cornerstones. These features of haunting will also constitute the site of intellectual and political agency within "hauntology."

Haunting is also unsettling to the very degree that a past remark or event or figure hovers over the present, thereby unsettling the line between past and present. To be haunted often entails being touched or suffused by something that one cannot quite recall, to feel the importance of something that one has laid aside or tried to forget. It is to recognize that there is something occupying the present from the past whose shape or meaning eludes us. So haunting takes place between history and memory; it is simultaneously an achievement of memory and a failure of memory with regard to some significant historical effect. As an achievement, it keeps the phenomenon alive and potent; as a failure of memory, it indicates or points toward a history that it cannot fully conjure or command. Disavowed, the haunting will undo the present as it works according to its own logic, yet avowed, it does not make perfectly clear what its meaning and effects are. This is the conundrum set for us by affirming hauntology as historiography.

On Derrida's second and more diagnostic point, concerning the "out-of-jointness" of the present, we must make brief examination of Derrida's invocation of Hamlet's time as an image of our own. *"The time is out of joint."* Derrida reads, rereads, and overreads this phrase from Hamlet to allow it to converge with the promise of a reformulated temporality for justice heralded by spectrality. He queries whether the remark invokes time in the sense of *"le temps* itself, the temporality of time, or else what temporality makes possible (time as *histoire,* the way things are at a certain time . . .), or else, consequently, the *monde,* the world . . . our world today, our today, currentness itself," and settles on the possibility that it is all three.[21] He exploits the diverse French translations of Shakespeare's phrase—a time that is off its hinges, broken down, out of sorts, upside-down, askew—to reflect on the different dimensions of temporality and decenteredness the phrase elicits. Derrida is especially drawn to Gide's translation: "Cette époque est déshonorée [this age is dishonored]," because it combines a strong ethical and political meaning—a sense of moral decadence, of corruption of the polity, of dissolution or perversion of customs—with the more general observation that things are not going as they ought to go.[22] It is this condition of being internally broken apart (disjointed) in the sense of being in disharmony with our own values, or off-center with regard to our own principles and institutions, that Derrida seizes upon as the diagnostic moment connecting Shakespeare with Marx with Derrida's own reading of the injustice of our own time. This moment, Derrida insists, calls for a different order of justice, a justice that breaks with the current order of things even as it strikes continuity between past, present, and future. But what Derrida calls the out-of-jointness of time is crucially distinguished from a notion of a time in "crisis." The former indicates a more subtly corrosive condition than the latter; it suggests a time that is wearing badly, a time whose languages have grown thin or hypocritical, whose practices have grown hollow, whose ideals are neither realized nor perhaps any longer suit the age.

What conventionally sets time right again, Derrida argues, is the law, but law's traditional connection with vengeance, and even with blood revenge, can only perpetuate the out-of-jointness of the times because it addresses only its symptoms. (This would seem to be indicated by the boundless litigiousness of the present age, especially from those aggrieved by the current order of justice.) Justice cast in legal terms repeats the fundamental principles and practices of the current order of justice and thus condemns us to the out-of-jointness of our time. A formulation of justice intended to rectify the disjointedness of the times must rely on something other than the law; in Derrida's formulation, it must be beyond right, debt, calculation, and vengeance. "Otherwise justice risks being reduced once again to juridical-moral rules, norms, or representations, within an inevitable totalizing horizon. . . ."[23] Derrida seeks a noncontemporaneous idiom for justice, one that embraces out-of-jointness as itself the spur to justice and as the mode of a detotalized condition of justice. A detotalized justice is necessarily in a state of what Derrida calls "disjointure": it is reconciled to the indeterminacy of specters, the endless commerce of specters, the indeterminacy of the past, and of the past's relationship to the present. It challenges us to fashion justice from the material of the specters of the past and present, honoring the dead, attending to the not-yet-born, but all this with minimal leaning into metaphysical or epistemological foundations.

What has Derrida offered in this admittedly partial and self-serving reading of Marx, one that makes deconstruction not only compatible with but something of a necessary heir to Marx? [24] This reading, so patently against the grain, highlights in Marx's thought the very ghosts that Derrida knows Marx avers: "Marx does not like ghosts . . . he does not want to believe in them. But he thinks of nothing else." [25] As a study of Marx, this reading culls the immateriality that haunts Marx's materialism, the spirit that haunts his empiricism, the magic that haunts his Real. But what Derrida offers as well is the tentative beginnings of a historiography for historical political consciousness in the time after progress. He offers strategies for developing historical consciousness that rely neither on a progressive historiography nor on historical determinism more generally, strategies for conceiving our relation to past and future that coin responsibility and possibilities for action out of indeterminacy.

WALTER BENJAMIN'S "THESES ON THE PHILOSOPHY OF HISTORY"

Thinking involves not only the flow of thoughts but their arrest as well. Where thinking suddenly stops in a configuration pregnant with tensions, it gives that configuration a shock, by which it crystallizes into a monad. A historical materialist approaches a historical subject only where he encounters it as a monad. In this structure he recognizes the sign of a Messianic cessation of happening, or put differently, a revolutionary chance in the fight for the oppressed past. He takes cognizance of it in order to blast a specific era out of the homogeneous course of history blasting a specific life out of the era or a specific work out of the lifework. As a result of this method the lifework is preserved in this work and at the same time canceled; in the lifework the era; and in the era, the entire course of history. The nourishing fruit of the historically understood contains time as a precious but tasteless seed. [26]

For Walter Benjamin, the conundrum of modern history is its stormy forward movement absent a telos. But the conundrum of radical political action (contra Marx historiographically, while linking arms with him politically) lies in the need to break this stream of history, to interrupt or arrest historical process in order to inaugurate another possibility or "actuality." What Marx, after Hegel, called world historical events, do not for Benjamin fulfill history's mission but explode historical processes, reroute history, even begin it anew.

Benjamin's critical engagement with the notion of progress, on which he considered all modern strains of philosophy and political life to rest, was by no means a simple rejection of historical process. To the contrary, the backward-looking angel of history both sees and feels the terrible press of history, a "single catastrophe which keeps piling wreckage upon wreckage," a storm that "has got caught in his wings with such violence that he can no longer close them" but can do nothing to stop that force.[27] Indeed, it is not the task of the angel but of an ill-defined "us" to interrupt this force, to seize moments in the present as possibilities for action. Thus, Benjamin argues, "the awareness that they are about to make the continuum of history explode is characteristic of the revolutionary classes at the moment of their action."[28] Great revolutions, he recalls, always introduce new calendars, thereby marking the interruption of one trajectory of history and the inauguration of another.

Benjamin seeks to formulate "interruption" not only as the spirit and metaphor of revolutionary politics, but as everyday politics. He seeks to deploy "interruption" or "blasting open the continuum of history" as a kind of persistent revolutionary political orientation that breaks both with the notion of progress and with its cousin, uniquely "ripe" revolutionary conditions, even as it attends closely to historical configurations of opportunity or possibility. The "arrest" of history that revolution achieves not only sets history's sails in a new direction (as opposed to the progressivist view that revolution is a teleological conclusion of a historical process), but indicts a fundamental premise of progress, namely that more just and felicitous times have steadily displaced more impoverished ones. For Benjamin, the past is not an inferior version of the present, but an exploitable cache of both traumatic and utopian scenes. Thus, the theological moment that Benjamin believes inheres in all revolutionary hopes pertains to traces of the good life left behind, preserved and cultivated as imagistic memories. These are the traces that would inspirit revolutionary action, and it is precisely the ideology of progress that eliminates these traces from view. What Benjamin terms the revolutionary-historical "tiger's leap into the past" is thus the grand revolutionary gesture, at once political and intellectual, of disinterring repressed emancipatory hopes and experiences from their tombs under the putative march of progress. As Lutz Niethammer phrases it: "Benjamin's hope is that . . . it will be possible . . . to bring time to a halt . . . and to reach beyond the most insupportable conditions to assist the species-recollection of the good life . . . as the guide to human action. Through his tiger leaps, the historian must stand at their side and blast the repressed hopes out of the progress-leveled past."[29]

This "tiger's leap" is a complicated one, however, for, as Benjamin notes, "it takes place in an arena where the ruling class gives the commands,"[30] and the trick is to seize the interruption of history from the maw of bourgeois co-optation. When Benjamin adds that "the same leap in the open air of history is the dialectical one, which is how Marx understood the revolution," he is identifying the struggle between revolutionary and bourgeois forces as a struggle that is not only over the present, but over the meanings of history as well.[31] History interrupted is a fecund political moment, but it comes with no guarantees, with no absence of struggle and no certainty about the outcome. That is why he refers to it only as "a revolutionary *chance* in the fight for the oppressed past."[32]

But how paradoxical is the notion of historicized political consciousness poised for action that Benjamin develops! Deeply attuned to the possibilities that history presents and that can be created within it, it is also committed to a kind of "forgetting" in which history is not simply "blasted apart" but "gaily parted with." Thus, the historical memory Benjamin cultivates as political possibility in one moment is literally exploded by revolutionary action in another. History is not simply "realized" by revolutionary action but invented, reworked, and also destroyed by it.

For a clearer view of this paradox, and its importance in developing a politics "after history" that also draws its energies from historical consciousness, we need to tarry longer with Benjamin's famous enigmatic angel. The figure of the angel in Benjamin's ninth thesis on the philosophy of history carries (but does not exhaust) Benjamin's critique of progress and thus contributes to a reframing of the problem of political knowledge and political action in the era of *posthistoire*.[33] Gershom Scholem's genealogy of Benjamin's crafting of this figure (from Klee's *Angelus Novus*, which Benjamin owned, as well as from other sources) is immensely helpful in this regard, as is the reading of the ninth thesis by Lutz Niethammer. Scholem begins by noting that the word for "angel" in Hebrew also means "messenger," and adds that in one strain of Jewish tradition, each of us is said to have a personal angel that represents our secret self in a problematic way: this angel can enter into opposition to and tension with the human to whom it is attached.[34] So Benjamin's messenger of history, harboring history's secret meaning, immediately casts history as tragic, propelled toward a future to which its back is turned, and carrying meaning only as a witness to catastrophe. The secret truth of history is at best a negative one, centered on this nebulously defined catastrophe; but perhaps more important, history's "secret" is that its movement has no meaning at all. The messenger of history is also paradoxically mute: it cannot speak to the future, even as history is implicated in the future. That is, history has bearing on the future insofar as the storm from Paradise (which Benjamin, borrowing from Krause, casts as "both origin and goal") is blowing toward the future.[35] But the angel cannot look there, it cannot speak, nor can it intervene in the storm into which it is only and always blown backward.

Paradise, Scholem suggests in his reading of Benjamin, is the primal past of man as well the utopian image of our future redemption.[36] But the storm prevents the angel—history's meaning—from doing this redemptive work. The angel cannot "stay, awaken the dead, and make whole what has been smashed," which Benjamin claims is its yearning, because there is a forward (nonprogressive) press of history, and because the angel is powerless and speechless. The angel is pushed toward a future into which it does not gaze, cannot gaze, but cannot not go, and also looks out over a past that it cannot redeem even as it longs to do so. The angel, however, sees history for what it is: "one great catastrophe," the ruins of freedom unrealized.

Lutz Niethammer also approaches Benjamin's angel theologically, but from a different angle. Why, Niethammer asks, does Benjamin give us the image of an *angel* of history, when, on the one hand, historians usually choose muses as their higher beings, and when, on the other, angels in the Bible and in the Jewish tradition generally relate to God or humanity, but not to history? What the Hebrew Bible knows is the past, and this knowledge "is typically denoted by the same word that refers to what the face is turned towards in attention; while the word for the future also signifies what is hidden behind one's back."[37] Niethammer concludes, "The position and line of vision of the new (or still young) angel in the storm thus evoke the religious tradition, as does the storm itself."[38] The line of vision of the angel is thus precisely at odds with the secular dynamic of progress and reason constitutive of the Enlightenment. It is a vision that draws from its knowledge of paradise again, both an archaic and a utopian knowledge, or from the hopes and dreams of humankind. But disenchantment, itself occasioned by the idealization of progress and rationality, depowers this tradition's insights and instigations, indeed overwhelms them as if by a storm, a storm that makes ruins of everything, including messianic hopes and dreams. The tradition of religious redemption (and hence religious inspiration) has become impotent: "The victims [of the history of progress] no longer have access to the power of religious redemption; for in the raging wind of disenchantment the angel is driven up and away."[39] Under the hegemony of progress, the divine messenger is incapable of action and redemptive politics is impossible. Only the rupture of progressive ideology, the "arrest" of historical process, permits the redemptive powers of hope, dream, and utopian passion a place on the political and historical stage. Only then can history be rewritten as a different future is coined from the present. But this also suggests that the rupture of history and progressive ideology simultaneously constitutes a theological and a secular opening for political understanding and action. It is an opening for both the messianic dreams and the human crafting that are erased by progressive historiography and politics. Thus does postfoundationalism become simultaneously spiritual and historical; its challenge to historical automatism reactivates the figures banished by that automatism: conscious and unconscious memories, hopes, and longings.

Together, Scholem's and Niethammer's interpretations suggest that while progress may be a delusion, it has functioned as a powerful ideology that has both displaced the Edenic elements of the past and destroyed the memory of their existence. With the force of a storm, "piling wreckage upon wreckage," it has rendered theological yearnings impotent on earth. The angel who represents these yearnings and who alone apprehends the limitations of an Enlightenment perspective, sees the ruin of this course of history but is powerless to express its insight and is itself a passive wisp in the winds of this history. Yet the figure of this melancholy angel does not mean that Benjamin abandons the project of redemption and revolution. Rather, Benjamin's reformulated dialectical materialism, far too heavy with messianic and literary tropes to be acceptable to most Marxists, poses the prospect of simultaneously interrupting the continuum of history and redeeming the past.

Revolution and redemption at once, and achieved through one another—it is hardly the most intuitively credible moment of hope issuing from Benjamin's despairing vision. To increase its credibility, we must leave the ninth thesis and investigate further both Benjamin's critique of progress and his formulation of dialectics. In the thirteenth thesis, Benjamin offers a terse, threefold critique of the conception of progress as it appears in the social democratic theory of his milieu. The social democrats, he claims, understand progress as "first . . . the progress of mankind itself . . . second . . . [as] something boundless, in keeping with the infinite perfectibility of mankind . . . [and third] . . . as irresistible, something that automatically pursues a straight or spiral course."[40] Each of these predicates, Benjamin remarks, "is controversial and open to criticism."[41] But his critique exceeds one that would simply point out the groundlessness of the various premises of progress, and instead aims at "what they have in common: The concept of the historical progress of mankind cannot be sundered from the concept of its progression through a homogeneous, empty time. A critique of the concept of such a progression must be the basis of any criticism of the concept of progress itself."[42]

What Benjamin names homogeneous, empty time is precisely the opposite of historical time. Time, he insists, is always "filled by the presence of the Now," meaning that it always has particular content that itself gives meaning to time, rather than the other way around. Time does not exist in some transcendental status outside of the particular present ("the time of the now"), investing it with questions, meaning, or projects. Thus, the fundamental trouble with all notions of historical progress is their imbrication with a false transcendentalism—progress inevitably transpires above human consciousness, activity, and concerns. Within a progressive metanarrative, time is unstructured by anything other than progress, and historical memory or consciousness imagines itself to be unstructured by the present, to be unsituated and unsaturated. Benjamin's objection to progressive historiography, then, is not simply its groundlessness as historiography, but the havoc it wreaks with a historically oriented political consciousness. Rather than focusing this consciousness on the parameters of the present, rather than licensing it to evoke and create historical memory, progress lifts consciousness out of time and space, and treats past, present, and their relation as givens.

The problem of developing a political consciousness oriented to historically shaped possibility is further illuminated in thesis 8, which immediately precedes Benjamin's invocation of the angel of history.

The tradition of the oppressed teaches us that the "state of emergency" in which we live is not the exception but the rule. We must attain to a conception of history that is in keeping with this insight. Then we shall clearly realize that it is our task to bring about a real state of emergency, and this will improve our position in the struggle against Fascism. One reason why Fascism has a chance is that in the name of progress its opponents treat it as a historical norm. The current amazement that the things we are experiencing are "still" possible in the twentieth century is *not* philosophical. This amazement is not the beginning of knowledge unless it is the knowledge that the view of history which gives rise to it is untenable.[43]

Like Derrida, Benjamin insists that it is not history that "ends" in the twentieth century but a certain concept of history that reaches the limits of tenability, a concept that nonetheless continues to grip political thinking and reaction even in its ghostly form, producing "amazement" and literal dumbfounding. Progress, so often understood by radicals and reformers as a wellspring of political hope, functions in just the opposite way in Benjamin's view. Progress reconciles and attaches its adherents to an inevitable (even fatalistic) and unwittingly normative account of political formations and events. The hopefulness that a progressive view of history offers is both delusional and ultimately conservative, precluding a politics devoted to bringing about the "state of emergency" that breaks with this present or "blasts open the continuum of history."[44] Moreover, Benjamin argues, while it is the downtrodden who often cling hardest to the progressive promise, progress always measures the condition of the dominant class and is part of the ideology constituting its dominance as natural.[45] For Benjamin, the ratification of the bourgeoisie offered by a progressive historiography pertains to its articulation of an ideology that erases the condition of the defeated or the oppressed in the name of a historical automatism, that is, a process with no agent, no powers, and most important, no victims—or at least none for whom anyone or anything is accountable.

It is this seamless narrative—reinforced by one version of dialectical materialism but challenged by Benjamin's version—that Benjamin seeks to disrupt with both alternative historical images and new sites of political possibility. Historical materialism has to abandon the epic element in history. It blasts the epoch out of the reified "continuity of history." But it also blasts open the homogeneity of the epoch. It saturates it with *ecrasite,* that is, the present.[46]

The destructive or critical impetus in materialist historiography comes into play in that blasting apart of historical continuity which allows the historical object to constitute itself. . . . Materialist historiography does not choose its objects casually. It does not pluck them from the process of history, but rather blasts them out of it. Its precautions are more extensive, its occurrences more essential.[47]

This "blasting open" or "blasting apart" that Benjamin identifies as the work of the historical materialist is neither objective nor simply invented. Rather, it is a very specific kind of interpretive work, one that affirms historical contingency in its vision, acknowledges the element of invention resulting from this contingent quality, yet insists on the materiality of the past that it glimpses and renders in the present. It insists, in other words, on the material unfolding of the past, but distinguishes this material unfolding from the bearing of the past on the present, and from our grasp of the past in the present.

In thesis 6, Benjamin states, "To articulate the past historically does not mean to recognize it 'the way it really was' (Ranke). It means to seize hold of a memory as it flashes up at a moment of danger."[48] This formulation of history as fleeting, appearing in fiery but transitory images, and as both capturing and signaling a moment of danger (the danger of being colonized, of rendering both interpreter and the past "a tool of the ruling classes") is a recurring one in Benjamin, and corresponds directly to the project of undoing the inevitability or the givenness of the present with historical memory. The blasting that Benjamin invokes both seizes upon and opens possibilities in the present, in what Benjamin called "this particular Now," which are then "actualized." The "possible" in Benjamin, according to Wohlfarth, "is both a measure and a gift"—a measure of the contours and contents of the present, but also a gift to the would-be revolutionary who would make a different present.[49] "True actuality," Wohlfarth adds, is untimely yet historically located—it stands both "in" and "against" its time; thus actuality "must be 'wooed' from unfruitful surfaces."[50] What Benjamin calls "the truly actual," intimations of another reality that can only be actualized or realized through political transformation, lodge in "the oddest and most crabbed phenomena" yet "point from the heart of the present beyond itself."[51] Again, revolutionary possibility does not simply ripen once and for all, but rather, takes specific shape in a specific time and is given this shape, at least in part, by revolutionary actors and historians. "Actuality, thus conceived, is a matter of actualizing the specific potential of this particular now."[52]

At this point, we are well suited to understand another of Benjamin's insistent connections between revolutionary historical consciousness and theological work. In Appendix A of the "Theses on History," Benjamin writes:

> Historicism contents itself with establishing a causal connection between various moments in history. But no fact that is a cause is for that very reason historical. It became historical posthumously, as it were, through events that may be separated from it by thousands of years. A historian who takes this as his point of departure stops telling the sequence of events like the beads of a rosary. Instead, he grasps the constellation which his own era has formed with a definite earlier one. *Thus he establishes a conception of the present as the "time of the now" which is shot through with chips of Messianic time.*[53]

Grasping the constellation that our own era has formed with a definite earlier one entails grasping the extent to which (selected elements of) past and present ignite each other, resemble each other, articulate with one another, figure meaning in one another. It allows the past to illuminate the possibilities of the present, and especially to open hope in the present. This in turn allows the present itself to emerge as a time in which redemption—that is, connection of a particular political formation in the present with a particular formation of oppression in the past—might be possible. This articulation of past and present constitutes those "chips of Messianic time" that redeem not all of history once and for all, but rather, history in particular patches and segments. Benjamin's reformulated dialectical materialism abandons the totalized project of nineteenth-century dialectics, even as it refuses to abandon its redemptive aim.

Consider again those elements of modern historiography that Benjamin criticizes. "Historicism," "empty time," "eternity"—these are Benjamin's pejorative names for conceptions of history that misrepresent both the powers constitutive of the past and the possibilities of opening a different future. But more than misrepresentations, they are also sites of political corruption or disorientation, sometimes dangerous ones. Recall his claim that "nothing has corrupted the German working class so much as the notion that it was moving with the current," a current Benjamin names "empty time" because it is divorced from "this particular Now," the diverse elements that constitute a present that might be other than itself.[54] As with Derrida's emphasis on the spectral nature of Marxist historiography, Benjamin here claims to be offering a way of reading and enacting Marx, rather than departing from him. The dialectics he takes over and radically reworks from Marxism does not refer to the process by which history moves but rather aims to capture a peculiar meeting of past and present that occurs in the *image* of the past as a "blazing up." In *The Arcades Project,* Benjamin attempts to explain why:

> It isn't that the past casts its light on the present or the present casts its light on the past: rather, an image is that in which the *Then* and the *Now* come into a constellation like a flash of lightning. In other words: image is dialectics at a standstill. For while the relation of the present to the past is a purely temporal, continuous one, the relation of the Then to the Now is dialectical not development but image, leaping forth. Only dialectical images are genuine images; and the place one happens upon them is language.[55]

For Benjamin, dialectics defines the transformation achieved by the encounter of past and present, and image is the frozen expression of this encounter. In what he sometimes calls "true historical materialism," Benjamin claims, "history breaks down into images, not stories," and it is the very transduction of images for stories that constitutes the immanent critique of the concept of progress that Benjamin insists is levied by dialectical materialism. Benjamin's materialism entails a certain appreciation of the empirical truth of the past, but dialectics complicates this truth with its recognition of the past's play in the present as selective, interpreted, and imagistic. Similarly, while Benjamin's dialectical materialism converges with what Marxists call material conditions of actions, it distinguishes these conditions from the particular way in which the past presses on the present. He is thus differentiating three elements frequently collapsed by Marxists into one: the materialism of the past (a question of what happened), the materialism of the present (a question of what historical conditions shape contemporary political possibility), and the way in which past and present take their shape from one another in political consciousness (a question of memory and consciousness). In Benjamin's rendering, dialectics functions as a name for the process by which some element of the past is made to live in the present, is ignited by the present, and transforms present and past in this illumination. The past can have occurred without memory, but it cannot live in the present without memory, and, importantly, historical memory is conveyed imagistically. Benjamin makes this claim with particular sharpness in response to a reprimand from Horkheimer in which the latter argues that "the assertion of [the] incompleteness [of history] is idealistic, if completeness isn't included in it. Past injustice has occurred and is done with. The murdered are really murdered. . . . If one takes incompleteness completely seriously, one has to believe in the Last Judgment. . . . Perhaps there's a difference with regard to incompleteness between the positive and the negative, such that only injustice, terror, and the pain of the past are irreparable. . . ." Here is Benjamin's rejoinder:

> The corrective to this line of thought lies in the reflection that history is not just a science but also a form of memoration. (*Eine Form des Eingedenkens*). What science has "established," memoration can modify. Memoration can make the incomplete (happiness) into something complete, and the complete (suffering) into something incomplete. That is theology; but in memoration we discover the experience (*Erfahrung*) that forbids us to conceive of history as thoroughly a-theological, even though we barely dare not attempt to write it according to literally theological concepts.[56]

As with Derrida's conception of history as haunting the present, history as images can never add up to a coherent totality but rather is always "incomplete." Dialectical images evoke particulars of the past that bear on the present, that "blaze up" in the present, and that tear up the conventional conception and relation of present and past. Derrida and Benjamin share this rejection of historical totalization in favor of a fragmented and fragmentary historiography, and both do so, somewhat perversely, in the name of Marx. Indeed, Benjamin is unapologetic about his insistence on the imagistic dimension of historical recognition—its truth-value pertains precisely to its transitory, partial, and contingent character. In his notes on method in *The Arcades Project,* he says he wishes to demonstrate "that the materialistic presentation of history is imagistic in a higher sense than traditional historiography."[57] And he insists that the materialistic presentation of history is paradoxically more attuned to the Real to the extent that it cultivates the expression of the connection of past to present in an image, which is the medium of individual and collective memory and experience.

While this emphasis on the conjuring of historical images places dialectics in a register far more subjective than that of Marx, it is a subjective register of a very particular sort. We have already seen that dialectics, for Benjamin, does not represent an objective process of development in the world, but is rather a name for the play of history in the present, the play between present and past in a particular political moment, a play that transforms past and present into the "Then" and "Now" as a form of mutual illumination. Heavily dependent upon memory, this play is also fueled by anxiety about certain losses in the past and about losing position in the present, and hence by anxiety about the capacity to make a future. But if imagistic history is subjective, the form of this subjectivism is, importantly, not individual. History does not simply draw on memory but produces it (and in this, Benjamin adds, presumes "destruction"); it is the phenomenon that places the past in a "critical condition"[58] by attending to those "jags and crags that offer a handhold to someone who wishes to move beyond them."[59] Here, we are inevitably reminded of Foucault's genealogies, which are intended, inter alia, to articulate political possibilities in the present by telling alternative histories of the present, by producing a historical ontology of the present, one that reveals the fissures and breaks in the production, thereby interrupting both a seamless narrative of the past that yielded the present and a seamless architecture of the present. By featuring memory as a production rather than a given, by activating it as a strategic force that is engaged in "the fight for the oppressed past," by being instructed in it and cultivating its possibilities, we open "the strait gate through which the Messiah might enter."[60]

An appreciation of Benjamin's interest in cultivating historical memory designed to disrupt the givenness of the present enables us to make a final turn toward his political critique of a melancholic relationship to the political present. Benjamin seeks to discern a way in which lost moments in the past, rather than being treated as lamentable and unrecoverable on the one hand, or as superseded by progress on the other, might be cultivated as incitations in the present. What Benjamin tendentiously names "Left melancholia" remains bound to a notion of progress, and hence to the movement of "empty time" in which opportunities missed are permanent and unrecoverable. If, however, history does not move toward a goal, if it does not unfold according to a plan, then "every historical moment has its own revolutionary chance including, therefore, those moments where possibilities are severely reduced."[61] By contrast, Left melancholia represents a refusal to come to terms with the particular character of the present, that is, a failure to understand history in terms other than "empty time" or progress. It signifies as well a certain narcissism with regard to one's political attachments and identity that exceeds any contemporary investment in political mobilization, alliance, or transformation.[62]

The irony of melancholia, of course, is that attachment to the object of one's sorrowful loss supersedes the desire to recover from this loss, to live free of it in the present, to be unburdened by it. This is what renders melancholia a persistent condition, a state, indeed, a structure of desire, rather than a transient response to death or loss. In Freud's 1917 meditation on melancholia, he reminds us of a second singular feature of melancholy: It entails "a loss of a more ideal kind [than mourning]. The object has not perhaps actually died, but has been lost as an object of love."[63] Moreover, Freud suggests, the melancholic will often not know precisely what about the object has been loved and lost: "This would suggest that melancholia is in some way related to an object-loss which is withdrawn from consciousness, in contradistinction to mourning, in which there is nothing about the loss that is unconscious."[64] The loss precipitating melancholy is more often than not unavowed and unavowable. Finally, Freud suggests that the melancholic subject low in self-regard, despairing, even suicidal, shifts the reproach of the once-loved object (a reproach leveled for not living up to the idealization by the beloved) onto itself, thus preserving the love or idealization of the object even as the loss of this love is experienced in the suffering of the melancholic.

Now why would Benjamin use this term, and the emotional economy it represents, to talk about a particular formation on and of the Left? Benjamin never offers a precise formulation of Left melancholy. Rather, he deploys it as a term of opprobrium for those more beholden to certain long-held sentiments and objects than to the possibilities of political transformation in the present. Benjamin is particularly attuned to the melancholic's investment in "things." In the *Trauerspiel,* he argues that "melancholy betrays the world for the sake of knowledge," here suggesting that the loyalty of the melancholic converts its truth ("every loyal vow or memory") about its beloved into a thing, indeed, imbues knowledge itself with a thinglike quality.[65] Another version of this formulation: "In its tenacious self-absorption [melancholy] embraces dead objects in its contemplation."[66] More simply, melancholia is loyal "to the world of things,"[67] suggesting a certain logic of fetishism, with all the conservatism and withdrawal from human relations that fetishistic desire implies contained within the melancholic logic. In the critique of Kästner's poems wherein Benjamin first coins "Left melancholia," Benjamin suggests that sentiments themselves become things for the Left melancholic, who "takes as much pride in the traces of former spiritual goods as the bourgeois do in their material goods."[68] We come to love our Left passions and reasons, our Left analyses and convictions, more than we love the existing world that we presumably seek to alter with these terms, or the future that would be aligned with them. Left melancholy, in short, is Benjamin's name for a mournful, conservative, backward-looking attachment to a feeling, analysis, or relationship that has been rendered thinglike and frozen in the heart of the critic. And if supplementation from Freud is helpful here, then this condition presumably issues from some unaccountable loss, some unavowably crushed ideal, an ideal that lives in empty time rather than the time of the Now.

To "stand entirely to the left of the possible" is the stance of the Left melancholic, a stance that prefers a particular analysis, that prefers brooding on the losses this analysis documents to seizing and developing the prospects of political transformation in the present. This is the stance of the "revolutionary hack," and contrasts with that of the thinker-activist, who would "stand to the left within the possible." [69] It would be a mistake to misread Benjamin's critique of Left melancholia, however, as an argument for reconciliation with the conditions of the present or with a rejection of the place of historical memory in shaping the possibilities of the present. Here again is that most difficult paradox in Benjamin's formulation of the bearing of history on the political present: we must cultivate memory while we foster a means of "gaily parting with the past." [70] We must reconcile ourselves to parting with our past—and here Benjamin quotes Marx and not Nietzsche—if we are to do the work of mourning rather than cultivate melancholia, the latter being the condition that binds us to the past as a collection of things, as a way of knowing, such that we are complacent about the present. But parting with the past does not mean forgetting it; rather, it involves what Benjamin terms "mindfulness," a particular form of remembering aimed at rendering history "an outrage to the present." [71] Bolz and van Reijen elaborate:

> The contemporary accentuates the present as something that is historically crucial, as a crisis. History can do it justice not as a science but only as a "form of being mindful." Mindfulness means remembrance stretched by forgetting; here, forgetting should be understood not as not-remembering, but as counter-remembering. In mindfulness, what has been experienced is not pinned down but opened up to its pre- and post-history. But this also means that through mindfulness past suffering is experienced as something unfinished. [72]

Suffering that is not yet finished, of course, is not only suffering that must still be endured, but suffering that can still be redeemed, that need not be concluded as an episode of suffering but might develop another face. Making a historical event or formation contemporary, making it "an outrage to the present," and thus exploding or reworking both the way in which it has been remembered and the way in which it is positioned in historical consciousness as "past," is precisely the opposite of bringing that phenomenon to "closure" through reparation or apology (our most ubiquitous form of historical political thinking today). The former demands that we redeem the past through a specific and contemporary practice of justice; the latter gazes impotently at the past even as it attempts to establish history as irrelevant to the present, or at best, as a grievance in the present. Hence Benjamin's sense of history as both an "activation of the past" and a convocation of demands upon the present, both an accusation against the present and a challenge to set understandings of the past. Hence, too, his insistence on the possibility of redeeming the past (which is actually a transformation of the past) through revolutionary action in the present.

The memoration that Benjamin locates at the nexus of historical understanding and political consciousness is neither an individual nor an institutional nor a collective memory of "what really happened," but is rather a dynamic, episodic, agentic, and imagistic form of remembering that counters the force of one conjuration of the past with another. It is simultaneously a coming to terms with our losses, and a redemption of them through the cultivation of a different version of them achieved in a re-articulation of past and present. What Benjamin offers, then, is not so much a way (for historians) to do history as a way (for political actors) to think historically, a way to have historical consciousness about the shape of contemporary political life—its openings or possibilities. He offers a way also to address history as we make a future not just a method of consulting the past but a means of redeeming or transforming it, thus a way of recovering the past that paradoxically loosens its grip on our political psyches at the moment it is addressed consciously and deliberately.

Taken together, Benjamin's strange and incomplete historiography and Derrida's "hauntology" certainly will not satisfy those who want scientific, systematic, or empirically precise formulas for the bearing of the past on the present. Nor will it satisfy those who are inclined to believe that *posthistoire* means we are without responsibility to history and are unclaimed by it, that we spring free of history into a present where we can conjure meanings and possibilities as we wish. It won't satisfy unreconstructed liberals, for whom the continued claim of progress, and belief in the autonomy of the will, renders history largely irrelevant to political life except as episodes of trauma or greatness, episodes to recoil from or to emulate. And it won't satisfy unreconstructed Marxists, for whom history is always so heavy and determining, radically constraining the scope of possibilities in the present. But it may offer a guiding sensibility to those who wish to discern a ground for political action that attends to history once history appears without a distinct shape and trajectory. This would seem to be the glimmer of possibility offered by these two scholars of literature and philosophy, these postmaterialists who work more in language and image than in historical data, these post-Marxists who want to extend, revive, and enliven the Marxist project with figures that Marx could not avow, even as he spawned them. Taken together, the reflections of Derrida and Benjamin tender not a new conception of historical development, but novel touchstones for political consciousness that would dwell in history rather than taming, jettisoning, or submitting to it. It is a consciousness that simultaneously seeks to ignite the past and to open a path for departing from it, that conjures the power of the past while resisting any preordained implications of that power for the making of a more just future. It may even be a political consciousness that offers modest new possibilities for the practice of freedom.

NOTES

1. Walter Benjamin, "Theses on the Philosophy of History," in *Illuminations*, ed. H. Arendt (New York: Schocken Books, 1969), 257–58.

2. Irving Wohlfarth, "The Measure of the Possible, the Weight of the Real, and the Heat of the Moment: Benjamin's Actuality Today," *New Formations*, special issue, "The Actuality of Walter Benjamin," no. 20 (Summer 1993): 2.

3. Sheldon Wolin, "Political Theory: From Vocation to Invocation," in this volume.

4. Ibid.

5. Ibid.

6. Ibid.

7. Michael P. Steinberg, "Introduction," *Walter Benjamin and the Demands of History*, ed. M. P. Steinberg (Ithaca, N.Y.: Cornell University Press, 1996), 15.

8. *Specters of Marx: The State of the Debt, and the Work of Mourning, and the New International*, trans. P. Kamuf (New York: Routledge, 1994), xvii.

9. Ibid., xvii.

10. Ibid., xviii–xix.

11. Ibid., xx.

12. Ibid., 6.

13. Ibid., 13.

14. Karl Marx and Frederich Engels, "The Manifesto of the Communist Party," in *The Marx-Engels Reader,* 2d ed., ed. R. C. Tucker (New York: Norton, 1978), 473.

15. *Specters of Marx, 6–7.*

16. Ibid., 4.

17. Ibid., xix.

18. Ibid., 45.

19. Ibid., 10.

20. Ibid., 15.

21. Ibid., 18.

22. Ibid., 19.

23. Ibid., 28.

24. Mark Poster's reading of *Specters of Marx* emphasizes strongly Derrida's (and deconstruction's) claim to be Marx's proper heir: "Derrida boldly proposes to improve upon Marx, to eliminate his 'pre-deconstructive' limitation, to 'radicalize' him, and calls for 'a new International' that will instantiate 'a new Enlightenment for the century to come.'" Poster in "Textual Agents: History at 'The End of History,'" in *"culture" and the Problem of the Disciplines,* ed. J. C. Rowe (New York: Columbia University Press, 1998), 217.

25. *Specters of Marx, 46–47.*

26. "Theses on the Philosophy of History," in *Illuminations,* ed. H. Arendt (New York: Schocken Books, 1969), 262–63.

27. "Theses on History," 257.

28. Ibid., 261.

29. Lutz Niethammer, *Posthistoire: Has History Come to an End,* trans. P. Camiller (London: Verso, 1992), 119–20.

30. "Theses on History," 261.

31. Ibid., 261.

32. Ibid., 263.

33. This critique is often (mis)read through Theodore Adorno's rejoinder to it in "Progress," republished in English in *Benjamin: Philosophy, Aesthetics, History,* ed. G. Smith (Chicago: University of Chicago Press, 1989), 84–101.

34. Gershom Scholem, "Walter Benjamin and His Angel," republished in English in *On Walter Benjamin: Critical Essays and Recollections,* ed. G. Smith (Cambridge: MIT Press, 1988), 65.

35. Benjamin, "Theses on the Philosophy of History," 261.

36. "Walter Benjamin and His Angel," 83.

37. *Posthistoire,* 111.

38. Ibid.

39. Ibid.

40. Ibid., 260.

41. Ibid., 260.

42. Ibid., 261.

43. "Theses on the Philosophy of History," 257.

44. Ibid., 262.

45. Marx makes a similar point in his claim that "each new class which puts itself in the place of one ruling before it, is compelled . . . to represent its interest as the common interest of all the members of society . . . it has to give its ideas the form of universality and represent them as the only rational, universally valid ones." *The German Ideology*, in *The Marx-Engels Reader*, 2d ed., ed. R. C. Tucker (New York: W. W. Norton, 1978), 174.

46. "N: [Re The Theory of Knowledge, Theory of Progress]" [an excerpt from *The Arcades Project*], in *Benjamin: Philosophy, Aesthetics, History*, ed. G. Smith (Chicago: University of Chicago Press, 1989), 65.

47. Ibid., 66.

48. "Theses on History," 255.

49. Wohlfarth, "The Measure of the Possible," 2.

50. Ibid., 4.

51. Ibid., 5.

52. Ibid., 2.

53. "Theses on History," 263.

54. Ibid., 258.

55. "N . . . ," 49.

56. Ibid., 61.

57. Ibid., 51.

58. Ibid., 60.

59. Ibid., 64.

60. "Theses on History," 264. The longer passage from which this phrase is drawn is instructive: "We know that the Jews were prohibited from investigating the future. The Torah and the prayers instruct them in remembrance, however. This stripped the future of its magic, to which all those succumb who turn to the soothsayers for enlightenment. This does not imply, however, that for the Jews the future turned into homogenous, empty time. For every second of time was the strait gate through which the Messiah might enter."

61. Wohlfarth, "The Measure of the Possible," 2.

62. For Benjamin's bewitching formulation of the "Then" and the "Now" as political terms unapproachable by "Past" and "Present," see "N," especially pages 49, 51–52, and 80.

63. "Mourning and Melancholia," *The Standard Edition of the Complete Psychological Works of Sigmund Freud*, trans. J. Strachey (London: Hogarth Press, 1957), vol. 14, 245.

64. Ibid., 245.

65. *The Origin of German Tragic Drama,* trans. J. Osborne (London: Verso, 1977), 156–57.

66. Ibid., 157.

67. Ibid., 157.

68. "Left Wing Melancholy," republished in *The Weimar Republic Sourcebook,* ed. A. Kaes, M. Jay, E. Dimendberg (Berkeley: University of California Press, 1994), 305.

69. Wohlfarth, "The Measure of the Possible," 3.

70. "N . . . ," 55.

71. Norbert Bolz and Willem van Reijen, *Walter Benjamin,* trans. L. Mazzarins (Atlantic Highlands, N.J.: Humanities Press, 1991), 19.

72. Ibid.

J . PETER EUBEN

3 // THE POLITICS OF NOSTALGIA AND THEORIES OF LOSS

Is this the promis'd end?
—Kent in *King Lear*

On February 17, 1970, Michael Eugene Mullen, Sergeant First Class, Sixth Infantry Division, was killed in Vietnam. As the eldest son of Peg and Eugene Mullen, he was expected to inherit the Iowa farm that had been in the family for five generations. For the Mullens, Michael's death seemed the death of the future, as it did for so many Vietnamese and Americans. It disrupted the continuity of life, uprooting them from the ground that had defined their lives. At least in our civilized times, the young are not supposed to die before the old, and parents are not supposed to outlive their children. Except of course in times of war.

For the Mullens, particularly Peg, finding meaning in their son's death became a way of life. At first that meant reconstructing the specific circumstances of his death: How did he die? At what time and place? Who was with him? Did someone hold and comfort him as he faced his final ordeal? No detail, however incidental or ordinary, could be left out as Peg tried to connect the story of his short life, which she knew, with the story of his death, which she did not.

But the Army stonewalled. They evaded her questions or answered them dishonestly. And they had good reason to, since Michael Eugene Mullen had been killed by drunken American gunnery; he had died by what the army called "friendly fire." In a war noted for its euphemisms, this may have been the most perverse, since it allowed the Army not to count Michael's death as a casualty of war. In the gruesome game of body counts, his didn't count at all.

Driven by grief, outrage, and loss, Peg, like many others of her generation, became politicized. She began to organize Iowa farm families against the war.

The Mullens took out a half-page advertisement in the *Des Moines Register* on April 12, 1970. On page five of the news section there was a half-inch-high banner headline:

"A SILENT message to the fathers and mothers of Iowa." and then below it in smaller boldface type:

> We have been dying for nine, long, miserable years in Vietnam in an un-declared war . . . how many more lives do you wish to sacrifice because of your SILENCE?

Off to the right of "Silence" was a small black cross and beneath it, the epitaph "Sgt. Michael E. Mullen—killed by friendly fire." "Then," says C. D. B. Bryan, from whom I take these details, "came the crosses."[1]

> Row upon row of crosses, fourteen rows containing forty-nine crosses each, a fifteenth row with twenty-seven and space left open for more. Their ranks, so starkly aligned and black against the bleak white page, suggested a photo-graphic negative of some well-kept battlefield cemetery viewed from afar.

"These 714 crosses," a legend explained, "represented the 714 Iowans who have died in Vietnam." Near the bottom left-hand corner of the page was printed: "In memory of Vietnam War Dead whom our son joined on February 17, 1970."

Peg not only became politicized; she simultaneously became "theoreti-cized" in the sense that the loss of her son generated a passion to find mean-ing in his death by asking increasingly comprehensive questions about the nature of our public life. Naturally enough the questions began with a de-mand for details about his death. But they soon expanded in scope into ques-tions about the Vietnam War and war in general, about patriotism and demo-cratic accountability, and eventually to questions about American political culture and political realism. It seemed that only complete knowledge of the structure that shaped her son's life could provide solace for the absurd cir-cumstances of his death.

I do not mean to romanticize Peg Mullen (or the 1960s), though I do admire her persistence and politics and share her sense of loss. Her relentlessness could be wearying while her obsessive preoccupation with Michael's death unnerved even members of her immediate family. There is, naturally enough, more than a little rage and desire for revenge mixed in with her grief.

Still less do I mean to argue that when Peg became theoreticized she suddenly became a philosopher. Obviously she never wrote anything remotely like *The Republic*, and while the loss of her son politicized her life, the loss of Socrates (as *The Seventh Letter* tells it) depoliticized Plato's. Still, it is worth recalling that Socrates was in the streets rather than in the academy, and that the conversation in Book I of *The Republic* is about everyday matters in everyday language. Indeed, one of the interlocutors defends a notion of justice as helping friends and harming enemies, which Socrates critiques by raising questions about how we can distinguish our "true" or "real" friends from our false and seeming ones.

My point in beginning with Peg Mullen is threefold: She represents a response to loss without nostalgia; her reaction to Michael's death suggests why and how personal, political, and epistemological dimensions of loss are more than contingently related, though less than necessarily; and, most significantly, because her story can be read as a parable about the emergence of political theory in classical Athens and its reemergence in otherwise disparate historical settings. At a minimum it reminds us that people were and are driven to theorize by a need to make sense of a world that suddenly appears out of joint as they themselves come to feel displaced in it. More generally, I want to argue that while philosophy may begin in wonder that things are the way they are (Aristotle), or may be a preparation for death (Plato), or the acceptance of finitude, much political theory begins with loss. Loss animates it as an enterprise and forms its problematic.[2]

To claim that political theory emerges and reemerges from a sense of loss does not tell us very much unless we can specify how particular theorists understand and represent that loss. Do they present it as an aberration in a trajectory of progress or as endemic to "the human condition"? What rhetorical or poetic devices, what metaphors or prophetic intonations do they use to dramatize the loss they confront and promise to move beyond or redeem? Do they embrace, indulge in, or resist nostalgia, counsel accommodation, endorse revolutionary praxis, or posit some purer realm unsullied by the messiness or undisturbed by the frailty of this world?

Why does loss so often haunt even the most utopian theoretical visions? Unlike functionalist discourse, which assumes that loss can be erased without a trace, Freud's work suggests that oblivion is not an irremediable absence but a presence absent only from itself, a veiled surface sheltering what would only have been repressed, the crudely healed scar of an amputation forever memorable[3] like the cherry-choke tree on the back of Sethe in Toni Morrison's *Beloved*. Is that the case with political theories?

We also need to know how various theorists (Plato, Machiavelli, and Marx, for instance) pictured and then responded to the absences and erasures loss represents, and what filled the spaces in life and thought left empty. How did they confront narratives of inevitable decline (or indeed progress) of fate or history that would have made their theoretical endeavors futile?

Finally, we need to know not only what is lost but who loses what and who loses most. Peter Laslett writes about a "world we have lost," a world in which "the whole of life went forward in the family, in a circle of love, familiar faces, known and fondled objects, all to human size."[4] Robert Wiebe tells a similar story about late-nineteenth-century America, which he calls a "distended society." Nationalization, industrialization, mechanization, and urbanization led to a profound sense of "dislocation and bewilderment." As men inadvertently shaped a world that required them to range farther and farther from their communities, "they tried desperately to understand the larger world in terms of their small, familiar environments,"[5] to master a now impersonal world using the customs of a face-to-face community. While such stories and the contrasts they provide may well be an essential component of critiques of the present, they can easily encourage a nostalgia that underemphasizes how inscribed hierarchies of class, race, gender, ethnicity, and religion were part of that "naturalized" past.

But this knowledge cannot just be about losses publicly recognized. It must include those that cannot be acknowledged or grieved over. Judith Butler writes about preemptive loss and a mourning for unlived possibilities. "If this [homosexual] love is from the start out of the question, then it cannot happen, and if it does, it certainly did not. If it does, it happens only under the official sign of its prohibition and disavowal."[6] Her argument challenges us to identify circumstances where loss is effaced, to ask about absent presences, and to distinguish between loss and constitutive absences.

In what follows I want to offer four such narratives of loss: the synchronic (Homer and tragedy); the philosophic (Plato in *The Republic*); the perspectival (Machiavelli's *Prince*); and the diachronic (Marx and modernism). Each narrative tells a story about theory and loss, and each tells us something about the power and danger of nostalgia. None is purely what I say it is, and not all are given equal space. This is especially true of the last, which is most familiar.

SYNCHRONICITY

In pre-Platonic Greek thought loss is generally conceived synchronically (from the Greek *su–n,* meaning "along with, in the company of, or side by side with," and *chronos,* meaning "time") rather than diachronically. Though the life of man is likened to the cycles of nature (the word "hero" is related to words having to do with the seasons),[7] there is no notion of a historical process analogous to a natural one. And despite the fact that Hesiod describes a Golden Age from which his own has degenerated and figures from Nestor (in the *Iliad*) to the orator Demosthenes refer to earlier better times, they do not refer to an initiatory moment outside of history that might provide a transcendent moral ideal to be recaptured or redeemed.[8] Because there was no sense of processes such as capitalization, disenchantment, or degeneration, there could be no redemptive moment when loss would be made good and the tragedy of human agency erased.

With no significant idea of afterlife (except in certain mystery cults), what counted was what men did in this one; and what counted in this life was excellence in words and deeds. Only the brilliance of one's achievements, especially on the battlefield, and the courage shown in the face of death could give one a second life on the lips of men. It was honor and glory that gave meaning to life and defined the human condition. Since the gods were immortal they were immune to the ravages of old age and the finality of death. It was the intense Greek awareness of both that heightened their sense of beauty and their equally intense sense of loss. In choosing a short, glorious life Achilles preserves his virility, strength, and beauty; through death he becomes fixed in a beauty of an unending youth.

But the *Iliad* is a poem of loss: of men and cities, of friends and family, of life itself. Achilles poses this logic of loss and recompense in the starkest terms: life for song, home and old age for *kleos* (fame, glory, renown). "Achilles," Simon Goldhill writes, "can only carry into battle on his shield a representation of a social world he cannot take part in," but that we are reminded of by his foil Hector.[9]

There are, of course, moments of respite and relief: Hector with his wife and son, the reconciliation scene between Priam and Achilles, instances of ransom and recognition of guest friendship. But they just make the sense of loss all the more acute.

By the epic's end the world is in flames. Hector has been killed; his city will soon be sacked and destroyed; Achilles has finally avenged the loss of his beloved Petroclos, but that, he knows, is the prelude to his own death. Loss is victory's companion, death and weakness shadow mastery and strength. We are all equal in the end, Achilles complains. Even the greatest of Greek warriors and the son of a goddess confronts the pathos of death, the sudden change from the brightness of life to meaningless existence, from the joy of friendship and the responsibility of family to forsaking and being forsaken by them. Like Michael Eugene Mullen, these men die far from home and family, and no one, not their comrades nor their loved ones, can help them or make good their loss.[10] That is why the Funeral Games, a ritual of loss in book 23, along with the mourning for Hector in book 24 constitute an epitaph for everyone in the epic as well as for those mortals hearing of their deeds in song. The last line of the *Iliad,* "Such was the burial of Hector, breaker of horses," really is the end.

But not quite. The deeds of heroes live on as long as there are bards to tell their stories and audiences to hear and think about them. For example, one of the most vehement controversies about the *Iliad* concerns the episode where Odysseus, Phoinix, and Ajax come to offer Achilles recompense for Agamemnon's insult in hopes of inducing him to rejoin their ranks and reverse their flagging fortunes. Achilles rejects their offer with a violence of and to language that is unique in the epic, and he goes so far as to contemptuously dismiss the heroic ethic of which he is the supreme exemplar. No gifts can compensate for such an insult, no glory is worth a life if he like any other man dies in the end. Though this scene is distinctive for its intensity it is, nonetheless, typical in the way it draws its readers/listeners into evaluating *kleos* with Achilles and makes us active participants in the "debate" he is having with himself and the three ambassadors about what sort of life is most worth living.[11]

The synchronic nature of loss and gain in the *Iliad* means that endings are also potential beginnings. For as death stalks life, so life is present in the living traditions of storytelling. Just as there are no necessary beginnings—the *Iliad* starts in the middle, and tragedians reinterpreted the mythic traditions that were themselves polyvocal—there are no final endings, and those that are "forced," such as the deus ex machina in Euripidean plays, merely serve to emphasize the artificiality of an order that appears out of nowhere. Works like the *Iliad* and the *Odyssey* satisfy not only our desire for an ending but also a desire for the not-ending, the unendable, at the same time.[12]

The *Odyssey* is a story of a homecoming (*nostos,* from which "nostalgia" comes), which immediately sets it against the ethos of the *Iliad,* where Achilles rejects his *nostos* in favor of immortal glory.[13] Though home is the objective of Odysseus's journey and the end of his story, yet the end of the story is not the end of the journey, despite the fact that we have every reason to expect it to be. Having revealed himself, taken Penelope to bed, and had his revenge on the suitors, Odysseus engages in one more act. In the words of Margaret Anne Moody: "Having regained his own house, Odysseus leaves it to venture into the fields to find his humble father, the farmer, digging, in a tattered and dirty chitton." In contrast to the trials of Odysseus's journey home and the heroic ferocity of his revenge, Laertes is antiheroic. It is not just that he is, in terms of the poem, something of an embarrassment, but that he "casts our minds to the future, in which Odysseus himself will no longer be the middle-aged hero he is now, but an old man without the strength of arm to bend his bow."[14] Though there is a parallel scene in the *Iliad* where Priam and Achilles look upon one another's beauty as the latter remembers his father and so his own mortality, Priam is a majestic even if a pitiable figure. Not so Laertes.

Perhaps the fullest articulation of synchronicity in Greek literature can be found in what is commonly known as the "choral ode in praise of man" in *Antigone.* The first thing to say about the ode is that it is not in praise of man but about what is strange and alien about human beings. I quote from the Grene translation:[15]

Many the wonders, none
is more wonderful than what is man.
This is it that crosses the sea
with the south winds storming and the waves swelling,
breaking around him in roaring surf.
He it is again who wears away
the Earth, oldest of gods, immortal, unwearied, . . . [368–74]

The tribe of the lighthearted birds he snares
and takes prisoner the races of savage beasts
and the brood of the fish of the sea,
with the close-spun web of nets.
A cunning fellow is man. His contrivances

make him master of beasts of the field
and those that move in the mountains.
So he brings the horse with the shaggy neck
to bend underneath the yoke;
and also the untamed mountain bull;
and speech and windswift thought
and the tempers that go with city living
he has taught himself, . . . [384–89]

He has a way against everything,
and he faces nothing that is to come
without contrivance.
Only against death
can he call on no means of escape;
but escape from hopeless diseases
he has found in the depths of his mind.
With some sort of cunning, inventive
beyond all expectation
he reaches sometimes evil,
and sometimes good.

If he honors the laws of earth,
and the justice of the gods he has confirmed by oath,
high is his city; no city
has he with whom dwells dishonor
prompted by recklessness. [393–408]

The Greek *deinos* (strange, wondrous) and its cognates refer both to that which inspires awe, such as technical ingenuity, intelligence, mastery, resourcefulness, and daring, and to that which inspires dread, such as the monstrous, evil, self-annihilating, and violent. These double meanings are played out in the ode (as well as in the ode's place in the play as a whole).

Human beings alone can master nature and use her for their own purposes. They are not, as animals are, passive "victims" of nature's imperatives or at the mercy of oceans, winds, and brute strength or dependent on nature's largesse. Their ingenuity harnesses nature's creatures and power; they plow the earth with oxen, trap birds and fish to eat, build shelters to protect themselves against the elements, invent medicines against disease. More than that, they have taught themselves language, thought, and civic virtue, creating cities that provide power, camaraderie, and a space for law and justice. Only death thwarts their power; only against death is human ingenuity helpless. And even death need not be the end. Those men fallen in war, Thucydides' Pericles tells his compatriots, "offered up their bodies for the common good and took for themselves that undying praise and that most distinctive tomb—not the one in which they lie, but the one in which their fame remains to be eternally remembered in words and deeds on every fitting occasion" (II, 43).[16] The polis, Hannah Arendt argues after quoting Sophocles' version of Silenus (that not being born is best, and second best is to die as soon as possible), "is the space of men's free deeds and living words which could endow life with splendor" (ton bion lampron poieisthai).[17]

But then there is the other meaning of deinos. Humans may tame the sea but they cannot tame their own passions. When men use nature to enhance her offerings they assault her, and mastery over nature and nature's creatures is a constant temptation to tyranny, as suggested by the fact that Antigone is likened to a bird and Creon seeks to yoke her (as well as others) as men do animals. How much pride can man take in his self-taught language, his reason, and his civic virtue if he has also "taught" himself how not to listen, how to turn such achievements to his own selfish purposes, using them, as Creon does, as instruments of oppression and violence?

Humans are the only creatures of nature who are unnatural in the sense of re-creating themselves against as well as with nature. This means that their home, their city, the place of justice, freedom, and power, is also a "sign" of their homelessness. We are also unnatural in the knowledge of our own mortality, which means that death is our traveling companion and haunting double. Thus our greatest achievements—freedom and knowledge—leave us absent to ourselves, necessarily divided and multiple, unsettled and unsettling. The question is whether we can acknowledge our condition without melancholy, nostalgia, or resentment.

In the Iliad loss is endemic to the human condition. In it the inequalities evident to us in the treatment of Thersites, the dependent status of women, and the often lethal disparities of prowess pale before the shared recognition of mortality. We may well regard the heroic ethic as murderous and self-destructive. Indeed the Iliad itself regards it that way even as it projects and instantiates it. Yet there is something to be said for a response to human finitude that avoids melancholy and nostalgia, ressentiment and redemption.

Though tragedy, as represented by the choral ode, also linked achievement and loss, the themes of the play together with the conditions of its performance give wider opportunity to human action.[18] However transgressive our achievements may be, we are capable of an agency not present in the *Iliad*. In this regard one could say that tragedy exists halfway between the pretheoretical, self-contained world of epic and the transformative aspirations of Platonic philosophy. If drama does not envisage overcoming this world to produce new values, new men, and a new order, it does believe that things as they are—particularly Athenian political life—might be otherwise and better.

In the case of tragedy the issue of who loses is more prominent and so politicizes the idea of synchronicity and "the" human condition. Though it is not clear whether such prominence altered political practice, tragedy dramatizes loss by depicting its consequences for women, slaves, and barbarians. At least in the confines of the theater and dramatic festival, the excluded and the closeted appear on stage. In this space and moment the defeated survive; the indigestible, unassimilated and cross-grained, and otherwise effaced possibilities have at least a shadowy presence. And while it is true that a tragic sensibility precludes the idea of redemption, the beauty of its poetry provides a redemptive moment by transforming suffering and loss into a story of human endurance. In this respect at least, political theory carries forward a bardic tradition. Theorists too are singers of songs, even if the hero is Socrates rather than Achilles and the audience is philosophers rather than the *aristoi* or *demos*.

THE PHILOSOPHIC NARRATIVE

Plato is thought to have ended all this because his rejection of tragedy and epic in the name of an ontologically grounded morality transmogrifies synchronicity into a toxic vision of the human condition. To leave the cave is to ascend from the everyday world, with its fleeting appearances, clashing opinions, and moral confusions, to one in which moral and political judgments are univocal. In terms of *Antigone*, one could say that Plato believed that Creon had the right instincts but the wrong character and insufficient knowledge to accomplish what he intuitively knew had to be done. Order and harmony are indeed the goals of politics, but they cannot be found in or founded upon the world as presently constituted and understood.

Though much can be and has been said for this reading of *The Republic*, I believe it underestimates the continuities between epic tragedy and philosophy while overestimating Plato's rejection of synchronicity. An alternative reading of the dialogue suggests how Plato displaces synchronicity by incorporating its rhythms and sensibility into philosophical dialogue. This process of displacement is Plato's response to a loss that, not unlike that of Peg Mullen, is at once personal, political, and epistemological.

Sheldon Wolin emphasized the continuities between epic and theory in his discussion of "epic political theory." In Plato, epic theory has three dimensions. First, it imitates the heroic aspiration of achieving some memorable deed whose greatness will live on in the stories men (and women) tell about it. But here the theory is the deed. "If the great words failed to be translated into reality," Wolin writes, "if society could not be made into the image of the world, the world might endure nonetheless as a memorial to the aspirations of thought." [19] Thus theory provides a "pattern of the good society which cannot be erased by forgetfulness or destroyed by history" and the tradition of political theory becomes a form of storytelling. Secondly, as this suggests, epic theory is an attempt to redeem in thought what is denied in practice. In these terms *The Republic* is a meditation on and response to Plato's failure at Syracuse, and Plato is a theorist out of frustration rather than aspiration. Finally, the epic dimension of theory refers to its transformative ambition to recast all social relationships, revolutionize our conception of knowledge, and provide a new vision of the destiny of the human soul.

While *The Seventh Letter* [20] provides evidence for Wolin's argument that *The Republic* was, in part, a response to Plato's failure at Syracuse, the *Letter* also suggests another factor: the Athenian treatment of Socrates. In the *Letter* Plato says that the idea of the philosopher-king came to him because of the harassment of Socrates by his oligarchic friends and relatives and the trial and conviction of Socrates by the restored democracy. It was because of this that Plato drew back from entering Athenian public life.

"The more I reflected upon what was happening," Plato writes, "on what kinds of men were active in politics, and upon the state of our laws and customs," the more he realized "how difficult it is to manage a city's affairs rightly." Indeed, the corruption of the city's laws and customs "was proceeding at such amazing speed that whereas at first I had been full of zeal for public life, when I noted these changes and saw how unstable everything was, I became . . . quite dizzy." [21] This did not stop him from reflecting on how to make the city more just, but it did make him wary enough to wait for the ideal moment. But after further reflection and perhaps continued disappointments, he reluctantly concluded that all existing states are so badly governed that the "ills of the human race" would be perpetual until "either those who are sincerely and truly lovers of wisdom come into political power, or the rulers of our cities, by the grace of God, learn true philosophy." [22]

In this story political theorizing emerges from a sense of loss analogous to that suffered by Peg Mullen. In both cases personal loss is also political and epistemological: political in the sense that America and Athens forfeited their moral claim to patriotic attachment; epistemological in the sense of a felt need to discover the truth behind shifting appearances. For Peg as for Plato, the dizzying quality of events pushed them to seek firmer ground for belief and action.

As *The Seventh Letter* makes clear, Socrates' death signified a twofold loss: that of a moral exemplar, teacher, guide, and friend; and for Plato, that of an opportunity for honor, power, and achievement a political career promised. Together they created not only a sense that something irretrievable had been lost and the world diminished by it but a pervasive sense of loss in excess of anything in particular.

How did Plato or rather how does *The Republic* respond to this sense of loss? It does so in three ways. The first, which conforms to the conventional reading of the dialogue, generates a contrast between, on the one hand, a political domain of unreality, deception, mutability, and loss, and on the other, an ultimate changeless reality in which loss is a noncategory. The second represents the way in which a synchronic relationship is established between the conventional reading and elements in the text that challenge and interrogate it. The third is represented by a displacement of synchronicity into dialectic and dialogue.

The first response to loss is to create a world that would never kill another Socrates. This is the world ruled by philosopher-kings, themselves "selfless instruments of timeless truths." [23] In this world Socrates would be vindicated and avenged largely at the expense of democracy. Indeed, the ideal state with its harmony, unity, and naturalized hierarchies founded on moral certainty seems a virtual inversion of what we know about Athens, especially as it is presented in the portrait of democracy in book 7.

Yet vindicating and avenging Socrates seems to require his erasure. For the Socrates who is conducting the dialogue would be superfluous if not dangerous in the society that dialogue creates. We know that Plato went to Syracuse in the hopes of turning a tyrant into a philosopher-king. But we also know, or have reason to believe—based on what "Socrates" says in the *Apology* and *Crito*—that Socrates would never have gone to Syracuse and would not endorse the idea of a philosopher-king. Nor is there evidence in these early dialogues that Socrates had anything like a theory of the forms and a view of moral certainty that is entailed by it.

The second response speaks to the paradox of a vindication that is also an erasure. Here Socrates continues to do in death what he did in life: talk to everyone he meets about the choices they have made and do not know that they are making. Here his death dramatically frames the themes and urgency of the dialogue. His loss is a constantly felt absence drawing the search for understanding and knowledge forward, exploring alternative narratives in which the death of Socrates can be given meaning. Here Socrates lives on in the dialogue with the interlocutors, with Plato and with us.

In this voice loss does not generate visions of redemption and certainty. For all of Socrates' clear endorsement of moral principles about virtue being knowledge, accepting injustice being done to one rather than committing it, "he" is aware of the contingent nature of every moral claim. Political theory is not a preparation for death or a gesture of contempt toward the world of becoming. It is the carrying on of talk, speech, and dialogue without end.[24]

The significance of aporetic dialogue lies in the possibility that while we do seek closure we also seek the continuation of life that the inconclusiveness of dialogue represents. So we come to endings only to defer them by finding ways for the talk to begin again. If the real ending is death, then resistance means life: of a text, of its readers/interlocutors, and of its argument. In these terms Socratic political theory as embodied in this second voice is not a preparation for death but an affirmation of life.[25]

If my argument about the two voices in *The Republic* has merit, then the synchronicity banished in the first voice reappears, not so much in the second alone, as in the tension between the two. As with Homer and *Antigone*, achievement is shadowed by transgression, gain accompanied by loss. The gains: intelligence, rationality, intellect, certainty, and with them redemption against the vicissitudes of becoming; harmony and order, goodness and justice, and the achievement of community. Yet against this assertion of mastery and hope is the insufficiency of mortals, which guarantees the incompleteness if not the futility of the quest. But "insufficiency" begs the question insofar as it ignores the loss and erasure "Platonic" philosophy demands:

citizenship, friends, family, the body, the pleasures of particular places and people, the texture of ordinary recognitions and loves.

What synchronicity exists in *The Republic* is subject to philosophical interrogation as it obviously is not in epic and tragedy. Homeric heroes live on in the stories of glorious deeds passed on from generation to generation. The reality of those deeds, their "ontological" ground, depends upon a world of comrades and friends, of action and publicity, and of singers whose formulaic retellings were this worldly, however much inspired by the muse. Characters could protest against the injustice—even absurdity—of the heroic ethic, as Achilles does in book 9 of the *Iliad*. But there was no other ethos for him to embrace, no other superior life available to him as there is for philosophers in *The Republic*. And though Achilles may envy the gods their immortality, he knows and even prides himself on the fact that he, not they, must pass the ultimate test of courage when encountering death. Because mortals exist in time and places with others, synchronicity literally defines the human condition. The question is whether this itself represents a falling away and an insufficiency to be remedied. Certainly there are ways in which *The Republic* suggests it does; that the frailty and darkness of life as exemplified by politics can and must be redeemed in order for men to have an end to what Plato calls "the ills of the human race."

PERSPECTIVALISM

Like Plato, Machiavelli became a theorist by default. Though one cannot imagine the former seconding the latter's declaration that he loved his country more than his soul—not only because care of the soul trumps patriotism for Plato but because he advised foreign princes—both were driven to theoretical reflection by a sense of loss that was at once personal, political, and epistemological. The personal aspect was Machiavelli's being forced out of office, thereby being denied access to the realm in which he felt most alive. The sense of political loss had a general as well as a specific aspect. The general one concerned the tenuous status of republicanism, not merely at the moment and in Florence, but in the face of emerging political forms of monarchical states. The specific one concerned the disarray of Florence and Italy as a whole. Ravaged by petty quarrels, random violence, narrow ambition, and an interfering church strong enough to prevent common action but too weak to actually undertake it, both city and nation were incapable of maintaining their liberty. The loss was epistemological in the sense that men had forgotten how to gain political knowledge and what was distinctively political about it.

As was the case with Plato, these crises induced a dizziness that paralyzed understanding and action. Here is J. H. Plumb on politics in Renaissance Italy. I quote at length.

"Horror waits on princes," wrote Webster, the Elizabethan dramatist for whom the bloodstained annals of Italy had a compulsive fascination. Certainly, the way to power was strewn with corpses; men murdered their wives, wives poisoned their husbands, brother slaughtered brother, family ranged against family, city sacked city. In 1402 the chief members of the ruling house of Lodi were burned alive on the public square; at Bologna in 1445 the people, enraged by the slaughter of their favorite family, the Bentivoglio, hunted down their enemies and nailed their steaming hearts to the doors of the Bentivoglio's palace, as a token of their love.

Yet Bologna was a tranquil city compared to many, and even bloodless when matched with Foligno; there a noble—Pietro Rasiglia—cuckolded by his prince, took his vengeance. He flung his faithless wife from the turrets of his castle and killed two brothers of the Prince. Retribution rapidly followed. The whole Rasiglia clan, men, women, and children, were butchered and chopped up; their joints, hung like meat, were paraded through the streets. Of course, the ghoulish chroniclers liked to heighten the horror, and their macabre imaginations rioted in sadistic fantasy. [Plumb is not doing too badly either.] Yet all allowances made, politics became a murderous game in which death in bed came only to the skillful or the lucky. The savagery used by men in pursuit of power was due to the nature of society and the prizes which it offered.[26]

Here is the opening of Machiavelli's famous chapter 25 on *fortuna* in *The Prince:*

It is not unknown to me that many have held, and still hold, the opinion that the things of this world are controlled by Fortune and by God, that men with their wisdom cannot control them, and on the contrary, that men can have no remedy whatsoever for them; and for this reason they might judge that they need not sweat much over such matters but let them be governed by fate. This opinion has been more strongly held in our own times because of the great variation of affairs that has been observed and that is being observed every day which is beyond human conjecture. Sometimes, as I think about such things, I am inclined to their opinion. Nevertheless, in order that our free will not be extinguished, I judge it to be true that Fortune is the arbiter of one half of our actions, but that she still leaves the control of the other half, or almost that, to us.[27]

Given such unprecedented, relentless, rapid, and violent changes, many are tempted by intellectual and political fatalism. Now Machiavelli does not dismiss this view out of hand. In fact, he admits his own susceptibility to it. Yet he does not give in to it, because doing so would insure it was true, since there is always a self-fulfilling dimension to political beliefs. A theory, or at least a political theory, does not merely describe the world but carries prescriptive force in the sense of creating an imaginary future which either invites or discourages theoretical and political agency. Nor is Machiavelli willing to join those who, because so much seems beyond human control, give up the idea of control altogether. A demand for mastery is so easily disappointed that endorsing it becomes a recipe for cynicism and passivity. The challenge then is to accept contingency without a longing for certainty, to explore the moral possibilities of politics without endorsing an antipolitical moralism.

Machiavelli likens fortune to a river whose elemental power threatens to overwhelm every obstacle unless one takes the precaution of building dikes and levees. If rightly constructed, such precautions will not only limit nature's destructiveness but can even turn its elemental power to constructive purposes. This image implies two things: that fortune presents opportunities for as well as dangers to the exercise of human power (*virtù*); and that fortune is not just external natural forces but includes the adequacy of human responses to them. The domination of *fortuna* then signifies human failures.

What then are Machiavelli's precautions against the domination of *fortuna*? Wherein does his theoretical *virtù* lie? How does he propose to provide men with the intellectual and political wherewithal to act in the face of this seemingly implacable rush of events without falling into the destructive dialectic of mastery and abasement? He has, I believe, five related strategies: the use of realism; a critique of moralism; an antinostalgic reading of the past; a proposal for and definition of political knowledge; and the substitution of renewal for redemption.

The first precaution Machiavelli takes is his use of realism. To say that Machiavelli uses realism as a strategy to shore up human agency and direct the elemental forces of nature (including a Prince's passions for power and glory) means that he is no realist. This is not to deny that he has a pessimistic view of human nature, believes that the ends justify the means, regards violence as a necessary dimension of politics, sees politics as a limit on morality rather than vice versa, thinks politics involve disguise and deceit, insists that a single-minded commitment to goodness brings failure rather than success, endorses the significance of will and passion in politics, claims intentions or the state of one's soul are largely irrelevant political considerations, or thinks that in politics men need to rely on the instincts of a fox and the animal power of a lion. It is to insist, in the first instance, that we need to be leery in our assertions about someone who advocates disguise, deceit, and changing with the times. It is, in the second place, to remember that Machiavelli advocates views that qualify this realism. For instance: that men can become republican citizens and so better than their nature; that only a few very extraordinary ends justify any means; that one should use violence and cruelty economically; that his critique of morality is (I shall argue) a critique of moralism; that his insistence that politics requires disguise and fraud draws attention to the rhetorical and theatrical dimensions of political activity; that his division of goodness and success must be reconciled with the way he comes to insist that the Prince must moderate his excesses so as to maintain his power and ensure glory, thus providing a prudential grounds for morality; and that emphasis on will and passion (as with other of his ideas) is not limited to realists.

What I am arguing is that realism is Machiavelli's strategy for getting himself heard against the competition of others and allaying Medici suspicions. One way of doing both is to make what he says seem necessarily true and obvious while insisting that the means by which such obvious truths are discovered—such as extensive study of the past and an ability to see from high and low—are not. In this regard consider the lengths to which Machiavelli goes in the "Dedication" to *The Prince* to distance himself from those self-indulgent advisors who lard their advice with rhetorical embellishments. By contrast he has "neither decorated nor filled it [his work] with fancy sentences, with rich and magnificent words, or with any other rhetorical or unnecessary ornamentation. . . ."[28] His own rhetoric denies that he has any; *The Prince* is simply a reflection of reality. Thus the words he uses represent the facts of the world. No interpretation intervenes to distort his mapping of the political forces and presentation of the choices a prince must make. His competition may need copious references to ancient authority to establish their own. But he does not, which is why he has exactly two such references in the entire *Prince*. His authority comes from verisimilitude. His talent is packaging such truths in a terse easy-to-read tool kit for princes on the go.[29]

Consider in this regard the utter confidence evinced in chapter 1. In a few brief sentences Machiavelli maps the political terrain. "All states and all dominions . . ." he begins, and the rest of this very short chapter divides every political regime that ever existed into a few categories.

The second precaution Machiavelli makes is a critique of moralism. Moralism is the declaration of absolutes in a world of contingencies, a dogmatic idealism indifferent to political realities, and an otherworldliness that has corrupting influences it does not acknowledge.

Moralists say "never" and "always." They are committed first to the purity of their intentions and state of their soul, and are only secondarily, if at all, concerned with the consequences of their righteousness.[30] At the level of abstract principle at which they think, they need not ask how the morality they embrace came into the world. If they dared to ask, they would be forced to acknowledge that great states are almost always founded on violence, and that without the existence of such states moral life could not be lived. It would then follow that it is self-contradictory to criticize what makes morality possible on moral grounds. Politics must be a limit on morality before morality can be a limit on politics.

Moralism includes the fetishism of ideals. If one writes to be useful rather than just to spin out intellectual fantasies, one must be attentive to how truths and ideals can be made effective. That means that truths and ideals must arise out of the political world itself. If they do not, if the imagined political societies are only wishful thinking, they can never come into existence, though the desire and belief that they can will have real deleterious political consequences. "For there is such a gap between how one lives and how one ought to live," Machiavelli famously writes, "that anyone who abandons what is done for what ought to be done learns his ruin rather than his preservation; for a man who wishes to make a vocation of being good at all times will come to ruin among so many who are not good. Hence it is necessary for a prince who wishes to maintain his position to learn how not to be good, and to use this knowledge or not according to necessity" (126–27). As several commentators have pointed out, Machiavelli is not recommending that one abandon what ought to be altogether, but is insisting that any political vision must be accountable to and for the world it seeks to transform. Nor is he advocating being evil. Rather, he insists that when necessity requires it a strategic use of not being good is the only way to make goodness real. Any prince who refuses to abide by these dicta will lose his power and likely increase the evil and violence in his city.

Much of this critique of moralism and idealism is present in Christianity.[31] Like idealism, Christianity is otherworldly but ignores confronting the worldly implications of its unworldliness. For instance, its counsel of humility promotes passivity and subjection to authority, thereby leaving the worst men free to dominate politics and discouraging "good" men from trying to alter whatever political circumstances happen to exist. This not only increases the immorality of human life, it also insures political miscreants against (conventional) "moral" reproach. The language of Christian virtue, in promoting respect for existing authority, allows the rich to present themselves as the wise protectors of the people's liberties, and encourages the poor to accept this self-serving self-presentation.[32]

Despite its otherworldliness, moralism provides a reading of the past that legitimates certain attitudes toward the present and expectations about the future. In its hands history becomes a morality play where good and evil battle for supremacy. States like Rome and Sparta, or figures like Brutus and Romulus, are either pure or corrupt, righteous or damnable. The result is a nostalgia that reinforces the passivity already made attractive by the dizzying pace of change. It is against such nostalgia that Machiavelli offers a political reading of the past, a specific idea of political knowledge, and the notion of renewal as a political response to loss.

The problem is not that people ignore the past, but that they are in thrall to a sanitized version of it. Some are titillated by past deeds and actors as if they were watching a play that had little import beyond the moment of performance. Others aestheticize the past in the double sense of admiring its literature and art while ignoring its politics, and by purging politics of power so it can be viewed as a work of art. By depoliticizing ancient societies they separate politics and culture, education from political education, in the way the ancients themselves did not do even when their self-presentation might indicate otherwise. Still others philosophized the ancients, again in a doubled sense of only reading philosophers and reading them as philosophers, even when they were responding to political crises. In these terms imaginary republics such as one finds in The Republic become even more rarefied. As

Claude Lefort reminds us, "The classical search for the best government proceeded from the experience of and the critical reflection on corrupt regimes." For Machiavelli "the assumptions of the ancient philosophers have come to justify new forms of corruption." Still others worshiped the past as constituting a new religion not in the pagan civic sense Machiavelli commends but in a Christianized secular sense. Thus Greece or Rome, Athens or Sparta, the Roman Republic or Empire become transcendent moments of perfection compared to which we mere mortals are utter failures.[33] We unworthy ones cannot hope to compete with such achievements. Better to let things be as they are and take pleasure in the contemplation of a greatness that is totally beyond our ken.[34]

It is against such paralyzing nostalgia that Machiavelli offers a political reading of the past.[35] That reading has critical and constructive moments. The critical one begins with a denial that the inferiority of the present is a necessary and permanent condition. If one learns the "right" things from the past, the present can become its equal or even surpass it, given that the past did not have itself to study. Since human nature is largely constant and the central questions of public life recur in every epoch, the past becomes a repository of political experiences for the present. What this implies is that any dismissal of one's time in some grand gesture of ennui or contempt is a foppish luxury.

To indulge in such posturing is to embrace a debilitating self-loathing while encouraging a corrosive cynicism. Such melancholic displays are a pathological response to loss analogous to the one Freud analyzes in "Mourning and Melancholy." There, he describes the melancholic as someone who so fixates on an actual loss that it promotes a profound impoverishment of the ego. That is because melancholics engage in self-flagellation, proclaiming their moral inferiority and worldly incapacities. Such impassioned self-abasement seems so excessive, so radically disproportionate to what occasioned it, that the patient seems delusional. But, Freud insists, if we look further, we find that while the most violent of their self-condemnations does not fit them, it does fit someone else whom the patient loved or may still love, so that the self-reproaches are masked accusations against a lost love object. More than that, the melancholic's sense of loss eventually expands beyond the death of a loved one to include every situation in which the "patient" feels slighted, neglected, or disappointed.[36] In political terms the nostalgic's contempt for his age is an act of aggression and resentment, a pique and irritation at not being more honored.

The constructivist moment involves a narrative of Roman history that contests the reigning one, and the creation of true fictions that exhibit the principles of successful action in the past in order to enable similar ones in the present.

Machiavelli had his own ideal to compete with those imaginary republics he scorns in *The Prince*. His ideal is Rome. But not the Rome of contemporary humanists, who presented the Roman republic as a harmonious community guided by the wisdom of the Senate. His ideal Rome was full of social divisions and class antagonism, and these, not unity and order, are what made Rome great. Those who celebrate the intrinsic virtue of Roman institutions or the virtuous nature of her citizens ignore the role such quarrels played in avoiding tyranny and license, as well as in contesting an authority that would, left to its own devices, have become too petrified to adjust to the times. In this narrative the usual story of the agitations of the people destroying an otherwise peaceful and good city are seen to be self-serving *and* politically naive.

Machiavelli's writings are full of stories about successful and unsuccessful actors and ventures. Such stories are playlets that dramatize events while distilling the principles of action operative in them. The point of these dramas is to teach not just precepts of right action, but the political sensibility that made those actions and actors successful (barring completely unforeseen strokes of fortune). And the past is essential for such teaching since the present lacks inspiring examples of *virtù*. The combination of this arduously gained knowledge of great deeds of the past together with extensive experience of the present is the gift Machiavelli offers to Lorenzo in the form of *The Prince*.

The claim Machiavelli makes here, that political knowledge comes from being able to inhabit two times, is complemented by his claim that it also requires the ability to inhabit two places. Here is the famous passage in the Introduction to *The Prince* where Machiavelli likens himself to a landscape painter.

Neither do I wish that it be thought presumptuous if a man of low and inferior station dares to debate and regulate the rule of princes; for just as those who paint landscapes place themselves in a low position on the plain in order to consider the nature of the mountains and high places, and place themselves atop mountains in order to study the plains, in like manner, to know well the nature of the people one must be a prince, and to know well the nature of princes one must be of the people. [78]

Because the prince occupies one position only, his power is also his power-lessness, since he lacks the double perspective that would enable him to change with the times and sustain his position. For the same reason he lacks the crucial political knowledge of the impressions he makes on others. In these terms political power and political knowledge require the ability to look down from on high and up from below, in contrast to the morally and epis-temologically privileged position ascent and height have in *The Republic* and the Christian theology of heaven and hell. The epistemological implication is that political knowledge is built up discursively rather than deduced from a metaphysical, theological, or ontological premise. The equally radical politi-cal implication is that those who are low have a part of political knowledge as essential as the part held by those who are of higher status.[37]

This does not mean Machiavelli is a partisan of the people. Though he praises their virtues, his commitment is neither to them nor to the prince but to their mutual recognition of the shared dependency that is the ground of political power. To the prince Machiavelli promises power and glory. But to get that he must moderate some of his excesses, for the same reason per-formers modify their performances to receive the applause they crave. So the prince must be moral, or rather must be seen to be moral, or at least not too immoral, if he is to be successful—a not inconsiderable limitation when ap-pearance is the only thing that counts. To the people Machiavelli shows two things: that the prince's dependence on them means they have more power than they know; and how to make political rather than moralistic judgment of princes.

There is a sense in which the dual perspective that defines Machiavelli's notion of political power and knowledge extends to his idea of founding. That sense can be defined in terms of Hannah Arendt's characterization of Roman politics. At the heart of that politics, "from the beginning of the re-public until the end of the imperial era" stands the conviction of the sacred-ness of foundation. Unlike for the Greeks, for whom the founding of a body politic was a common occurrence, foundation for the Romans was the "central, decisive, unrepeatable beginning of their whole history, a unique event."[38]

Founding figures prominently in Machiavelli's thought as well, and the

Roman founding is the one that matters above all others. At one and the same time he perpetuates the sacredness of foundations in the Latin sense of religion (re-ligare, meaning "to be tied back, obligated, to the enormous, almost superhuman, and hence legendary effort . . . to found for eternity")[39] and undercuts it. The founding story he chooses to tell (there were alternatives) is that of fratricide. On the one hand the killing of a brother dramatizes, as does Brutus's killing of his sons and Lucretia's suicide, the sacrifice great republics require. Yet fratricide is also a story likely to provoke skepticism toward sacredness, given Augustine's use of fratricide as a reason to condemn the pretensions of Rome and of politics generally. Thus, while the founding is necessary, it is not a moment of perfection and unity to be revered. What can it mean to be "tied back" and "obligated" to this legendary founding of Rome? This attitude toward foundation is consonant with three other aspects of his thought: his rewriting of Roman history to emphasize the role of division and conflict in sustaining Roman power; the cynical way he tells the story of Numa pretending to cavort with a nymph[40] as a strategy to establish religion in Rome; and his insistence on the inseparability of good and evil.

If good and evil are inseparable, there can be no apocalyptic endings any more than there can be pure beginnings, and redemption narratives are read out of politics. Of course Machiavelli is no more above using the language of redemption when it accomplishes a worthy end (witness the last chapter of The Prince) than he is above advising the prince to use whatever means necessary to establish and maintain his power.[41] But the invocation of the Christian prophecy of the Second Coming in that chapter in an appeal to the Medici has the same distancing effect that the story of fratricide and the origins of Roman religion has in the founding mythology. What is notably absent in Machiavelli is any narrative of redemption, any story of final deliverance and perfection, atonement and harmony, salvation and moral certainty.

What Machiavelli offers in place of redemption is the idea of renewal. One reason for Rome's longevity was her ability to deal with those crises that threatened the disintegration of the city. That she was able to deal with them in ways that exorcised corruption while invigorating the citizenry had to do with her institutions, the virtue of individuals produced by them, and their ability to remind their compatriots what it was they shared that made their liberty and power possible. Such reminders did feature recourse to the founding myth. But given the substance of that myth any invocation of community, let alone brotherhood, would be highly problematic.

One can think of renewals as replenishing and reviving civic virtue through continuous rearticulations of origins that respond to the exigencies of changing times. Though such renewals are most dramatic where the city's existence is in the balance, Machiavelli's idea of renewal is more extensive in two respects. To begin with, because politics is at every moment poised on irresolution, each decision is a form of renewal, not necessarily because of what is decided, but because the very act of decision reaffirms and exemplifies the liberty of a free people to decide for themselves. Secondly, there is the sense in which renewal is an appeal to the culture that institutions create from the actual but varyingly corrupt practices those institutions now sanction. While the Romans and Machiavelli emphasize institutional politics, institutions, like the prince, have a propensity to become ossified unless there is a way of reconstituting them, of having something like a Jeffersonian revolution every generation. Some of this flexibility was provided by the mixed nature of the Roman constitution itself and its provision for extraordinary powers in times of crises. But some of it came from the political culture, which was at once fuller and more formless than even these emergency powers.

Machiavelli's notion of renewal allows for the significance of appeals to common origins without reifying them, to foundations that acknowledge those conflicts communities write over in their subsequent history, and to beginnings that must be begun again. In this he recognizes the need for invoking the past in a political way that forestalls nostalgia and narratives of redemption. Lacking a story of inevitable progress or decline, he restores the idea of synchronicity while emphasizing the political dimension present in its Greek meaning.

I have argued that Machiavelli uses realism as a way of establishing his theoretical bona fides and allaying Medici suspicions. I have also suggested that he is sympathetic to the sense of futility that came over his contemporaries in the wake of the wildly fluctuating vicissitudes of fortune. Though one must always be alert to the strategic dimension of Machiavellian thought, especially in *The Prince,* there seems to be an element of desperation to his realism there, as if he needs to reassure himself as much as his compatriots that there are still spaces for political and theoretical *virtù.* Given the unanticipated consequences of our deeds (what Weber called the ethical irrationality of the world), exaggerated by particular historical circumstances, there is a question of whether politics, particularly republican politics, is possible (which is why Francisco Guicciardini regarded Machiavelli's republicanism as utopian). Think, for instance, about the degree of mastery and accuracy of prediction necessary to realize Machiavelli's advice about well-used cruelties and economical use of violence. Suppose, for instance, that a virulently imperialistic fascist regime were to come to power in Russia. Would we then look back at 1989 as a disaster? Does not Machiavelli's advice require a degree of foresight that, if we looked too closely, would intimidate action in the way he wishes to avoid?

If this reading has any merit, Machiavelli's realism is born of desperation as much as of confidence, is as much a prophecy of hope and an act of faith as evidence of mastery and control. It is also a readmission, however inadvertent, of the tragic synchronicity of the choral ode against the philosophical tradition's efforts at erasure.

But it would be too unperspectival to leave matters here. For despite a resonance with Aristotle, Machiavelli asks a new kind of question: Does division and conflict necessarily and always signify corruption, or can it be a sign of political and intellectual vitality?

Here is Claude Lefort:

For the thinker, is the experience of conflict not a source of endless questioning? For the political actor, is it not a reason for accepting ultimate indeterminacy, whenever he is confronted with the requirements of judging and acting? For the city, is it not an incentive for his historical creation? [42]

Peg Mullen, Plato, and Machiavelli all attest to the profound disorientation that attends loss. Plato, in his reaction to the treatment of Socrates, and Machiavelli, in his response to the pace of change, admit to feeling dizzy and momentarily incapacitated. Neither gives in to those feelings (nor does Peg Mullen, for that matter), unless one reads *The Republic*'s philosophical rejection of politics as doing so. But Machiavelli does something more: he enables us to see why even such rapid changes are or must be seen to be opportunities for *virtù*; and he allows us to see his susceptibility to the lure of nostalgia and redemptive hopes in the face of such transformations before insisting that they lead to political disaster.

DIACHRONICITY

In some respects Marx's famous description of capitalism as revolutionizing economic and social life, creating constant uncertainty by dissolving every relationship while preventing any new ones from solidifying, reads like a gloss on Machiavelli's discussion of *fortuna*.[43] Yet for Marx Machiavelli's turn to Rome is a kind of nostalgia. Here is Marx in "The Eighteenth Brumaire of Louis Napoleon" on the distraction of republican rhetoric in the French Revolution.

> The tradition of all the dead generations weighs like a nightmare on the brain of the living. And just when they seem engaged in revolutionising themselves and things, . . . they anxiously conjure up the spirits of the past to their service and borrow from them names, battle slogans and costumes in order to present the new scene of world history in this time-honoured disguise and this borrowed language. Thus Luther donned the mask of the Apostle Paul, the Revolution of 1789 to 1814 draped itself alternately as the Roman Republic and the Roman Empire, and the Revolution of 1848 knew nothing better to do than to parody, in turn, 1789 and the revolution tradition of 1793 to 1795.[44]

The leaders and parties of the Revolution who performed "the task of their time in Roman costume and with Roman phrases" diverted attention from the mundane sobrieties of commercial reality surrounding them.

Marx's rejection of Machiavelli's political use of the past is possible because he erases the problem of *fortuna* that haunted Machiavelli with the process of dialectical materialism. It is true that the vividness of Marx's description/evocation of capitalism's human costs is unsurpassed. But the synchronicity present in *Antigone*'s choral ode is effaced by a narrative of historical progress in which God's curse on Adam and Eve that they and all their progeny are fated to enmity, sexual inequality, and unceasing, unproductive, and unrewarding labor is redeemed by capitalism and communism. In this diachronic narrative, loss and pain, alienation and contradiction are redeemed by the certainty of a better future. Even death itself seems to dissolve in a vision of agency where men and women are able to integrate identity and activity, being and doing, in demystified form, when change means liberation and renewal.[45] The idea and expression of loss becomes delusional and pathological.[46] To the extent that one loses a sense of loss in Marx and Enlightenment thought generally, to that extent the story I have told about political theory belongs in the dustbin of history.

Until quite recently neoliberals and globalizers extended this narrative not so much by standing Marx on his head as by rewriting his final chapter. Thus Victor Nee has argued that it is state socialism that is an outdated transitory mode of production whose internal contradictions have led to capitalism. It is state socialism, not capitalism, that "appropriates surplus directly from the immediate producers and creates and structures social inequality through the processes of reallocation."[47] But the Fukuyamian moment has passed, brought up short by Russian collapse and the retrenchment in the market "successes" of the Czech Republic, Hungary, and Poland. Despite its apologists, globalization as process ideology where corporate giants have "the technical means and strategic vision to burst old limits—of time, space, national boundaries, language, custom, and ideology"[48] is increasingly seen as politically disabling. The existence of unaccountable corporate power and the dizzying pace of change it demands have left men and women with a sense of loss analogous to that discerned by Wiebe and Laslett in the previous century.

Two things complement these developments of late-twentieth-century capitalism. The first has to do with modern notions of time. Of all historical periods, modernity, Terry Eagleton argues, is the only one to designate itself in terms of a dazzling, dismaying experience of time that is no longer located in history, habit, or custom but in their opposite. "The modern," he writes, "is that which reduces everything which happened up to half an hour ago to an oppressive traditionalism," an ironic self-representation given that nothing is more time-honored than efforts to break with the past.[49] Secondly, there is a vertiginous historicizing that reveals every thought, feeling, attribute, and event to be a historical construction with its own particular formation and trajectory. In this narrative, nature, God, citizen, and self are presented in an assemblage of ideological symptoms and cultural practices that, precisely because they are invented by power, lose any political innocence they may have had.[50] As the previous discussions indicate, I have considerable sympathy for such skepticism and the genealogical analyses that often accompany it (though I do think Machiavelli escapes their strictures). But too often the critique of nostalgia is too impatient with the sense of loss that makes it attractive to many and compelling to a few. Though usually critics of Enlightenment thought, genealogists sometimes assign the same rhetorical function to "nostalgic" that their theoretical opponents assign to "unrealistic" or "irrational." Finally, the precipitous critique of nostalgia intimidates the naming of loss, and thereby contributes to what might be called the nostalgia of the present. This is particularly so when present conditions of fragmentation are projected back onto all previous ages.

This impatience is more problematic when, as now, a sense of loss pervades or informs our public discourse. For example, family incomes have largely remained stagnant despite the increase in two-earner households. The result has been that many Americans have lost their sense of getting ahead and have developed a fear for their children's financial future. More generally, there are the unrelenting pace and demands of globalization, the lamented end of what Henry Luce dubbed "the American Century," Samuel Huntington's disappointment that the revolutionary hopes of 1989 have ended not in exultation or harmony but in delusion and bloody local conflicts, Robert Bellah's conviction that our spiritual life is utterly "impoverished," and Alasdair MacIntyre's complaint that not only is morality not what it once was, but what once was morality has, for all intents and purposes, disappeared. In sum, modernization is a bill of goods with the price left off. Since America was the harbinger of the modernized future, such disillusionment affects us most of all. We are no longer a new world dedicated to spreading liberty everywhere. We are no longer innocents with a special mission and vision of the future. But if our motives are no purer than others', if we are not exceptional and a vision of the future, then we must renounce any special moral mission in the world. Such renunciation brings mortality to center stage. When revolutionary hopes are crushed and projects for reform are frustrated, erasure of pain and loss is less successful. Perhaps part of the cynicism, apathy, dystopianism, and commodification of religion adhered to dogmatically is the return of the repressed in the form of a tragic sensibility.

CONCLUSION

How might political theory deal with this sense of loss while resisting both an enervating nostalgia and a redemptive politics? To begin with it might explore the distinctively political dimension of such loss. By this I mean three things: examine historically and comparatively those conditions that have called such responses forth; rearticulate a notion of politics as preeminently concerned with a public realm, as distinct from but not opposed to "the" private realm; and attend to the way inequalities of power and wealth must shape any analyses of or responses to loss. Secondly, it might explore what may be a prototypical American way of dealing with loss, that is, not dealing with it at all. Whether it is Tocqueville's discussion of how Americans are in constant motion, or the harsh lesson of equality of opportunity for those who lose the race, or quarantining signs of mortality by having the aged, diseased, infirm, senile, and dying put in special places run by professionals, this is not a nation that understands loss publicly. In this regard political theory might explore public forms of grieving, allowing us—"we the people"—to confront loss, integrate it, but also move on from it, as Sethe and Paul D seem to do in Toni Morrison's *Beloved*. Thirdly, political theory might do the same with genealogy, so that "real" loss, including the sort Butler discusses, can be acknowledged. This means talking again about the common good, public-spiritedness, civic virtue, citizenship, public freedom, and power as part of what Simon Critchley calls an "austere messianism."[51]

Finally, political theories may need to reject the fetishism of the present as well as narratives of inevitability for Machiavellian reasons. That means generating critiques of the present drawn from the past and finding spaces for theoretical and civic *virtù* no matter what the pace of change and no matter how deep the crisis. For, as Sheldon Wolin has reminded us, the Chinese "have a way of writing the word 'crisis' by two characters, one of which signifies 'danger,' the other 'opportunity.'"

NOTES

1. C. D. B. Bryan, *Friendly Fire* (New York: Putnam, 1976), 139–40.

2. This does not mean that all theories can be read as (or as part of) a narrative of loss, or that any theorist can be wholly read that way. Nor would I deny that the very act of writing about loss is often an act of compensation and redemption, no matter what the explicit argument.

3. Nicole Loraux, *Mothers in Mourning*, translated from the French by Corinne Pache (Ithaca, N.Y.: Cornell University Press, 1998), 83–84.

4. Peter Laslett, *The World We Have Lost: England before the Industrial Age* (New York: Scribner's, 1965), 5.

5. Robert Wiebe, *The Search for Order: 1877–1920* (New York: Hill & Wang, 1967), 12.

6. Judith Butler, *The Psychic Life of Power: Theories in Subjection* (Stanford, Calif.: Stanford University Press, 1997), 139.

7. In Homer, *he–ro–s* is related to *ho–re–*, meaning "season," especially the season of spring, so that a hero is seasonal "in that he comes into his prime, like flowers in the spring, only to be cut down once and for all." See Seth Schein, *The Mortal Hero: An Introduction to Homer's Iliad* (Berkeley and Los Angeles: University of California Press, 1984), 69. In my view Schein's book is far and away the best introduction to *The Iliad* available in English.

8. Hesiod is, wrongly I believe, sometimes considered an exception to this statement.

9. Simon Goldhill, "Intimations of Immortality: Fame and Tradition from Homer to Pindar," in his *The Poet's Voice: Essays on Poetics and Greek Literature* (Cambridge: Cambridge University Press, 1991), 76.

10. Schein, 72. The wrath of Achilles is also the wrath of his mother, Thetis, who was forced to marry a mortal man. In Loraux's words: "Homer has displaced the wrath from a mother to her son and because the maternal me–nis 'becomes absorbed in the actual wrath of her son' we credit the hero with a Great Mother's wrath without seeing that mourning and wrath are undivided between the mother and son," 49. (She is quoting Laura Slatkin's "The Wrath of Thetis," *Transactions of the American Philological Association* 116 [1986]: 22.)

11. Goldhill, 86.

12. See Margaret Anne Doody, "Finales, Apocalypses, Trailings-off," *Raritan* 15, no. 3 (Winter 1996).

13. See the discussion of this in Goldhill, 93–94.

14. Doody, 28–29.

15. Sophocles, *The Complete Greek Tragedies,* 2d ed., ed. David Grene and Richard Lattimore, trans. and with an introduction by David Grene (Chicago: University of Chicago Press, 1991).

16. Blanco translation of Thucydides' *The Peloponnesian War,* ed. Walter Blanco and Jennifer Tolbert Roberts (New York: W. W. Norton and Co., 1998).

17. Hannah Arendt, *On Revolution* (New York: Viking Press, 1963), 285. The line is spoken by Theseus in Sophocles' *Oedipus at Colonus.*

18. I have discussed this at length in *The Tragedy of Political Theory,* chaps. 1 and 2.

19. Sheldon Wolin, *Hobbes and the Epic Tradition of Political Theory* (Los Angeles: University of California Press, 1970), 6.

20. Though there are serious questions about the authenticity of *The Seventh Letter* I think the same conclusions about *The Republic* and Syracuse can be made more circuitously by relying on other sources.

21. 325 b–c. I have relied on the Morrow translation (New York, 1962).

22. 325 d–e. Cf. *The Republic,* 473d, 487e, 499b, 501e.

23. The phrase is Sheldon Wolin's from *Politics and Vision: Continuity and Innovation in Western Political Thought* (Boston: Little, Brown, 1960), chap. 2.

24. I have discussed the aporetic quality of *The Republic* in *The Tragedy of Political Theory,* chap. 8.

25. Doody, 42–43.

26. J. H. Plumb, *Renaissance Italy* (New York: American Heritage, 1961).

27. *The Portable Machiavelli,* trans. and ed. Peter Bondanella and Mark Musa (New York: Penguin Books, 1980), 159.

28. *The Prince,* 78. See the perceptive analysis of Machiavelli's realism in Robert Hariman, *Political Style: The Artistry of Power* (Chicago: University of Chicago Press, 1995).

29. If I am right in following Hariman on this point, Machiavelli moves from being a successful realist to being an unsuccessful republican in the sense that his means *(The Prince)* to an end *(The Discourses)* became the end. While we take Machiavelli's realism as his final word and reject politics because it relies on deceit, power, and appearances, he saw this as a spur to political engagement. Thus he has contributed to a political cynicism he was trying to combat. Since it is *The Prince* and not *The Discourses* that is honored as a "great book," few people aside from political theorists know anything about Machiavelli's views of civic virtue, the dignity of citizenship, public-spiritedness, confrontational politics, the people as the appropriate repository of liberty, and civic religion.

30. The most powerful modern restatement of Machiavelli's views on this subject remains the concluding section of Max Weber's *Politics as a Vocation.*

31. See *The Discourses,* especially 297–99.

32. See Claude Lefort, "Machiavelli: History, Politics, Discourse," in *The States of "Theory": History, Art, and Critical Discourse,* ed. and with an introduction by David Carroll (New York: Columbia University Press, 1990), 113–24.

33. Lefort, 138.

34. Machiavelli's critique of religion parallels Marx's argument about God. We project our powers onto an alien being and need to recover them for ourselves. Capitalism's corrosive effect on religious belief and affiliation is "progressive" in this respect.

35. In a discussion of "high minded nostalgia," Mary Beard argues that ever "since the Romans it has been an underlying tenet of most classical scholarship that the present generation is strikingly less capable than its predecessors at the job of preserving and passing on the great traditions, that 'we' unlike our illustrious forebears are simply not up to it" ("Not You," *London Review of Books* [January 23, 1997]: 10–11). If Beard is right, then Machiavelli learned about the problem of nostalgia from the Romans.

36. Sigmund Freud, "Mourning and Melancholia," in *The Freud Reader,* ed. Peter Gay (New York: W. W. Norton, 1989), 584–89. Freud has a quite different analysis in *The Ego and the Id.* On the significance of the differences, see Butler, 132–41.

37. Machiavelli implies that the dual perspective essential for political knowledge and power was institutionalized in the Roman mixed constitution. Because that constitution was composed of (at least) two classes, each of which stood for different principles (the Senate for tradition, authority, order, property, and continuity, the people for innovation and liberty) and interpreted events in those terms, Rome was

able to change with the times. In other words, a healthy society like Rome has no need of the theorist's special qualifications as they are presented in the image of the landscape painter.

38. Hannah Arendt, "What Is Authority?" in *Between Past and Future: Eight Exercises in Political Thought* (New York: Penguin Books, 1977), 120–21.

39. Ibid. No doubt Machiavelli also chose fratricide to contest Augustine's version, which he would have seen as a further instance of Christianity's political naïveté.

40. See *The Discourses* I, xi.

41. Of course, if I am right that Machiavelli finds prudential reasons why the prince must modify his immoral impulses, then this is far less of a blanket endorsement than it seems.

42. Lefort, 124.

43. Marx, "Manifesto of the Communist Party," in *The Marx-Engels Reader*, 2d ed., ed. Richard Tucker (New York: W. W. Norton, 1978), 475–76.

44. In ibid., 595–96. With this description Marx "transformed, by a sort of reverse rhetorical alchemy, the golden *exempla* of humanist favor into the leaden burdens of a dead past" (Kristie McClure, "Affect in Action: Figurae, the 'Community Sense,' and Political Prose," paper delivered at the American Political Science Association Meetings, September 1998). For Machiavelli this *was* often a result of invoking Rome, but it need not be the one.

45. See Jonathan Dollimore, *Death, Desire and Loss in Western Culture* (New York: Routledge, 1998).

46. I do not mean to exaggerate. Religion for Marx was delusional only in the sense that the objective conditions that brought it into being and made it an opiate would be transformed. Moreover, many criticisms of Marx come from Marx himself, which is why he denied that he was a Marxist.

47. Victor Nee, "A Theory of Market Transition: From Redistribution to Markets in State Socialism," *American Sociological Review* 54: 663–81.

48. See the "Introduction" to *Global Dreams: Imperial Corporations and the New World Order*, by Richard J. Barnet and John Cavanagh (New York: Simon & Schuster, 1997).

49. "Newsreel History," *London Review of Books* (November 12, 1998): 8.

50. See Elaine Showalter, "Foucault in America," *Times Literary Supplement* (November 28, 1997): 28.

51. See the discussions in Simon Critchley, *Very Little—Almost Nothing: Death, Philosophy, Literature* (New York: Routledge, 1997), 2–3, 24.

PART III

THINKING IN TIME

4 // CAN THEORISTS MAKE TIME FOR BELIEF?

This is an essay on political theory, and an expression of respect for Sheldon Wolin and the work he has done to make the "calling" of theory, as he described it, a worthy one. It shares his assumption that theory should be something more than a method that "avoids fundamental criticism and *fundamental commitment*."[1] However, I begin by making another assumption as well: that Wolin's talk of "fundamental" criticism and commitment shares something—a posture, at least, if not a position—with those beliefs called fundamental, or "fundamentalist." To be clear, this is not a claim that Wolin is a closet religious fundamentalist, as the term is commonly (and pejoratively) bandied about in contemporary American politics. In the lead essay to this volume, Wolin indicts religious and patriotic fundamentalism as a "twisted" expression of resentment and loss; and to the extent that his reference is to any number of expressions of cultural paranoia and nostalgia current in Western society today, I would agree with his assessment.[2] My point is a more narrow claim: that it is impossible to articulate *fundamentals* without also articulating (and legitimating) a belief. Not all beliefs assume the existence of fundamentals, of course; one can be orthodox or even extreme in one's political or religious beliefs, without assuming a fundamentalist posture. But the reverse is not true: to talk honestly about adopting fundamental positions and making fundamental critiques cannot help but reveal one as at least a potential believer—as one who accepts and invites the possibility of fundamental propositions, not just as cultural or structural expressions, but as *truths*.[3] And claims to believe or at least allow for such truths are not well received in theory today, which tends to view such affirmations as, at the very least, untheoretical.

By "fundamental belief" I mean a comprehensive outlook that has both ethical and ontological dimensions. Generally (but not always), such outlooks take on a theistic cast, and it is that sort of belief which most interests me here. Claims about the marginalization of religion are nothing new, of course, and have only become more common in recent years.[4] But rather than take up the much-discussed moral divide assumed by so many to exist between the philosophy of secular Athens and the religion of pious Jerusalem,[5] I would like to explore a subtle methodology implicit in modern life, a hidden assumption that I think theory often unconsciously supports, thus undermining its own potential.

Usually, belief is considered a private as opposed to public mode; the public articulation of fundamental beliefs is seen, politically at least, as an intrusion. The liberal ideal suggests that those who wish to communicate comprehensive, fundamental beliefs should first submit them to a rational "filter," eliminating those elements that do not match the overriding political assumption that, as "self-authenticating" individuals, we can adjudicate or mitigate truth-claims as our interests dictate.[6] Many theorists, to be sure, have strongly denounced this vision of modern discourse and the public sphere; Wolin himself, in reference to the often illiberal worldview of "democratic localists, socialists, radical feminists, Christian fundamentalists, Black Muslims, or Jewish Hasidim," has challenged how modern liberalism "creates cultural pressures to restrain the individualism that forms so fundamental a part" of liberal accounts in the first place.[7] But this attack on liberal practice does not result in all these (and other) comprehensive possibilities being made equally available, much less equally regarded, by political theory. Whatever the substance of its critiques, theory's *way* remains, by and large, *disbelieving.*

To question such practices is not to dismiss them: in a world where some fundamentalist believers feel impelled to violence, there are good reasons for theory to be liberal, and thus, in a particular way, disbelieving. But Stephen White reminds us that "we live in 'late modern' times . . . [with] a greater awareness of the conventionality of much of what has been taken for certain in the modern West."[8] His observation regarding our "lateness" highlights the concerns of this essay: the conventionality of theory's way, and the complication it presents to many believers, is best understood in terms of time.

POLITICAL THEORY AND THE PROBLEM OF TIME

Quoting Suzanne Langer in his classic text *Politics and Vision,* Wolin suggested that it is through a "temporal order of words," made concrete via our institutions, that "the activities of individuals and groups are connected."

It is within this already established political time that theorists are able to "make meaningful assertions . . . [about] the 'things' or phenomena of political nature."[9] He elaborated on this relationship in a recent on-line essay: political time, he writes, "requires an element of leisure." It is a temporality "conditioned by the presence of differences and the attempt to negotiate them," requiring a discursive, deliberate pace.[10] Such a requirement suggests a temporal arrangement that takes an intentionally ecumenical approach to difference. The arrangement must be pervasive and inclusive, one that conditions and is shared by all the various actors and phenomena that are affected by political concerns, making them available for negotiation and compromise. Also, the arrangement should be pluralistic (implying that anything might at another time be otherwise) and fallibilistic (implying that any judgment might at another time be wrong). Presumably, without such a temporal order theory will not be able to engage in the process of articulation and critique. It needs time to be homogeneous; that is, unvarying and accessible and commensurate for all.

There is a challenge to this arrangement in "the temporalities of economy and popular culture." These new arrangements, outgrowths of late capitalist development, prize innovations over conclusions, and result in an "instability of political time" wherein the sort of temporality necessary to "a common narrative . . . formerly a stable element in conceptions of the political" is replaced by the process of fashion: invention, enlargement, and rapid replacement. Theory, when governed by this notion of time, must customize, frequently, quickly, or face obsolescence.[11] Standing against this sort of momentum requires a resourcefulness that political theory is often hard-pressed to muster.

But if theory can find itself subjected to an accelerated temporal mode that complicates its best efforts, theory itself can make temporal demands on yet other ways of being. Or, to put it more carefully, the temporality assumed, however unintentionally, by many theorists buttresses a subtle sort of dominion, excluding temporalities that are not entirely compatible with the homogeneity theoretical discourse usually presumes. The temporality of political theory expects that our discourse will be orderly, that no options will be foreclosed or conclusions granted on the basis of claims that deny the need for reflection or the wisdom of the admonition "in due course."[12] Such orderliness, among other guises, may be discerned in the modern state as Max Weber described it.

The point here is to make clear a problematic in the theoretical endeavor.

In order to theorize persuasively about difference, at least in the manner traditionally understood, a certain attitude toward time, an assumption of openness and evenness, is taken by many to be a sine qua non; one of the ontological basics of any proper theoretical process. Yet that very attitude toward time, demanding that every commitment be a plural, fallible, potentially interchangeable one, is a creature of the modern liberal public sphere, and involves a way of discourse that is fundamentally at odds with many forms of belief.

Engaging this problem requires several steps. First, there should be an investigation of the relation between time, the public sphere, and religious belief, so as to understand both the origin and the significance of belief's complaint with modernity and its theoretical supports. Second, other accusations against modernity that complicate the vocation of theory warrant consideration, to see how they relate to the obstacles that theory unknowingly places in belief's way. Third, postmodern notions of temporality need to be taken up, to see if there are alternative presumptions that would make theory less party to modern homogeneity and thus less reducible to a mere method. Finally, in light of these alternatives, I will suggest not only how theory's ways might be made compatible with belief, but also how belief might deepen theoretical discourse's resources. Again, the point is not to force political theory to accommodate certain substantive beliefs, but rather to make the theoretical vocation more open to *believing*. The implication here is that while the wise citizen or theorist need not be a believer, theory itself is wise only insofar as it learns to take seriously the belief that the time in which we live may be something other than an empty vessel for modern theorists to fill.

RELIGIOUS TIME AND THE PUBLIC SPHERE

Charles Taylor notes that the public sphere, which he defines as a "common space" that allows citizens "to meet through a variety of media . . . to discuss matters of common interest and thus to be able to form a common mind about these," is "not only a ubiquitous feature of any modern society," but also central to the whole premise of self-government.[13] Drawing heavily on the work of Jürgen Habermas, Taylor sees the real genesis of liberal theory in the North Atlantic world to be the emergence . . . of a new concept of public opinion. . . . [While the earlier] "opinion of mankind" was supposed to have passed down in each case from parents and elders, in a myriad of unlinked acts of transmission, public opinion was deemed to have been elaborated by a discussion among those who held it, wherein their different views were somehow confronted, and they were able to come to a common mind. The opinion of mankind is probably held in identical form by you and me, because we are formed by the same socializing process. We share in a common public opinion, if we do, because we have worked it out together.[14]

This was a vital innovation, and it did not come about suddenly. The rise of literacy, the development of theories of popular sovereignty, the rational possibilities discerned within the human and natural worlds—all these revolutions of the late medieval era and the Enlightenment played their part. Through them, the basics of the liberal worldview were established. Of course, these revolutions carried a particular cost: Taylor points to the work of Michael Warner, who succinctly observed that the old unity of the medieval world—the fabled Great Chain of Being—was ultimately replaced with a new unity: "the ideal of a [traditional] social order free from conflictual debate" was made over into an "ideal of debate free from social conflict." That is, public opinion was not to result from a harmonious social world that maintained itself through the power of (and struggles over) traditions and authority, but from a harmonious debate that maintained itself by severely restricting appeals to "pre-public" forms of tradition and authority. Rather than a unity of all, a unity of debate involving all.[15]

For the old substantive unity to be imitated by a methodological one, the theoretical range of this debate had to be coterminous with the boundaries of the community in question, both physically and temporally. While the idea of a public debate that includes all persons has taken much time and conflict to be fully realized (and some would argue we are still far from such a realization), once it began its march no serious argument opposing the participation of any significant group capable of discourse has had much success. Similarly, claims to temporal exclusions have had difficulty resisting the force of modern public debate. Notions that societies might be constituted by a belief that "transcends contemporary common action" because its origin is literally "time out of mind" have had a hard time in the post-eighteenth-century Western world. Such determinations would be outside the temporally constituted process of debate; they would suppose a unity that preceded the modern, procedural one. This is why Taylor calls the public sphere *secular*:

> [I use the world *secular*] in spite of all the misunderstandings that may arise . . . [T]he original sense of *secular* was "of the age," that is, pertaining to profane time. It was close to the sense of *temporal* in the opposition temporal/spiritual. . . . Modern *secularization* can be seen from one angle as the rejection of divine time and the positing of time as purely profane. Events now exist only in this one dimension, in which they stand at greater and lesser temporal distance and in relations of causality with other events of the same kind. The modern notion of simultaneity comes to be, in which events utterly unrelated in cause or meaning are held together simply by their co-occurrence at the same point in this single profane time line.[16]

The practical meaning of this change is better understood when one is confronted with an example of how "temporal calculations," as it were, came about before the development of the modern public sphere. Erich Auerbach describes the sort of consciousness involved:

> If an occurrence like the [biblical] sacrifice of Isaac is interpreted as prefiguring the sacrifice of Christ . . . then a connection is established between two events which are linked neither temporally nor causally—a connection which it is impossible to establish by reason in the horizontal dimension. . . . It can be established only if both occurrences are vertically linked to Divine Providence, which alone is able to devise such a plan of history and supply the key to its understanding. . . . [The] here and now is no . . . mere link in an earthly chain of events, it is *simultaneously* something which has always been.[17]

This simultaneity is not reductive, but substantive; it suggests a unity between a person and the world's beginning and end. The unity of public opinion, on the other hand, is methodological; it makes the past a resource, the future an unending continuation of the same. This transformation was hardly an immediate one, but it was inexorable; by the beginning of the eighteenth century, residents of colonial Massachusetts would look back with confusion on the assumptions of the Puritan founders a mere two generations before. It should also be noted that simply because medieval Christian Europe provides us with important examples of Benjamin's "vertical" simultaneity does not mean that "horizontal" simultaneity is only to be found in Western liberal states. Wherever theories of liberalism and modern nationalism have taken root, temporal transformations have also, whatever awareness of time and concomitant forms of belief may have previously prevailed. Benedict Anderson takes up Benjamin's notion of modernity as a "homogenous, empty time" and uses it to explore various material components of the public sphere, like newspapers and novels. He discerns similar dynamics at work in a great diversity of authors and sources: Honoré de Balzac, nineteenth-century Filipino novelist Jose Rizel, Mas Kartodikromo, a late-nineteenth-century Indonesian storyteller, and the *New York Times*. In each case, Anderson demonstrates a reigning sense of "temporal coincidence," wherein all activity is the "steady, anonymous" methodological movement of a calendar.[18] It makes possible the imagination of a new sort of ordering, a unity of discussion and discourse and process, which binds people together as theoretical sovereigns while liberating them from, or at least making unnecessary, the more substantive binding beliefs of the past.

The significance of Wolin's comments regarding political theory should now be apparent. If theory does have, as he suggests, a preservative function in relation to time—that is, a concern and interest in maintaining a temporality that is sufficiently regular so as not to interrupt the joint imagining of a political identity and community—then theory itself, at least as traditionally practiced, is an accomplice to the creation of the modern liberal worldview and the consequent emptying of time. Political theory, to be sure, need not be liberal or even modern. But even deeply revisionist philosophies of history and politics are more often than not wholeheartedly committed to a way of theorizing that rejects as truly untranslatable and incommensurable those fundamental beliefs that would discount or deny the inexorable pace of modern discourse.[19] Theorists who claim to break with modernity while still assuming that *all* differences, including believing ones, are temporally equal, are perhaps operating a tad disingenuously. They are exclusionary just the same.

But how much—or how little—exclusion does that disingenuousness actually cover? Perhaps believers *have* in the majority of cases, especially in the West, accommodated their fundamentals to a modern "public" sense of the divine. This is, by implication, the argument recently made by Stephen Macedo. Arguing for a "transformative constitutionalism" that would result in a healthy, manageable diversity of religious belief, Macedo writes that believers in America have had to and should have to accept a "compartmentalization of [their] political and religious views"—that is, a separation of belief from the public realm. Such compartmentalization requires that religiously oriented temporal commitments be abstracted from the pluralistic and fallibilistic temporal commitments that must dominate politics. If this means political irrelevance as the "price of assimilation into the American way of life," it is a price that Macedo, citing Will Herberg, nonetheless believes has been accepted by just about everybody—"though perhaps not Fundamentalists as of yet," he generously adds.[20]

"Political irrelevance" may be an extreme formulation of liberalism's demands, and Macedo in fact backs away from it somewhat. And in any case, liberalism's demands are not theory's demands—though as an endeavor supportive of and situated within the public sphere, theory *has,* as I have argued, embraced at least some of the conventions of liberal discourse. A revealing comment by Brian Barry makes this plain. He wrote that "a submission to [journals like] *Philosophy and Public Affairs* or *Ethics* that consisted in the derivation of various conclusions from some sort of religious fundamentalism would be so far from the shared premises of all previous contributors that it simply would not get a look."[21] This may not be a recipe for total political irrelevance: after all, most voters do not read *Philosophy and Public Affairs* or *Ethics* (or any academic journals, for that matter). Still, it does represent the sort of obstacles that stand in the way of the theoretical expression of belief.

When theory's heretofore overwhelming (even if unstated) demand for a shared, revisable temporality is played out in a religiously and normatively diverse polity like our own, the greatest frustration will involve those who contend that time has already been "constructed"—that is, ordered, set, or fixed.[22] There are innumerable ways in which this belief has been and can be expressed: in doctrines of a preexistence or a cycle of reincarnation or a final judgment, in assertions of prophecy or destiny. Collectively, these beliefs often involve some form of millenarianism or transfigurism—a hope for or fear of salvation or transformation at a particular moment in time. This entails a concomitant conviction that certain conditions are *fundamental* to either achieving the right state or being in the right place at that moment, which is what gives their normative commitments their particular character. In the United States alone a host of Christian groups—ranging from smaller sects like the Mormons, Seventh Day Adventists, Old Order Amish, Mennonites, Jehovah's Witnesses, and Christian Scientists to numerous mainline Evangelical Protestant churches, as well as certain Catholic and Eastern Orthodox congregations—include various "fundamentalisms" in their belief systems. So do a wide variety of Orthodox Jews, conservative Muslims, and members of numerous new religious communities. Looking abroad, one may include revivals of Restorationist Zionism, Shi'ism, Buddhism, and Sikhism in the broad fundamentalist spectrum.

Contemporary fundamentalism is to a degree a "fighting" posture; fundamentalists today "no longer perceive themselves as reeling under the corrosive effects of secular life. On the contrary, they perceive themselves as fighting back, and doing so rather successfully."[23] It is this fighting that makes them so suspect. A degree of antinomianism almost always attends nonliberal temporalities; fundamentalist beliefs that assert that time has been fixed generally suggest that the act of orientation toward that moment of personal or collective end will lead in social directions divergent from society as a whole. Therefore, fundamentalists fight against the tide; indeed, what they fight against is the very rhythm of tides and tempos—deliberate, negotiable, revisable, repeatable—that stands as a theoretical support to the modern order.

The theorist looking to reconsider her possibly unconscious allegiance to the secular temporality of modernity might first rightly insist on asking one question: whether the antinomian fighting that fundamental beliefs may give rise to might do too much damage to the public at large to make their inclusion worthwhile. I would acknowledge the problem, but also insist that there is a wide range of things that might be "damaged." On the one end, there is that overly touted "bipartisanship" which is so often acclaimed as essential to "getting work done for the American people," and whose loss is so often blamed on fundamentally minded "single-issue" legislators.[24] On the other end, though, is the relative civil peace of the modern West, ever fearful (and properly so) of sectarian violence.

Many fundamentalist believers have suffered violence, physical and institutional, at the hands of our polity: one thinks of the nineteenth-century persecution of the Mormons because of their polygamous practices, which almost drove the church to the point of dissolution; or, over a hundred years later, of the lumber companies that clear-cut a forest held to be sacred by a Native American cult, despite acknowledging that doing so might cause that faith to simply disappear.[25] Unfortunately, these experiences have not prevented some believers from succumbing to the lure of violence as well. Of course, many who claim to speak on behalf of believers are not advocates of a different temporality at all, but reactionary, substituting a desire to turn back the clock for the determination to look beyond it; theorists and others concerned about the possible fragmentation of our polity should always keep in mind that the first does not equal the second.[26] Nonetheless, the threat remains, and in this regard one must not ignore the value of the public sphere as presently constituted. The painstaking and careful work of theists like Charles Taylor is again of use here: believers, if they are to make their case against the temporal demands of liberal modernity, must recognize that much was gained, in terms of both ethics and faith, when the churches themselves no longer authoritatively, punitively, set the public pace.[27]

If the matter really was purely a conflict between a secular, liberal temporality and a radical, sectarian, believing one, most Americans (including the majority of churchgoers) would declare it no contest. Few people, after all, felt a loss at the death of David Koresh, much less saw that debacle as a political matter.[28] But the choice, fortunately, is not either-or. There are resources in the language of belief that can accommodate the ultimate requirements of public opinion, without being excused from the process of building that opinion. No doubt the "fundamental commitments" and "fundamental critiques" Wolin called for will be unsettling. But is being unsettled such a disreputable possibility? Theorists have been discomfiting modernity for decades now, with little sign of letting up. Moreover, theory "deals also in possibilities; it tries to state the necessary or sufficient conditions for attaining ends which . . . are deemed good or desirable."[29] It is possible that the temporal struggle of theory today—against the antithesis of belief, an economic polity that rushes onward without reflection—may be aided through an engagement with belief. Fundamentalists, after all, have been attempting to change time for centuries; while political theory, as it has developed in the West, for all its vaunted bellicosity in regard to issues of political authority, civic participation, and political justice, has been surprisingly amenable to being put on modernity's clock.

MYTH, BELIEF, AND THE PROBLEM OF MODERNITY

Many theorists, uncomfortable with belief, celebrate myth. Myth presumably allows us contact with archaic potentials within ourselves. Unlike fundamental beliefs in substantive unities prior to our temporal boundaries, myths are very much in our grasp—playthings that can be rehearsed and revised and reattributed to no end. They are, presumably, a safe belief. Max Weber, however, points out the consequences:

> We live as did the ancients when their world was not yet disenchanted of its gods and demons, only we live in a different sense. As Hellenic man at times sacrificed to Aphrodite and at other times to Apollo, and, above all, as everybody sacrificed to the gods of his city, so do we still nowadays, only the bearing of man has been disenchanted and denuded of its mystical but inwardly genuine plasticity. Fate, and certainly not "science," holds sway over these gods and their struggles. . . . Many old gods ascend from their graves; they are disenchanted and hence take the form of impersonal forces. They strive to gain power over our lives and again they resume their eternal struggle with one another.[30]

What Weber calls a "mystical but inwardly genuinely plasticity" we might call a "believing soul." The rite of sacrifice was a meaningful rite, and its performance, whether for Greek cult priests or Confucian scholars, had a shaping, ordering, binding power. Such is the etymological origin of "religion": *religare*, "to bind up together." Souls were knit together with others and with their gods through ritual and belief. Weber believed that disenchanted man lacked the inclination toward shaping. Our relation with our contemporary "gods," especially our civic ones, is impersonal—not even science affords us much power over them. Wolin notes in regard to this passage that "while the old personifications of power have given way to depersonalized conceptions of power [he suggests modern capitalism and technology], that change is less striking than the change in the internal life of man."[31]

Of course, human beings in this late modern age still have their rituals, but to what end? The ritual notion of power originally involved an act of orientation and discipline. While inwardly shaped by religion, so would one be instructed in outward boundaries as well—temporal, social, and physical. And in identifying boundaries, one would be set in a proper (that is, empowering) relationship with an existing order. However powerful the realities confronted were believed to be, there remained an *affirmative* aspect to them, a conscious act of internal construction and mediation. Individuals reached out and jointly adjusted themselves to others and the world, binding themselves to a unity that may well have been impossibly restrictive, but was nonetheless reciprocal; power was both imparted and received.[32] Today we are still bound—but the binding involved is more subtle, impersonal, and passive than before. As such, it teaches us little—about our relationships with each other, the world, or even our own bodies. As Talal Asad suggests, the ritual practices of our day are no longer assumed to create or transform (that is, "shape") our moral capabilities, but rather simply to "invent representations," which we may reject or embrace as we prefer.[33] While modern rituals bespeak a larger reality—a generally homogeneous one—they also insist on an individuality and anonymity: anyone can do them, and mostly we do them alone. Consequently our civic posture is reactive, and politics goes on autopilot, legitimated through our very withdrawal from the ritual responsibilities and possibilities of the group:

> The . . . autolegitimacy of the political [is] the expression of power in an age of high technology that has nullified the traditional notion, as old as the tradition of Western political theory itself, that power emanates from the community. Compared to the microchip, a vote represents a negligible quantum of power.[34]

When political time is threatened by the evanescent pace of the modern economy, the rapidity and lack of reflection within the polity allow for the quick manufacture of culturally constituted temporalities, all equally transient. Weber insists that "in the last analysis" the state is the only viable modern political association, and cannot be understood in terms of ends; rather, it can "only be defined sociologically in terms of a specific means."[35] When one speaks of the "ends" in politics, one usually thinks of Aristotle and the telos. But it might be beneficial also to think of "ends" in the sense of temporal endings. A state without an ending, where there is only the "slow, strong drilling through hard boards" without end, without the ability to conceive what Wolin called in a different context an "end-fulness," is certainly safe from the threat of enchantment.[36] But is it safe from the tempos of power, should they accelerate beyond our ability to control them? Probably not.

The point should be clear: the homogeneous and capacious temporality of the modern world gave human beings unprecedented room to move, but it also allowed them to move so far away from their embodied selves, each other, and any sense of ends that the binding power of belief, expressed through rituals and community action, was drastically diminished. Contemporary myths may be sufficient for some—the most self-confident, the most socially integrated and successful—to overcome this absence, but not all.

Was the modern emptying of time really central to the development of a mechanistic worldview that challenged fundamental belief? In a fascinating discussion toward the end of *Being and Time,* Martin Heidegger considers our thinking about time and the consequences thereof. Temporality, he asserts, was originally an awareness of time that was inseparable from a simultaneously revealed awareness of the world around us: there was a unity of existence that was made present to us in our own embeddedness in temporal events. Technological development allowed for the creation of sundials and ever more sophisticated clocks; but time then became more an entity in itself rather than a discovered thing in a given set of relationships. Further advances made temporality ever more abstract, revealed in increasingly impersonal relations: "using time," "taking time," "wasting time," and so forth. Our sense of time becomes relatively narrow, in that all time seems similar:

> When we use a clock in ascertaining what o'clock it is, we say—whether explicitly or not—"It is *now* such and such an hour and so many minutes; *now* is the time for . . ." or "there is still time enough *now* until . . ." When we look at the clock and regulate ourselves *according to the time,* we are essentially saying "*now.*" Here the "now" has in each case already been understood and *interpreted* in its full structural content of datability, spannedness, publicness and worldhood. This is so "obvious" that we take no note of it whatsoever; still less do we know anything about it explicitly.[37]

Without the possibility of believing that time is connected to us and the world, the ability to understand time as anything other than an isolating "now" becomes harder to maintain. Once time manifested a unity wherein the world, its past and future, could be conceived as a significating "vertical" moment. After the advent of the technological worldview, however, time became an unending "horizontal" simultaneity posing as a presence that we are constantly trying to fill—and inevitably, that which fills it fastest, and fullest (the most emphatic "now"), will dominate. This is not an explicitly technological consequence, but rather a metaphysical transition. Hans-Georg Gadamer suggests that Heidegger's thinking about being and time was in fact originally inspired by the "distortion" that he believed metaphysical thinking had wrought on religion. The "experience of time that Heidegger recognized in St. Paul," Gadamer writes, sounding a little fundamentalist himself, was a temporality that allowed for a "time beyond all time," a "Second Coming that cannot be expected, a coming that is meant as parousia and not as presentness."[38]

Theory's position today is surely a difficult one. On the one hand, the modern worldview has allowed its harmonized temporality and deliberate inclusion of difference to shape pluralistic and liberating public habits, all of which have allowed theoretical discourse to proliferate; on the other hand, this slow but sure replacing of any belief in ends with fallibilistic presumptions has left us unmoved or uninvolved in substantive, collective rituals, leaving us all (including theorists) open to an impersonal, automatic temporal acceleration against which we have only weak, individualistic myths to keep us secured. Theory's acquiescence to a temporality that denies presumptive closure works at least partly against its own preservative function; as Wolin wrote in the elegiac essay that opens this volume, the political theorist today has unconsciously "replicated the pace of technological change: he and she are synchronous with the utopia," meaning the present world, and the overpoweringly crisis-proof system it appears to represent.[39] Wolin suggests that in the midst of what is fundamentally a temporal dilemma, something old must be invoked: not a new revolution, for revolution has already been appropriated into a commercial myth, but rather something collective and ritualistic and unexpected: something, perhaps, like belief.

THEORETICAL DISCOURSE AND THE
POTENTIAL OF PUBLIC BELIEF

In the introduction I noted that the demand for homogeneity and its inevitable dismissal of fundamentalist perspectives is not uniform throughout the discipline; there are theorists who have challenged the denial of fundamental concerns, and have admitted certain comprehensive worldviews into their discussions. One sees this not only in Wolin and other radical democrats, but in the work of many Nietzschean-inspired theorists as well.[40] But that challenge has been too often selective—when it comes to real questions of temporality, belief has only rarely been admitted to the theoretical table. Those fundamental beliefs that do not directly threaten the temporal proceduralism of modernity are more and more frequently being included, it is true. But what of orthodox Islam's insistence on the definitive revelation of Mohammed? Or the persistence of individual inequality in the Hindu worldview? More to the point for Americans, what about the Evangelical belief in scriptural infallibility, the Anabaptist insistence on embodied social discipline, or conservative Catholic claims to papal authority? None of these issues is new to constitutional scholars, who have dealt with interpretations and implications of the First Amendment and the nonestablishment clause throughout the history of our nation. But in political theory, in the actual discourse and critique of politics, the earnest invocation of belief is only beginning.[41]

Even if we agree to hold fast against believers who see the public sphere as just another space for coercion, and even if we acknowledge the potential that fundamental beliefs have to expand our challenge to Weber's iron cage, the actual *expression* of belief remains problematic for theorists. The particular construction of public opinion that modern political theory both supports and assumes began with innovations in how human beings communicated. Open dialogue between citizens is an obvious component of this. Of course, citizens engaged in a dialogue may well choose to make space within their polity for a belief that can express itself only in some mystic fashion, but it will not contribute much by way of public concerns if it is not comprehensible to others. Some might assume that by that criterion all religious beliefs are thereby emptied of theoretical relevance: for are not all religious claims conveyed in a closed, uncompromisable language? Some are, it is true. But not all prophets mutter nonsensically, and not all believing language is unreasonable.[42]

Some of those who have approached this issue with some sympathy for fundamental belief are Michael Perry, Sanford Levinson, and Stephen Carter.[43] All of these writers explicitly challenge the necessity of constituting public opinion in the exclusionary sense heretofore discussed. However, they also ground their argument on a rational ideal that assumed a "coherence" among comprehensive visions of the good. For them, a rational religious vision would be one that followed the basic liberal agenda of avoiding claims that consider themselves either infallible or given. If a belief does not adhere to these standards, it is not publicly "accessible," and thus would be out of place in liberal society.[44]

Certainly speech should be publicly intelligible. Discourse that is inscrutable, or violently exclusivist, will not bring anything to the public and may take a good deal away from it. But we should not too casually limit ourselves to a model of public discourse such as Perry's. There are, he maintains, four types of political dialogue: *declaring* reasons for supporting a particular political choice, *persuading* others to support that choice, *justifying* the reasons for such a choice, and *deliberating* about choices.[45] This is a good list. But what about *witnessing*? Why is it not tolerable for an individual to speak directly and solely of her beliefs, in a public forum and in a political manner, in order to *testify* to the truth of the particular choice the speaker has come to as she understands it? In short, what about the most original and unmodern sort of believing: testimony? Is such a way of speaking completely without theoretical content?

The act of witnessing is an act that, by and large, eschews appeals to rational belief; it is an attempt to connect on a fundamental level. It is this level that David Smolin sees as discriminated against by the modern public sphere. In a review of Perry's book, Smolin contends that Perry has tried to redeem liberal politics rather than rethink it. Commenting on Perry's insistence that "there is more . . . to participating in ecumenical dialogue than simply making one's claims accessible to the public," and that dialogue that appeals to sources of authority or experiences that are not common outside one's historical community is not "tolerant" and therefore not quite accessible enough,[46] Smolin writes:

> Perry . . . appears to define tolerance by his prior commitment to individual autonomy. Indeed, Perry's commitment to individual autonomy is so profound that he reads into "authentic religion" a commitment to the self-revising autonomous individual. The intolerant, then, turn out to be all who reject this radical conception of individual autonomy. Since a commitment to tolerance can require an intolerance of the intolerant, Perry's ecumenical politics is actually an explicit justification for liberalism's traditional exclusion of non-liberal cultural groups. . . . To allow Perry's version of "public accessibility" to govern the debate about [liberal theory] is simply another way of requiring that fallibilism and pluralism win.[47]

Smolin does not deny Perry's arguments in toto: he freely admits, for instance, that dialogue over fundamentals requires a degree of civility, of "sincerity and honesty,"[48] especially when one is engaged in specific exploratory dialogue with a political opponent or observer about one or another activity in the public realm. But Smolin's argument is that asking for more than such sensitivity, assuming some sort of orderly standards for forms of belief, will necessarily be exclusivist. Smolin believes that we must take seriously the possibility of real competition in the public sphere—that fundamentalist Christianity, for example, be "allowed to win" if Americans respond to testimony in such a manner.[49]

In short, Wolin unapologetically calls for a dismissal of the leisurely temporal order (which has acted perhaps too leisurely against the increasing speed of the contemporary world) and for a willingness to accept that "religious and cultural conflict will continue in our society in virtually all areas of public concern."[50] The conflict should be restricted by a sense of civility, but not directed away from particular conclusions or arguments by methodological, much less institutional, restrictions. This is hardly a call for civil war. Indeed, it may be a call for more dedication *to* civil society. As Stephen Carter argued in a subsequent, much more persuasive book, the witnessing role of believing individuals and communities, even to the point of civil disobedience and disturbance, is crucial to a society's health; within a liberal polity, it is the *dissent* of the governed that prevents the law from becoming an oppressive fundamentalism all its own.[51] Moreover, there are possible unities, even civil ones, beyond that assumed by a procedural, uninterruptable temporality. As Kenneth Strike suggests, liberals like Rawls (and, I would add, their unknowing defenders) underestimate the ability of people with fundamental disagreements to engage in "argumentative reciprocity."[52] As one analysis of the contributions that fundamental, temporally challenging beliefs (in this case, Anabaptist discipline) may make to political (especially post-Nietzschean) discourse put it, "differences do not preclude conversation around interesting affinities."[53]

A dialogic approach to the articulation of divergent beliefs and the incipient community such acts of dialogue invoke is actually suggestive of political "expressivism"—a sort of aesthetic unity grounded in the nature of language and how it shapes, through the transformation of shared contexts, our behavior and sense of self.[54] Making this sort of agonistic civility into a reality will surely not be easy; boundaries will always have to be drawn, and then re-drawn, and many efforts to resolve this or that issue will no doubt come to naught. On the other hand, though, such involving adjustments may ultimately serve a sort of ritualistic function, by making us real participants in the discussion, rather than passive applicators of quaint theoretical claims.[55]

CONCLUSION

We have reached a point where theory seems exhausted—not because it has nothing more to say, but because its attachment, however reluctant or disavowed, to the conventions of the modern liberal state has allowed it to proliferate, like widgets on an assembly line, going nowhere. Wolin, in obvious frustration, mourns as a probable result the passing of political theory as a calling.[56] He comes close to, but does not quite articulate, the problem that this essay diagnoses—that temporality, and specifically theory's commitment to an uninterruptable and dependable version of it, is the conveyer belt upon which all too many theorists are sitting. It's time to get off. Without question, it will be quite a leap—a leap of faith, in fact.

A theorizing that could also be believing would not necessarily result in unmodern, illiberal conclusions: civility and respect for persons, after all, were enlightened values long before such principles were codified (and thus set at a distance) by the rise of rights-talk. Perhaps the finest argument for why these virtues, so central to ordinary life in the modern world, may attend a discourse that admits comprehensive, fundamental beliefs was made by a distinctly unmodern thinker: Saint Augustine, who pointed out that conflict itself can in some circumstances be called peaceful:

> As, then, there may be life without pain, while there cannot be pain without some kind of life, so there may be peace without war, but there cannot be war without some kind of peace, because war supposes the existence of some natures to wage it, and these natures cannot exist without peace of one kind or another.[57]

The implication here is that even conflicts have a particular order to them; that order which Augustine described as affecting even the most savage animals and monstrous men. In our everyday lives, even if we live unjustly, there is a striving for peace, for the maintenance of order. By extension, a just conflict would be one that respects that peace, that order, which exists within the actual performance of the conflict itself. It would not be a methodologically imposed unity of debate of the sort that has come to dominate with the rise of the modern public sphere, but a sense that, within the theoretical vocation, discourse has an integrity all its own, one that is not likely to dissolve simply because of the inclusion of temporal perspectives claiming that time will meaningfully end, rather than continue on, always unresolved. That claim will never be demonstrable in some rigorous fashion; it will always be only a belief. But beliefs can be testified to, and such testimony is not without its own theoretical heft. Granting this does not and should not open *all* forms of modern discourse to alternate temporalities—just as the crowded theater remains the wrong place to shout "fire!" so would there be many times and many places where simple civility would suggest that fundamental critiques and commitments would be uncalled-for. Theory, though, is special vocation, and should not be limited by unnecessary external, temporal restrictions. In the end, it is unlikely any accommodation with fundamentalist beliefs will dilute theory, or lessen either its challenge to contemporary society or its (not much practiced) ability to speak peaceableness to power. On the contrary, such comprehensive views may strengthen political theory, by lending it the conviction necessary to engage a state that has long since outsped it, and thereby testify against it, with a sense of belief on its side.

NOTES

1. Sheldon S. Wolin, "Political Theory as a Vocation," in *Machiavelli and the Nature of Political Thought,* ed. M. Fleisher (New York: Atheneum Press, 1972), 28, italics added.

2. Sheldon S. Wolin, "Political Theory: From Vocation to Invocation," this volume; in regard to the misuses of nostalgia in politics today, see J. Peter Euben's contribution to this volume, "The Politics of Nostalgia and Theories of Loss."

3. Leon Wieseltier suggests this definition in his essay "The Jewish Face of Fundamentalism," in *The Fundamentalist Phenomenon: A View from Within; A Response from Without,* ed. Norman J. Cohen (Grand Rapids, Mich.: Eerdmans Publishing Company, 1990), 193.

4. The best-known treatments of this topic are probably Richard John Neuhaus, *The Naked Public Square: Religion and Democracy in America* (Grand Rapids, Mich.: Eerdmans Publishing Company, 1984), and Stephen L. Carter, *The Culture of Disbelief: How American Law and Politics Trivialize Religious Devotion* (New York: Basic Books, 1993).

5. Consider the position of Leo Strauss, especially in *Spinoza's Critique of Religion,* trans. Elsa M. Sinclair (New York: Schocken Books, 1965)—see 29, where he writes: "The antagonism between Spinoza and Judaism [and hence between philosophy and religion] is ultimately not theoretical but moral." This essay, setting aside the issue of morality for the moment, seeks to argue that the conflict really does have a theoretical side, after all. See also Strauss, "Jerusalem and Athens: Some Pre-

liminary Reflections," in *Studies in Platonic Political Philosophy*, ed. Thomas Pangle (Chicago: University of Chicago Press, 1983).

6. See John Rawls, *Political Liberalism* (New York: Columbia University Press, 1996), 32 and passim.

7. Sheldon S. Wolin, "The Liberal/Democratic Divide: On Rawls's *Political Liberalism*," *Political Theory* 24 (February 1996): 103–4.

8. Stephen K. White, "Weak Ontology and Liberal Political Reflection," *Political Theory* 25 (August 1997): 502–3.

9. Sheldon S. Wolin, *Politics and Vision: Continuity and Innovation in Western Political Thought* (Boston: Little, Brown & Co., 1960), 7; quote from Suzanne Langer, *Philosophy in a New Key* (New York: Mentor, 1952), 58–59.

10. Sheldon S. Wolin, "What Time Is It?" *Theory & Event* 1: 1, 3–5.

11. Wolin, "What Time Is It?" 3, 6–7; see also this volume's "From Vocation to Invocation."

12. In contrast to the desire to approach problems "theoretically" or with a leisurely pace, one is reminded of Martin Luther King's classic *Why We Can't Wait*. John Rawls, among other liberals, has praised King and the Abolitionists for speaking comprehensively, and religiously, to "an unjust political society," even though he asserts that today the exclusion of fundamental commitments from public discourse is necessary for political justice. Andrew Murphy has noted the confusion that attends Rawls's attempt to make space for the religiously motivated (and in the case of the Abolitionists, sometimes apocalyptic) pronouncements of these individuals in his otherwise secular model. See Rawls, "Introduction to the Paperback Edition," *Political Liberalism*, lii, iii n. 27; Andrew R. Murphy, "Rawls and a Shrinking Liberty of Conscience," *Review of Politics* 60 (Spring 1998): 264 n. 39.

13. Charles Taylor, "Liberal Politics and the Public Sphere," in *New Communitarian Thinking: Persons, Virtues, Institutions, and Communities*, ed. Amitai Etzioni (Charlottesville: University Press of Virginia, 1995), 185–86.

14. Taylor, "Liberal Politics," 187–88; see also Jürgen Habermas, *The Structural Transformation of the Public Sphere*, trans. Thomas Burger (Cambridge, Mass.: MIT Press, 1989).

15. Taylor, "Liberal Politics," 192; quote from Michael Warner, *Letters of the Republic* (Cambridge, Mass.: Harvard University Press, 1990), 46.

16. Taylor, "Liberal Politics," 197–98.

17. Auerbach, quoted in Walter Benjamin, *Illuminations* (London: Fontana, 1973), 265.

18. Benjamin, *Illuminations*, 263; Benedict Anderson, *Imagined Communities*, rev. ed. (London: Verso, 1991), 22–36.

19. My description of the perceived "untranslatable and incommensurable" divide between the ways of theory and the ways of belief is, of course, an allusion to Alasdair MacIntyre, who has written at length on the dynamics of cross-cultural understanding. His observation about the difficulty of broaching fundamental differences, to say nothing of temporal ones, is a humbling reminder: "Whether in

advancing their own enquiries or in criticizing their rivals, the adherents of each point of view tend to discuss at any length only with those with whom they are already in *fundamental* agreement" (MacIntyre, *Three Rival Versions of Moral Enquiry: Encyclopaedia, Genealogy, and Tradition* [Notre Dame: University of Notre Dame Press, 1990], 7).

20. Stephen Macedo, "Transformative Constitutionalism and the Case of Religion: Defending the Moderate Hegemony of Liberalism," *Political Theory* 26 (February 1998): 72, 68.

21. Brian Barry, "The Light That Failed?" *Ethics* 100 (1989): 163–64.

22. The conception of time as unified, as opposed to unending and undefined, is hardly the final criterion of whether a religious movement is "fundamentalist" or not, but it is very close to a common denominator. To assert that certain possibilities are inevitable—that certain sins will be punished, and certain works will be blessed, for instance—is to make a commitment to an unrevisable God or divine power; something whose purposes will be fulfilled, no matter what else is tried or embraced or discarded in the meantime. The most comprehensive and sympathetic work on fundamentalism in America and abroad is the Fundamentalism Project, a collection of four volumes edited by Martin E. Marty and R. Scott Appleby, including research by numerous scholars on the global rise of fundamentalist beliefs and the challenges they pose to modernity in a variety of contexts, including politics, education, family and social issues, gender roles, scientific research, military service, etc. The first volume, which includes the coeditors' important introductory essay, is *Fundamentalisms Observed* (Chicago: University of Chicago Press, 1991).

23. Ibid., ix.

24. This is not to dismiss the importance of working across political or religious divides in order to accomplish common goals: this was perhaps the most central assumption and hope held by the Founders when they crafted America's national legislature. But "where there is no consensus, or where consensus is available only at a level of such generality that it is morally and politically banal . . . [the better approach is], surely, a sharpening of distinctions and a war of ideas, followed by what used to be known as leadership." Leon Wieseltier, "Total Quality Meaning," *New Republic*, July 19 & 26, 1993, 18.

25. See *Reynolds v. United States*, 98 U.S. 145 (1879), and *Lyng v. Northwest Indian Cemetery Protective Association*, 485 U.S. 439 (1988). Excellent summaries of these and other legal battles involving minority faiths can be found in Frederick Mark Gedicks, *The Rhetoric of Church and State: A Critical Analysis of Religion Clause Jurisprudence* (Durham: Duke University Press, 1995).

26. It is important to distinguish "conservative" from "reactionary" thinking, since many (if not most) fundamentalist believers affirm a variety of conservative cultural and social views. Rather than viewing a reactionary posture as simply an extreme form of conservatism, one should understand it as a particular (I think somewhat incoherent) species of fundamentalism that sees the antithesis of the tempos of modern life in some bygone manifestation of it (the 1950s, for example).

Conservative thought, in general, simply wants to slow down the pace of change, and does not challenge the temporal, technocratic, and procedural imperatives that take us from one "era" to the "next." Edmund Burke is a good example. Whatever his religious beliefs, it seems that his attachment to the old order was premised on his understanding of what good politics required (respect for tradition, etc.), not on any distrust of the way of politics itself. Such conservative thought is an important and useful part of the discipline, but it does not in itself—as most fundamentalist believers should recognize—unsettle the temporal norms of modernity, as I am suggesting needs to be done.

27. This idea is discussed implicitly throughout Taylor's *Sources of the Self: The Making of Modern Identity* (Cambridge, Mass.: Harvard University Press, 1989); for a more explicit discussion of this theme, see Taylor's recent address, "A Catholic Modernity?" in *A Catholic Modernity? Charles Taylor's Marianist Award Lecture,* ed. James L. Heft (Oxford: Oxford University Press, 1999).

28. It should be noted that David Koresh and the Branch Davidians deserved a good deal more from political theorists—and the American public—than they received. It does no disservice to the government agents who died in the standoff that the government began to note that the visionary spirituality they faced, which issued in gun collecting, reclusiveness, harem building, rambling sermons on the apocalypse, and general pugnaciousness (but, it must be said, no evidence of the alleged child abuse, nor of the violent, revolutionary intentions the Branch Davidians supposedly harbored), was itself a legitimate, comprehensive view of the world. Surely, as Leon Wieseltier observed, "Ranch Apocalypse [the name given to Koresh's church-commune] could not have been expected to enjoy much of a claim on the liberal imagination." Nonetheless, the seventy-two bodies hauled out of the burning ruin testified to a failure of both theory and practice, a failure to consider that, if not Koresh himself, then at least the possibility of Koresh, the possibility of spiritual eruption and radical temporal determination, has been present since the beginning of American society, and for that reason ought to be respected by political theorists, for its genealogy if not for its content. See the powerful essay by Wieseltier, "The True Fire," *New Republic,* May 17, 1993, 25–27.

29. Wolin, *Politics and Vision,* 13.

30. Max Weber, "Science as a Vocation," in *From Max Weber,* ed. Hans Gerth and C. Wright Mills (New York: Oxford University Press, 1946), 148–49.

31. Sheldon S. Wolin, "Postmodern Politics and the Absence of Myth," *Social Research* 32 (Summer 1985): 222.

32. See Eliot Deutsch, "Community as Ritual Participation," in *On Community,* ed. Leroy S. Rouner (Notre Dame: University of Notre Dame Press, 1991).

33. Talal Asad, *Genealogies of Religion: Discipline and Reasons of Power in Christianity and Islam* (Baltimore: Johns Hopkins University Press, 1993), 78–79 and passim.

34. Wolin, "Postmodern Politics," 227.

35. Max Weber, "The Profession and Vocation of Politics," in *Political Writings,*

ed. Peter Lassman and Ronald Spiers (Cambridge: Cambridge University Press, 1994), 310.

36. Weber, "Vocation of Politics," 369; Wolin, "Postmodern Politics," 225.

37. Martin Heidegger, *Being and Time,* trans. John Macquarrie and Edward Robinson (New York: Harper & Row, 1962), 469 and passim.

38. Hans-Georg Gadamer, "The Religious Dimension," in *Heidegger's Ways,* trans. John W. Stanley (Albany: State University of New York Press, 1994), 174–75.

39. Wolin, "From Vocation to Invocation," this volume. Wolin discusses at length in this essay the bind described above, though in slightly different language. He notes the "symbiotic relationship" between the proliferation of opportunities of theorizing (which he calls "overtheorization") and the domination of the world by "premeditated change." Regretfully, he does not note how theory's own temporal assumptions help perpetuate this condition, though his idea of "invocation" does have certain implicit temporal characteristics.

40. Perhaps the most perceptive work being done in this area is by William Connolly. His recent books *Identity\Difference: Democratic Negotiations of Political Paradox* (Ithaca: Cornell University Press, 1991) and *The Ethos of Pluralization* (Minneapolis: University of Minnesota Press, 1995) strive to imagine a democratic way of being that would accommodate even fundamental differences. It is debatable exactly how Connolly's "agonistic" temporality would relate to the issue of belief; however, the title of his latest work, *Why I Am Not a Secularist* (Minneapolis: University of Minnesota Press, 1999), published too recently to be considered here, does give believers some reason to hope.

41. Some fascinating first steps in this direction include Roxanne L. Euben, "Comparative Political Theory: An Islamic Fundamentalist Critique of Rationalism," *Journal of Politics* 59 (1997); Daya Krishna, "Democracy and Justice: Presuppositions and Implications," in *Justice and Democracy: Cross-Cultural Perspectives,* ed. Ron Bontekoe and Marietta Stepaniants (Honolulu: University of Hawaii Press, 1997); Thomas Heilke, "On Being Ethical without Moral Sadism: Two Readings of Augustine and the Beginnings of the Anabaptist Revolution," *Political Theory* 24 (August 1996); and Stanley Hauerwas, "The Kingship of Christ: Why Freedom of 'Belief' Is Not Enough," in *In Good Company: The Church as Polis* (Notre Dame: University of Notre Dame Press, 1995).

42. Sometimes all that matters is who is doing the talking, and how. David Koresh, up until the FBI stopped talking and prepared to attack, may have ranted luridly about the seven seals in the book of Revelation to the negotiators he felt were determined to destroy him, but he reportedly maintained a cordial, intelligent relationship with the local sheriff throughout the standoff.

43. See Michael Perry, *Love and Power: The Role of Religion and Morality in American Politics* (New York: Oxford University Press, 1991); Sanford Levinson, "Religious Language and the Public Square," *Harvard Law Review* 105 (1992): 2061–79; and Carter, *The Culture of Disbelief.* Stanley Fish discusses some of these same authors, and makes an argument similar to my own, in his latest book, *The Trouble with*

Principle (Cambridge, Mass.: Harvard University Press, 1999), though his challenge to theory arises from his understanding of language, rather than temporality.

44. Perry, *Love and Power,* 52–65, 100–105.

45. Ibid., 45.

46. Ibid., 106, 195.

47. David M. Smolin, "Regulating Religious and Cultural Conflict in a Postmodern America: A Response to Professor Perry," *Iowa Law Review* 76 (1991): 1080, 1086.

48. Ibid., 1074.

49. Ibid., 1103. This is the fundamentalists' strongest challenge to modernity, and it elicits liberal theory's most naked defenses. Levinson readily admits that his willingness to argue in favor of greater consideration of fundamentalist beliefs is contingent upon living "in a country . . . where it is simply unthinkable that the members of a particularistic religion could ever capture national political institutions." Macedo goes further: happily embracing modernity's demands, he asserts that liberalism has an interest in replicating itself, and that we "should not be concerned to make it . . . easy for Fundamentalist Protestants . . . to pass along their beliefs to their children." See Levinson, "Religious Language," 2077; Macedo, "Transformative Liberalism," 73.

50. Smolin, "Religious and Cultural Conflict," 1095.

51. Stephen L. Carter, *The Dissent of the Governed: A Meditation on Law, Religion, and Loyalty* (Cambridge, Mass.: Harvard University Press, 1998), 94–99 and passim.

52. Kenneth A. Strike, "Must Liberal Citizens Be Reasonable?" *Review of Politics* 58 (1996): 41–51.

53. Heilke, "On Being Ethical," 512.

54. See again Taylor, *Sources of the Self,* and numerous essays in his collection *Human Agency and Language* (Cambridge: Cambridge University Press, 1985).

55. A good place to see how such discussions might begin is Richard Flathman's reply to Stephen Macedo's aforementioned argument for "transformative constitutionalism." See Flathman, "'It All Depends . . . On How One Understands Liberalism': A Brief Response to Stephen Macedo," *Political Theory* 26 (February 1998): 81–84. Flathman defends on Nietzschean grounds a "free-spiritedness" in our polity's pluralism, without particular regard for ensuring a "healthy" versus an unhealthy diversity. Flathman's negative equivocation of Macedo with communitarian critics of liberalism misses the point: a community itself, however constituted, can also be freely chosen, and the quest to discover communitarian virtues (which often include socially conservative principles central to fundamentalist belief systems) within a pluralistic order is entirely in line with the freedom Flathman encourages. Of course, freedom and community, just like temporal homogeneousness and a belief in a closed, alternative temporality, will conflict, and Macedo is right in suggesting that Flathman is not thinking about the consequences of that complicated struggle he celebrates. Macedo, "Reply to Flathman," *Political Theory* 26 (February 1998): 85–89. But Macedo's ignorance of the power of testimony and the legitimacy of the change it may bring is not good thinking either.

56. Wolin, "From Vocation to Invocation," this volume. Again, Wolin comes very close to the present essay's focus on temporality at times, especially when he comments, like Stephen White, that we are "late in the day." But he does not consider how the fundamentalism that he earlier (perhaps too easily) dismissed might, in a specific but very real way, enable theory to engage more than puerile myths, and instead help connect all of us with, as Wolin suggested, quoting Antonio Gramsci, our "traditional ideologies."

57. Augustine, *The City of God*, trans. Marcus Dods (New York: Modern Library, 1993), book XIX, chap. 13, at 690.

DAVID PAUL MANDELL

5 // THE HISTORY OF POLITICAL THOUGHT AS A ''VOCATION''

A Pragmatist Defense

Genetic method was perhaps the chief scientific achievement of the latter half of the nineteenth century. Its principle is that the way to get insight into any complex product is to trace the process of its making,—to follow it through the successive stages of its growth. To apply this method to history as if meant only the truism that the present social state cannot be separated from its past, is one-sided. It means equally that past events cannot be separated from the living present and retain meaning. The true starting point of history is always some present situation with its problems.
—John Dewey[1]

Much as it was in the late sixties, when Sheldon Wolin published "Political Theory as a Vocation," the place of the study of the history of political thought within the wider discipline of political science is uncertain.[2] In that essay, Wolin defended political theory as one of the last redoubts against positivist social science. Political theory, he argued, provides the social sciences in general and political science in particular with a sense of history and a sense of normativity; the tradition of political theory retains the visionary impulse that the narrowly empirical social sciences have lost and reminds us of such questions as what constitutes political order, what is the good life, and what is justice.

While much of Wolin's analysis remains valid, the state of the social sciences differs considerably from when he wrote his essay. Narrowly positivist approaches, although still dominant, have lost their hegemony. Over the last few decades interpretivist methods have made strong inroads in the social sciences, and political science and sociology have fruitfully cross-fertilized with history and anthropology.

Why has political theory not been a prime beneficiary of this "linguistic turn"? After all, it is political theorists who have, among political scientists, most cultivated the art of reading and interpreting texts. While many individual political theorists—including theorists I discuss in this essay—have borrowed and benefited significantly from this linguistic turn, the turn has not led to a significant renewal of interest in the history of political thought, nor improved the status of political theory within the discipline of political science. Amid the clash between "positivists" and "interpretivists," historians of political thought seem to have gotten lost. As greater attention is devoted to the discursive construction of all forms of social existence, the importance of the kinds of texts to which political theorists have traditionally devoted themselves is called into question. The political theory canon has not been so much deconstructed as it has been overwhelmed by the textuality of everyday life.

In this essay, I argue for an approach to the history of political thought that preserves its practical value. I argue that a particularly important task for historians of political thought is to sort out the relationship between past arguments and present concerns; it is to determine which of our inherited understandings remain valuable resources and which ought to be discarded. An approach that focuses either exclusively on historical continuity or exclusively on discontinuity and difference cannot take up this critical task.

In defending the history of political thought, I have chosen a somewhat unlikely ally—the pragmatist philosopher John Dewey. Dewey—at least according to one common interpretation—appears as the very embodiment of Wolin's antithesis to the "theorist," the villainous "methodist." The methodist embraces the methods of the natural sciences—particularly the methods of physics—as models for the human sciences. He or she focuses on practical problem solving and social control rather than developing epochal visions of social order that radically break with the present. But at the same time, he or she is present-minded and consequentialist, unconcerned with the past and "relatively indifferent to context."[3] History and tradition are to be overcome; they are obstacles rather than contributions to the future. The methodist is above all an instrumentalist in search of "short cuts"—quick, simple, and efficient means of achieving predetermined ends.

These caricatures of the methodist capture some real elements of pragmatism, including Dewey's pragmatism. Dewey's instrumentalism, his belief in the unity of the sciences and his account of intelligence as a tool for solving problems, seem to place him in the camp of the positivist social scientists rather than ally him with historians of political thought. This one-sided view of pragmatism and of Dewey is easily refuted. Pragmatism is more concerned with the development of values, the place of culture, and the problems of interpretation than "methodist" versions of pragmatism allow. Nonetheless, it is lessons from this instrumentalist, consequentialist, problem-solving side of pragmatism, I argue, that historians of political thought most need to learn. The full value of the history of political thought can be realized only if its students can learn to use "the past for a resource in a developing future."[4]

I argue that pragmatism provides a way of utilizing the past as such a resource. Dewey's own essays on the history of philosophy and the history of political thought are models of this approach. In his "reconstructions" of Western epistemology, of philosophy, and especially of liberalism, Dewey does not simply sweep away past conceptions, beliefs, and ideas. Rather, Dewey conducts a productive dialogue with the past in which he separates elements of the past that need to be preserved and built upon from those that have outlived their purpose and ought to be discarded. To put it simply—if somewhat cryptically—Deweyan historical reconstruction is the disentangling of the past that is past from the past that is still present.

I begin by contrasting Dewey's method of historical reconstruction with two prominent contemporary approaches to the history of political thought that also have pragmatist foundations—Quentin Skinner's historicism and Richard Rorty's recontextualism. I have chosen these two approaches because they represent two opposing views of the relationship of past and present. For the Skinnerian historicist, I argue, the past is permanently separated from the present, and therefore cannot be used as a resource in the present. For the Rortian recontextualist, past and present are suspect distinctions. The past can be addressed only as texts read by and for us. As a consequence, the crucial pragmatist sense of problem solving—of overcoming while preserving the past—is lost. Thus, unlike Dewey, both Skinner and Rorty have an inadequate understanding of the practical relationship between past, present, and future. After identifying the inadequacies of Skinner's and Rorty's approaches, I then return to Dewey's reconstructive method, and develop a model of the historian of political thought as "an intellectual coalition builder." I end by demonstrating how Dewey's own reconstruction of liberalism exemplifies this approach.

THINKING FOR OURSELVES:
QUENTIN SKINNER'S HISTORICISM

Over the last few decades, Quentin Skinner has provided what has been undoubtedly one of the most influential models of how to conduct the study of the history of political thought. In such works as *The Foundations of Modern Political Thought* and *Machiavelli*, and most recently in *Liberty before Liberalism*, Skinner has not only demonstrated the merits of a contextual approach to the history of political thought, but also suggested the importance of such contextual analysis for contesting some of our most taken for granted understandings of politics.[5] He has argued for the importance of "Roman liberty" and against the strictly negative conceptions of liberty that dominate contemporary liberal political discourse. And he has suggested that the history of political thought is uniquely equipped to help us see these limitations. However, my focus is not on Skinner's historical writings, but on his methodological essays. In focusing on how Skinner *says* we should carry out research in the history of political thought, rather than on how Skinner actually carries out such research, I hope to demonstrate a tension within his work, a tension that prevents him from drawing the present-minded lessons that he wants us to reach.

In his methodological essays, Skinner argues for the primacy of historical contextualism. Historians of political thought, he argues, must avoid anachronistic claims and acknowledge that "no agent can eventually be said to have meant or done something which he could never be brought to accept as a correct description of what he had meant or done."[6] Anachronistic interpretations of texts can be avoided and the history of political thought placed on the right track, Skinner argues, only if we have a correct understanding of language. Language must be seen as a tool. The basic question for the historian interpreting a text is not what the text means, but what the author of the text intended to do in producing it. This claim rests on an essentially pragmatist understanding of language: language succeeds not by representing but by doing. A vocabulary is adequate not because it corresponds accurately to an external world of things, but because it allows us to achieve our intended goals. While Skinner gleans this insight not from Peirce, James, or Dewey but from Wittgenstein and J. L. Austin, it is still that of the pragmatists.[7]

From this understanding of language as a tool follows a number of other important pragmatist propositions. Like the pragmatists, Skinner argues that "there are no perennial problems in philosophy," and few truths that are "wholly tenseless."[8] Rather, particular vocabularies are developed to address particular problems within particular contexts. The veracity of a claim is relative to these vocabularies and contexts.

Like a good pragmatist, Skinner also shows, as Charles Taylor notes, "how inextricably entwined the explanatory and the evaluative are in all languages of politics."[9] Political texts are political acts intended to convince, to motivate, and to instigate action. Hobbes's "science of politics" is also a call for a politics of a certain kind; it is impossible to firmly and absolutely separate his analytical and normative claims. The same holds true of other political theorists. Understanding an author's explanatory claims also entails coming to grips with his or her evaluative goals.

While Skinner accepts these basic pragmatist principles, he draws from them rather narrow methodological conclusions. His main concern is with *how* to study the history of political thought, and not *why* to study it. He largely brackets the more basic pragmatic question of the worthiness of the enterprise. His methodological essays are aimed at other practitioners of the discipline, and not at those who call the entire project into question. Similarly, while he places great importance on the contemporary concerns of the authors whose texts he interprets, he is extremely wary of contaminating historical inquiry with our own contemporary problems and desires—of reading back our own concerns and interests into the past.

Such presentist contamination takes, for Skinner, two primary forms. The first arises when historians search the past for the sources and origins of contemporary doctrines, looking for "precursors" and "anticipations" of such ideas as the separation of powers or judicial review. This leads to the perpetual danger of reading our own expectations into past texts.[10]

Such approaches not only introduce misleading anachronisms but are also dangerously teleological. If we devote attention only to authors we see as having contributed to what we take to be valuable, we will have a rather flattened view of the history of political thought. History will appear unnaturally linear and logical; it will be left sanitized, devoid of all its contingencies, inadvertent misappropriations, and accidental conjunctures. Such histories will also suggest that the views we now hold to be true are the only ones that we possibly could have come to accept as valid. In making the present appear inevitable, such histories naturalize our current understandings. As such, these histories are the enemy of the kind of "liberal irony" that Skinner—as well as Rorty and Dewey—defends.[11] Such histories fail to reflect how contingent our own understandings of the world are, and thus fail to argue for the tolerance that we ought to have for those who lack those understandings.

The second kind of anachronism has another source. It is the product of political theorists who see themselves as exploring the variety of human responses to the universal questions of political thought. Such theorists often see themselves as historicists. One of the lessons allegedly learned from this kind of history is that human communities have had radically different answers to such questions as: What is justice? and What does human nature allow? Skinner argues that theorists who explore the variety of answers to these questions fail to recognize the even more radically variable usage of such basic concepts as "nature," "justice," and the "state."[12] Skinner concludes not only that there are no universal answers to these fundamental questions, but that no such universal questions exist—at least in any meaningful or robust sense.[13] Instead of either a continual progression of development or an endless rehashing of shared problems, history is a sequence of disjoint and distinct "episodes in which the questions as well as the answers frequently change."[14]

I do not dispute Skinner's basic guidelines for interpreting historical texts, although I take them more as helpful tips than as logically necessary precepts. Instead, I want to focus on the inadequacy of Skinner's answers to two related pragmatic questions: (1) why we should study the history of political thought, and (2) how our own concerns should shape how we carry out this enterprise.

Skinner does recognize that it is impossible to completely separate our own interests from the concerns we engage with as researchers. We study something only because we believe it to be of value; "the decisions that we have to make about what we study must be our own decisions, arrived at by applying our own criteria for judging what is rational and significant."[15] Skinner's historian must sever his or her own value judgments from the judgments he or she makes while conducting research; this severing tacitly depends on the distinction between fact and value—on evaluative versus explanatory language. While Skinner claims to reject this distinction, his methodological precepts very much presuppose it. The choice of the object of study is inescapably a choice of value. However, once the object has been chosen and the research commenced, all values must be checked at the door. It is our present judgment of what is of importance that makes the texts of Machiavelli, Hobbes, and Dewey worthwhile topics of research. But these values do not tell us anything about how we should read or interpret these texts.

No matter how problematic this antipragmatist divorce of fact and value is in general, it has a particularly enervating effect on the study of the history of political thought. We must have some sense of how the answers we come up with at the end of our research address the concerns that motivated us to undertake the research in the first place. Skinner provides us with little or no guidance on how to take this final and essential step. While he quickly dismisses any suggestion that he renders the study of the history of political thought an antiquarian and irrelevant discipline, he never adequately refutes the charge. If his methodological claims are really true, what can we learn from the study of early modern understandings of liberty? How should an understanding of the civic republican tradition lead us to rethink our own democratic institutions?

The most substantive explanation Skinner gives as to why the history of political thought is of value is that it teaches us the relativity of our own views. We learn from the history of political thought the radical otherness of other places and other times; we discover "not the essential sameness, but the essential variety of viable moral assumptions and political commitments."[16] Historical knowledge helps us denaturalize the present, revealing the fundamental contingency of our beliefs. This is certainly an invaluable lesson, worthy of frequent repetition. However, if this is the sole message of the history of political thought, then the discipline is a one-trick pony. What is the significance of the actual research if it always brings us to this same conclusion? Furthermore, this role as the ambassador of contingency and historical difference places the historian of political thought outside contemporary political debates. He or she is left only to chastise the actual participants, warning them of their hubris and pointing out to them the relativism and limits of their own claims. The historian can help us to

> attain a greater degree of understanding, and thereby a larger tolerance, for various elements of cultural diversity. And above all, we can hope to acquire a perspective from which to view our own form of life in a more self-critical way, enlarging our present horizons instead of fortifying local prejudices.[17]

But a Skinnerian historian of political thought has nothing to contribute to the debate itself. Skinner cannot directly enter into the present because he inadvertently destroys any notion of an intellectual or political inheritance. All we have received from the past is a set of terms whose original contexts, and therefore, whose original use, we have forever lost. The origins of these terms tell us little or nothing about the adequacy of their current use.

Skinner's radical historicism ironically leads to an ahistoric treatment of the present. The arguments and understandings, and the problems and contexts, of earlier times do not haunt us. Past answers to past problems cannot help us to find answers to our own. As Skinner dryly concludes, "We must learn to think for ourselves."[18]

For anyone familiar with Skinner's historical work, his defense of republican political engagement, and his attempt to revive preliberal understandings of liberty, my accusation that Skinner's historical work is "apolitical" or at least politically detached seems unfair. Skinner's historical essays are often quite present-minded. However, as I noted earlier, my criticisms are not with these essays, but with the methodological writings that allegedly support them. I have argued that Skinner's methodological claims, rather than providing the foundation for his political project, in fact undermine it. Skinner's essay "The Idea of Negative Liberty: Philosophical and Historical Perspectives" provides a good example of the difficulties in drawing the conclusions he wishes us to draw if we accept his own methodological precepts. According to Skinner, both defenders of negative liberty, such as Isaiah Berlin, and critics, such as Charles Taylor, agree that we can connect a concept of individual liberty with virtuous acts of public service only if we posit an "idea of objective human flourishing."[19] Skinner argues that this is a false link, and that it is possible to make positive arguments for political participation that do not depend upon any metaphysical claims about objective human interests and the good. In order to defend this claim, Skinner turns to the history of political thought, arguing that "this quest will bring us to a line of argument about negative liberty which has largely been lost to view in the course of the present debate, but which serves to cast some doubt on the terms of the debate itself."[20] Skinner's quest for such an understanding of liberty takes him to Machiavelli, who speaks of "liberty as a matter of being independent of other social agents, and in consequence able to pursue one's own ends."[21] But Machiavelli also recognizes that this liberty can be safeguarded only through republican institutions and the preservation of the civic virtues that these institutions demand. Contrary to contemporary assumptions, it is possible, as Machiavelli shows us, to defend simultaneously both a duty of public service and also an understanding of liberty as the pursuit of ends that we have chosen for ourselves.

Why must we go back to Machiavelli in order to prove that a link that we see as logically necessary is merely contingent? Why doesn't Skinner simply "think for himself"? Skinner does address this question. His answer is that while conceptual analysis is important, history can add something else. While an analysis of the concept of negative liberty could show the logical possibility of an alternative use, "it is apt to seem much less convincing to suggest that a concept *might* be coherently used in an unfamiliar way than to show that it *has* been put to unfamiliar but coherent uses."[22] I think that this is a legitimate answer to the question. But can Skinner defend it on his own methodological grounds?

Here one might accuse Skinner of the fallacy of pseudo-historicism that he has so carefully cautioned others against. Why are we to believe that the same concept, and not simply the same term, is in use? That Machiavelli speaks of liberty does not prove that he means the same thing that we mean when we speak about liberty. Skinner suggests in his methodological essays that our working assumption should always be that there is conceptual discontinuity. Indeed, the fact that liberty is used in a way that we generally think is incoherent suggests that a different concept is in use. Skinner's assumption that we are working with the same concept may or may not be correct. I am not so concerned with the validity of this claim. My argument is that Skinner does not provide us with tools for answering this question. If we cannot answer this question, and determine whether or not the concepts that theorists from the past are using are the same as our own, we cannot make any judgment about the relationship between the coherence of past beliefs and the coherence of our own. He is only able to provide reasons why we should have some detachment from our own modern understanding of liberty, recognizing that there are conceptions that were once historically viable. He is not—if we take his methodological claims seriously—able to cast doubt on the validity of the conception of liberty with which we now live. He can demonstrate only the historical relativity of understandings, not their present inadequacy.

While he has written that the study of the history of political thought will illuminate "what is necessary and what is the product of our contingent arrangements," he has also concluded that almost nothing is necessary and almost everything is contingent.[23] We can agree with Skinner that the contingent predominates over the necessary, but unlike Skinner, we can also argue that much of this contingent past remains inevitably part of the present. It is this latter claim, I argue, that Dewey forces us to address. However, reading the past as part of the present does not mean obliterating the distinction between past and present. This obliteration, as I will demonstrate in discussing Rorty, has its own dangers.

PRAGMATISM WITHOUT PROBLEMS: THE CONSEQUENCES
OF RICHARD RORTY'S RECONTEXTUALISM

While the description of Skinner as a pragmatist may have seemed counter-intuitive, the identification of Richard Rorty with pragmatism has come to seem oddly natural. Over the last few decades Rorty has probably done more than anyone else to restore the popularity of pragmatism. However, the images and connotations Rorty's pragmatism evokes differ radically from the common stereotypes of pragmatism that prevailed up until the sixties. Rorty has—to a remarkable degree—divorced pragmatism from "method-ism." While pragmatism was once often treated as a species of positivism, it is now often thought of as a code word for interpretivism and relativism. Pragmatism's associations with purely instrumental rationality, the scientific method, and programs of technocratic social control have given way to iden-tifications with moral and cultural relativism, antirealism, and antifounda-tionalism, and the primacy of "texts" over "facts."

Thus it would seem that if anyone can provide a plausible pragmatist ac-count of the history of political thought, it would be Richard Rorty. Rorty's call for the "reweaving" of inherited narratives, his account of inquiry as "re-contextualization," and his claim that liberalism, rather than standing in need of a fundamental diagnosis, is merely due for a "poeticized" redescription, all seem like pragmatist calls for appropriating the past as a resource for the future.[24] He seems to give the history of political thought the sense of pur-pose that Skinner cannot provide. Indeed, Rorty has no problem violating Skinner's strictures against reading past texts in terms of present-day con-cerns. He finds nothing wrong with describing "the problems and data of all earlier epochs in a single up-to-date, commensurating vocabulary" or claim-ing that "what Aristotle was looking for was what Newton found, or that what the Roman plebeians were trying for was what the United Auto Workers later got."[25]

However welcome Rorty's redescription of pragmatism is, it has come at a price. Like Skinner's, Rorty's methodological precepts end up undermining the kinds of political projects in which he wishes to continue to engage. In jettisoning some of pragmatism's more disagreeable associations he has also diluted its more laudable and valuable impulses. As pragmatism becomes more about cultural redescription and the reweaving of narratives, it becomes less about the use of intelligence as a tool to solve problems. The sense of a problem situation—the moment when our habits no longer yield the results we intend, and we are forced to consciously confront and reassess them, as well as the ends they assume—is lost. It is this loss, I argue, that prevents Rorty from generating an adequately pragmatist understanding of the value of the history of political thought. Like Skinner's, Rorty's view of historical interpretation renders the past an unusable resource for the future. This is not, as it is with Skinner, because the past is permanently lost to the present. It is instead because past and present in Rorty's hands lose their distinctiveness. The question of which problems are and which are not still with us cannot be raised in any meaningful form. As a result, Rorty's judgments are oddly retrospective. Dewey's claim that thought is inescapably prospective gets lost.

For Rorty, pragmatism can be reduced to a single principle: it is "simply anti-essentialism applied to notions like 'truth,' 'knowledge,' 'language,' 'morality,' and similar objects of philosophical theorizing."[26] We should abandon "attempts to get back behind language to something which 'grounds' it, or which it 'expresses.'"[27] The validity of vocabularies rests not on how well they "correspond to the world," but on their efficacy as tools. We should think of "language as a way of grabbing hold of causal forces and making them do what we want, altering ourselves and our environment to suit our aspirations."[28]

How do we judge how effective a theoretical construct or a particular language is in helping us to solve our problems? How do we tell how efficacious a particular vocabulary is in bringing about our desired ends? In addressing these questions, Rorty's approach suddenly loses its pragmatist force. While Rorty defends Dewey's depiction of language as a tool rather than as a picture, he warns against phrasing this analogy "so as to suggest that one can separate the tool, Language, from its users and inquire as to its 'adequacy' to achieve our purposes."[29] Instead of inquiring as to how efficaciously a vocabulary serves our purposes, we should play texts off one another, and in the process produce new texts and new vocabularies. Philosophical problem solvers should give way to cultural reweavers.

This linguistic recasting of pragmatism shapes Rorty's entire understanding of the problem of doubt. Despite his antirealism, Rorty has embraced pragmatism's antiskepticism more than he has its fallibilism; he treats fallibilism as a doctrine—as the claim that we should not take ourselves too seriously and instead should always embrace our beliefs with a sense of irony. While we should always recognize that we could be wrong, Rorty never describes a situation in which we actually discover ourselves to be wrong. He does not treat doubt as an actual experience.[30] He acknowledges that in the end we may reject even our most basic beliefs and decide that the views we once strongly held were mistaken or that what we once took to be facts were just opinions. But he always describes this reassessment as a kind of looking back. We find ourselves using a new vocabulary and inhabiting a new way of life in which we discover that we can get by just fine without our old beliefs. It is only after we have started using the new vocabulary that we realize that we had cause to abandon the old. The psychological state of doubt or confusion is thus surprisingly absent from Rorty's account. Rorty, like Peirce, James, and Dewey, rejects the philosophical doubt with which Descartes begins his meditations. At the same time, he does not seem to admit the real and everyday doubt that the other pragmatists see as the starting point of all inquiry. There is no moment where we find that our beliefs and habits have broken down and that we are confronted with a world—a set of problems and questions—with which we are unfamiliar and in which our old habits no longer produce the outcomes we intend.

I do not want to suggest that these "problems and questions" are self-evident. The whole point of inquiry—including historical inquiry—is to develop an interpretation of what these problems and questions are. The historical enterprise is particularly useful in helping us to interpret what exactly these questions are by providing us with critical distance. The historical perspective helps reveal the taken-for-granted assumptions that underlie our beliefs. It also allows us to recognize ways of organizing and thinking about the world and about what is of value that is not readily apparent from our own parochial view. Thus, the past can also provide us with critical resources for engaging with the present—critical resources that enable us to question our chosen ends and aspirations. Much like Sheldon Wolin, Rorty correctly suggests that there is a close connection between the art of historical and textual interpretation and the art of imagination. And this imagination is important for developing a wider sense of what our current problems are. What I want to emphasize is that Rorty removes the psychological state of doubt that prompts the search for the questions and problems in the first place, and that unites our imagination with our critical faculties. Without the sense of doubt, the imaginative positing of hypothetical alternatives can create only an ironic detachment from the present, and not a critical engagement with its problems.

The closest Rorty comes to such a moment of doubt is in his description of intercultural contact. While the process of translation that ensues may lead to a transformation of our own vocabularies, it never leads to even a temporary sense of breakdown. The recognition of the transformation is retrospective; it is a matter of looking over one's shoulder to see how comfortable one has become with the new vocabulary that one finds oneself speaking. In playing cultures and vocabularies off one another, we produce new and better ways of speaking and acting. These are "not better by reference to a previously known standard, but just better in the sense that they come to *seem* clearly better than their predecessors."[31]

What are the consequences of Rorty's recasting of pragmatism for the study of the history of political thought? Without the experience of doubt we forgo the impetus for treating thought as a tool for solving problems. Without the sense of thought as a tool for solving problems we lose the possibility of explaining the historical transformation of concepts and ideas that Dewey's pragmatism provides. Once we give up the notion of "adequacy to achieve a purpose" it is impossible to explain how and why concepts lose their resonance, their sense of "doing something" and making worlds possible. Instead of showing the contingency of ideas—how they are the products of specific historical conjunctures that may or may not still persist—Rorty renders them arbitrary, and thus unexplainable. We ironically lose a sense of history, and are left only with a tale of endlessly shifting vocabularies. While we can "reweave" and "recontextualize," we cannot in any meaningful sense "reconstruct." Rorty's usages of texts are obviously present-minded in a way that Skinner's are not. However, their availability to us has nothing to with their historical character. They are unmediated entities that we can make use of as we please. Absent is a sense of the past as an inheritance that we simultaneously inhabit and have left behind.

However, Rorty does not completely reject textual interpretations that take historical context seriously. With his typical intellectual generosity, he finds room for Skinner's style of "historical reconstruction." He sees it along with "rational reconstruction" and *"Geistesgeschichte"* as one of three legitimate genres of intellectual history:[32]

Rational reconstructions are necessary to help us present-day philosophers think through our problems. Historical reconstructions are needed to remind us that these problems are historical products, by demonstrating that they were invisible to our ancestors. *Geistesgeschichte* is needed to justify our belief that we are better off than those ancestors by virtue of having become aware of those problems. [67–68]

Rorty sets a place for almost everyone at the historian's table, but does not really expect much dialogue to ensue. While both rational and historical reconstructions have something to tell us, it is unclear whether they have anything to tell each other; "[w]e should do both of these things, but do them separately" (49). How we historically reconstruct a text neither limits nor constrains how we can put it to use. The historical reconstruction only reminds us of what all good ironists already know—that people in other places and times speak with entirely different vocabularies.

The consequences of this merging of past and present are especially problematic when Rorty turns to "our traditions" as "cosmopolitan bourgeois liberals." Rorty's allegiance to Dewey is neither purely methodological nor purely philosophical. It is also political. Like Dewey, Rorty defends an "American anti-ideological liberalism." In contrast to those who castigate liberals for their lack of "philosophical depth," Rorty argues that this "shallowness" is a virtue. Liberals, rather than succumbing to this criticism and seeking stronger and more secure foundations for their beliefs, should, like Dewey, embrace liberalism as a kind of American faith, validated only by its accomplishments.[33] Rorty suggests that only this faith in ourselves and our past can inspire political engagement. Political activism requires a certain kind of national pride.

But how do we unite Rorty's ironic detachment with this active political engagement? Political engagement in the ends seems for Rorty to be simply a matter of faith, a result of choosing the right texts that will inspire us to action. In *Achieving Our Country,* Rorty tries to assemble a workable past that will help the American Left out of what he sees as its current malaise and passivity.[34] The past Rorty addresses—traditions of American Leftist thought—is not to be confronted so much as it is to be sifted through in search of inspirational material. Rorty does pick and choose what understandings of the past to resuscitate, favoring John Dewey, Walt Whitman, and Herbert Croly over Henry Adams and C. Wright Mills. However, the choice has little to do with the adequacy of their thought to the present. Rather, it is a choice of psychological disposition, of optimism over pessimism. While Whitman, Croly, and Dewey choose to be agents, Adams and Mills resign themselves to being spectators. While reading the former can inspire action, reading the latter can only lead to despondent resignation.[35] But since activism is always to be preferred to passive resignation, this is an ahistorical decision that has nothing to do with needs peculiar to the present. While Rorty thinks that there is much about American society that ought to be reformed, he leaves little room for a critical rethinking of existing political understandings, no need to move beyond the liberalism we have inherited from Dewey, no need to say anything beyond what Dewey said about the relationship of individual and society.[36]

However, Rorty's understanding of Deweyan liberal inheritance contrasts sharply with Dewey's understanding of his own relationship to the liberal political thought he has inherited. Rorty ignores the extent to which Dewey sees liberalism in crisis—as confronting a series of problems that we have no choice but to address.[37] Simply embracing liberalism as "our beliefs," Dewey argues, can lead only to political and social stagnation—it is to transform what was once a radical doctrine into a defense of the status quo. We can keep liberalism alive only if we can disentangle those liberal tools that were once of use but have now become obstacles from those that remain of value. In other words, we must engage in a historical reconstruction of liberalism.

DEWEY'S PRAGMATIST RECONSTRUCTION OF HISTORY: DISENTANGLING PAST AND PRESENT

I have so far criticized two approaches to the history of political thought that share pragmatist premises. While both Skinner and Rorty adapt pragmatist insights, neither develops an approach to the history of political thought that is pragmatic in the broader and more vernacular sense. Neither explains why the study of the history of political thought is a practical activity, nor how it can help us address our own problems. As I have demonstrated, Skinner and Rorty fail to develop a practical understanding of the history of political thought for opposite reasons. For Skinner, because the past is thoroughly lost to the present, it cannot speak to present concerns. For Rorty, there is no meaningful distinction between past and present. The past, therefore, loses its leverage on the contemporary world.

I now argue that pragmatist principles—as John Dewey demonstrates—can, in fact, lead to a more practical understanding of the relationship between past, present, and future. That history ought to be a practical, future-minded enterprise follows, of course, from Dewey's stipulation that thought always ought to be practical and future-minded. As he notes: "If [the past] were wholly gone and done with, there would be only one reasonable attitude towards it. Let the dead bury the dead." [38]

However, pragmatism can give substance to this truism. A more nuanced understanding follows, as I will argue, from three basic premises to which Dewey, as well as other pragmatists, generally adhere: contingency, contextual relativism, and fallibilistic antiskepticism. [39] The belief in contingency is the belief that the universe is full of possibilities and that its shape is not permanently fixed. It is possible to have a world organized differently than the one we now inhabit. The contextual relativist claims that the validity of our beliefs rests not on a fixed relationship to an external world, but on the situation in which they occur, and on our own purposes and aspirations. Truth assertions are valid only in relation to a particular context. The fallibilistic antiskeptic claims that while we ought to recognize that any of our beliefs could be wrong, it is meaningless to think that we are wrong about everything. [40]

While Dewey, Skinner, and Rorty all emphasize contingency, Dewey puts a slightly different emphasis on it. Dewey's contingency is not the contingency of the Rortian ironist; it is not just the recognition that because our beliefs, communities, and most basic commitments could have been something other than what they are, we must hold on to them with a certain detachment. For Dewey, contingency is instead a precondition of meaningful action. Only if the universe is not "finished" can we shape it into something of value. "Contingency," Dewey notes, "is a necessary although not a sufficient condition of freedom." [41] Without contingency we cannot fashion our own history.

Contextual relativism helps explain the pragmatist attitude toward historical difference. Contextual relativism follows from the pragmatist treatment of ideas as tools. For the pragmatist, thought is a practical activity; it is "doing," not "representing." The warrant of our assertions is not their "correspondence to the world" but their efficacy in bringing about the "world in the making" that we desire. Thus, the validity of our thought is always relative to a context—the context of problems we wish to solve and the resources that we have available. It is this contextual relativism that explains historical difference—different contexts produce different problems, and therefore yield different intellectual tools.

While contextualism explains pragmatism's approach to historical difference, it is pragmatism's fallibilistic antiskepticism that explains its emphasis on historical continuity. While Dewey celebrates our Promethean powers to shape the world to our own vision—to transform contingency into opportunity—he also recognizes the limits of our capacities. Because our beliefs are always open to revision, they must always be accepted as provisional. We have no certainty that even our most firmly held and basic beliefs will not eventually be discredited. Belief, as James notes, is just a temporary moment of equilibrium before new experiences force us back into thought.

However, we cannot hold all of our beliefs in suspension at once. The pragmatist is also an antiskeptic. This kind of doubt is purely "philosophical," a speculative mode we can engage in only as a thought experiment; it cannot serve as an impediment to action. Real doubt, like belief, requires justification. We question our beliefs when confronted with a problematic situation in which our understandings fail to produce the results we intend. In trying to identify and solve the problem, and in rethinking the belief thus cast into doubt, we must assume the validity of our other beliefs. These momentarily unquestioned beliefs provide the semi-stable foundation upon which we do our thinking. Thus, it is impossible for us to simply escape our inherited understandings, and assume a "view from nowhere."[42] For Dewey, there is no a prioristic reason, but only intelligence grounded in the here and now. But the here and now is the product of the past. Beliefs are habits of thought that we have acquired from past experience. Thinking requires thinking *through* these established beliefs. We must recognize, to quote Dewey, that "[p]hilosophers are parts of history, caught in its movement; creators perhaps in some measure of its future, but also assuredly creatures of its past."[43]

The developmental model of the history of ideas I have been suggesting might evoke images of evolutionary biology. Given Dewey's great admiration of Darwin, and his belief that he was expanding Darwin's insights into other fields, this should come as no surprise. However, the model of evolution evoked is one that emphasizes contingency rather than historical necessity. According to Dewey, Darwin brought philosophy back into the experiential world characterized by change. For Dewey, the evolutionary idea of progress is not as important as that of continual transformation.[44] The lesson of evolution is not so much that life steadily progresses, but that life forms need to continually modify themselves and adapt to ever-changing environments.

Furthermore, the mere presence of a particular structure in a given environment does not mean that it is necessarily an adaptation to *that* environment. Evolutionary development yields both vestigial structures and structures that are the contingent by-products of other structures and do not themselves serve any function, what Stephen Jay Gould and Richard Lewontin refer to as "spandrels."[45] Evolution does not start each time anew, but builds upon inherited material. As a result, existing structures may be the unintended by-products of other evolutionary adaptations, or leftover adaptations to conditions that no longer obtain. Thus, the biological world is full of panda's thumbs and retinal blind spots, structures that serve no present function.

While the analogy should not be pushed too far, the history of thought exhibits similar patterns. Our inherited beliefs are the contingent answers to problems that may or may not still persist. Thus, the mere existence of a habit or belief does not prove it to be useful. However, as has already been noted, we cannot simply break with the past. While we must begin our own investigations with these beliefs, we need not assume their validity for us. Furthermore, like the origins of vestigial structures and spandrels, the origins of our habituated beliefs may not be readily apparent to us. Thus, we often hold on to beliefs, without any real sense of what they do or of why they ever really made sense. Determining the present worth of an idea, concept, or institution often requires first recovering the original context in which it was developed. In order to have a sense of its adequacy to the present, it is important to know what problems it was originally designed to solve.

This analogy also helps us to see how ideas become associated. Traditions come to us in bundles—what Skinner refers to as "ideologies," but what might be better thought of as coalitions. Historical reconstruction helps us to identify these coalitions. The treatment of sets of inherited beliefs as coalitions points to a number of important factors that empower present-minded historical reconstruction. First, the construction of these coalitions is political; actors construct these coalitions through processes of contestation, negotiation, and even bargaining, and they construct them in order to achieve particular purposes. The connections between the ideas that constitute these coalitions are not logical necessities, but political creations; as Dewey notes of the contradictory nineteenth-century liberal alliance of utilitarian economics and natural law, "What is logic between friends?"[46] Second, because these connections are "political" and not "logical," they are at least somewhat contingent. Liberalism and empiricism were mutually supportive beliefs not because of any necessary relationship, but because of the structure of a particular context. Third, these coalitions are historically transient. With new contexts and new aspirations, new coalitions form.

This description of ideologies as coalitions acknowledges the place of human agency—these coalitions are crafted by humans to serve human purposes. However, I do not want to give the impression that they are simply willed—that such coalitions can be taken apart and put together with ease.[47] Such coalitions solidify and harden. They become taken for granted, and appear natural. Instead of a collection of friendly allies, they come to seem like logically necessary wholes. We come to believe that if we accept one component of the coalition we must buy the entire package. As such, these coalitions can also restrict our agency—we become trapped by creatures of our creation. Thus, an essential part of pragmatist historical reconstruction is to reveal these coalitions as coalitions—to use, through historical interpretation, the discontinuity of the past as leverage on solidified understandings of the present.

The pragmatist reconstructive historian of political thought is, thus, a coalition builder. The dissolution of old ideological coalitions and the formation of new ones is neither automatic nor spontaneous; it requires active critical work—the purging of former associates, the reforging of ties with old comrades, and the inclusion of new and formerly unimaginable allies. While it is a project oriented toward the future, it is also very much historical. It requires precisely those judgments about the relationship of past, present, and future that Skinner and Rorty proved unable to make. It requires decisions about what parts of the past should be left behind and what parts need to be brought forward into the future. As Dewey writes: "Essential philosophic reconstruction will regard intelligence not as the original shaper and final cause of things, but as the purposeful energetic re-shaper of those phases of nature and life that obstruct social well-being."[48]

This reconstructive approach to the history of political thought is certainly not the only one. Nor is the study of the history of political thought valuable only to the extent that it helps us build these new intellectual coalitions. However, pragmatist reconstruction does suggest an important way in which history remains an active participant in our own current political debates. Moreover, it is a pragmatic present-minded approach that still takes history seriously—where neither texts nor ideas of the past can be transferred or transported directly into the present. Understanding the historical context in which a concept, idea, or ideology developed helps us to determine whether it is something we should hold on to or something we should let go of. It is precisely because we must—as political actors ourselves—make these kinds of judgments about our own relationship to the past that the history of political thought remains an invaluable enterprise.

RECONSTRUCTING LIBERALISM

In this section I would like to give a brief example of Dewey's own use of this approach to the history of political thought. In a number of his most important essays, including *Liberalism and Social Action* and *The Public and Its Problems,* Dewey tries to develop a liberalism adequate to the problems and concerns of the first half of the twentieth century. In developing this liberalism, Dewey deploys the kind of historical reconstruction I described in the previous section; he undertakes a dialogue between past and present in order to determine how to critically make use of our political inheritance and bring liberalism forward into the twentieth century. In reconstructing the history of liberalism he not only "reweaves" the story of its development, but also argues in favor of abandoning much of what has become part of the liberal tradition. He acknowledges that "liberalism has had a chequered career, and that it has meant in practice things so different as to be opposed to one another." However, only by confronting this checkered past can liberalism remain a positive force; the "location and description of the ambiguities that cling to the career of liberalism will be of assistance in the attempt to determine its significance for today and tomorrow."[49]

Like many political theorists and social critics of the early decades of the twentieth century, Dewey sees liberalism in crisis.[50] Liberalism has lost its crusading spirit—once a tool wielded *against* authority, it is now a tool *of* authority. What had been a revolutionary doctrine is now the official dogma of the status quo.[51] Dewey recognizes that this transformation of liberalism is not simply a misappropriation—the co-optation by the powers that be of a formerly antithetical and hostile discourse. Rather, the historical character of liberalism has made this deployment of liberalism possible. The twentieth century, Dewey argues, demands new forms of political, social, and economic organization. However, liberalism's tactical individualism—its polemical treatment of the individual as presocial, self-sufficient, and rationally autonomous—undermines such constructive projects. These tools that were so useful for tearing down old structures have become impediments for building new ones; liberalism's language of autonomous individualism has become a barrier for thinking through the social preconditions of individual liberty.

Liberalism developed as a tool for fighting the European social orders of the seventeenth and eighteenth centuries and their associated forms of arbitrary government, political and religious intolerance, ascriptive hierarchy, and professional and trade monopolies. The idea of the natural rights of individuals provided a useful means of contesting authority. Early liberals, such as Locke, argued that because the individual was prior to society, only those institutions that could be justified in terms of individual rights were legitimate. But in making such forms of social organization suspect, it cast suspicion on all forms of association that were not solely and directly the product of individual contractual agreement. Liberalism, Dewey concludes, was individualistic in the sense that it was "opposed to organized social actions":[52]

> Born in revolt against established forms of government and the state, the events which finally culminated in democratic political forms were deeply tinged by fear of government, and were actuated by a desire to reduce it to a minimum so as to limit the evil it could do.[53]

It was for this contingent reason that liberal freedoms were cast in negative terms; "[t]here was no logic which rendered necessary that appeal to the individual as an independent and isolated being."[54]

Dewey puts this history of liberalism to two kinds of use. Like Skinner and Rorty, Dewey uses history to denaturalize the present, and show the contingency of our beliefs and commitments. Liberalism's traditional ahistoric self-understanding, Dewey argues, helps explain how it so easily transformed itself from a revolutionary force to a defender of the status quo; while defending change, it was able to envision it only as unfolding upon a single path; because it saw itself as positing the true and absolute doctrine of liberty as embodied in natural rights, it was unwilling to allow this doctrine a natural evolution of its own:

> But disregard of history took its revenge. It blinded the eyes of liberals to the fact that their own special interpretations of liberty, individuality and intelligence were themselves historically conditioned, and were relevant only to

their own time. They put forward their ideas as immutable truths good at all times and places; they had no idea of historic relativity, either in general or in its application to themselves.[55]

However, this insight is only a prologue to actual reconstruction. Only by identifying the contingency of liberalism's attachment to an atomistic individualism, an empiricist theory of knowledge, and a laissez-faire doctrine of economics can Dewey begin to build a new "renascent liberalism." Only by showing the conditions that led to such skepticism toward the use of public power can Dewey argue for a liberalism free from these vestigial attachments. Only then can Dewey build upon liberalism's traditional defense of human liberty and its call for the active use of human intelligence. In arguing for this reconstructed liberalism, Dewey is not just seeking new means for achieving old ends. He is also advancing a new understanding of social cooperation and extending the demands of social equality; these are advancements that both grow out of classical liberalism, and also—unlike Rorty's current engagement with liberalism—extend its limits.

THE HISTORY OF POLITICAL THOUGHT AS A PROFESSION?

The way I framed the problems confronting the study of the history of political thought at the beginning of this essay might have suggested the title "the history of political thought as a profession" rather than "the history of political thought as a vocation." The problems facing political theory today are seemingly as much disciplinary as they are anything else. The question for historians of political thought often seems to be how to talk to other social scientists—in both their positivist and their interpretivist forms. Wolin's intention in his essay on the vocation of political theory was less to defend an enterprise within the university than to preserve a form of critical thought for society at large. Political science served as a synecdoche for a technocratized world.

I hope that it is clear now that my aspirations are also not narrowly disciplinary. The basic lesson of pragmatism is that thought is a practical activity and the history of political thought too can assist in the development of a better future. There is also a second lesson that I think should be drawn from pragmatism. Political theory ought to be as much about everyday problems as it is about epochal visions. This is not to denigrate or ignore the importance of vision and of imagination, but to suggest the kind of vision with which we can most productively engage. The claim that Dewey was interested more in "method rather than vision" in the history of philosophy is not completely accurate.[56] We should be suspicious of this distinction, as Dewey suggested that we should be of most dualisms. We must make sure that our visions not only make sense of our past, but also direct us toward a better future.

NOTES

1. John Dewey, *Democracy and Education* (New York: Free Press, 1916), 214.

2. "Political Theory as a Vocation," *APSR 63* (1969): 1062–82.

3. Ibid., 1071.

4. *Democracy and Education*, 79.

5. *The Foundations of Modern Political Thought*, 2 vols. (Cambridge: Cambridge University Press, 1972); *Machiavelli* (Oxford: Oxford University Press, 1981); *Liberty before Liberalism* (Cambridge: Cambridge University Press, 1998).

6. "Some Problems in the Analysis of Political Thought and Action," in *Meaning and Context: Quentin Skinner and His Critics,* ed. James Tully (Princeton: Princeton University Press, 1988), 104.

7. "Meaning and Understanding in the History of Ideas," 61, and "'Social Meaning' and the Explanation of Social Action," 79. On the similarity between Wittgenstein's and pragmatism's emphasis on practice see Hilary Putnam, "Was Wittgenstein a Pragmatist?" in *Pragmatism: An Open Question* (Oxford: Blackwell, 1995), 27–56.

8. "Meaning and Understanding," 66.

9. "The Hermeneutics of Conflict," in *Meaning and Context,* 220.

10. "Meaning and Understanding," 31–34.

11. Skinner would probably reject this description of himself as a purely *liberal* ironist. However, while I cannot fully explore this argument here, I would like to suggest that his historical contextualism is more compatible with liberal irony than it is with the kinds of republican engagement for which Skinner expresses admiration in his historical essays. See "The Republican Ideal of Political Liberty," in *Machiavelli and Republicanism,* ed. Bock, Skinner, and Viroli (Cambridge: Cambridge University Press, 1990).

12. "Meaning and Understanding," 65, and "A Reply to My Critics," 283.

13. As such Skinner challenges not only the political theory of Leo Strauss, but also the more historically minded political thought of Wolin. Cf. *Politics and Vision: Continuity and Innovation in Western Political Thought* (Boston: Little, Brown, 1960),

3–4. For Strauss's claim that "political philosophy is not a historical discipline" see *What Is Political Philosophy?* (Chicago: University of Chicago Press, 1988), 56–77. However, the positions of Strauss and Skinner are more similar than they might at first appear. Both agree that historical research can "only be preliminary and auxiliary to political philosophy"—i.e., that historical research cannot provide answers to our own political questions.

14. "A Reply to My Critics," 234.

15. "Some Problems in the Analysis of Political Thought and Action," 100–101.

16. "Meaning and Understanding," 67.

17. "A Reply to My Critics," 287.

18. "Meaning and Understanding," 66.

19. "The Idea of Negative Liberty: Philosophical and Historical Perspectives," in *Philosophy in History*, ed. Rorty, Schneewind, and Skinner (Cambridge: Cambridge University Press, 1984), 197.

20. Ibid., 202.

21. Ibid., 206.

22. Ibid., 198.

23. Cited in James Tully, "The Pen is a Mighty Sword: Quentin Skinner's Analysis of Politics," in *Meaning and Context*, 19.

24. "Inquiry as Recontextualization: An Anti-dualist Account of Interpretation," in *Objectivity, Relativism and Truth* (Cambridge: Cambridge University Press, 1991), 93–110; "The Contingency of Liberal Community," in *Contingency, Irony and Solidarity* (Cambridge: Cambridge University Press, 1989), 53.

25. "Pragmatism without Method," in *Objectivity, Relativism and Truth*, 68–69.

26. "Pragmatism, Relativism and Irrationalism," in *The Consequences of Pragmatism* (Minneapolis: University of Minnesota Press, 1982), 162.

27. *The Consequences of Pragmatism*, XX.

28. "Texts and Lumps," *Objectivity, Relativism, and Truth*, 81.

29. *The Consequences of Pragmatism*, XIX.

30. Rorty's treatment of doubt as an abstract idea rather than as a concrete experience is also noted by Richard J. Bernstein in "Rorty's Liberal Utopia," *Social Research*, vol. 57, no. 1 (Spring 1990): 58–59.

31. *The Consequences of Pragmatism*, XXXVII. Emphasis in original.

32. "The Historiography of Philosophy: Four Genres," in *Philosophy in History*, ed. Rorty, Schneewind, and Skinner (Cambridge: Cambridge University Press, 1984), 49–75. Rorty includes a fourth genre of intellectual history, doxography, in which the complete history of philosophy is told as the story of different answers philosophers have given to a specific set of questions that define the study of philosophy. He also argues that this fourth genre serves no legitimate purpose and should be abandoned.

33. "Pragmatism without Method," 76–77.

34. *Achieving Our Country: Leftist Thought in Twentieth Century America* (Cambridge: Harvard University Press, 1997).

35. Ibid., 9.

36. Ibid., 31.

37. Thus, Rorty has often been accused of political complacency. Sheldon Wolin levels this charge against Rorty with particular force in "Democracy in the Discourse of Postmodernism," *Social Research,* vol. 57, no. 1 (Spring 1990): 5–30. On the evolution of Dewey's radicalism into Rorty's conservatism, see Richard Shusterman, "Pragmatism and Liberalism: Between Dewey and Rorty," *Political Theory,* vol. 22, no. 3 (August 1994): 391–413.

38. *Democracy and Education,* 214.

39. For a concise summary of the basic principles of pragmatism see H. S. Thayer, *Meaning and Action: A Critical History of Pragmatism* (Indianapolis: Hackett Publishing, 1981), 419–31.

40. Hilary Putnam, *Pragmatism,* 20–21.

41. *The Quest for Certainty* (New York: G. P. Putnam's Sons, 1929), 249.

42. The expression is, of course, Thomas Nagel's. *The View from Nowhere* (Oxford: Oxford University Press, 1986).

43. "Philosophy and Civilization," in *John Dewey: The Political Writings,* ed. Debra Morris and Ian Shapiro (Indianapolis: Hackett Publishing Co., 1993), 32.

44. "The Influence of Darwin on Philosophy" in *The Influence of Darwin on Philosophy and Other Essays in Contemporary Thought* (New York: Henry Holt and Co., 1910), 1–19.

45. "The Spandrels of San Marco and the Panglossian Paradigm: A Critique of the Adaptationist Programme," *Proceedings of the Royal Society of London,* series B, vol. 205, no. 1161 (1979): 581–98.

46. *The Public and Its Problems* (Athens: Swallow Books/Ohio University Press Books, 1954/27), 91.

47. Rorty, in his account of textual reweaving, implicitly assumes that such reconfigurations are easy and that pieces may be reassembled at will.

48. *Reconstruction in Philosophy* (Boston: Beacon Press, 1948/1920), 51.

49. *Liberalism and Social Action* (New York: G. P. Putnam's Sons, 1935), 3.

50. For the British New Liberal equivalent to this Progressive interpretation of the crisis of liberalism, see Hobhouse, "Liberalism," in *Liberalism and Other Writings,* ed. James Meadowcroft (Cambridge: Cambridge University Press, 1994), 8–9; J. A. Hobson, *The Crisis of Liberalism* (London, 1909).

51. *Liberalism and Social Action,* 1–2.

52. Ibid., 5.

53. *The Public and Its Problems,* 86.

54. Ibid., 87.

55. *Liberalism and Social Action,* 32.

56. John Herman Randall, Jr., "Dewey's Interpretation of the History of Philosophy," in *The Philosophy of John Dewey,* ed. Paul Arthur Schilpp and Lewis Edwin Hahn (LaSalle, Ill.: Open Court Press, 1939), 79.

PART IV

POLITICS AND THE ORDINARY

Part One: The Geometry

6 // POLITICAL THEORY FOR LOSERS

I am Defeated *all the time; yet to Victory I am born.*
—Ralph Waldo Emerson

But what of invocation, of that which signified that something irreplaceable
had gone, perhaps fled, and, as a result, the world has been diminished?
—Sheldon Wolin

TRY AGAIN, FAIL AGAIN

How might the experience of loss be theorized? This question is posed by
Sheldon Wolin as he opens a series of reflections concerning what he sees as
the recent shift from vocation to invocation in contemporary political theory.
The question is relevant to him because he believes that the incorporation of
loss in the modern world until now has been the task of conservatives, and
he seeks to break their hold on the subject of loss so as to enable democrats
to think of ways to recover from our losses. The recovery of an appropriate
way to acknowledge loss might be the role of the democratic political theorist
in an epoch when tribulation is marked by the disappearance of many of the
qualities of life that conservatives would never memorialize, but democrats
should grieve, if only they knew how.

In this essay I want to resist Wolin's response to this question, to depart
from his path of memorializing loss and instead to advertise another path
political theorists might take. I want to stake a different claim as to how loss
might be reckoned, marked, and made available for return. To do so I want
to match the experience of loss that Wolin describes with other losses experienced by another American democratic thinker, Ralph Waldo Emerson,
who in confronting the perils of his time and his hurt, especially and most
fatefully on the cusp of private and public life, found another path of thinking

and acting that enabled him and may encourage us to continue in front of our losses. To supplement and enrich the tonalities of Emerson's sense of the possibility of gain from loss, I want to compare Emerson's thought on loss to that expressed in an essay by W. E. B. Du Bois in which Du Bois also memorializes loss while deepening an understanding of it through a process of (dis)embodiment. Finally, I want to ask how a kind of invocation of loss that emerges from Emerson and Du Bois might turn us toward politics as a way of practicing freedom, rather than away from politics as an expression of liberal abandonment.

I agree with Wolin that the role of the political theorist is not to engage in a fatuous invocation of theory coming to the aid of democracy—a formulation he bleakly rejects in the conclusion of his jeremiad—but I would suggest that one role the theorist is well situated to perform is an insistent professing, an enactment, an ongoing demonstration of the capacity of everyone and anyone to reinspirit life in the face of loss. In fulfilling this role, I believe that the vocation of the theorist is to attend every bit as much to the diurnal turns of fortune as to the prophetic modes of irredeemable loss. For the same reason I believe that to cast off the everyday so as to engage in the epochal is a step that democratic thinkers cannot afford to take (though I think we can duly respect those who claim to hear the footfalls of time more distinctly as a consequence of maturity, especially when contrasted to those whose maturity is late—perhaps arrested—or worse, premature). The attendance of the everyday is, I think, an important point of the matter, the endless end of democratic life. And to the extent that one crisis or another—what Walter Benjamin once called the permanent state of emergency[1]—compels a turn away from the everyday and toward epochal pretensions, democratic life is imperiled as much by the distracted attention we pay to the conditions of emergency as it is by the fact of emergency itself. Put another way, the pure prophecy of the jeremiad is a poisonous brew, and while the *pharmakon* of theory must have room for poison—which is also a strong medicine—it ought to be doled out with care for the patient, with the most effective therapeutic touch, for otherwise it may leave us in a state where the medicine works and the patient dies.

I certainly do not wish to contest the argument Wolin develops concerning the current condition of democracy in the United States. His assessment of the antidemocratic bias of the contemporary political economy—which secures the fruits of the labors of the many for the few through the "systematization of loss," as he puts it—seems an apt and accurate reckoning of the miserable condition of substantive democracy in the United States. The gap between rich and poor grows larger, a deepening corruption of values among those who imagine themselves in charge of the rest of us—often glossed over by sanctimonious professions of concern regarding the values the rest of us should live by—proceeds apace, and everyday life is increasingly normalized and spectacularized. In fact, Wolin spares the more tender sensibilities of many of us by barely mentioning some of the more outrageous systemic injustices perpetuated by the American state in the name of its citizenry during the thirty-year interval between the appearance of "Political Theory as a Vocation" and his current reassessment of the conditions of the times.[2] For instance, in 1969, the prison population in the United States was well below 200,000 people. By 1997, that population had grown to about 1.7 million, almost a tenfold increase.[3] In 1980, the average chief executive officer of a corporation in the United States was paid about thirty times what the average employee of a corporation was. In 1998, CEOs were paid two hundred times the amount of the average employee.[4] Generally, a pattern consistent with the development and management of populations through a systematic monitoring of spaces and the micro-control of economic activity dominates life in these United States, and the racialization of class distinctions advances in pace with the growth of minority populations.[5]

Of course this same period has also seen major advancements in the cultural, political, and economic standing of oppressed racial, ethnic, and gendered groups in the United States. We might trace the vibrancy of contemporary American culture in large part back to the hard-fought struggles for political rights on the part of African Americans, Chicanos, women, and gays.[6] But those well-earned advancements are fragile and only partially secured, and these days are endangered as a consequence of the development of a renewed politics of resentment. In response to what they perceive to be a threat to their hegemony, many of those in positions of privilege try to mobilize intensely powerful hatreds. To the extent that they succeed, they are about to put continual pressure on those who have made gains in the recent past. Their actions, whether they be in the form of attacks on affirmative action in the name of a fictive racial color blindness, or assaults on cultural pluralism in the name of a recrudescent nationalism, threaten to undermine the gains of many of the previously injured while demonizing future generations. Indeed, the paradoxes that have attended the advancements of some members of these wounded groups in the face of the continued devastations of others may be a constitutive element of the limited forms of political activity currently available to democrats.[7]

Wolin gestures toward the institutional situation of theory itself as a source of concern regarding the repression of opportunities for political expression. Of the fact that the denizens of American colleges and universities have been swept up in processes by which the academy has become relatively isolated from important sites of contestation and struggle there can be little doubt. But in his threnody Wolin oversimplifies the complex character of the paths of intellectual inheritance in the late twentieth century. He strongly argues that the permutations of theory from the 1960s to the present can be attributed primarily to various adaptations to the pace of technological change. But this is a dubious proposition. When Heidegger famously stated that "the essence of technology is by no means anything technological," he meant at least in part to caution thinkers not to be distracted away from the more pressing problems of existence, nor to think that we have successfully confronted problems associated with meaning and our knowledge of it by developing technology-driven arguments to determine the shape of change and the influence of one thing on another, or the influence of things on thinking.[8] It is the very thingness of the world that has become a concern for those of us who worry about what happens when change becomes normal, as Wolin succinctly puts it. But to focus argument so extensively on the proliferation of means—a topic I take up again below—is to neglect pressing questions about the various relationships of those means to ends. It may be that Wolin's focus on means is a sign of a weakness that is present in the move from vocation to invocation: that is, the emergence of a too intensive concern with the inroads of methodism—most fully highlighted in "Political Theory as a Vocation"—may itself defer or obscure a necessary confrontation with the substance of the epochal problems Wolin has always wanted us to address. It may as well allow us to simply accept that all political theory must be biased toward a concern with the epochal, a claim I want to challenge.

It may be that the possibilities of both vocation and invocation are threatened less by specific manifestations of injustice than by the suffocation of meaningful responses to them. Wolin seems to attribute the problem of meaninglessness to the energetic theorizations of postmodernists and rational-choice theorists in their respective "overtheorizations" and their alleged reductions of all change to simple appearance and disappearance as much as to the evolving condition of the world(s) theorists inhabit. But this answer seems to be indiscriminate, conflating reponses to the condition in which we find ourselves to the condition itself.

What if we were to think about this matter in a slightly different way, to relieve ourselves—if only momentarily—of the burden of the reflexivity of political theory, and work from another premise, thinking that instead of the problems we face being a consequence of theorizing itself, they may be the result of a loss of meaning that occurs regardless of our theorizing? This would be the sort of loss that continuously fronts our theorizing in such a way as to leave us bewildered, unable to think about how to go on. Then we might think of the terms of our bewilderment in ways that allow us to escape, if only temporarily, what might be called the integrative bias of the epochal theorist. For while our bewilderment is partly a consequence of the numbness many democrats have experienced in response to the unrelentingly hostile and often duplicitous attacks on nonmoraline theory by reactionaries, it is also a result of what we might call a loss of metaphorical purchase. This loss registers itself not as a failure of theory itself but as a manifestation of the "danger" Heidegger identifies in his meditation on technology, as a way our thinking is continuously being reduced to a relentless positivity.

Thomas Pynchon described in compelling terms the eerie sensibility underlying such a loss of metaphorical purchase in 1967, two years before Wolin's first essay concerning the fate of political theory. In *The Crying of Lot 49*, the heroine, Oedipa Maas, discusses entropy with John Nefastis, who has a machine that he claims can do the work of Maxwell's Demon, gathering information while losing entropy, and all because the equations for the loss of energy and the loss of information look alike.

> "Entropy is a figure of speech, then," sighed Nefastis, "a metaphor. It connects the world of thermodynamics to the world of information flow. The Machine uses both. The Demon makes the metaphor not only verbally graceful, but also objectively true."
>
> "But what," she felt like some kind of heretic, "if the Demon exists only because the two equations look alike? Because of the metaphor?"
>
> Nefastis smiled; impenetrable, calm, a believer. "He existed for Clark Maxwell long before the days of the metaphor."[9]

Those things that exist *for* us—before the relevant metaphor comes into being through parallel yet disconnected experiences—are not yet available *to* us, and when they become available *to* us—after metaphor—they cease to be available *for* us. This paradox makes the task of invocation perilous. We may find ourselves lost between past and future, and unable to acknowledge the extent to which our present is thus diminished. But the fact of our incredibly shrinking past and future might also work to help transform the work of invocation into the conversion of despair into hope, because this always partial and incomplete process, as Wolin emphasizes, while entailing the remembrance of the loss of metaphorical certainty, also involves the finding (founding) of a will to live through the skepticism that the loss of certainty in past and future itself entails.[10] If this turn—this trope—were unavailable to us, the wisdom of Silenus would surely prevail. The overcoming of skepticism (the overcoming of entropy), as Pynchon noticed, takes the form of a demonic hope we might hold as theorists, to work through the powers of skepticism, not to emerge into a new Kingdom of God, but to try again, and fail again, to borrow from Samuel Beckett's invocation.

Fail again. The word "lose" expresses the experience of devastation, ruin, misery, but it is also noted by the *Oxford English Dictionary* as being a term of praise, of renown and fame. "Loss" expresses dissolution—with all of its ambiguities, since dissolution and solution, dissolving and solving, etymologically mean the same thing—but it also in its archaic sense expresses the breaking up of the ranks of an army.[11] Out of a sense of loss we might be tempted to break up the army of theory, to dissolve the cadres of thinking current deployed. But our army of tropes and metaphors might be redeployed instead. We redeploy our tropes (we support our troops) in our various attempts to recover from our losses, we return to the scene of the crime of consent, we give the lie to our failure in the very enunciation of it.[12] Try again.

Try again, fail again. What could be a better motto for political theorists?

PEDAGOGIES OF GRIEF

Emerson shocks his readers by comparing the death of his son Waldo to a bankruptcy of his debtors, claiming that the loss of property entailed by their failure to pay him might inconvenience him but would "leave me as it found me,—neither better nor worse. So it is with this calamity: it does not touch me: some thing which I fancied was a part of me, which could not be torn away without tearing me nor enlarged without enriching me, falls off from me, and leaves no scar. It was caducous."[13] Much has been observed of this section of the famous essay "Experience," especially two sentences that frame this observation, two of Emerson's most mysteriously truthful sentences. A sentence after: "I grieve that grief can teach me nothing, nor carry me one step into real nature." A sentence before: "The only thing that grief has taught me is how shallow it is." In both of these sentences grief is paradoxically proposed as its lack, as a lesson not to be learned, a shallow appearance, and this lesson of lack is connected to all of experience.

There are different ways through this pedagogy of grief. One way is to ask what it means to take a step or to be carried a step into real nature. Then one might think back to Emerson's opening lines of "Experience," asking where we find ourselves, and answering that we find ourselves in a series, on a stair. We might notice, with the help of Stanley Cavell's reading of Emerson, that the term "series" might suggest the writing of a philosophy in a series of essays, the subject of which is to be the very possibility of writing one's experience, of writing one's philosophy.[14] We might notice as well that at the heart of this essay, Emerson comments that when he is thinking, conversing with a profound mind, he becomes apprised of his "vicinity to a new and excellent region of life." Persisting in this thinking leads him further into this region, allowing him insight.

But every insight from this realm of thought is felt as initial, and promises a sequel. I do not make it; I arrive there, and behold what was there already. I make! O no! I clap my hands in infantine joy and amazement, before the first opening to me of this August magnificence, old with the love and homage of innumerable ages, young with the life of life, the sunbright Mecca of the desert. And what a future it opens! I feel a new heart beating with the love of the new beauty. I am ready to die out of nature, and be born again into this new yet unapproachable America I have found in the West.[15]

This finding, this founding, is a departure from nature, it is taking steps in experience, and away from the deadness of thoughtlessness. It is also a realization of what it might mean to think of something as unapproachable, and hence points us toward a never-to-be-completed project of rebirth and renewal. This is Emerson's claim for philosophy in America, an America unapproachable, to be found(ed) again, renewed every day, amended as we will it to become through the diurnal turnings of each and every one of us.[16] America as an unknowable destination is the ground the democratic theorist would claim in overcoming loss, a haunted ground for the invoking theorist, a phantom ground for the vocational theorist, a mysterious ground for the agonistic theorist, and yet for all a place from which we might move forward, to turn and hence to act together and apart.[17]

Such movements may be good for the morale of those of us who theorize—and perhaps such a result should not be underestimated for that reason—but they do not yet help us understand how we are to remember the past, surely a first step in invocation. In fact, to the contrary, Emerson's play with the relationship between experience and experimentation in another key essay, "Circles," leads in a different direction when he writes,

> But lest I should mislead any when I have my own head and obey my own whims, let me remind the reader that I am only an experimenter. Do not set the least value on what I do, or the least discredit on what I do not, as if I pretended to settle any thing as true or false. I unsettle all things. No facts to me are sacred; none are profane; I simply experiment, an endless seeker with no Past at my back.[18]

While we might note how strongly this passage subverts any simple idea of the self-possessed individual that many attach to Emerson, in "Circles" the presence of the present and its opening to the future seems to leave almost no room for an invocation of the past. (In his description of a passage from *Walden,* Cavell suggests that this intensive focus on the present as an experiment is an expression of Thoreau's mysticism, and encompasses simultaneously two moods, one of absolute hope and another of absolute defeat.)[19] This presentist sensibility is reinforced by Emerson in "The American Scholar" when he writes, "Give me insight into today and you may have the antique and future worlds." This passage is an indicator of how Emerson addresses the tragedy of a diminished past and an unknown future, not by repudiating the relationships of the past and future to the present, but by notifying us that we can best remember the past by a constant fidelity to the present, a present we may (or may not) overcome in a future as yet unmarked.

But what means are available to us when we try to overcome this relentless present, this aphasia that seems at points to prevent us from learning from experience? To turn to the epochal for the meaning it may provide as a counter to the meaninglessness of experience is one resolution of the paradox of presentism. This is a path that Wolin has explored in various ways. But Wolin has also been deeply skeptical of the possibility—for denizens of the modern era at least—that a thought entangled in the troubles of the present may permit a turn toward the positive without provoking a deep desire to escape the predicament of living together. For Wolin, this tradition of political thought—we might call it liberalism, in Leo Strauss's sense—even in its negative moments, as in Hobbes's enunciation of an apolitical utopia in his Leviathan, tempts the theorist to try to overcome the inevitable instabilities of politics through an epochal act of renunciation. "The political epic of the anti-hero proves, in the end, to be an attempted epitaph to politics, another denial of the ancient hope of a public setting where men may act nobly in the furtherance of the common good, another way of absolving men of complicity and guilt for their common predicaments."[20] Here, and elsewhere, Wolin seems to identify the remainder of experience in opposition to the specifically epochal event, opposing the claims of "the political" to the force of the intensifying administration of the world in modern life.[21] The political pathway between administration and epoch, or between what might be called the "normalized and the eventful,"[22] may be difficult to discern. But in tracing that pathway it may be possible to think yet again about another means of comprehending experience so as to allow it to turn us toward a politics of the ordinary, as opposed to a politics of the epochal.

A way of thusly comprehending experience entails taking further steps in Emerson's pedagogy of grief, trying to complement Emerson's turn toward this new yet unapproachable America by deepening his sense of what it means to approach the unapproachable. To do so it is useful to develop a fuller understanding of what it might mean to be untouched.

Emerson claims that the calamity of the death of his son leaves him untouched, with no scar. "It was caducous," he writes. It falls away from him, and there is no sign that his son was ever there in the first place.[23] Emerson is untouched, and in being untouched he is untouchable. The untouchable is a figure of isolation, of absolute loneliness. Another clue to the meaning of being untouched is provided in Emerson's seemingly offhand observation: "Was it Boscovich who found that bodies never come in contact? Well, souls never touch their objects."[24] ("Touch" is a word that comes from the old French *toucher,* which is related to the Italian *tocco,* to knock, stroke, and *toccare,* to strike or hit, both of which emphasize the violence of contact. The violence of touch, the contact with corporeality, is a refusal by the Emersonian soul, a refusal that may be overcome some other place, in some other way, perhaps by someone else. For me, it is addressed from within the space created by Michel Foucault's lingering attachment of the soul to the body in *Discipline and Punish*.) [25]

These two observations, concerning the caducous character of his loss—the calamity of his son's death—and the strange "fact" of souls never touching their objects, might be seen as adumbrating Emerson's transcendentalist understanding of the fate of spirit in the play of philosophical understanding. "Caducous" means the falling off of a limb, but it also means fleeting, and being subject to "falling sickness," that is, susceptible to epilepsy. Epilepsy is classically known as the disease of prophecy, contracted by those who would be seers. A "cad" holds as its primary meaning that of being "a familiar spirit," even as its most contemporaneous meaning is that of an ungentlemanlike betrayer of the affection of women. The word "cadaver" suggests a body from which the spirit has flown. "Cad" is closely associated with the word "cadet," which means "youngest son." "Cadre," the framework for the organization of a troop regiment, is also associated with "cad." So there is something about the caducous character of the loss of Waldo that turns Emerson to thinking about spirit, not simply the lost spirit of his son, but the loss of spirit that is constitutive of our ongoing failure to experience truly. We cannot experience truly without spirit: this insight is one of Emerson's lessons to Nietzsche. The invocation of loss for Emerson must be an incantation of spirit, like a prayer, or it is no invocation at all, simply a howling in the night, timeless, spaceless, desolate.

Emerson turns toward the West, not to fulfill a utopian vision, but to conjure a spiritual approach to true experience through a process of returning. Against the idea that Emerson suggests that there is a realm of thought on a higher plane than the world of experience, or more plainly put, against the notion that a neo-Platonic realm of mental self-reliance renders all attempts to act upon the world a necessary corruption of the highest form of self-reliance, his conjuring of spirit can be thought of as a way of diminishing our ever-present presence, our never-to-be-completely-overcome temporal and spatial isolations. This conjuring is realized, always incompletely, in what might be called the Emersonian event. [26] In the concluding passages of "Experience" Emerson gestures toward the means through which we might act upon the world, not through "manipular attempts to realize the world of thought" [27] but through a realization that the influence of what we are to know on the world remains open to us as a question. As it is an open question, the means of moving to address or front it is a practice of patience.[28] "Patience and patience, we shall win at the last." This patience is necessary if we are to live our skepticism, and not deny it or repress it. But what are we to win? "[A]nd the true romance which the world exists to realize, will be the transformation of genius into practical power."[29]

For some, practical power is utility, and would seem to be the obvious end of a useful political theory. For those attracted to this kind of relevance, a political theory for losers might strive to turn losers into winners, and would do without the need to invoke the memory of loss. But while such a theory would try to forget or suppress loss, it would not hope to memorialize loss, because for the utilitarian, memorializing could only be understood as sinking into a morass of regret. Such a forgetfulness is not the practical power Emerson would have us invoke. A theory of action is required, but such a theory would not begin by turning the idea of power into a utility. But neither would such a theory limit action to the confines of the realm called "the political." Attempts to limit action might be comprehended as examples of what Emerson referred to as the clutching at objects that lets them slip through our fingers, the evanescence and lubricity of those objects being "the most unhandsome part of our condition."[30] We would be better off if we came to understand our unhandsome condition in its fullness, to acknowledge the insight that directness and clarity are not the most valuable of values when it comes to the actions that mean the most to us. We might better realize that, in Emerson's terms, "our relations with each other are oblique and casual."[31]

"Thinking is a partial act," Emerson writes in "The American Scholar." Living is the total act.[32] Living is beyond capture by our direction, living is a totality that we cannot claim for any partial purpose, no matter how important that purpose is. It is at this turn in his thought that Emerson moves from transcendence to immanence, from the untouchable to the embrace of corporeal life. To acknowledge thusly the partiality of action is to come to terms with the futility of total thought, and to turn from the absolute isolation of untouchability to the partial actions indefinitely available to us. This formulation helps us to dissolve the tendentious distinction that we commonly make between mind and body, allowing us to acknowledge that "words are also actions, and actions are a kind of words."[33]

Our words are actions and our actions are words that we put into play in order to realize the world. And yet the world is an intractable and unjust place. If the invocation of loss performs the work of mourning and allows us some means to advance through the world by acts of transformation, we will be on our way to reinspiriting the world. This reinspiriting might even be identified as the ethical task of the political theorist, for all the rest of the work that theory entails presumably can be done by historians, psychologists, and scientists. "Never mind the ridicule, never mind the defeat: up again, old heart!"[34] The heart turns, overcomes its losses, and moves forward. It does so through the resources of the actions of words, through the tropes (turns) that mark and record, remember us, in the common wealth of language and experience.

In and through democracy the possibility of returning is a mode of invoking that may be indefinitely available to anyone who takes steps. In a time when democracy seems to be in recession, what resources are available to take such steps, and for whom? Democratic claimants of Emerson's inheritance might be able to take heart by observing the reckoning of loss undertaken by W. E. B. Du Bois.

UNHOPEFUL HOPE

As Emerson grieved the loss of his son, Waldo, so too did Du Bois grieve the loss of his son, Burghardt. Du Bois's reflection on the death of his son takes up but a few pages of The Souls of Black Folk. But it might serve as a response to Emerson's working through grief. Du Bois's grief strongly contrasts to Emerson's, which seems to depend extravagantly, if silently, on the privileges Emerson enjoyed as a free white male New England property owner, as someone who could look forward to the abolition of slavery as the achievement of justice, who, while feeling the pain of the slave as a silencing of the processes by which we all might be free, nonetheless was privileged to observe all of this from the comfort of his home in Concord, Massachusetts. But Du Bois, a Harvard graduate and a leading intellectual of his age, did not enjoy the privileges of an Emerson, and this was only because he was a Negro, a colored person. So if we are to acknowledge his loss, we must try to reckon into the calculus of loss this horrible stain of injustice as a part of the experience of Du Bois and not of Emerson. And as democratic theorists, we must try to reckon not only his loss, but his loss as multiplied by the losses of millions of others who one by one have so suffered it directly as its most prominent victims, and indirectly as witnesses who have so far been muted in response to the damage it has done to us, and partially, as our collective inheritance of a culture. This loss must become something else than it is if we democrats are to turn our losses into gains. If we hope to take steps in Du Bois's experience of grief, our first step must be to acknowledge how all of us are stained by the specific pain of that which he has experienced and we have witnessed.

Another way of putting this is to suggest that Du Bois's reflection on the death of his son is informed by the double-consciousness that racism imposes as a life condition for all of those who are subject to its regime—which means all of us who think we have inherited something from the culture of the United States—as we look backward to the moment of freedom from a life of de jure segregation.[35] Then we might ask, in what way does the fact of racism make a difference for the experience of grief? Perhaps most important for Du Bois, the formulation of grief is already written into the life of the child who is mourned. Du Bois grieves upon the birth of his son.

> Within the Veil was he born, said I; and there shall he live,—a Negro and a Negro's son. Holding in that little head—ah, bitterly!—the unbowed pride of a hunted race, clinging with that tiny dimpled hand—ah, wearily!—to a hope not hopeless but unhopeful, and seeing with those bright wondering eyes that peer into my soul a land whose freedom is to us a mockery and whose liberty is a lie, I saw the shadow of the Veil as it passed over my baby, I saw the cold city towering above the blood-red land.[36]

Du Bois grieves his son upon the occasion of his son's birth! He sees something like the inversion of a redemption narrative taking place, undertaking a measure of the estate of his son in a loss that predates his son's birth. Echoes of the experience of Moses and of the Exodus narrative are clear, if complicated. A shadow passes over this baby, the Veil condemns this firstborn child to a life like death. A flight is in the offing, but where are the people to go?

The influence of Emerson is also clear. Du Bois's "hope not hopeless but unhopeful" echoes Emerson's "I grieve that grief can teach me nothing." The clinging hand is the unhandsome condition of the seeker of certain truth. An unhopeful hope is what Du Bois is to offer his firstborn son as the legacy of the wise father. "I too mused above his little white bed; saw the strength of my own arm stretched onward through the ages through the newer strength of his; saw the dream of my black fathers stagger a step onward in the wild phantasm of the world; heard in his baby voice the voice of the Prophet that was to rise within the Veil."[37]

The step Du Bois imagines is transposed across generations. If Emerson wants us to try to intensify our presence in the present, Du Bois asks us to imagine the futures that might emerge as the inheritance of the present, imagining what the opening might hold for those who may escape the confinement of a present built upon a sordid past. Du Bois's historical imagination socializes the journey of recovery in a manner that complements but extends the Emersonian imagination of the social as the return to us of our rejected thoughts with an alienated majesty. The depth of alienation becomes tragic, the majesty historic. This is a staggering step, but a step nonetheless, into a new world. For Du Bois this new yet unapproachable America becomes the wild phantasm of the world. The Emersonian practice of patience is stretched, extended from one generation to the next, as the everyday is preserved within the hardship of the smallest movement forward. And the modesty of Emerson—"I know better than to claim any completeness for my picture. I am a fragment, and this is a fragment of me"[38]—is stretched as well, in Du Bois's notice of the hard indifference of death as life goes on all around it. In describing the moment of Burghardt's death he writes, "The day changed not; the same tall trees peeped in at the windows, the same green grass glinted in the setting sun."[39] Against this tragedy there is the duration of the day, indifferent, a sky, the same sky, everywhere he goes.

The days of Du Bois are not the same as the days of Emerson. How could they be? The difference between them is inscribed in the divisions that constitute the shadow of the Veil. The color line, which had not yet harmed the boy in his young life—"in his little world walked souls alone, uncolored and unclothed"—caught up to him after death, a moment too late to hurt him, but ever decisive for his wise father. As the dead firstborn's family proceeded through the streets of Atlanta to bury him, they heard the pale-faced men and women utter the word that measures the distance from one side of the Veil to the other, an indefinitely open, infinitely deep divide: "Niggers!"

We could not lay him in the ground there in Georgia, for the earth there is strangely red; so we bore him away to the northward, with his flowers and his little folded hands. In vain, in vain!—for where, O God! Beneath thy broad blue sky shall my dark baby rest in peace,—where Reverence dwells, and Goodness, and a Freedom that is free?[40]

A word is an action, and an action is a word. A word propelled the family to the North to bury young Burghardt, but Du Bois is not so foolish as to think he will find relief there: there is no freedom that is free. Again, we must account for this difference, and in doing so take upon ourselves the stain of racism as our debt, and hope that it will enable us to acknowledge the indefinitely deeper grief of Du Bois.

Where does this compounded grief leave Du Bois? Where does he find himself? Does he have anywhere to turn? The final paragraph of this chapter, in its conventional expressions of a parent's wish ("If one must have gone, why not I?"), seems to be far from the invocation Emerson makes on behalf of his Waldo, but its final note of encouragement echoes Emerson and suggests a metaphor for comparing two equations of America.

> The wretched of my race that line the alleys of the nation sit fatherless and unmothered; but Love sat beside his cradle, and in his ear Wisdom waited to speak. Perhaps now he knows the All-love, and needs not to be wise. Sleep, then, child,—sleep and waken to a baby voice and the ceaseless patter of little feet—above the Veil.[41]

Du Bois was Wisdom, his wife was Love, and with his death their son knows All-love and has no need to be wise. Whose baby's voice will it be, whose little feet will patter above the Veil? Is not Du Bois himself in death to be stripped of his wisdom, and hopefully born again; will he not be clapping his hands in infantine joy at this America that does not yet exist for him except in visions of an after-death? "Nothing is left us now but death. We look to that with a grim satisfaction, saying, there at least is reality that will not dodge us," writes Emerson in his essay of grief.[42] What is this after-death for which we are to be prepared to die? For Du Bois it is the way to be above the Veil, the pain of a deeply invidious distinction. For Emerson, it is the finitude that grounds the indefinitely open approach to the possibility that we might attain some measure of hope in our hopeless situation. Both of them call it God, but I believe that both of them prepare us to get over that belief in favor of a truer romance.

For Emerson, the overcoming of the reality that will not escape us, the predictable ordinary of temperament, that lord of life, is also death, the determination of our fate, with one exception. "In every intelligence there is a door through which the creator passes."[43] This is the passage of Spirit, the moment of return, the spiritual being, that which is its own evidence. The passage of spirit might allow us to die out of Nature and be born again. And so too for Du Bois, who sees in the Sorrow Songs the gifts of story and song, of sweat and brawn, and of Spirit. He asks, "Would America have been America without her Negro people?"[44] Du Bois will be born again with a baby voice, come into his own as an American, when the possibility of the Afterthought becomes, again like a prayer, born in the Wilderness.

Hear my cry, O God the Reader, vouchsafe that this my book fall not still-born into the world-wilderness. . . . Thus in Thy good time may infinite reason turn the tangle straight, and these crooked marks on a fragile leaf be not indeed
THE END[45]

TURNING TOWARD POLITICS

We are the readers, the gods for whom these words are written, and every day we turn a new leaf. The leaves of Walden, the leaves of grass, the vinelands of California, the hemp that forms the ropes on which strange fruit is hung as Du Bois composes his book and life. The possibility of being free in an America not yet approachable, to be born again, not stillborn but facing the endless writing of ourselves, turning our tropes into troops, our cadets into cads, allowing the grief to fall away, and the spirit to come in—this is the hardest work we can possibly do. This is a practical power that we realize in the discourses of freedom available to us as a specific inheritance of American political thought. It will perhaps someday make it not matter to be American, which is perhaps the best that we can hope for.

The losses that Emerson and Du Bois sustained are profoundly ordinary. Whatever sense we might come away with from the records of their struggles—from the crooked marks on fragile leaves—we might acknowledge that they more or less sustained the capacity to see the worst and offer more than that for our consideration. If we are to understand them as references, as guides, we need to try to think an amazingly shocking thought: that even now, even after Auschwitz, even after Hiroshima, even after Stalinism, even after Tiananmen Square, even after bleeding Africa, even after Iraq, even after Kosovo, even after the mushrooming carceral, starving children, dispossessed families, cynical capital, even after every conflagration we might take note of that stands as an unanswered accusation that the twentieth century has been the bloodiest in history, and even after we succeed in connecting its bloodiness to Du Bois's prophecy concerning the color line, the worst is still not that bad, at least not yet. "This time, like all times, is a very good one, if we but know what to do with it," is what Emerson writes in front of slavery, in anticipation of or prophecy of civil war.[46] And perhaps we might remember that it was Adorno, Wolin's muse of loss as he reaches for some conclusion, who once wrote in the aftermath of so much of this devastation that "philosophy is the most serious of things, but then again, it is not all that serious."[47]

We are still here. When we turn back to the world from the place of losers, we might know that we will inevitably be returning again to a place of loss. The turn toward the world from a place of loss is the turn toward politics, toward constructing common and uncommon spaces of agonistic exchange and misunderstanding, of revelation and projection, of new coinages and destructions, partial and fragmentary, neither utopian nor dystopian, but, as Wolin seems to suggest, and Emerson would endorse, encompassing both. For those purposes, we engage in politics not only when we act together, but when we act apart. The injustices we struggle to ameliorate and rectify, the capacity for connection and openness we seek to cultivate, the pleasures we might take in the variety of adventures in becoming—adventures that we might acknowledge as being indefinitely available to anyone and everyone, and that we might intuit as the democratic inheritance—are the constitutive elements of political gesture and conspiracy. When we conspire, we breathe together, we inspirit each other, and so ourselves.

The role of theory in all of this political movement and agitation may be to help us take steps, to provide us with some aid in reckoning where we are and in what directions we might go to find spirit. After some centuries of ascendancy we democrats might find ourselves in a state of loss, a state of retreat in the face of the failure of both epoch and organization to settle that which cannot be settled, and these times, in the face of that failure and the fallout of repressions of various sorts that accompany failure, may be when theory is most needed.

Wolin concludes his reflections on the current moment of political theory by suggesting that the old needs to be reconsidered. A fine word, "reconsider"; the root of "consider," "sider" means star, and the word is thought to have originated as a term in augury, in the predicting of fortune through the constellations of the stars and the entrails of sacrificial animals. The method of negative dialectics considers constellations of meaning. Somehow we turn back in the realm of prophecy, to looking again to the stars, to overcoming or reconsidering our recent turns of fortune. In our reconsideration of the old, we might find something new, and the sidereal turns of theory should enable us to see, if only faintly, as if by starlight, the outlines of the woods through which we walk.

NOTES

The author wishes to thank William Connolly, Jason Frank, George Kateb, and John Tambornino for advice on the first draft of this essay.

1. See Walter Benjamin, "Surrealism," "The Last Snapshot of the European Intelligentsia," and "Critique of Violence," in *Reflections,* ed. Peter Demetz (New York: Harcourt, Brace, Jovanovich, 1978). Also see Giorgio Agamben, *Homo Sacer: Sovereign Power and Bare Life,* trans. Daniel Heller-Roazen (Stanford: Stanford University Press, 1998), 12.

2. See Wolin, "Political Theory as a Vocation," *American Political Science Review,* vol. 63, no. 4 (December 1969): 1062–82.

3. See "Nation's Prisons and Jails Hold More Than 1.7 Million," and linked materials, from the Bureau of Justice Statistics, U.S. Department of Justice (www.ojp.usdoj.gov/bjs/). One might consider population increase as being accountable for some of this growth, but the population of the country has increased slightly less than 30 percent during this period.

4. Kevin Phillips, "Commentary," *Morning Edition,* National Public Radio, July 24, 1998.

5. For an earlier analysis of the unfolding of these processes, see Thomas L. Dumm, "The New Enclosures," in Robert Gooding-Williams, ed., *Reading Rodney King, Reading Urban Uprising* (New York: Routledge, 1993).

6. For a study that performs such a tracing, see George Lipsitz, *Time Passages: Collective Memory and American Popular Culture* (Minneapolis: University of Minnesota Press, 1990). Another, more recent, study traces some of the complex expressions of loss as well as gain in American folk music more specifically, and connects key questions of the American transcendentalist tradition to popular culture very powerfully. See Greil Marcus, *Invisible Republic: Bob Dylan's Basement Tapes* (New York: Henry Holt, 1997).

7. For discussions of the politics of identity and difference see William E. Connolly, *Identity: Democratic Negotiations of Political Paradox* (Ithaca: Cornell University Press, 1991), and Wendy Brown, *States of Injury: Power and Freedom in Late Modernity* (Princeton: Princeton University Press, 1995).

8. Martin Heidegger, "The Question Concerning Technology," in *Basic Writings*, ed. David Farrell Krell (New York: Harper and Row, 1977), 287.

9. Thomas Pynchon, *The Crying of Lot 49* (New York: Bantam, 1967; Windstone edition, 1982), 79.

10. Here I am obliquely gesturing to Stanley Cavell. Much of what I have to say below in regard to the sense of loss in Emerson's "Experience" depends on Cavell's essay "Finding as Founding: Taking Steps in Emerson's 'Experience,'" in *"This New Yet Unapproachable America": Lectures after Emerson after Wittgenstein* (Albuquerque: Living Batch Press, 1989).

11. All definitions and etymologies of English words in this essay are derived from the *Oxford English Dictionary*.

12. See Avital Ronell, *Finitude's Score: Essays for the End of the Millennium* (Lincoln: University of Nebraska Press, 1994), especially "Support Our Tropes," and "Activist Supplement, I."

13. Ralph Waldo Emerson, *Essays and Lectures* (New York: Library of America, 1983), Essays: Second Series, "Experience," 473.

14. Cavell, "Finding as Founding," 89.

15. Emerson, "Experience," 485.

16. This sentence so slavishly impersonates the words that Cavell emphasizes in his reading of Emerson that I feel a certain embarrassment. I am also strongly influenced and reassured in the power of Cavell's understanding of Emerson by Simon Critchley's reading of Cavell in his remarkable study, *Very Little . . . Almost Nothing: Death, Philosophy, Literature* (New York: Routledge, 1997), especially 125–38.

17. The idea of turning as acting is addressed in Thomas L. Dumm, "Resignation," *Critical Inquiry* 25, no. 1 (Fall 1998).

18. Emerson, *Essays and Lectures*, "Essays: First Series," "Circles," 412.

19. Cavell, *The Senses of Walden,* expanded edition (Chicago: University of Chicago Press, 1992), 9–10.

20. See Sheldon Wolin, *Hobbes and the Epic Tradition in Political Theory* (Los Angeles: William Andrews Clark Memorial Library Seminar Papers, 1970), 50.

21. See Wolin, *Politics and Vision* (Boston: Little, Brown, 1960), chap. 10, "The Age of Organization and the Sublimation of Politics."

22. See Thomas L. Dumm, *A Politics of the Ordinary* (New York: New York University Press, 1999), chap. 1.

23. In his biography of Emerson, Richardson notes that Emerson returned to open young Waldo's coffin long after the boy's burial, just as he had done after his first wife's death. This not uncommon practice of the era is nonetheless fraught with disturbing implications concerning the desire to mark the present even in the face of the material decomposition of a body. See Robert D. Richardson, Jr., *Emerson: The Mind on Fire* (Berkeley: University of California Press, 1995), Prologue.

24. Ibid., 473.

25. See Foucault, *Discipline and Punish: The Birth of the Prison,* trans. Alan Sheridan (New York: Pantheon Press, 1977). He asks, "What would a non-corporeal pun-

ishment be?" (16). For a discussion of the corporeality of power in Foucault that connects parallels but controverts Emerson on this point, see Dumm, *Michel Foucault and the Politics of Freedom* (Thousand Oaks: Sage Publications, 1996), 79–96.

26. For a gloss on the politics of the Emersonian event, see Cavell, "What Is the Emersonian Event? A Comment on Kateb's Emerson," *New Literary History* 25 (1994): 951–58.

27. Emerson, "Experience," 492.

28. Cavell, "Finding as Founding," *"This New Yet Unapproachable America,"* 95–96.

29. Emerson, "Experience," 492.

30. Ibid., 473. The sentence is: "I take this evanescence and lubricity of all objects, which lets them slip through our fingers when we clutch hardest, to be the most unhandsome part of our condition." For a thorough gloss on this sentence, see Cavell, *Conditions Handsome and Unhandsome: The Constitution of Emersonian Perfectionism* (Chicago: University of Chicago Press, 1990), "Aversive Thinking," esp. 40–41, and *"This New Yet Unapproachable America,"* "Finding as Founding."

31. Emerson, "Experience," 473.

32. Emerson, *Essays and Lectures,* "The American Scholar," 62.

33. Emerson, *Essays and Lectures,* "Essays: Second Series," "The Poet," 450. One might contrast this dissolution of the difference between mind and body with Wolin's division of labor and power between mind and body in the conclusion of "From Vocation to Invocation." "[The theorist's replication of the pace of technological change] means, among other things, they have aligned themselves with a future that identifies the future, not with the elevation of the brawny but with the brainy classes. While the brainy classes live lives of permanent revolution, the masses, who represent the stuff of democracy, live at the opposite end of that revolutionary pole described by Gramsci, 'detached from their traditional ideologies.'" (20). A gentle response to this characterization might be, "Neither brawny nor brainy be." A harsher response might highlight the condescension to ordinary people implied in the assumptions underlying the articulation of this division.

34. Emerson, "Experience," 492.

35. The corrosive effect of the regime of legal segregation on the citizenry at large has been discussed at length by George Kateb, *"Brown* and the Harm of Legal Segregation," in *Race, Law, and Culture: Reflections on Brown v. Board of Education,* ed. Austin Sarat (Oxford: Oxford University Press, 1997).

36. W. E. B. Du Bois, *The Souls of Black Folk,* ed. and with an introduction by David Blight and Robert Gooding-Williams (Boston: Bedford Books, 1997; originally published 1903), chap. 11, "Of the Passing of the First Born," 160.

37. Ibid.

38. Emerson, "Experience," 491.

39. Du Bois, "Of the Passing of the First-Born," 161.

40. Ibid., 162.

41. Ibid., 163.

42. Emerson, "Experience," 473.

43. Ibid., 475.

44. Du Bois, *Souls of Black Folk,* XIV. "The Sorrow Songs," 193.

45. Du Bois, *Souls of Black Folk,* "The Afterthought," 195.

46. Emerson, "The American Scholar," 68.

47. Theodor Adorno, *Negative Dialectics,* trans. E. B. Ashton (New York: Seabury Press, 1973), 14.

7 // FEMINISM'S FLIGHT
FROM THE ORDINARY

A celebrity feminist of the postmodern variety goes to a conference on "identity" in New York City. After presenting a paper charting the demise of the category "women," she is confronted by a hostile member of the audience who accuses her of betraying feminism. Feminism, the practice, needs a subject called women, declares the irate spectator; a subject that feminism, the theory, has dissolved in its skeptical flight from the ordinary. In a voice pitched well above the ordinary, this spectator emphatically asserts her confidence in the existence of "real women" (like herself), and concludes by asking the speaker: "How would you know that there are women right here in this room?" To this agitated rhetorical query the weary postmodern feminist replies rather matter-of-factly: "Probably the same way you do."

How did we get here? What sort of problem are we—that is, feminist theorists like myself who go to such conferences—trying to address when we ask of each other: Are there women in this room? What *kind* of question is this? What *sort* of answer are we looking for? What did the irate spectator want of the postmodern feminist? What did the postmodern feminist want of the irate spectator?

I begin with this event in order to introduce the question of feminist theory and its relationship to the ordinary and to feminist practice. Although the history of second-wave feminism has been characterized by a persistent questioning of this relationship, the last decade has witnessed a fairly dramatic escalation of the stakes of theorizing. Indeed, the debates have taken on the tone of a war of differences in which each attempt to theorize is subjected to accusations that more or less cluster around two problems: (1) the problem of political exclusion (claims to the category "women" bring with them a normative conception of women, i.e., white, heterosexual, middle class); (2) the problem of political skepticism (refusals of the category undermine the existence of feminism's collective subject). There is a general sense that feminist theory, which once stood—or so it is said—in a symbiotic relationship to feminist practice, has lost its footing in the ordinary and has spun a web of overly complex concepts that only a handful of overpaid professors can understand and that bear little if any relation to women's daily lives.

Whereas the task of early feminism was to produce a comprehensive if not universal explanation of women's daily lives, the call today is for a practice of feminist theorizing that is more attuned to differences among women, hence to the particular, the local, and the specific case. This shift in focus—initiated in the early 1980s by the critiques developed by "women of color" and pursued in rather different directions by feminists working under the sign of postmodernism—is far too complex to outline here. What I should like to emphasize, however, is the extent to which the rejection of women both as a unified category and as the subject of feminism has produced, in turn, not only a longing for concepts that could speak to, without hypostatizing, the shared experiences of women in a global context, but also an attenuation of what is often assumed to be the skeptical character of postmodernism. Unlike some critics of the linguistic turn in feminism, I do not see these developments as tantamount to an admission of the political incoherence of critiques of the subject-centered paradigm of reason and of signification, critiques that inspire some of the most important texts in contemporary feminist theory. I take this project to be not only a strongly argued one in the history of philosophy (which hardly begins with postmodernists) but also a departure point for thinking politically. I see these developments, rather, as evincing deep uncertainty about what feminist theory is (what counts as theory) and about the relationship of feminist theorizing to the worldly context of feminist practice and women's lives.

Although I am sympathetic to the call for attending to difference in contemporary feminist theory—especially as it has unmasked a false and racially marked homogeneity in the most fundamental categories of feminism—I am led to question the extent to which that call in turn masks not only political matters of social hierarchy, as a range of critics have recently argued, but also the discontents of feminist theorizing itself. It is as if the concept of difference were a magical substance that could not only eviscerate the legacy of exclusion in feminism but also settle fundamental questions about what theory is and how it relates to practice. I suspect, for instance, that one of the reasons for the uses and abuses of postcolonial feminist writings (which yield such figures as the "Third World Woman") is that we (feminist theorists, including myself) look to those writings to save us from the consequences of a certain tendency of theorizing, namely, what Wittgenstein calls our "craving for generality" or, what amounts to the same thing, "the contemptuous attitude towards the particular case."[1] This craving is not a natural human disposition but the product of centuries of philosophical and political thinking; it is a disposition to generalize, to which feminists, working with that inheritance, are by no means invulnerable. I am thus suggesting that what drove some feminists to produce unified categories that did not attend to the particular case was in part this craving for generality, a craving that animated the hegemonic strand of the feminist theoretical enterprise through the mid-1980s and that continues to haunt it today, if only in the form of its nemesis, be that skepticism or radical particularism.

What interests me in these debates is the unspoken wish that feminist theory can, and ought to, explain why the world is the way it is, as well as provide a kind of "super-idealized guidance," to borrow David Pear's phrase, on how we can change it.[2] I call this wish the desire for solace, a desire that would be satisfied by, and thus incessantly searches out, the perfect theory; the same desire that, in its nostalgic mode, yearns for the supposedly "golden days" when theory existed in a symbiotic relationship to practice. The phenomenal success of Judith Butler's *Gender Trouble,* as well as the spirited critiques of the applicability of her performative theory of gender to the ordinary world of feminist politics, speaks not only to the author's polemical brilliance but also to our desire for just such a theory (even when, as in Butler's case, the theorist herself calls into question our nostalgia and wish for guidance).[3] Is this desire unreasonable? Hasn't second-wave feminist theory itself incited our desire for solace by generating a long chain of causal explanations of women's oppression, which, if rightly understood, could be rightly remedied? Notwithstanding the fact that few feminist theorists writing today would so much as dare speak of the origin or cause of (all) women's suffering, I am led to ask whether the wish for solace, which structures the relationship between feminist theory and practice, has really changed. The frustration that many feminists feel when reading academic feminist theory reflects partly the disappointed expectation that theory ought to grow out of feminist practice—but only partly. The real problem, I submit, lies in the assumption that feminist theory can and ought to translate into a more coherent feminist politics because politics itself is an epistemic practice, a practice of knowing.

I want to contest this conception of feminism as an epistemic practice and the guiding role it assigns to theory in feminist politics. On the contrary, I hold that feminists, as political actors, "know not what they do," as Hannah Arendt once described political actors,[4] and, further, that the sort of action that brings about real social and symbolic change has little to do with knowledge, that is, with the cognitive practices of adducing evidence, establishing truth or falsity, providing justification or nonjustification. I do not deny that (some) feminists are knowledge producers, working to transform, in the broadest sense, what we know and how we come to know it, as well as the relationship between knower and known. I do not deny the value of that work. But I do contest the idea that the work of feminism is first and foremost at the epistemic level; and, more exactly, in Susan Hekman's recent words, that "feminist politics are necessarily epistemological."[5] Although I recognize that part of what motivates the epistemic impulse in feminism is the need to authorize political claims in the coinage of modern scientific rationality and its practices of justification, I am critical of the idea that political claims can or ought to be redeemed as claims to knowledge and truth. The sense that they must be so legitimated inevitably leads feminism in the direction of either strong or weak versions of both foundationalism and skepticism, and away from politics.

In the feminist debates of the 1990s, epistemic commitments include the obsessive focus on foundations, to the virtual exclusion of everything else: defending them or critiquing them on the basis of what they authorize and what they foreclose. Whatever position one takes in this acrimonious debate, both sides seem to share (even when they assert otherwise) the assumption that political claims are at bottom knowledge claims; hence, what must either be protected (in the view of some feminists) or questioned (in the view of others) is a foundation, a piece of (noninferential) knowledge. On the one hand, this debate over foundations in feminism has been immensely productive inasmuch as it has brought to light a series of exclusions (e.g., racism and heterosexism) that were associated with a feminism whose organizing principle was "women and their interests." On the other hand, this same debate has been influenced by more general, problematic assumptions concerning the nature of critical reflection. As James Tully has shown in an article dealing with Wittgenstein and political philosophy, these assumptions include both the notion that there is a sharp distinction between our everyday practices and the practice of critical thought, and the idea that our words and acts are rational only insofar as we can give reasons for them.[6]

From the debates over *The Second Sex* to the debates over *Gender Trouble*, this conception of critical reflection has strongly influenced our understanding of the tasks of feminist theory. Notwithstanding the call for theory to be grounded in the everyday practices of women's lives, there is a persistent tendency to understand feminist theory as that which cuts through the taken-for-grantedness of our two-sex system, largely by revealing the ungrounded character of our prereflective agreement in judgments. The problem with this notion of theory as a critique of our customary ways of acting and thinking arises when the practice of critical reflection is seen as being somehow of an entirely different order than that of all other (nonreflective) practices. This view of feminist critical reflection as an interpretive enterprise that is non-continuous with customs and habits has contributed to two mistaken assumptions: (1) that the two-sex system is fundamentally a problem of epistemic claims that can be unsettled by classically skeptical questions about the possibility of knowledge or truth, and (2) that such skeptical questioning defines the task of feminist theory, which unsettles our prereflective habits and customs and in turn sets the agenda for feminist political practice.

What I find curious about the debate over foundations is, first, that the project of feminist critics of foundationalism, as I understand it, by no means includes the elevation of theory as an autonomous critical practice—indeed, as I have already suggested in connection with Butler, just the opposite may be the case—and, second, that those same critics were hardly blind to the noncognitive dimensions of the two-sex system. The performative theory of gender developed by Butler, for example, includes phenomenological features that are irreducible to knowledge claims. Even the far more empiricist work of the feminist biologist Anne Fausto-Sterling acknowledges the extent to which the broader symbolic framework that she is criticizing for limiting embodiment to two sexes also limits the political effect of her own claim that there are at least five.[7]

Nevertheless, to enter the fray of contemporary feminist theory is to find oneself witness to the conference scenario described at the beginning of my essay, a scenario in which the cognitive issues dominate: the postmodern feminist stands accused of denying that women exist; that is, of a failure to register a being whose existence, it is claimed, ought to be given in the simple act of perception. This feminist and her theory are guilty of effacing the empirical and thus, on this view, the political reality of women by placing into radical question every knowledge claim, including the claim "There are women in this room." This accusation inevitably elicits either a weary re-sponse in the form of a joke or a counterattack in the form of "How do *you* know (that there are women in this room)?"—an attack that then proceeds to unmask the exclusions that are integral to the knowledge claim. And so it goes, in a never-ending circle of accusation and counteraccusation, with both sides talking past each other. Feminists can break out of this circle, but we need to recognize, first, that the most important issues for us concern not foundations and justified knowledge claims but ungrounded frameworks and groundless actions, and second, that behind our claims to knowledge lies an underarticulated demand for both alterity and plurality, a demand that shifts the emphasis of skeptical questioning in feminism from the epistemological to the ethical and the political.

FROM FOUNDATION TO FRAMEWORK

In order to clarify the limits of the debate over foundations in feminism, I want to begin with what seems to be a tension in Judith Butler's early work between, on the one side, an epistemological skepticism, which would "re-veal" that gender identity is not metaphysically secured or naturally given and thereby destabilize it, and, on the other side, her account of gender iden-tity as something that is produced and sustained, not through a set of beliefs or theories or knowledge claims, but through an exceedingly complex and differentiated set of daily acts that are utterly groundless, wholly without (and without need of) justification. Whereas Butler's mode of epistemologi-cal skepticism about the truth of gender often sounds as if unmasking knowl-edge claims were the real task of feminist critique—thus giving rise, in the view of critics like Joan Copjec, to the charge of voluntarism: we can unmake gender by exposing it as fully contingent[8]—her phenomenological account suggests that the issue is not one of exposing the limits of knowledge but rather one of interrogating the noncognitive dimensions of gender as lived experience, as well as the exclusions and failures that attend it.

It is the former, cognitive, dimension of Butler's critical questioning that I want to discuss in this context, inasmuch as it has generated controversy over the empirical question of women as the subject of feminism. We shall find that the debate over Butler's critique remains entangled in the problems asso-ciated with the classical skeptical attack on foundations and the certainty of knowledge. These problems concern not only the sense of exhaustion and worldlessness that goes under the name of skeptical despair but also the intrinsically self-defeating character of skepticism's negative thesis that we cannot know anything with certainty.[9] By questioning every claim to knowledge, classical skepticism undercuts its own legitimacy. A feminist critical practice that followed the skeptical path would likewise land in the inevitable aporia of a critique that destroys its own foundation. A feminism driven by epistemological skepticism, as critics are fond of saying (wrongly, in my view) of postmodernism, could not coherently make counterclaims, let alone justify them.

The point here is not to refute skepticism (an impossible task, as Wittgenstein well understood) or to argue for a renewed practice of epistemic justification (as feminists like Sandra Harding, Lorraine Code, Susan Hekman, and Nancy Hartsock, among others, seem to suggest), but to indicate the limits of the entire classical skeptical problematic for articulating questions of gender and power. What this problematic cannot account for is the fact that the varying types and degrees of our certainty (in the two-sex system) generally consist in the absence of doubt rather than in the logical or empirical refutation of doubt. Whereas the skeptic assumes that certainty is more or less of one kind, and that doubt can in principle be raised about anything, anywhere and at any time (e.g., doubting the existence of the external world while sitting alone in your study), Wittgenstein calls our attention to the different kinds of certainty that we experience and to the specific conditions under which our doubts can arise. There is the kind of analytic certainty that we express in propositions like "Two plus two equals four." There is the certainty that we have about propositions that we have never so much as articulated, such as "The front door to my house does not open onto an abyss." Then there is the even deeper certainty that, as Jules David Law explains, "concerns matters we would not know how to doubt—certainties for which we couldn't even imagine or construct a recognizable counterbelief." Wittgenstein gives an example of this sort of certainty when he "asserts the impossibility of clearly and genuinely doubting that he has a hand."[10] As we shall see, Wittgenstein does not rule out the possibility of doubting even these propositions, but instead "wrestles with the hypothetical questions of what would have to be the case for our deepest beliefs or certainties to be invalidated."[11] In the process, however, he radically questions our (skeptically inflected) understanding of what a doubt is and under what conditions it can be raised.

Wittgenstein's work on certainty takes up the challenge of skepticism by focusing our attention on the series of assumptions that do not enter our frame of reference as objects that are contemplated, defended, or contested (like a foundation), objects that are instead the invisible "scaffolding of our thoughts,"[12] the ungrounded ground that doesn't get questioned and that keeps our various language games going. As I have argued elsewhere in connection with the later Wittgenstein, the deeply entangled concepts of sex and gender are held in place not only by a series of propositions that can at any moment be doubted, refuted, verified, or confirmed—in a word, known—but also by a whole series of "hinge propositions" (e.g., "I have two hands"; "The world has existed for a long time"), which are not indubitable in the strong epistemic sense that the foundationalist demands and the skeptic contests, but which are unlikely candidates for doubt under ordinary conditions.[13] These propositions form, as it were, the groundless framework (constituted through actions) rather than a foundation (constituted by reasons) within which we play the language games of doubting, and distinguish true and false.[14]

Our framework of sex and gender is in no way immutable; but to say as much does not mean that, being groundless, it is contingent in the increasingly facile contemporary sense of "constructed" and therefore fully contestable and resignifiable. That is because what stands fast for us is not a foundation, a piece of noninferential knowledge, as the skeptical problematic would have it. Rather, "our ground," as Jules David Law explains,

> is composed of various things: some memories, some empirical facts, some physical sensations, some names of things, some mathematical propositions. The self-referring character of this ground derives from the fact that it is not simply a set of facts, but a set of activities (construed in the widest sense—for example, thinking, remembering, calculating, examining, talking . . .) which we have learned to perform without questioning. . . . Certainty is not a decision to accept [as the classical skeptical paradigm would suggest], but an acceptance that is never questioned.[15]

In other words, this acceptance comes not through intellectualist argument or persuasion but through a series of acts or trainings in which the meanings of words are intimately connected to human practices. As Wittgenstein writes: "Children do not learn that books exist, that armchairs exist, etc. etc. they learn to fetch books, sit in armchairs, etc. etc."[16]

Following Wittgenstein I argue that hinge propositions are not fixed but indeterminate, and, further, that reasons, arguments, facts, and figures are necessary but insufficient to bring about genuine change in our two-sex system of reference. It will be more than a matter of demonstrating that, scientifically speaking, there are at least five sexes rather than two (Fausto-Sterling);[17] it will be more than a matter of producing a more truthful correspondence between representation (Woman) and empirical reality (the plurality of women); it will be more than a matter of a better argument or better evidence. It is important for feminists to point out empirical exceptions to the two-sex system (e.g., intersexuals, transsexuals, lesbians); but if these exceptions seem limited in their ability to unsettle the deeply imbricated hinge propositions—"There are males and there are females; there are men and there are women"—it may be because we never learned those propositions as empirical ones. The idea that once we have all the facts and figures before us we can unmask the falsity of the two-sex system assumes that the fundamental problems that this system raises for us are empirical. But are they?

Although the answer to this question is too complex to elaborate here, I would like to emphasize the extent to which the debate over foundations in feminism keeps us tied to explanatory hypotheses and empirical explanations insofar as it continues to pose the central problems of feminism in epistemic terms. (Thus even a feminist theorist like Butler, who clearly eschews straightforward empirical accounts of the two-sex system, winds up having to answer the question: Are there women in this room?) My turn to Wittgenstein on the question of certainty (and its difference from knowledge) stems from my general sense that although contemporary feminist theory is exasperated and disappointed at the failure of empirical knowledge to address core questions about sexual difference, it remains hostage to the epistemic orientation, largely out of fear of the political consequences of the anti-epistemic (postmodern) one.

Raising the question of certainty and the conditions of doubt in non-epistemic terms, as I would like to do, means first of all that a feminist theorist like myself must take adequate account of her embeddedness in a system of hinge propositions that (at any given moment) is not doubted and that makes possible the doubts that I do raise. If Wittgenstein is correct to argue that where there is no certainty there is no doubt, or, if you doubted everything, you would not get so far as doubting anything, what does this mean for feminist theory? What does it mean to say that at any given moment the (feminist) language game of doubting rests on a series of hinge propositions that themselves are not doubted, and that the absence of doubt shows itself not in what we think but in how we act, without reasons or justifications? What would it mean for our understanding of the relationship between theory and practice if we were to restructure feminism on the grounds not of epistemological hypotheses but of ungrounded yet irreducible human actions? What does it mean for the whole "problem of foundations" in current feminist theory if we say, with Wittgenstein's interpreter Stanley Cavell, that our relation to the world and to others "is not that of knowing, anyway not what we think of as knowing"?[18]

The difficulty I have with the feminist debate over foundations is that those who question them seem to assume not that one could doubt everything at once (all the words in my sentence) but that everything can be doubted (every word can in principle be doubted). On this view foundations may and do exist, but, as pieces of knowledge, they are at best "contingent" (Butler).[19] Following Wittgenstein's remarks on what stands fast for us, I want to reconsider the tenacity of our two-sex system as a problem not of what is grounded (the foundation debate) but rather of what is groundless—that is, as part of a system of reference that forms the framework for feminist criticism. If the "system of reference one adopts in order to judge reality cannot be evaluated in terms of its correspondence or lack of correspondence to reality," as Jacques Bouveresse interprets Wittgenstein,[20] it may not matter, finally, whether the feminist biologists discover five sexes or even fifty, because within *our* system of reference there will only be two sexes (or one, following Luce Irigaray). Feminist appeals to the counterfacts of biology or social exceptions to the rule of sex/gender tend to be absorbed into the model and thus neutralized by it. Such appeals, moreover, are quite limited in their ability to change my world-picture, partly because I did not get that picture by satisfying myself of its accuracy or agreement with reality. I do not say that we cannot change that world-picture, that system of reference. But I do insist that change in our form of representation is extraordinarily difficult, certainly far more difficult than recent debates over foundations in feminist theory sometimes make it out to be.

Put somewhat differently, the limit of the feminist project that I want to address concerns the implicit assumption that the problem with the category of women is that we have treated it as essential, homogeneous, and fixed, and that what we now need to do is to make it "a site of permanent openness and resignifiability."[21] But what if what stands fast for us does not yield in this intellectualist way to our interrogation? If what holds our two-sex system in place is not in fact a piece of noninferential knowledge, then the feminist project of revealing foundations as contingent and contestable is limited at best. To question the two-sex system in this way is important inasmuch as large components of that system are composed of knowledge claims, empirical propositions that are not static and that can and ought to be contested. But we should be clear about the limits of this critical project: it does not (and by definition cannot) even touch the groundless framework of our two-sex system; on the contrary, it is parasitic on that framework. Furthermore, it can blind us to that system's non-epistemic dimensions.[22] We should be wary of any move to naturalize this framework and to treat it as immutable, but we should also be wary of attempts to construe it in epistemic terms, which can be changed by demonstrating the failure of reasons and justifications. As I shall argue below, it is difficult to raise in an adequate manner the ethical and political questions of alterity and plurality in feminism if one remains riveted to the question of foundations and caught in the cognitive acrobatics that the defense or critique of them exacts.

A DIFFERENTIATED PRACTICE OF DOUBTING

I said earlier that Judith Butler's work raises a dimension of the two-sex system that is irreducible to knowledge claims and thus to her own epistemological skepticism. The central issue that animates her work is at bottom not the refutation of foundationalism but the exposure of the logic of exclusion. Rejecting the notion of subject-centered reason and signification that classical skepticism assumes, Butler's critical intervention consists in an effort to explore "cultural domains designated as culturally unintelligible and impossible" and to generalize the possibility of failure in the two-sex system in order to undo the notion of naturalized heterosexuality and same-sex identity.[23] In a passage that puts into question our ordinary criteria for determining sex difference, Butler explains the appeal of the extraordinary, the strange, in this way:

The point here is not to seek recourse to the exceptions, the bizarre, in order merely to relativize the claims made in behalf of normal sexual life. As

Freud suggests in *Three Essays on the Theory of Sexuality,* however, it is the strange that gives us the clue to how the mundane and taken-for-granted world of sexual meanings is constituted. *Only from a self-consciously denatu-ralized position* can we see how the appearance of naturalness is itself consti-tuted. The presuppositions that we make about sexed bodies, about them being one or the other, about the meanings that are said to inhere in them or to follow from being sexed in such a way *are suddenly and significantly upset* by those examples that fail to comply with the categories that naturalize and stabilize that field of bodies for us within the terms of cultural conventions. Hence the strange, the incoherent, that which falls "outside," gives us a way of understanding the taken-for-granted world of sexual categorization as a constructed one, indeed as that which might be constructed differently. [Em-phasis mine.][24]

One could hardly overstate this turn toward the "strange," the extraordi-nary, in Butler's work and in the major texts of feminist theory of the 1990s. The figure of the strange is clearly an attempt to imagine forms of life differ-ently, to sketch scenarios in which the things that seemed simply given and most certain to us turned out to be contingent, subject to change. Notwith-standing this impulse to break the hold of our cultural imaginary and reveal gender difference as mutable, I am led to ask whether this turn to the strange does not remain entangled in problematic assumptions about the nature of critical reflection. In the passage just cited, such reflection is understood as a "self-consciously denaturalized position." What would such a position actu-ally look like?

If Wittgenstein is correct to argue that doubt presupposes certitude, how could we possibly stand outside our forms of life and judge them to be arbi-trary (or, for that matter, nonarbitrary)? The point here is not to dispute the possibility of feminist critique but to question the assumption that it would take the form Butler suggests. Although it seems correct to me to argue that, in certain circumstances, the strange *can* help us to see "the taken-for-granted world of sexual categorization" as, if not exactly "constructed," then mutable, I cannot help recognizing (as Butler surely must) that, more often than not, the strange is simply absorbed into heteronormativity. Rather than assume that our two-sex system is "suddenly and significantly upset" whenever we are faced with the strange, then, we should ask: what are the conditions under which (1) something or someone even appears strange to us, and (2) the strange can occasion critical thought? To answer these questions we have to consider the context of practices in which we engage in the reasonably rare act of interpretation.

We can better understand the complexity of the act of interpretation if we examine Butler's example of drag as an imitative practice in light of Wittgenstein's remarks on following a rule in *Philosophical Investigations*. In *Gender Trouble*, drag serves as the paradigmatic instance of the "strange" that calls forth the act of interpretation that puts into question the naturalness of our two-sex system: *"In imitating gender, drag implicitly reveals the imitative structure of gender itself as well as its contingency,"* she writes.[25] It is important to see that, on Butler's account, drag not only reveals to the spectator the illusion of gender as an original and abiding identity, it also serves—crucially, in fact—as the paradigm for understanding that gender is a performance rather than an essence, *"a stylized repetition of acts."*[26]

Let us assume for a moment that drag introduces doubt about our two-sex system where there was certainty, and that it calls forth an interpretation where we would otherwise find an unreflective act of perception. What happens when we try to understand ordinary cases on the model of what Butler herself calls the strange? What happens when we try to understand gender by way of drag? We can approach these questions by considering Wittgenstein's suggestion that "the sense of the given as commonly held forms of behavior greatly limits the sphere in which the problematics of interpretation apply."[27] In contrast to the traditional conception of critical reflection, Wittgenstein argues that interpretation [*Deutung*], which, in passage 201 of the *Philosophical Investigations,* he explains as "the substitution of one expression of the rule for another," is called for only when our normal procedures break down, where there is a sense of doubt and we do not know our way about. What happens when we apply interpretation to ordinary cases of rule-following, he suggests, is that we end up misunderstanding and intellectualizing what it means to follow a rule. We ascribe the activities of justification and explanation to a practice (rule-following) that, he argues, remains unmediated by either. To know how to do something (read a signpost, play chess, calculate, sing a tune) does not entail an interpretation.

Following Wittgenstein's remarks on the difference between interpretation and rule-following, I want to examine the implications of trying to understand gender on the model of drag. The problem is not simply, as Butler's critics would have it, that drag is not exactly an effective political means for undoing gender; it is that what really matters for understanding gender precisely as a series of repeated and largely unreflective acts—which I take to be her major contribution to feminist theory—does not apply to drag: namely, interpretation (assuming once again, with Butler, that drag introduces such doubt). Even if one agreed that drag incites the act of interpretation (under what conditions?), which in turn gives rise (in whom?) to critical reflection about gender norms, it does not follow that gender is *like* drag, or that the latter exposes the imitativeness of the former. The critical reflection supposedly gained in thinking about or witnessing a drag performance itself is parasitic on the wide range of nonreflective techniques and abilities that compose the motley of practices that we associate with gender. As part of what James Tully, following Wittgenstein, calls the "vast and diversified landscape of rule-following," these practices are "not reducible to the behaviorist's causal compulsion of habit."[28] The tendency to understand rule-following in terms of the force of conditioning and as being at odds with the act of critical reflection leads to claims (e.g., *"In imitating gender, drag implicitly reveals the imitative structure of gender itself as well as its contingency"*) that are simply too general to be useful and that divert our attention from the question: What are the conditions of doubt?

Needless to say, the conditions of doubt cannot be formulated as a universalizable proposition. It is possible to imagine, for example, a situation in which a drag performance raised existential questions about gender identity for one person, confirmed what a second already thought, and was consumed as a bawdy spectacle by a third. But the matter here concerns more than the subjectivist aspects of doubting. I mentioned earlier that the limitations of the strange to disrupt our ordinary practices concern the limits of doubt. It is important to see that, according to Wittgenstein, it is not that we *cannot* doubt something, as if someone or something were preventing us from doing so, but that under ordinary circumstances we do not doubt it. There will be contexts in which the word "woman," for example, will not raise questions for me (i.e., when I describe to my friend, a woman, the woman sitting next to me on the plane), and there will be contexts in which that same word does raise such questions (e.g., when I hear my male colleague describe the same woman). Furthermore, the limits of doubt are also its conditions. What this means for a practice like drag is that the conditions for doubting gender are none other than the language game of gender itself. To argue, then, that a drag performance reveals the imitative structure of gender—reveals gender as nothing other than a performance "without which there would be no gender at all"—simply misses the extent to which what gets "revealed," should one wish to remain with this language, is irreducibly entangled with what does not get "revealed." Simply put: your certainty in gender allows you to doubt gender. The corrosive sense of an all-consuming doubt that haunts feminist debates over the category "women," the sense that, once we so much as doubt the category, we will lose our grounding and be unable to act, remains within the skeptical problematic, in which the need to interpret sets off a chain reaction of interpretations in which all is put into doubt.

Skepticism is devastating. It produces a sense of loss and disaster. The pathos that characterizes the category-of-women debates in contemporary feminism is testament to the extent to which the classical skeptical problematic continues to define the terms of the discussion. This is true despite the fact that theorists who criticize subject-centered reason and representation (like Butler) hardly see the limit of knowledge as a deficiency or failure, in the way classical skepticism does. Instead they see that limit as an opportunity to articulate alterity and plurality.[29] Notwithstanding this crucial difference between skepticism and what goes under the sign of postmodern feminism, the category-of-women debates are characterized by the sense of an all-consuming doubt that undermines feminism. If we want to understand this pathos rather than merely ridicule it, we need to look more closely at our practices of doubt.

The skeptical sense of an all-consuming doubt is precisely what haunted the scene of the conference in New York City with which I began this essay. To concede, in response to the irate spectator, that one knows, in the same way that she does, that there are women in the room, is to make the familiar conciliatory gesture of the skeptic: of course we can agree that, *for all practical purposes,* there are women. Should I assert more forcefully, and not only for practical purposes, that there are women, don't assume that my certainty is like that of "Two plus two equals four," or "I am forty-two years old," or "I ate spaghetti last night." "The kind of certainty is the kind of language-game," says Wittgenstein. "We remain unconscious of the prodigious diversity of all the everyday language-games because the clothing of our language makes everything alike."[30] But I hear, from feminist quarters, the objection posed by the philosopher's persistent interlocutor: "'But if you are *certain,* isn't it that you are shutting your eyes in face of doubt?' They are shut."

What can it mean to say, with Wittgenstein, that one's eyes are shut to doubt? According to Stanley Cavell: "His eyes are shut; he has not shut them."

To say as much is to say "that one can, for one's part, live in the face of doubt. But doesn't everyone, every day? It is something different to live without doubt, without so to speak the threat of skepticism. To live in the face of doubt, eyes happily shut, would be to fall in love with the world."[31] Although Cavell is far less troubled than I am by locutions such as "our form of life," his reading of Wittgenstein raises an important issue for feminists: namely, how we might doubt fundamental aspects of "our form of life" like the two-sex system and yet not fall prey to the despair of skepticism (which generates the inevitable objections of the irate spectator). What has been at issue all along, after all, has not been whether gender conventions are certain in the sense of being permanently beyond all dispute, but rather, what disputing them would entail.

Wittgenstein's remarks about two-thirds of the way through *On Certainty* exemplify the practice of doubting that I have in mind. As Jules David Law astutely notes, "After dismissing specific doubts as incoherent or unimaginable, he almost inevitably turns around and asks if after all they are not imaginable in some bizarre way."[32] The doubts Wittgenstein raises include everything from questioning whether he really lives in England to questioning his name and his sex.[33] In each case he also explores the various ways in which he might respond to his doubt: "What if it *seemed* to turn out that what until now had seemed immune to doubt was a false assumption? Would I react as I do when a belief has proved to be false? Or would it seem to knock from under my feet the ground on which I stand in making judgements at all? . . . Would I say 'I should never have thought it!' or would I (have to) refuse to revise my judgement because such a 'revision' would amount to annihilation of all yardsticks."[34] One way of responding to this threat to his world-picture, says Wittgenstein, would be to doubt his doubt: "If something happened (such as someone telling me something) calculated to make me doubtful of my own name, there would certainly also be something that made the grounds of these doubts themselves seem doubtful, and I could therefore decide to retain my old belief." Another way would be to experience a conversion.[35] And so on.

The point in all these examples is that certainty is not of one kind, and neither is doubt. Among other distinctions to consider here, there is the difference between what Wittgenstein calls "comfortable certainty" and the "certainty that is still struggling."[36] As Jules David Law rightly argues, this distinction "is crucial because it reflects the different degrees of mental exertion involved in different kinds of doubt or certainty. There are many different kinds of mental 'comfort' and 'struggle'—many different procedures and degrees of exertion involved in shutting out doubt."[37] Thus it is not a matter of having one's eyes happily shut, as Cavell suggests, but of the wide variety of degrees and strategies humans develop in order to doubt and to live with their doubts. What Wittgenstein teaches, then, is that "different amounts of mental energy are required to meet different challenges to our habitual ways of thinking, and not all challenges are 'simply' accommodated or rejected."[38] This differentiated account of the practices of doubting, it seems to me, is far more useful for feminists than an account that offers us all or nothing.

FROM KNOWLEDGE TO ACKNOWLEDGMENT

Our sense that the feminist practice of doubting entails all or nothing is what generates the impasse in the category-of-women debates and what led to the standoff at the conference in New York City. I asked earlier, What did the postmodern feminist and the irate spectator want of each other? If the one doubts and the other affirms that there are women in the room, what sort of knowledge is each seeking? Is this knowledge of material objects? But knowing that there are women in the room is not like knowing that there is a table in it. There are ordinary criteria for knowing that, just as there are for sex difference. I can push hard on those criteria, and they will disappoint me, give me reason to doubt. But to discover that our criteria falter—to discover that there are XY chromosomal women and XX chromosomal men, for example—what is that to discover? That one cannot say with certainty that there are women in the room? Sure, I can claim that. I can be a skeptic, insist on opening my eyes to doubt, but at some point I will have to come out of my study and make peace with the irate spectator who, holding fast to her metaphysical crutches, has closed her eyes to doubt, not in the sense of living in the face of it, but in the sense of living without it. "For all practical purposes, I know the same way you do," I say. My pragmatic concession to her commonsense way of knowing won't change anything, however, if what we both are seeking turns out to be not knowledge in the sense of criteria that would not disappoint but acknowledgment in the sense of the recognition of our separateness.

Isn't the question, "Do I know of the existence of others?" really the question, "Do others know of my existence?" as Cavell suggests?[39] Couldn't we say that feminist questions about the category "women" are really questions not about the existence of the group but about the acknowledgment of those so classified; that is, recognition of them as separate and unique persons? The issue of acknowledgment, which concerns the recognition of separateness and difference (i.e., a woman is not a "little man" and not another woman either) is, for me, the fundamental problem that opened second-wave feminism, and that continues to haunt it in the form of the category-of-women debates. Feminism begins with the demand for separateness and difference— think of Beauvoir—but is always torn between affirming women's existence (in the familial form of a gigantic sisterhood) and denying it (in the skeptical form of a criteria crisis). Both the affirmation and the denial amount to a displacement of the very problem of separateness that they seek to address. Whether one "converts metaphysical finitude into intellectual lack," as Cavell says of the skeptic, or converts it into intellectual plenitude, like the essentialist, one avoids the fundamental problem of others, especially other women.

The debate over the category "women," I want to conclude, converts the problem raised by other-mind skepticism into that raised by material-object skepticism. That is one reason why the question, Are there women in the room? gets posed and debated as if it were a question like, Is there a table in the room?—that is, as if it were a question about the existence of a material object, the answer to which would entail statements and proofs and justifications. The frame of contemporary feminist debates about the category "women," in other words, makes it seem as if one could know or doubt the existence of women as one knows or doubts that of a table. And once you assimilate the question of women's existence to that of a material object, skeptical doubts are bond to arise and, in turn, to provoke both the irate spectator's objection ("I see them with my own eyes") and the skeptic's pragmatic concession ("For all practical purposes, so do I").

I want to loosen the hold that epistemic concerns have on feminist theory because the incessant debate over criteria and foundations fundamentally misconstrues what it means to question our conventional ways of thinking, and because it displaces the political question of the different attitudes we take to different kinds of challenges.

NOTES

I wish to thank Teresa de Lauretis, Bonnie Honig, Gregor Gnüdig, Samantha Frost, Melissa Orlie, and George Schulman for their comments.

1. Ludwig Wittgenstein, *The Blue and Brown Books* (New York: Harper, 1965), 17, 18.

2. David Pears, *The False Prison: A Study of the Development of Wittgenstein's Philosophy* (Oxford: Oxford University Press, 1988), vol. 2, 488.

3. Judith Butler, *Gender Trouble: Feminism and the Subversion of Identity* (New York: Routledge, 1990).

4. Hannah Arendt, "'What Remains? The Language Remains': A Conversation with Gunther Gauss," in *Essays in Understanding, 1930–1954,* ed. Jerome Kohn (New York: Harcourt Brace & Co., 1994), 23.

5. Susan Hekman, "Truth and Method: Feminist Standpoint Revisited," *Signs: Journal of Women in Culture and Society,* vol. 22, no. 2: 341–65, 342.

6. James Tully, "Wittgenstein and Political Philosophy: Understanding Practices of Critical Reflection," *Political Theory,* vol. 17, no. 2 (May 1989): 172–204.

7. Anne Fausto-Sterling, "The Five Sexes: Why Male and Female Are Not Enough," *Sciences* (March/April 1993): 20–25. I discuss this article below.

8. Joan Copjec, "Sex and the Euthanasia of Reason," in *Supposing the Subject,* ed. Joan Copjec (London: Verso, 1994), 16–44.

9. These problems (exhaustion, worldlessness, self-defeating behavior) have been associated with postmodern thought *tout court.* Jürgen Habermas, to take the famous example, has argued that postmodern thinkers are caught in a performative contradiction: "The totalizing self-critique of reason gets caught in a performative contradiction since subject-centered reason can be convicted of being authoritarian in nature only by having recourse to its own tools." *The Philosophical Discourse of Modernity: Twelve Lectures,* trans. Frederick G. Lawrence (Cambridge: MIT Press, 1992), 185. For a strong response to Habermas's critique see Ewa Płonowska Ziarek, *The Rhetoric of Failure: Deconstruction of Skepticism, Reinvention of Modernism* (Albany: State University of New York Press, 1996), esp. chap. 3.

10. Jules David Law, "Uncertain Grounds: Wittgenstein's *On Certainty* and the New Literary Pragmatism," *New Literary History,* vol. 19, no. 2 (Winter 1988): 319–36, 321. For the passages on doubting one's hand, see Ludwig Wittgenstein, *On Certainty,* trans. Denis Paul and G. E. M. Anscombe (New York: Harper, 1972), §§ 24, 54, 125, 247.

11. Law, "Uncertain Grounds," 322.

12. Wittgenstein, *On Certainty,* § 211.

13. See my "Doing without Knowing: Feminism's Politics of the Ordinary," *Political Theory,* vol. 26, no. 4 (August 1998): 435–58.

14. It is important to distinguish Wittgenstein's notion of a framework or scaffolding from the philosophical notion of foundation. As P. F. Strawson writes: "It

is quite clear that Wittgenstein does not regard these propositions, or elements of the belief-system, as foundations in the traditional empiricist sense, i.e., as basic reasons . . . for the rest of our beliefs. The metaphor of a scaffolding or framework, within which the activity of building or modifying the structure of our beliefs goes on, is a better one." *Skepticism and Naturalism: Some Varieties* (New York: Columbia University Press, 1985), 16.

15. Law, "Uncertain Grounds," 322.

16. Wittgenstein, *On Certainty*, § 476.

17. See Anne Fausto-Sterling, "The Five Sexes."

18. Stanley Cavell, *The Claim of Reason: Wittgenstein, Skepticism, Morality, and Tragedy* (Oxford: Oxford University Press, 1979), 241.

19. See Judith Butler, "Contingent Foundations," in *Feminists Theorize the Political,* ed. Judith Butler and Joan Scott (New York: Routledge, 1992), 3–31. The problem with the idea of contingent foundations is twofold: (1) it remains within the epistemic framework of justification and grounds, and (2) it does not take adequate account of the conditions of doubt. The issue is not that we cannot doubt something but that we do not doubt it. Our doubting practices take place within a framework whose elementary propositions are not so much contingent as groundless.

20. Jacques Bouveresse, *Wittgenstein Reads Freud: The Myth of the Unconscious,* trans. Carol Cosman (Princeton, N.J.: Princeton University Press, 1995), 18.

21. Butler, "Contingent Foundations," 16.

22. I want to emphasize here that this framework is relatively stable but by no means solid. As I have argued elsewhere, Wittgenstein shows that the notion of a framework, in stark contrast to that of a foundation, is a shifting multilayered construct composed in part of hinge propositions that are by no means impervious to doubt, as if something were preventing us from doubting them. It is just that we do not doubt them at this moment. See my "Doing without Knowing," 445–47. Ludwig Wittgenstein, *Philosophical Investigations,* trans. G. E. M. Anscombe (New York: Blackwell, 1997), § 115.

23. Butler, *Gender Trouble,* 149.

24. Ibid., 110.

25. Ibid., 137.

26. Ibid., 140.

27. Charles Altieri, "Wittgenstein on Consciousness and Language: A Challenge to Derridean Literary Theory," *Modern Language Notes,* vol. 91 (1976): 1397–1423, 1406.

28. Tully, "Wittgenstein and Political Philosophy," 183.

29. On this crucial distinction between classical skepticism and postmodern criticism, see Ziarek, *The Rhetoric of Failure.*

30. Wittgenstein, *Philosophical Investigations,* 224.

31. Cavell, *The Claim of Reason,* 431.

32. Law, "Uncertain Grounds," 322.

33. On these doubts see my "Doing without Knowing," 444–46.

34. Wittgenstein, *On Certainty,* § 492. Quoted in Law, "Uncertain Grounds," 323.

35. Ibid., §§ 516, 578.

36. Ibid., § 357.

37. Law, "Uncertain Grounds," 324.

38. Ibid., 334.

39. Cavell, *The Claim of Reason,* 442.

PART V

POLITICAL KNOWLEDGE

MARK B. BROWN

8 // CONCEPTIONS OF SCIENCE IN POLITICAL THEORY

A Tale of Cloaks and Daggers

The increasing prominence of interdisciplinary research has challenged many of the familiar boundaries between political theory and other academic fields. Scholars calling themselves political theorists publish in outlets with little or no explicit connection to academic political theory, and authors from a wide variety of disciplines produce works of central importance for the field. One boundary has remained remarkably stable, however, and has played a central role in shaping the professional identity of political theory—the boundary between science and politics. This ancient conceptual boundary has been used since the nineteenth century to justify a disciplinary boundary between the humanities on one side and the natural and social sciences on the other. The science-politics boundary often sets the terms for debate on different approaches to the study of politics. It manifests itself most clearly in the current relationship between political theory and the natural sciences. The rigidity of this conceptual and disciplinary boundary contrasts markedly with the pervasive, if largely unacknowledged, practical collaborations between natural scientists and a wide range of social and political actors. These collaborations produce an increasing array of scientific and technological artifacts—computerized workplaces, genetically engineered foods, global warming—that are intimately bound up with political life. Although political theorists have formulated important critiques of concepts such as "scientific rationality" and "the technological society," they have often neglected the political dimensions of concrete scientific and technological artifacts. Political theorists, I argue, will have difficulty engaging the politics of these artifacts until they find ways of reconceiving the boundary between science and politics. This essay draws on the writings of Sheldon Wolin to discuss one way that contemporary political theorists have thought about science and politics, and then considers the implications of the alternatives posed by recent science and technology studies, focusing on the work of Bruno Latour.[1]

Concerning the attitude of social and political theorists toward the natural sciences, Latour provocatively remarks, "Either they respected them and tried to emulate them on their own territory; or they despised them and tried to be as immune as possible from them."[2] Within contemporary political science, proponents of behavioralism and rational choice have long seen themselves as emulators of the natural sciences. While few political theorists have "despised" the sciences, many have subscribed to conceptions of science and technology as either antipolitical, apolitical, or prepolitical.[3] These conceptions generally build upon the ancient Greek division between instrumental action (*technē*) and communicative action (*praxis*), often assuming that genuine politics is primarily concerned with the latter.[4] As students of the field have often noted, efforts to erect a wall between political theory and "positivist" approaches in social and natural science have usually assumed that positivist philosophy of science accurately portrays scientific practice.[5] What has gone relatively unnoticed is that this implicit acceptance of the positivist image of science has persisted alongside endorsements of *post*positivist conceptions of science as an interpretive, value-laden, practical activity. Despite their frequent assumption of a positivist view of science, political theorists have found in the postpositivist theories of Thomas Kuhn, Paul Feyerabend, and others a potent weapon in their struggles against the disciplinary ascendance of scientific approaches to political inquiry.

In short, contemporary political theory's relationship with science has been a cloak-and-dagger affair in which theorists have defended themselves against the criticisms of social and natural scientists with the claim that political inquiry is *essentially* different from science (the cloak), while simultaneously drawing on postpositivism to attack science for being less objective than it claims to be (the dagger). Political theorists have used the cloak to shield themselves from natural and social scientists, and the dagger to denounce the scientists' claims to superiority. Contemporary theorists have said, in effect, "Science and political theory are categorically different—and besides that, science is just as subjective as political theory!"

These claims do not *necessarily* conflict with each other, of course, and some scholars have elaborated theories of science that apply the dagger only to scientific method and the cloak to the resulting scientific knowledge. Karl Popper, for example, argued that while the process of scientific discovery may include subjective elements, it is still possible to provide objective justifications of scientific knowledge.[6] While this is not a logically contradictory conception of science, it assumes a categorical division between the context and content of science that has become untenable in light of recent work in science and technology studies. Moreover, when political theorists have drawn on theories of science to argue for a particular conception of their field, they have often applied both the cloak and the dagger arguments indiscriminately to science as a whole. This has involved theorists in the logical contradiction of claiming that science both is and is not categorically—i.e., essentially, ontologically—different from political theory.

One might forgive the contradiction that inheres in the cloak-and-dagger strategy toward science because it has been quite effective at defending political theory from (what often appears to be) the methodological imperialism of behavioralism, rational choice, and other methods that seek to imitate the natural sciences. However, this strategy has also had deleterious consequences for political theory. Political theorists' use of the cloak, I contend, has supported a stultifying methodological relativism that implicitly endorses the positivist image of scientific method, even while it rejects the application of this method to the study of politics. The cloak thus isolates political theory from the sciences, discouraging study of the political significance of scientific practices and findings. By the same token, political theorists have tended to use the postpositivist dagger merely to debunk the alleged objectivity of the natural and social sciences, often failing to explore the full implications of postpositivism. The dagger thus provides, ironically, a rationale for the cloak, insofar as it reveals the hypocrisy of the sciences' claims to objectivity, thus increasing political theorists' sense of alienation from the sciences. Postpositivist theories of science need to be seen not as rhetorical tools for academic turf battles, but as resources for illuminating the politically constitutive role of scientific practices.

I cannot determine how many contemporary political theorists write about science in the manner suggested, especially since what identifies a person as a "political theorist" is itself controversial. But the notion of a cloak-and-dagger strategy toward science can be used to raise important questions about how political theorists understand their vocation. The next section of this essay elaborates the cloak-and-dagger conceptions of science by associating each with a particular interpretation of Kuhn's *The Structure of Scientific Revolutions*.[7] The third section draws on examples from Wolin's writings to illustrate how some political theorists have employed these two conceptions of science. The fourth and fifth sections consider Latour's theory of scientific practice and its implications for political theory. Despite significant flaws, Latour's conception of science provides the resources for developing new relations between political theory and the natural and social sciences that might dispense with the problems created by the cloak-and-dagger strategy.

SCIENCE AS THEORY AND PRACTICE

In a 1968 essay, "Paradigms and Political Theories," and in his widely influential essay of a year later, "Political Theory as a Vocation," Wolin explores the implications of Kuhn's *Structure of Scientific Revolutions* for political theory.[8] As is well known, Kuhn argues that the history of science is characterized by a succession of "paradigms." Glossing over the many controversies surrounding this term, in Kuhn it generally refers to the explicit or implicit theories, methods, and standards of practice that guide and provide the means of evaluating scientific research. The vast majority of scientific activity, what Kuhn calls "normal science," aims to solve the puzzles posed by a particular paradigm. Every once in a while, however, the gradual accumulation of anomalous observations that do not quite fit the categories of an existing paradigm, accompanied by the development of new theories, together make up what Kuhn calls "revolutionary" science. Scientists working under the existing paradigm withhold professional sanction from those pursuing revolutionary science and use various means to enforce the existing paradigm. But if the revolutionary scientists acquire sufficient means of persuasion, their efforts lead to a "paradigm shift." Through a process that blends rational argument with psychological and sociological factors, a scientific discipline adopts the concepts and criteria of the new paradigm, which are largely incommensurable with those of the old.

Kuhn's book received widespread attention on account of its challenge to many of the basic views shared by most philosophers of science, including such rivals as Karl Popper and Rudolf Carnap.[9] Philosophy of science had long provided an intellectual justification for the social prestige of the natural sciences, and Kuhn's book was seen by many as a challenge to the widely assumed superiority of scientific modes of thought. Against reigning doctrine, which can be loosely labeled "positivist," Kuhn argued that science is not cumulative, does not follow a unified method, and can be understood only within a particular historical context. He also suggested that the history of scientific practice does not support most philosophers' assumption of a sharp distinction between observation and theory, or between discovery and justification.

As Joseph Rouse and others have noted, philosophers of science have usually interpreted Kuhn's book in terms of their assumption that science is primarily concerned with the truth of theories.[10] While scientists may engage in all sorts of activities, *real* science aims to articulate theories that provide the single best representations of natural phenomena. This assumption has led some philosophers of science to accuse Kuhn of describing theory choice as a fundamentally irrational matter of "mob psychology."[11]

The problem with this reading is that it assumes the very split between scientific theory and natural phenomena—what John Dewey called the "spectator theory of knowledge"—that Kuhn seeks to challenge. For Kuhn, in contrast to both Feyerabend and Popper, normal scientific activity, while perhaps ultimately aimed at discovering truth, is dominated by the goal of creating and manipulating phenomena.[12] With the exception of a few naturally occurring regularities (e.g., planetary motion, the tides, or certain behaviors among animals), nature is too complex and undifferentiated to present scientists with isolated phenomena ready for observation. The study of natural phenomena, therefore, goes hand in hand with their generation and standardization in the laboratory.[13] Articulating a paradigm thus requires a close interaction between theoretical and experimental work. Paradigms are, according to Kuhn, "accepted examples of scientific practice—examples which include law, theory, application, and instrumentation together."[14] Scientific facts are not only "theory-laden," but laden with skills and instruments as well. According to this reading, Kuhn's notion of a paradigm is best understood not as a theory shared by a scientific community, but as shared practices of research that may or may not be guided by theory.[15]

Against common misunderstandings, this emphasis on scientists' need to create the phenomena they study does not imply the philosophical idealist view that the world exists only in people's minds. While scientists make laboratory phenomena, nature sets limits on what they can make. The world is really "out there," but there is in principle always more than one theory that could effectively represent it. Neither individual genius nor nature alone determines the theories scientists adopt. The view that a constructivist epistemology implies an idealist ontology incorrectly assumes that knowing is something individuals can do by themselves.[16]

These two different readings of Kuhn—science as theory versus science as practice—loosely correspond to the cloak versus dagger conceptions of science discussed above. According to the cloak, scientists theorize about nature and nonscientists theorize about politics. According to the dagger, theorists of both nature and politics engage in practices that draw on many of the same intellectual and practical resources. Admittedly, it is easier to read Kuhn as a theorist of scientific practice from a contemporary perspective than it would have been when *Structure* was first published. Nevertheless, both interpretations are supported by Kuhn's text. Kuhn shares the interest of contemporary science studies in the practical dimensions of science, but he also adopts the positivists' concern with determining essential "demarcation criteria" that formally distinguish scientific from nonscientific theories. Within recent science studies, in contrast, the search for reliable demarcation criteria has been largely replaced by the study of how such criteria become established through social and scientific practices.[17] Before exploring the notion of science as practice in more detail, I want to examine how Wolin's treatment of the relationship between science and political theory draws on both these conceptions of science, with problematic results.

SHELDON WOLIN'S TWO SCIENCES

In each of the essays cited above, Wolin suggests an analogy between Kuhn's notion of revolutionary science and the practice of political theory, on the one hand, and between normal science and behavioralist political science on the other. Behavioralism, Wolin argues, fulfills many of Kuhn's requirements for a paradigm. Wolin's analogy has been criticized on a variety of grounds.[18] As far as I can tell, however, none of Wolin's critics has noted that he alternates between two different conceptions of science.

In both essays, Wolin uses Kuhn's critique of the spectator theory of knowledge to attack the boundary so dear to the behavioralists between the "hard" sciences and "soft" forms of inquiry like political theory. Wielding the postpositivist dagger, Wolin notes with evident pleasure, "Kuhn's analysis may produce some anxieties in the political scientist who had believed that scientific theories were, in some simple sense, symbolic representations of reality."[19] He drives the point home by considering how Kuhn would respond to political scientists who insist that nature imposes at least *some* limits on the range of potentially acceptable scientific paradigms: "His answer suggests that 'nature' does not constitute an obvious limit at all."[20] Wolin thus challenges the behavioralists' assumption that scientific knowledge simply mirrors nature.

Wolin reinforces his attack on the pretensions of behavioralism by explicitly pointing out the many similarities between political theory and the natural sciences. Going beyond the common assertion that scientific facts are always "theory-laden," Wolin argues that the behavioralist mentality

> poses a threat not only to so-called normative or traditional political theory, but to the scientific imagination as well. It threatens the meditative culture that nourishes all creativity. That culture is the source of the qualities crucial to theorizing: playfulness, concern, the juxtaposition of contraries, and astonishment at the variety and subtle interconnection of things. These same qualities are not confined to the creation of theories, but are at work when the mind is playing over the factual world as well.[21]

Similarly, Wolin claims that Kuhn's notion of a paradigm "invites us to consider Plato, Aristotle, Machiavelli, Hobbes, Locke, and Marx as the counterparts in political theory to Galileo, Harvey, Newton, Laplace, Faraday, and Einstein."[22] Both natural scientists and political theorists proposed new methods and criteria for understanding and interacting with the world. By showing that great scientists and political theorists share many skills and goals, Wolin undercuts the behavioralists' claims to have developed a superior method of studying politics.

Yet right alongside these efforts to reveal the similarities between political theory and natural science, Wolin draws a cloak around his vocation by invoking the familiar categorical division between science and politics. Having acknowledged the many capacities that natural scientists share with political theorists, he effectively contradicts himself by suggesting that in the case of natural science these capacities remain "extra-scientific."[23] Wolin then draws a parallel division between behavioralist political science and political theory. He writes, "The antithesis between political wisdom and political science basically concerns two different forms of knowledge."[24] Wolin defines "political wisdom" as analogous to Michael Polanyi's concept of "tacit knowledge," which is "suggestive and illuminative rather than explicit and determinative."[25] The notion of tacit knowledge then appears at the heart of Wolin's argument that political theory provides a form of knowledge categorically different from those of both natural and political science. Science's form of "methodistic truth," Wolin writes, can be "economical, replicable, and easily packaged," but "theoretical truth cannot, because its foundation in tacit political knowledge shapes it towards what is politically appropriate rather than towards what is scientifically operational."[26] Wolin does not acknowledge the irony in defending the positivist boundary between science and nonscience with a concept that Polanyi had used to challenge positivism![27]

Similarly, although Wolin humbles the behavioralists by highlighting the practical dimensions of science, thereby casting doubt on the sciences' objectivity, when he wants to defend the distinctiveness of political theory he endorses a theory-centered conception of science as a mirror of nature. Wolin repeatedly insists, for example, that whereas scientists change their theories to fit the world, political theorists (ought to try to) change the world to fit their theories.[28] "Although the scientist surely may claim for his theories the daring, beauty, and imaginativeness that are claimed for other forms of endeavor, he will concede that at some point his theory must submit to confirmation by the world."[29] This statement neglects the implications of Kuhn's claim that although scientists do look to the world for "confirmation," what confirmation means is specific to particular practical contexts. In characterizing the difference between science and nonscience in terms of whether priority is accorded to theory or to the world, Wolin assumes the spectator theory of knowledge challenged by Kuhn's conception of science as practice.

In sum, Wolin pursues a dual-track strategy against the behavioralists, drawing on two different interpretations of Kuhn to simultaneously challenge and endorse a categorical division between the methods of political theory and those of natural and political science. One might make the objection, noted above, that Wolin does not in fact employ two conceptions of science, but simply acknowledges a distinction between the subjective methods of individual scientists and the objective knowledge produced by science as a whole. Wolin does not consistently draw this distinction in his writings, however, nor does he explore the implications of this understanding of science for political theory.

My point is not that Wolin misunderstood Kuhn's theory of science. For one thing, as I suggested above, the conflicting interpretations of *Structure* can be traced in large part to the book's own ambiguities. Moreover, Wolin's essays need to be read in light of the widespread attacks then being made on political theory as an academic discipline. Wolin's appeal to two different conceptions of science allowed him to open up questions about the role of conventions in political science and to challenge behavioralist efforts to dominate the profession.[30] Indeed, thanks in part to Wolin's efforts, the number of articles, books, and conference panels devoted to political theory today is greater than ever before.[31] Sheer activity is no guarantee of institutional stability, but it seems that in contrast to the 1960s, political theory today holds a relatively secure spot in the American academy. Given this breathing room, political theorists have an opportunity to explore less problematic ways of challenging the continuing dominance of positivist approaches to the study of politics. It is therefore unfortunate that the cloak-and-dagger strategy evident in Wolin's essays of thirty years ago also appears in some of his more recent publications.

In an essay on Horkheimer and Adorno, for example, where he writes eloquently about the threats that instrumental reason poses for democracy, Wolin equates instrumental reason—reason in the service of calculation, self-interest, and efficiency rather than democracy, truth, or the good life—with modern technology and "the practice of positivist science."[32] Wolin does not consider whether either instrumentalism or positivism provides an adequate theory of scientific practice. This allows him to draw the familiar cloak around political theory, defending a conception of political reason categorically opposed to the alleged instrumentalism of science and technology: "The recognition of context is political reason honoring its debts. Instrumental reason, in the form of technology, is impatient with context and strives to be independent."[33] At the same time, Wolin does not forget the postpositivist dagger, remarking briefly, "It is, however, a special mark of those who practice instrumental reason that they are largely unaware of how it has been socially constituted, especially in its scientific form."[34] Wolin does not discuss the implications of this crucial point.

Similarly, in another essay, Wolin notes his continuing support for postpositivist theories of science.[35] This endorsement is accompanied, however, by references to "the technological thesis" of corporate and global capitalism in a "technologically driven society."[36] While these phrases certainly describe many people's perception of contemporary society, they also perpetuate the mistaken notion that technology is an autonomous social force rather than the product of political values and decisions. Wolin thus contradicts decades of research in the sociology of science and technology, despite his endorsement in the same essay of the Kuhnian conception of science that inspired much of this research.

Wolin's cloak-and-dagger strategy toward science is not his alone, of course, and it is not difficult to find examples in the writings of other prominent theorists.[37] At this point, however, one might rightfully ask: What exactly is wrong with the cloak-and-dagger strategy? If it proved rhetorically effective in the battle against behavioralism, why should we abandon it now when faced with the imperialist ambitions of rational choice?

One problem created by the cloak-and-dagger strategy lies in its restriction of political theorists' analyses of science and technology to questions of ontology, ideology, or the general character of modernity.[38] Contemporary political theorists have only rarely addressed the political dimensions of laboratory research or technological innovation, not to mention the mundane material objects of everyday life. In addressing the issue of political subjectivity, for example, a theme eliciting some of the field's most creative recent work, political theorists have usually restricted their attention to relations among subjects or subject positions. The relationship between subjectivity and the objectivity of science and technology rarely enters the picture. Few political theorists have shown interest in the possibility that "who we are is just as much at issue in the natural sciences as in those inquiries that make us directly into an object of study."[39]

The cloak-and-dagger strategy is also bound up with an academic politics of denunciation that has limited political theorists' explorations of postpositivist theories of science. Political theorists have primarily drawn on postpositivist insights to debunk the assumptions, methods, and conclusions of their scientistic colleagues—often quite effectively, as the discussion of Wolin's essays indicates. But like the toxic waste shipped to Third World countries that comes back on imported fruit, the effective attacks on behavioralism in the 1960s did not prevent positivist conceptions of science from later reasserting themselves in the form of rational choice. While the denunciations of positivism have helped save political theory from disciplinary annihilation, they have often presupposed, and hence strengthened, the very conception of science they attack. Indeed, in some respects, the estrangement of political theory from the sciences has gotten worse. As Wolin notes, "Yesterday's animosities, as well its areas of mutual concern, are today's indifferences."[40] While there have been some collaborative efforts, the relationship between political theory and political science today is frequently one of mutual suspicion and avoidance.[41] Political theory's relationship with the natural sciences is even more distant. In the following section, I suggest that political theorists can both deepen their critique of positivist social science and establish more productive relations with the natural sciences by extending the postpositivist concern with scientific practice.

BRUNO LATOUR'S ANTHROPOLOGY OF SCIENCE

One way of conceiving science as practice that might help political theorists move beyond the cloak-and-dagger strategy appears in recent science and technology studies. The work of Bruno Latour holds particular interest for political theorists, because he is among those attempting to develop an explicitly political, rather than sociological or linguistic, conception of the natural sciences. Much of Latour's work is addressed to the urgent question of how societies can better deal with those "hybrids" of science and society—such as AIDS, air pollution, or the ozone hole—that lie at the center of so many political controversies. He is also concerned, however, with the politics inhering in the most mundane daily artifacts, such as automobiles, buildings, or clocks.[42]

Latour's method for pursuing these concerns emerges from his attempt to understand "science in action," *before* facts become accepted as true. This requires above all that the study of science begin with, without remaining confined to, the practical perspective of scientists themselves. Latour thus contrasts his method with the "social realist" approach he associates with the Edinburgh and Bath schools of science studies.[43] Whereas most philosophers of science have been "natural realists," reducing scientific knowledge to a mirror of nature, Latour argues that social realists simply take the reverse approach, reducing science to a product of social structures and interests. Rejecting both social and natural realism, Latour argues for the view held by the scientists he studies: an "agnostic symmetric position" on the ontological question of what "really" makes up both nature and society. If scientists were either natural or social realists, he argues, if they believed scientific knowledge to be determined by either nature or society, they would not engage in the various practices of making knowledge; "they would just wait."[44] Latour also wants to avoid social and natural realism because they tend to force scholarship into endless debates on the essential qualities of nature or society, often forgetting the hybrid artifacts that are the ostensible topic of study. Nature and society, Latour argues, are not the *causes* of scientific knowledge, but the *consequences* of the activities of scientists and their allies. "We do not need to attach our explanations to the two pure forms known as the Object or Subject/Society, because these are, on the contrary, partial and purified results of the central practice that is our sole concern. The explanations we seek will indeed obtain Nature and Society, but only as a final outcome, not as a beginning."[45] Latour thus concentrates his efforts on tracing the concrete relations in which particular hybrid artifacts participate.

More specifically, Latour argues that both objective scientific facts and subjective free citizens are abstractions constructed through a dual process of "purification" and "mediation." In the mediation process, human and nonhuman "actants" establish alliances with other actants that support the abstract subject or object they seek to construct. Establishing a fact, as Kuhn showed, requires the support of the relevant scientific community. Latour goes beyond Kuhn, however, in arguing that establishing a fact also requires the support of many nonscientists. Technological inventions and scientific discoveries do not simply diffuse through the world on their own power, nor does the genius of those who initiated them suffice to establish their objectivity.

Latour has caused a lot of confusion with his actant concept.[46] Despite some misleading rhetorical flourishes, Latour uses the actant as a methodological rather than ontological concept. Unlike the "ecocentrist" thinkers with whom he is often identified, Latour does not seek a resolution of questions concerning the degree to which nonhuman entities have will or agency. Rather, he aims to evoke the perspective of science-in-the-making, prior to the establishment of a scientific fact. Latour uses the actant concept to acknowledge nature's independent influence on the construction of scientific knowledge, thus avoiding social realism, without falling back into the natural realist claim that scientific knowledge simply mirrors nature.

In his study of Louis Pasteur's discovery of the microbe, for example, Latour shows how only the implicit cooperation of a broad range of allies could socially establish Pasteur's discovery.[47] The transformation of "disease" from an individual affliction managed according to ad hoc local practices into a societal problem subject to scientific control relied upon civil servants and epidemiologists who collected and evaluated public health data. Recorders and epidemiologists were also needed to document the effects of Pasteur's techniques once their use had become widespread. Most important, Pasteur needed the support of the public hygiene movement to promote his ideas and techniques. Finally, Pasteur needed the "support" of the microbes themselves—i.e., he had to learn how to control them. He thus developed laboratory techniques for isolating microbes from their natural environments, allowing him to first study their behavior and then, once he had gotten them to "cooperate," control them in the world outside.

In contrast to Pasteur's success at forming alliances with civil servants, epidemiologists, hygienists, and microbes, private physicians long remained unconvinced by Pasteur's claims. They disputed the same evidence the hygienists considered indisputable. Because physicians worked in private settings with the idiosyncratic symptoms of individual patients, the indiscriminate application of laboratory vaccines to entire populations contradicted their professional interests and training. It was not until the Pasteurians had succeeded in redefining the physician's social role, from patient's confidant to guarantor of public health, that the physicians also adopted Pasteur's ideas. They did so on their own terms, however, focusing on those bits of knowledge and technique, such as the use of preventative serums, that they could mold to their clinical practices.

The alliances that establish scientific facts are eventually concealed, Latour argues, by what he calls the process of purification. The contingent victory of a hybrid alliance is recast as the heroic achievement of a scientific genius, such as Pasteur, who is portrayed as unlocking the secrets of Nature. "As long as controversies are rife, Nature is never used as the final arbiter since no one knows what she is and says. But *once the controversy is settled,* Nature is the ultimate referee."[48] The result is a scientific or technological artifact that would not exist but for the network of relations between social subjects and natural objects, but which, as it enters the circulation of daily life, is unmistakably an object and not a subject.

For Latour, then, facts, machines, and other purified constructs become established only gradually, and only insofar as they can continuously enlist the necessary alliances over time. If there is a shift in the chain of alliances, the artifact's self-evident objectivity is *practically* deconstructed. If the artifact happens to be a free citizen, such deconstruction can happen just as readily to the artifact's subjectivity. We can thus talk about the dehumanization or "objectification" of human subjects as the flip side of the "subjectification" of scientific facts. Both involve a practical deconstruction of the alliances that support a particular claim. For Latour, subjectivity and objectivity, politics and science, must be treated in tandem, as the endpoints of a continuum along which artifacts are established and maintained. This methodological postulate does not assume there are no differences between science and politics, only that the differences are practical rather than ontological.

The most important difference between politicians and natural scientists is that scientists have laboratories. By reducing the infinitely complex outside world to purified and manageable forms—figures, formulas, chemical stocks, laboratory-bred animals, etc.—scientists can gain control over things to a degree that nonscientists never can. Scientists can then practice manipulating the things brought in from outside, making as many mistakes as they wish. Social scientists also rely on the manipulation of standardized forms, as in the collection and analysis of statistics. But natural scientists have far greater freedom in this regard. Although political scientists can play with voting statistics as much as they like, they cannot produce or manipulate standardized human subjects in a laboratory.[49] By manipulating things in the lab, natural scientists learn to predict events. Predicting events outside the lab, however, requires extending the conditions of the laboratory itself. As Ian Hacking puts it, "Few things that work in the laboratory work very well in a thoroughly unmodified world—in a world which has not been bent toward the laboratory."[50]

In the first dramatic public trial of Pasteur's vaccine, for example, where he vaccinated half of the sheep at a farm in Pouilly-le-Fort, Pasteur had to first convince the farmers to provide laboratory-like conditions. The vaccinated and unvaccinated animals had to be marked and separated from each other; the animals' temperatures had to be measured and recorded daily; control groups had to be established. This export of the lab to the farm was a delicate affair: too many changes and the public would no longer perceive the trial as a "real world" application; too few and Pasteur would not be able to detect the vaccine's effects. More generally, Pasteur's knowledge of how to control microbes did not simply diffuse through an unchanged society. The breweries, hospitals, and milk-processing plants that wanted to control microbes and eliminate infectious diseases had to adopt many of the same techniques and apparatuses that Pasteur had used in his lab. This is where the "disciplinary power" of the sciences becomes effective, as explored by Michel Foucault.[51]

Latour often exaggerates his claims, and his account of scientific fact-making has important shortcomings.[52] Nonetheless, he has produced one of the most creative and provocative theories of science and politics currently on offer. Lacking the space to explore Latour's limitations in detail, I want to examine the implications for political theory of Latour's basic claim that the boundary between science and politics is always the product of negotiations in local contexts. This notion is not Latour's alone, but has become a central tenet of research on "boundary work" in recent science studies.[53] Unlike research on the conceptual logic of science and technology, studies of boundary work assign the task of demarcating science from nonscience to social actors rather than academics. The notion of boundary work does not imply that boundaries between science and politics are infinitely flexible. Indeed, it is widely acknowledged that scientists can establish boundaries around new facts only by means of old facts. These old facts become increasingly stable as new facts are built upon them. Although the boundaries between science and nonscience are *in principle* always open to challenge, in practice they often prove quite stable. The notion of boundary work suggests a number of ways political theorists might avoid the cloak-and-dagger strategy in their thinking about both natural and social science.

TOWARD NEW RELATIONS WITH THE SCIENCES

Latour's theory of science holds at least four implications for political theory: (1) a conception of universality that obviates the cloak-and-dagger strategy; (2) a need to integrate empirical research into conceptual analyses of science and politics; (3) a rejection of an academic politics of denunciation; and (4) an understanding of scientific practice as a potential site of political activity.

First, Latour's conception of science suggests a way of understanding scientific universals that works against the cloak-and-dagger strategy toward science. It seems clear that moving beyond this two-part strategy will require some way of acknowledging the best arguments for each part. The above discussion has presented a case for the claim that boundaries between science and politics can be determined only with reference to local practices rather than categorically (the dagger). It is undeniable, however, that natural science has generated knowledge of far wider applicability and social authority than other types of inquiry (the best argument, I think, for the cloak). As the above account suggests, Latour integrates these two claims by explaining scientific universality in terms of networks of relations. The Newtonian gravitational constant, for example, like the existence of Pasteur's microbe, can be verified "everywhere," but only by extending the networks of scientific instruments and social practices required for measuring and interpreting its effects.[54] At the same time, however, the gravitational constant has been verified so many times that to contest it has become practically impossible. But this is a question of what practice can achieve, not what Nature has revealed. Some might see this as a distinction without a difference, but it could make a lot of difference for political theory. If political theorists come to see how science can be simultaneously local and universal, they will have little need to alternate between the contradictory poles of the cloak-and-dagger strategy.

Second, Latour's conception of science implies that political theorists who want to understand the relationship between science and politics will need to either conduct or, more likely, draw upon empirical studies of scientific practice. As Latour puts it, the relational networks that produce our conceptions of science and citizenship "must be followed through and through, from the hot events that spawned the objects to the progressive cool-down that transforms them into essences of Nature and Society."[55] Political theorists have always used the work of historians, journalists, novelists, and others who concern themselves with the details of concrete events. Those interested in studying the politics of science need only extend their range of sources to include accounts of concrete scientific practices.

A third implication of Latour's work for political theory lies in his rejection of an academic politics of denunciation. Political theorists' use of post-positivism to debunk scientific methods as socially or historically "relative" has served theorists well in defending the professional status of their field, but it has also contributed to their isolation from the rest of political science, and from the natural sciences as well. According to Latour, methodological relativism only goes halfway. It denies that different fields of inquiry can be measured against a set of universally valid criteria—say, the ability to formulate falsifiable hypotheses—but it assumes that if there *were* a standard of measurement, it would be the one defended by the positivists. It thus accepts the positivists' terms of debate and ends up isolating each field within its own disciplinary dogmas. Latour calls this position "absolute relativism," and contrasts it with "relativist relativism."[56] The latter view acknowledges that any standard of measurement relies on a relational network. New modes of relation get haggled out all the time among different subfields of the humanities and natural and social sciences. Relations across the science-politics boundary, in contrast, have remained relatively fixed for a long time. If political theory is to establish less antagonistic modes of relation with political science, it must first articulate new ways of relating to the natural sciences, extending interdisciplinarity to those disciplines traditionally associated with the study and manipulation of nature.

Finally, Latour's theory of science suggests what may be a very problematic extension of political theorists' conception of politics itself. Is there a parallel between the behavioralists' attempt to reduce politics to a science and what appears to be Latour's effort to make all science political? Does viewing science as a potential site of politics threaten to contribute to what Wolin called the "sublimation of politics," emptying "the political" of determinate meaning and making impossible its earlier association with matters of general concern? [57] And without a determinate meaning of the political, how can political theorists develop a coherent conception of their vocation? These are serious questions, and I cannot address them here except to suggest that they assume two things: that political theorists are at liberty to determine their own conception of the political, and that a concern with local practices precludes attention to general public issues.

In *Politics and Vision*, Wolin characterized political theory as "a continuing form of discourse concerning what is political," but he also claimed that "the boundaries and substance of the subject-matter of political philosophy are determined to a large extent by the practices of existing societies." [58] This claim suggests that it is not due to "overtheoretization" that science has become increasingly political, as Wolin's essay in this volume would imply, but due to the insinuation into political life of an increasing array of hybrid artifacts. As Langdon Winner argues, "No longer will it suffice to seem ignorant or surprised as new technical devices are woven into the social settings one cares about—computers in schools, agile technologies in the workplace, Web browsers in the living room, or surveillance cameras in the mall." [59] Addressing oneself to the political dimensions of these hybrid artifacts does not entail a boundless notion of the political, nor an embrace of "politics" as the pursuit of private advantage. Nor does it imply a rejection of Wolin's concept of the political as a realm of deliberative and authoritative decisionmaking regarding matters of general concern. [60] The point is not that one can find politics *within* science, although one certainly can, but that many scientific practices have become intertwined with matters of concern to the political community as a whole. And while scientists do not make politically authoritative decisions, their professional authority often supports, and is supported by, those who do. Many hybrid practices that once belonged only to "science" now straddle the science-politics boundary, or move back and forth across it. Without a distinct concept of the political, political theory would indeed lose any sense of disciplinary identity. But the specific content of this concept can change. Political theorists can play a role in shifting the boundaries of the political, but they must also accommodate themselves to the changes brought about by concrete practices, including those of natural science.

Finally, Wolin is right to criticize the view, which he associates with postmodernism, that the only universal today is constant change. As discussed above, actants do produce universally true facts, as well as, if less frequently, free citizens. But such universals are best understood as the more-or-less vulnerable products of local practices. Scientific facts are universal not *in spite of* being constructed through local practices, but *insofar as* they are so constructed. One task for political theory is to illuminate the connections between these local practices and the universal facts they produce. By opening up the local construction of scientific facts to critical examination, political theorists can help citizens respond to the interactions between scientific practices and matters of general concern.

NOTES

Many people provided helpful comments on earlier versions of this essay. I would especially like to thank Benjamin Barber, Mark Button, Peter Euben, Jason Frank, David Guston, Timothy Kaufman-Osborn, Jill Locke, and John Tambornino.

1. For an overview of science and technology studies, see Sheila Jasanoff, Gerald E. Markle, James C. Petersen, and Trevor Pinch, eds., *Handbook of Science and Technology Studies* (Thousand Oaks, Calif.: Sage Publications, 1995).

2. Bruno Latour, "The Impact of Science Studies on Political Philosophy," *Science, Technology, and Human Values* 16 (Winter 1991): 6.

3. Simplifying greatly, these three conceptions of science and technology might be loosely identified with Herbert Marcuse, Jürgen Habermas, and Hannah Arendt, respectively.

4. On the problematic implications of this division, see Mary G. Dietz, "'The Slow Boring of Hard Boards': Methodical Thinking and the Work of Politics," *American Political Science Review* 88, no. 4 (1994): 873–86.

5. Following what I take to be general usage, I use the term "positivist" to refer

very broadly to any method of inquiry that purports to employ logically given procedures for producing objective knowledge that mirrors the external world. While this neglects important distinctions between empiricism and logical positivism, and between behavioralism and rational choice, it highlights their shared aspirations. On political theorists' assumption of the positivist conception of natural science, see John G. Gunnell, "Realizing Theory: The Philosophy of Science Revisited," *Journal of Politics* 57, no. 4 (1995): 924; Jeffrey C. Isaac, "After Empiricism: The Realist Alternative," in *Idioms of Inquiry: Critique and Renewal in Political Science,* ed. Terrence Ball (Albany: State University of New York Press, 1987), 190, 198; Richard Ashcraft, "One Step Backward, Two Steps Forward: Reflections upon Contemporary Political Theory," in *What Should Political Theory Be Now?* ed. John S. Nelson (Albany: State University of New York Press, 1983), 518–22.

6. Karl Popper, "Normal Science and Its Dangers," in *Criticism and the Growth of Knowledge,* ed. Imre Lakatos and Alan Musgrave (Cambridge: Cambridge University Press, 1970), 56–57. On the use of this argument by behavioralists to "co-opt" Kuhn, see David M. Ricci, *The Tragedy of Political Science: Politics, Scholarship, Democracy* (New Haven, Conn.: Yale University Press, 1984), 199–201.

7. Thomas S. Kuhn, *The Structure of Scientific Revolutions,* 2d ed. (Chicago: University of Chicago Press, 1962, 1970).

8. Sheldon S. Wolin, "Paradigms and Political Theories," in *Politics and Experience: Essays Presented to Professor Michael Oakeshott on the Occasion of His Retirement,* ed. Preston King and B. C. Parekh (Cambridge: Cambridge University Press, 1968), 125–52; "Political Theory as a Vocation," *American Political Science Review* 63, no. 4 (1969): 1062–82.

9. See Ian Hacking, *Representing and Intervening: Introductory Topics in the Philosophy of Natural Science* (Cambridge: Cambridge University Press, 1983), 1–17. For a discussion of why Kuhn "took" in the 1960s, see also Tracy B. Strong, *The Idea of Political Theory: Reflections on the Self in Political Time and Space* (Notre Dame, Ind.: University of Notre Dame Press, 1990), 7–11.

10. Joseph Rouse, "Kuhn and Scientific Practices," *Configurations* 6, no. 1 (1998): 33–50; *Knowledge and Power: Toward a Political Philosophy of Science* (Ithaca, N.Y.: Cornell University Press, 1987), chap. 2.

11. Imre Lakatos, "Falsification and the Methodology of Scientific Research Programs," in *Criticism and the Growth of Knowledge,* ed. Lakatos and Musgrave, 93, 178.

12. Phenomena are here identified not with the Kantian notion of sense experience, but with the more limited notion of observable natural regularities. On this point see Helen Longino, *Science as Social Knowledge: Values and Objectivity in Scientific Inquiry* (Princeton: Princeton University Press, 1990), 32–37.

13. See Hacking, *Representing and Intervening,* chap. 13.

14. Kuhn, *Structure of Scientific Revolutions,* 10; see also 26.

15. Rouse, "Kuhn and Scientific Practices," 35.

16. Hacking, *Representing and Intervening,* 220–32, 262–75; David Bloor, "Idealism and the Sociology of Knowledge," *Social Studies of Science* 26 (1996): 839–56.

17. See Thomas F. Gieryn, "Boundaries of Science," in *Handbook of Science and Technology Studies*, ed. Jasanoff et al., 393–443.

18. See Richard J. Bernstein, *The Restructuring of Social and Political Theory* (Philadelphia: University of Pennsylvania Press, 1976), 99–106; John S. Nelson, "Once More on Kuhn," *Political Methodology* 1 (Spring 1974): 73–104; J. J. Smolicz, "The Amorphous Paradigms: A Critique of Sheldon Wolin's 'Paradigms and Political Theories,'" *Politics* 6 (November 1971): 178–87.

19. Wolin, "Paradigms and Political Theories," 138.

20. Ibid., 138–39.

21. Wolin, "Political Theory as a Vocation," 1073.

22. Wolin, "Paradigms and Political Theories," 140.

23. Wolin, "Political Theory as a Vocation," 1072, 1073.

24. Ibid., 1070.

25. Ibid. See Michael Polanyi, *Personal Knowledge: Towards a Post-Critical Philosophy* (Chicago: University of Chicago Press, 1958).

26. Wolin, "Political Theory as a Vocation," 1071.

27. One might note that while Polanyi criticized the positivist conception of science and inspired later social studies of science, his notion that scientists rely on "tacit knowledge" also serves to insulate science from interference by outsiders who lack such knowledge.

28. Wolin, "Political Theory as a Vocation," 1079, 1080; "Paradigms and Political Theories," 144.

29. Wolin, "Political Theory as a Vocation," 1081.

30. See Sheldon S. Wolin, "History and Theory: Methodism Redivivus," in *Tradition, Interpretation, and Science: Political Theory in the American Academy*, ed. John S. Nelson (Albany: State University of New York Press, 1986), 62.

31. Both the vibrancy of contemporary political theory and, incidentally, its lack of attention to scientific practices are highlighted in Iris Marion Young, "Political Theory: An Overview," and Bhikhu Parekh, "Political Theory: Traditions in Political Philosophy," in *A New Handbook of Political Science*, ed. Robert E. Goodin and Hans-Dieter Klingemann (New York: Oxford University Press, 1996), 479–502, 503–30.

32. Sheldon S. Wolin, "Reason in Exile: Critical Theory and Technological Society," in *Technology in the Western Political Tradition*, ed. Arthur M. Melzer, Jerry Weinberger, and M. Richard Zinman (Ithaca, N.Y.: Cornell University Press, 1993), 173.

33. Ibid., 186.

34. Ibid., 173.

35. Sheldon S. Wolin, "Political Theory: From Vocation to Invocation," this volume.

36. Ibid.

37. See, for example, Chantal Mouffe, *The Return of the Political* (London: Verso, 1993), 14; Benjamin R. Barber, *The Conquest of Politics: Liberal Philosophy in Democratic Times* (Princeton: Princeton University Press, 1988), 16. A similar critique

of Charles Taylor's conception of natural science is made in Clifford Geertz, "The Strange Estrangement: Taylor and the Natural Sciences," in *Philosophy in an Age of Pluralism: The Philosophy of Charles Taylor in Question,* ed. James Tully (Cambridge: Cambridge University Press, 1994), 83–95. See also Strong, *The Idea of Political Theory,* chap. 3, which presents an account of the relationship between the scientific and political communities in some ways very similar to the one argued here (74–75). Ultimately, however, Strong seems to remain within a Kuhnian internalist account of the "normal" scientific community as essentially separate from the political community (102–5).

38. See, for example, Melzer, Weinberger, and Zinman, eds., *Technology in the Western Political Tradition.* In his introduction to this volume, Leon R. Kass rightly argues that technology must be understood as more than a collection of material artifacts, but like most contributors to the volume he largely ignores the material dimension and restricts his concerns to technology understood as "the disposition to rational mastery" (5). See also George Kateb, "Technology and Philosophy," *Social Research* 54 (Fall 1997): 1225–46. Kateb rightly questions the common equation of "the technological project" with "anger, alienation, resentment" (1245), but he appears uninterested in what he calls the "common sense" understanding of technology as problem solving. He focuses instead on the truly "philosophical" questions that "add depth": those basic passions that have "called forth" the "much larger and rather mysterious project" of modern technology (1125–27).

39. Rouse, *Knowledge and Power,* 183. There are exceptions, of course, many inspired by feminism, environmentalism, pragmatism, or Marxism. See, for example, Donna J. Haraway, *Modest_Witness4o@Second_Millennium.FemaleMan©_Meets_OncoMouse.Feminism and Technoscience* (New York: Routledge, 1997); Timothy Kaufman-Osborn, *Creatures of Prometheus: Gender and the Politics of Technology* (Lanham, Md.: Rowman and Littlefield Publishers, Inc., 1997); Richard E. Sclove, *Democracy and Technology* (New York: Guilford Press, 1995); Langdon Winner, *The Whale and the Reactor: A Search for Limits in an Age of High Technology* (Chicago: University of Chicago Press, 1986). Kaufman-Osborn offers some helpful speculations on the reasons underlying contemporary political theory's lack of interest in the politically constitutive role of technological artifacts (21–25).

40. Wolin, "Political Theory: From Vocation to Invocation," this volume. Moreover, as Geertz points out, the failure to forge thoughtful linkages across the boundary between science and politics lends credence to New Age efforts at achieving a vague synthesis through such fantasies as Zen physics or parapsychology ("The Strange Estrangement," 95).

41. See Joseph V. Brogan, "A Mirror of Enlightenment: The Rational Choice Debate," *Review of Politics* 58 (Fall 1996): 793–806; James Johnson, "Is Talk Really Cheap? Prompting Conversation between Critical Theory and Rational Choice," *American Political Science Review* 87 (March 1993): 74–86.

42. Bruno Latour, "Where Are the Missing Masses? The Sociology of a Few Mundane Artifacts," in *Shaping Technology/Building Society: Studies in Sociotechni-*

cal Change, ed. Wiebe Bijker and John Law (Cambridge, Mass.: MIT Press, 1992), 225–58.

43. Latour's criticisms of "social realism" are much contested. See David Bloor, "Anti-Latour," *Studies in the History and Philosophy of Science* 30 (March 1999): 81–112; Bruno Latour, "For David Bloor . . . And Beyond: A Reply to David Bloor's 'Anti-Latour,'" ibid., 113–29; H. M. Collins and Steven Yearly, "Epistemological Chicken," in *Science as Practice and Culture,* ed. Andrew Pickering (Chicago: University of Chicago Press, 1992), 301–26.

44. Bruno Latour and Michel Callon, "Don't Throw the Baby Out with the Bath School! A Reply to Collins and Yearly," in *Science as Practice and Culture,* ed. Pickering, 353.

45. Bruno Latour, *We Have Never Been Modern,* trans. Catherine Porter (Cambridge, Mass.: Harvard University Press, 1993), 79. See also Bruno Latour, *Science in Action: How to Follow Scientists and Engineers through Society* (Cambridge, Mass.: Harvard University Press, 1987), 96–100, 141–44.

46. For the charge that Latour anthropomorphizes nature, see Simon Schaffer, "The Eighteenth Brumaire of Bruno Latour," *Studies in the History and Philosophy of Science* 22 (1991): 174–92. For a defense, see Latour and Callon, "Don't Throw the Baby Out with the Bath School!" 356.

47. Bruno Latour, *The Pasteurization of France,* trans. Alan Sheridan and John Law (Cambridge, Mass.: Harvard University Press, 1988).

48. Latour, *Science in Action,* 97 (italics in original); see also 128–32; and *We Have Never Been Modern,* 10–11, 39–43.

49. For an account of the relationship between social and natural science that draws on Latour, see Rouse, *Knowledge and Power,* chap. 6.

50. Ian Hacking, "The Self-Vindication of the Laboratory Sciences," in *Science as Practice and Culture,* ed. Pickering, 59. See also Bruno Latour, "Give Me a Laboratory and I Will Raise the World," in *Science Observed,* ed. Karin D. Knorr-Cetina and Michael Mulkay (London: Sage, 1983), 141–70.

51. On the relationship between Foucault's notion of power and natural scientific practice, see Rouse, *Knowledge and Power,* chap. 7.

52. Some have found an untenable voluntarism in Latour's insistence on seeing social interests as a consequence rather than a cause of scientific fact-making. That is, Latour appears to ignore the possibility that scientists' interests can be understood as products of past social processes without necessarily reifying those processes. Similarly, Latour's account of fact-making alliances appears to assume that scientists are rational egoists, thus neglecting the cooperative dimensions of scientific inquiry. See James Robert Brown, "Latour's Prosaic Science," *Canadian Journal of Philosophy* 21 (1991): 245–61; Steven Shapin, "Following Scientists Around," *Social Studies of Science* 18 (1988): 533–50. For related criticisms of science and technology studies as a whole, which has often assumed a liberal pluralist conception of politics, see Langdon Winner, "Upon Opening the Black Box and Finding It Empty: Social Constructivism and the Philosophy of Technology," *Science, Technology, and Human Values* 18, no. 3 (1993): 62–78.

53. See Gieryn, "Boundaries of Science"; Simon Shackley and Brian Wynne, "Representing Uncertainty in Global Change Science and Policy: Boundary-Ordering Devices and Authority," *Science, Technology, and Human Values* 21 (Summer 1996): 275–302.

54. Latour, *We Have Never Been Modern*, 119.

55. Ibid., 135.

56. Ibid., 111–14; see also 43–46; and Bruno Latour, "A Few Steps toward an Anthropology of the Iconoclastic Gesture," *Science in Context* 10 (1997): 63–83. Latour's rejection of denunciation is more fully discussed in Robert Koch, "The Case of Latour," *Configurations* 3 (1995): 319–47, esp. 338–47.

57. Sheldon S. Wolin, *Politics and Vision: Continuity and Innovation in Western Political Thought* (Boston: Little, Brown and Company, 1960), chap. 10; "Political Theory: From Vocation to Invocation," this volume.

58. Wolin, *Politics and Vision*, 4, 6.

59. Langdon Winner, "Technology Today: Utopia or Dystopia?" *Social Research* 64 (Fall 1997): 1012.

60. Wolin, *Politics and Vision*, 6–10.

LON TROYER

9 // POLITICAL THEORY AS A PROVOCATION

An Ethos of Political Theory

IN HONOR AND MEMORY OF S. PAIGE BATY

Maybe the target nowadays is not to discover
what we are, but to refuse what we are.
—Michel Foucault

This essay seeks to disrupt what Mark Reinhardt aptly describes as "the tacit settlement established with the ebbing of the theory/science wars in the early 1970s that maintained a place for political theory in political science departments by consolidating a division of labor in which political theorists served as custodians of old texts while otherwise leaving the 'real world' to their 'empirical' colleagues."[1] As part of this effort, I turn to Sheldon Wolin and Michel Foucault to rethink the inheritance of Wolin's "Political Theory as a Vocation" and to examine the disciplinary tendencies that have emerged in its wake.[2] I inquire into what political theory might look like after Foucault, informed by Wolin, and reoriented toward theoretical projects that engage the political world and its practices. Building from a close reading of Wolin's seminal essay and a more recent one on Foucault, I identify a tension between the knowledge of the theorist and the technical knowledge of the methodist that later importantly informs Wolin's critique of Foucault. I explore this tension for what it reveals about the role of the contemporary political theorist via considerations of technical knowledge, Foucauldian "power/knowledge," and the disciplinary norms of political theory.

It is my contention that a key distinction between theorists and methodists strategically issued in "Vocation" has in the intervening years contributed to a vision of political theory that eschews engagement with political and historical phenomena. To unpack this unintended legacy, I apply Foucault's insights into power/knowledge to political theory as institutionalized within political science. In opposition to the primarily pedagogical role secured for theory in political science today, I propose that we reframe political theory as a *provocation* to a sometimes stultifying, unyielding discipline. Those who practice it should be provoked to propose countermemories of political knowing and practice, and to counter visions of politics by numbers. I draw support for this claim in the end from both Foucault and Wolin, returning to "Vocation" to see what alternatives it offers to the current state of political theory it has helped to create. In conclusion, I suggest that we "invoke" "Vocation," as Wolin himself suggestively does in this volume, and examine it for contributions to an "ethos" of political theory, one that I call "political theory as a provocation."

POLITICAL THEORY AS A VOCATION

What seems to have been forgotten is that one reads past theories,
not because they are familiar and therefore confirmative, but
because they are strange and therefore provocative.
—Sheldon Wolin

Wolin's intent in "Vocation" "is to sketch some of the implications of the primacy of method in the study of politics and to do it by way of a contrast between the vocation of the 'methodist' and the vocation of the theorist" (V 1062). By contrasting the two, Wolin intends to make an argument about qualities that separate the work of the theorist from that of the methodist and about the importance of the theorist's vocation. His essay serves as both a defense of theory and a warning of method, as he assumes that "the idea of method, like all important intellectual choices, carries a price . . ." (V 1062). Wolin's essay is as revealing on the question of what constitutes method as it is on what constitutes theory. In order to understand this, we must closely examine Wolin's treatment of method.

According to Wolin, political scientists' desire for rescue from professional vertigo by methods was spurred on by the belief that methods were neutral and philosophically uncontroversial. Wolin challenges this view on two counts: first, the teaching and use of methods by students surely informs "the way in which initiates will look upon the world and especially the political portion of it," and second, "the alleged neutrality of a methodist's

training overlooks significant philosophical assumptions admittedly incorporated into the outlook of those who advocate scientific inquiry into politics"
(*V* 1064). Methods frame how students and practitioners view the world.
Method "presupposes a certain answer to a Kantian type of question, What
must the world be like for the methodist's knowledge to be possible" (*V* 1064).

By casting doubt on the promises of method, Wolin also seeks to make
a case for the *bios theoretikos* by contrasting its lineage to that of the "*vita
methodica*" (*V* 1065). As Wolin writes, "while *philosophia* and its sister, *theoria,*
tended to stress the arduous difficulties awaiting those who sought truth, the
devotees of *methodus* began to emphasize the economy of being methodical . . ." (*V* 1066). Wolin notes that "method promised not only 'the use of
knowledge' but, above all, 'the *progression* of knowledge.'" Method was advocated for its utility and for its rigorousness. "Method came to mean, among
other things, a form of discipline designed to compensate for unfortunate
proclivities of the mind" (*V* 1067). One learned method by applying critical
doubt to what one claimed to know. More important for Wolin's argument—
issued as it was in a tumultuous era of U.S. politics and American political
science—method not only mastered those who wielded it; it also bore a
conservative politics. As Wolin notes, even method's great philosophical advocate, Descartes, "cautioned especially against bringing the new method
to bear upon questions of morality and practical action" (*V* 1067). Popular
morality and political ethics were off-limits to the methodist's examinations
because of the "fear of disorder" (*V* 1068). It was feared that the methodist,
doubt ridden and skeptical of tradition, would be likely to view current political and moral conditions as the "best" ones because they had proven their
practical worth, if not their perfection. Wolin identifies the problem with
such an arrangement: "What sort of political commitment is likely from a self
which has been purged of inherited notions, pledged to the support of existing political and moral schemes, yet inhibited by the belief that they are 'provisional'? A self of this type is likely to treat politics and morals in a way that
avoids fundamental criticisms as well as fundamental commitment" (*V* 1068).

This answer is crucial for Wolin because his defense of political theory is
also an indictment of political science. If the political scientist's adherence to
method is no longer viewed as neutral or philosophically bereft, it can also
no longer insulate him or her from criticism. Method's conservative character
is masked behind the appearance of scientific objectivity recast as method's
neutrality, which is then relied on by its practitioners not only to appear out-

side the mien of politics and philosophy but also to establish the "what is" of the political world as the "what ought to be." Far from constituting a neutral position, method binds the methodist to the world studied because he/she reconfirms it and calls for its continuation as the product of his/her empirical research. The methodist's belief that there is a "real world" to be studied empirically produces representations of only those aspects of the world that can be rendered in the spare language of empiricism. Wolin's calling into question of the "reality" of that world undermines the methodist's mission.

Both the questions confronting the methodist and the knowledge produced are technical, while the methodist's education accords to a model of training. Wolin writes, "The idea of training presupposes several premeditated decisions: about the specific techniques needed and how they will be used; about what is peripheral or irrelevant to a particular form of training; and about the desired behavior of the trainee after he has been released from his apprenticeship" (V 1072). Such training tends to produce methodists who view the products of the application of methods as plain empirical facts with little ambiguity or history. As a result, as Wolin notes, "an approach to the 'facts' consisting of statements which palpably lack precision, quantifiability, or operational value is said to be false, vague, unreliable, or even 'mystical'" (V 1071). The facts and statements of theory are transformed under the logic of method into these "unreliable" forms.

The demands of theory for its practitioners, on the other hand, require a wholly distinct view of knowledge, the world, history, and facts. Wolin asserts, "For the theorist, nothing is more difficult to appreciate than a fact, and nothing, it might be added, is more necessary as a condition for theorizing than that facts not be univocal" (V 1073). Theoretical "facts" are rich for interpretation; they demand not training in technique but immersion in historical detail, participation in philosophical debate, and appreciation of "the incoherence and contradictoriness of experience." Theoretical knowledge "tends . . . to be suggestive and illuminative rather than explicit and determinate" (V 1070). It focuses on "what is politically appropriate rather than . . . what is scientifically operational" (V 1071). Ruminative, deliberative, contemplative, and speculative, theoretical knowledge as constructed by Wolin offers not technical instruction but instead "cultural resources [that can be] itemized as metaphysics, faith, [and] historical sensibility . . ." (V 1074).

The first three sections of "Vocation" work to undermine the methodist's position while promoting that of the theorist by polarizing them. What this polarization establishes are two separate realms for the fields and their respective knowledges. It is assumed that there will be some traffic between the two realms—for how else would theory justify its continued presence in political science?—but each will maintain its own language, norms, and practices. There is much at stake in the question of why these principalities of knowledge are erected. Do the distinctions between theory and method reflect deep-seated differences or do they establish them? We must also ask who profits from the creation of a border and from its patrolling. It is my contention that the border does not safeguard vulnerable "ways of life" in the name of intellectual diversity so much as it creates formations of identity that circulate in the service of intellectual balkanization.

We must also question the distinction Wolin draws between the political theorists of today and the theorists they teach. The "vocation of the political theorist" looks little like the "nature and role of epic political theorists," to borrow the headings from Wolin's final two sections. As Wolin describes it, our vocation as contemporary theorists is primarily a pedagogical one. Today's theorists are those "who preserve our understanding of past theories, who sharpen our sense of the subtle, complex interplay between political experience and thought, and who preserve our memory of the agonizing effort of intellect to restate the possibilities and threats posed by political dilemmas of the past" (V 1077). We transmit the theories that others have created. While this is itself quite a task, it positions theorists as the bearers of esoteric knowledge whose main purpose is to initiate new converts. It does little to contest the theorist/methodist position other than reverse the normal hierarchy of knowledge recognized in political science. And it is also not clear that Wolin's original belief in the radical potential of political theory finds support in his treatment of the contemporary political theorist.

The epic political theorists aimed high; we teach. Wolin's defense of political theory threatens to deform and defuse it while trying to save it. This is not to say that his is not a brave, eloquent, thoughtful, and provocative argument. My qualm is whether it cedes too much ground by drawing too great a distinction between theory and method. In separating theory from method in "Vocation," Wolin relies on a key distinction between two forms of knowledge, tacit political (theoretical) and technical (scientific). This distinction is meant both to make a case for the special and intrinsic value of political theory and to call into question the status of technical knowledge. Wolin introduces a distinction that will not hold, and there is serious risk both to political theory and to politics if the distinction—what I shall term "the knowledge divide"—is rigidly maintained. This is not to suggest that there is no difference in the practices of theorists and methodists but rather to insist that no one is served by treating their knowledges or "truths" as fully distinct. This division between a knowledge that informs reflection and one that makes and implements policy does not serve us anymore; we serve it.

It is more likely that all facts are equally rich, but some are more easily transformed into statements, guidelines, and procedures; that is, "truth which is economical, replicable, and easily packaged, and truth which is not" (V 1071). Foucault offers a way of looking at all facts as "created" equal that allows us to historicize and contextualize the kind of knowledge that functions as "truth" in the university and elsewhere. His work provides insights that enable us to make an argument about political theory without falling into an overly rigid division between political theorists and the departments that house them. If we affirm an alternative view that all facts are historical and that even scientific data can be seen, upon closer inspection, to bear ideological and normative stamps, we open up new possibilities for theoretical commitments and practices. Wolin himself suggests as much when he writes,

> If facts were simply "there" to be collected, classified, and then matched with a theory . . . the political scientist might well declare, "Whether [a] proposition is true or false depends on the degree to which the proposition and the real world correspond." But although everyone is ready to acknowledge that facts depend upon some criteria of selection or significance, what is less frequently acknowledged is that such criteria usually turn out to be fragments of some almost-forgotten "normative" or "traditional" theory.[3]

This quote illustrates that it is not Wolin's position per se that I question here, but the bifurcated vision of knowledge that careless readers of his text have taken from "Vocation" and established in our field. For while Wolin appears to be drawing what lawyers call "bright lines" between scientific and theoretical knowledge, closer examination reveals a blurred, unstable boundary. It is along the fuzzy lines of the knowledge divide that I eventually bring Wolin and Foucault together on the question of what it is to "do" theory. First, however, the knowledge divide must be undone, and for that we must turn to Wolin's critique of Foucault.

Wolin's critique of methodism in political science resonates with Foucault's

critiques of disciplinarity and governmentality. While Wolin's project of elucidating a "vocation of political theory" would strike Foucault as odd, Wolin's
criticisms would find a welcome audience with him. Wolin's writings have
been both exposé and exposition of elite power and the radically undemo-
cratic practices that govern contemporary politics, and they share many of
the concerns of Foucault's analysis of disciplinary regimes, which are enacted
and fueled by purveyors of elite knowledge who shape and instruct contemporary life. That is why Wolin's scathing critique of Foucault, "On the Theory
and Practice of Power," presented in the collection *After Foucault*, comes as a
surprise.[4] One need not imagine a tight and reciprocal relationship between
their thought to find common sympathies. Wolin's reductionist and politically futile portrait of Foucault is so dismissive as to suggest less that Wolin
views him as politically naïve than that Wolin sees him as a kind of threat to
politics and to theorists. What is perhaps most disappointing is that Wolin's
objections to Foucault's conception of power largely concern its implications
for the theorist's vocation, not deficiencies in the conception itself.

The risk that Foucault poses to the account of the political theorist's role
advanced in "Vocation" can be summarized as follows: Foucault deals a devastating blow to the distinction between technical knowledge and theoretical
knowledge that "Vocation" enforces but cannot sustain. "Vocation" presumes
that such a division in knowledge is necessary in order to secure a place for
political theory in the academy, but tension underlying the piece reveals the
division to be in fact untenable. Foucault's treatment of power/knowledge,
which superficially resembles technical knowledge, along with his deep suspicion of "global theories," makes him look to Wolin like a barbarian at the
gate, a theorist who bears a methodist's traits and ways of life and so threatens
to bring an end to the theorist's own. The theorist's vocation, as envisioned
by Wolin, is based on a false binary that he sustains for perceived immediate
benefit but at considerable long-term cost. While a belief in the separate existence of "tacit political knowledge," which the theorist bears and inculcates
in students, serves to provide a defense for the traditional theorist's practices
(and so conveniently preserves both the works of epic political theorists and
the jobs of contemporary political theorists), it is primarily a defense in action, not a strategic offense. Although Wolin considers theoretical knowledge
superior to technical knowledge for politics, "Vocation" provides no strategy
for undoing the reign of technical knowledge in academia and life, generally,
or in political science and politics, specifically.

While the theorist can issue counterattacks across the divide, nothing in "Vocation" suggests that the theorist's tacit political knowledge should be used in his or her own investigations of matters that the knowledge divide puts squarely in the methodist's hands. Wolin berates political scientists for failing to address long-standing theoretical questions in their work (V 1074), but nowhere in "Vocation" does Wolin suggest that contemporary political theorists should take up investigations in light of political science's distortions caused by its adherence to method. While political science is taken to task for its empirical bent and distrust of "moral knowledge," or "'metaphysical' and 'normative' preoccupations," political theory receives no censure for its reluctance to engage empirical phenomena (in the form of historical research, analysis of political events, or what is called "data," for example) with its theoretical material.

Wolin cannot be seen to be an active part of political theory's silences; he himself in his life and work engaged historical and political events. It is all the more striking, then, that his essay has, in spite of its underlying philosophical tension and, I would assume, its author's intent, promoted professional norms of political theory that encourage political complacency, if not complicity. Foucault's insights into power/knowledge bring such norms into focus as the forms of discipline they are. His work also undermines attempts by political theorists to employ the knowledge divide as a form of security against attacks from those more technically inclined. For while Wolin issued the knowledge divide in a strategic manner to defend political theory at a critical juncture, today the divide acts to relieve contemporary political theorists from engagement with politics and historical phenomena. As such, the divide proves contestable inasmuch as it legitimates a vocation of political theory that imagines itself exonerated from engagement with contemporary politics or places itself beyond political contestation. After Foucault, political theory becomes risky again, not because it is under attack as it was at the writing of "Vocation," but because it offers an offensive position for political engagement.

POLITICAL THEORY AS A PRACTICE

Wolin's stated objections to Foucault are to his conception of power, his concerns about the totalistic nature of theory, the lack of a privileged theoretical position, and the reduced importance of the state in his study of power. They can be linked narratively as follows: Foucault proposes a totalistic theory of power that politicizes previously nonpolitical domains as it diminishes those domains previously deemed the most political (for Wolin, the state, along with its scientific apparatuses). He therefore invests every person and position with potential for the exercise of power while simultaneously denigrating the worth of traditional practices and global political theories for understanding power in this new way. This has particularly dire consequences for political theory because it politicizes the position of the political theorist as it calls into question the usefulness of his or her expertise for understanding power and politics. After Foucault, the political theorist confronts a sudden investiture of power at the same moment as he or she experiences a staggering divestiture of professional prestige and political agency qua theorist. In place of the surety and security of vocation, the political theorist—like other political subjects, but perhaps sensing it more keenly—is made aware of him- or herself as another operative in the intermeshing of disciplinary power and governmentality.

Wolin states that Foucault "almost singlehandedly . . . moved the discussion of that most elusive and illusive concept [power] from its modern or state-centered understanding to a postmodern or decentered version" (OT 179). Power for Foucault is everywhere, and he explodes the conception that power is something that one has, that can be lost or retained like an object, positing instead that power exists only in its exercise. In Wolin's words, "[for Foucault] there is no social space undefined by power relationships and no socially significant form of power which is not housed. It is a social world totally dominated by power but not necessarily a totalitarian world" (OT 186). This conception of power troubles Wolin in part because "Foucault's critique left standing some of the bastions of modern power while ignoring its peculiar dynamics. The best that it could produce was an insurrectionary gesture toward a corporatized world with no exits" (OT 179). Moving his sights from the state to society and the social formations of power, Foucault risks missing the "real" authors of oppression: "the seamless web of involvements between science, governmental bureaucracies, and business corporations . . ." (OT 187–88). As Wolin reads him, "for Foucault, the emphasis is on the repressive, dominating quality of power" (OT 198). Wolin's Foucault is a theorist of oppression, imagining all power as negative and finding evidence of its effects in all elements of life. Because "he offers no hope of escape," "Foucault seems to have repeated the same error of totalistic thinking with which he had taxed classic theory" (*OT* 186). Foucault's insistence on the ubiquity of power leads Wolin to assert that Foucault is proposing another totalistic vision of the political. Finding power everywhere precludes Foucault from imagining positions that are removed from its exercise—one of which, Wolin insists, is the political theorist's—and leaves him with a theory that cannot fundamentally alter the political system it critiques.

For Wolin, Foucault poses a problem for the political theorist on two fronts, one related to the status of "truth" and the other fixed on the historical effects of theory. On the topic of truth, Wolin maintains that "there is no exit [from power for the theorist] because Foucault has closed off any possibility of a privileged theoretical vantage point that would not be infected by the power/knowledge syndrome and would not itself be the expression of a Nietzschean will-to-power" (*OT* 186). Foucault disposes of what Wolin refers to here as "classic theory" (epic political theory in "Vocation") through his "rejection of the notion of theoretical truth independent of practices. . . . [Truth] is a product of the practices that make it possible" (*OT* 191–92). "[H]is attack was directed at the idea of theory as a representation of political totalities and the idea of the theorist as the creator of political truth" (*OT* 185). For Foucault, political theory is not removed from politics but is instead bound up with power in the same way that other discourses (psychiatry, political science, criminality, anthropology, delinquency, inter alia) are bound up with their proposed objects of study, constituting themselves as discourses through the naming and interrogation of a subject that is constituted through the procedures as a "problem" to be solved. The theorist and theory, politics and political theory, are for Foucault inextricably linked with each other: not in the sense that one term can be reduced to the other, but instead by the very fact that they cannot be separated. This view of political theory undermines what are for Wolin the theorist's particular attributes and tasks. Wolin believes that the "project of [political theory] as a practice—that is, the activity of theorizing—declares its autonomy from politics, its separate identity from political practices, even while it is prescribing them" (*OT* 192). Political theory requires for Wolin a critical distance from politics in order to give it the proper perspective from which to offer its evaluative and prescriptive commentary. This is so because "it is the nature of action to fall short of theory and it is the role of theory to declare that. Theory can only perform that critical function if it retains a separate identity. Otherwise, theory becomes *technē*, and the theorist becomes indistinguishable from the technician of power" (OT 193). Foucault threatens to transform the theorist into a "technician of power," according to Wolin, which is tantamount to turning the theorist into a methodist.

Beyond the implications of Foucault's treatment of "truth" (and knowledge) for political theory, there is a more general critique of the notion of theory itself. According to Wolin, "[T]heory signified in [Foucault's] eyes a totalizing system of thought, an all-inclusiveness that was at once authoritarian and ignorant . . . [and] theorists, according to Foucault, mostly ignore the relationships and systems of meaning which actually constituted human life" (OT 181). Theory is authoritarian in Foucault's depiction because, as Wolin describes it, "the theoretical project and the theoretical subject . . . are carriers of a state-centered, authority-centered politics that is inherently repressive" (OT 185). One can see here how Foucault's analysis of power informed his treatment of theory. If political theory preserved the idea of the sovereign state and the liberal individual in its texts, for example, it participated in the proliferation of state-centered views of power and sovereignty in society through the teaching of such texts. At the same time, theorists mulled over theoretical depictions of power that masked its existent forms in the world, and thus missed any chance of illuminating the question of power and elucidating its attributes. Convinced that classic theory could teach us little about power as it presently functions, Foucault sought to analyze power in the practices and transactions in which it was exercised and on display. To Wolin, it was as if Foucault "promised entry into the world shaped by technical knowledge and centralized state power. He rejected the ideal of theoretical knowledge and sought a conception that would bridge the gulf between knowledge and its application and thus would eliminate the traditional problem of the proper relationship between theory and practice" (OT 184). In this sense, Foucault considered theory to be a practice that, understood discursively, could be analyzed for its disciplinary predilections, power dynamics, critical incitements, and strategic exclusions. Since theory for Foucault lacks the protective cloak of tradition that "Vocation" drapes it in, it is vulnerable to the same kind of investigations to which Foucault subjects other disciplines.

Throughout Wolin's critique, it is as if Foucault were a traitor to the cause of political theory. "For Foucault there is domination but not betrayal or diminution because theory has been denied integrity. In fact, truth only becomes truth when it is integrated with practice and systems of power. The tensions between theory and practice have disappeared" (*OT* 193). Foucault is constituted as a threat to political theory precisely because he refuses to fall back on a division between theory and practice that has long marked political theory. Foucault does not register his shift in approach as a "betrayal" or "diminution" of theory, and thus reveals his failure to understand the vocation of political theory. Wolin frames Foucault as a threat to theory as great as method was in "Vocation." Method is practice informed by theory in the application of certain techniques to the empirical world in the investigation of political questions. Because Foucault is interested in examining techniques for what they reveal about power and politics, he is similarly dismissed by Wolin. With method, the cause for alarm was that there were practitioners who approached politics as if it were a technical problem to be overcome through the correct application of methods and technologies. Although Foucault could not stand in further contrast to such a position, Wolin makes him appear in one just as dangerous. Foucault does not investigate the question of power as an answerable one whereby techniques could be applied to "fix" the "problem." Instead, he analyzes political techniques, strategies, and logics *in order to undermine* the treatment of politics as though it were a problem that can be solved. To grasp this in all its weight, one needs to rebut the major tenets of Wolin's critique, for in order for Foucault to take on the appearance of a methodist, to have any resemblance whatsoever, a serious flaw in Wolin's interpretation must exist.

Foucault's conception of power is productive, not merely oppressive, although it can produce forms of oppression. "Power," states Foucault,

> must be analysed as something which circulates, never localised here or there, never in anybody's hands, never appropriated as a commodity or a piece of wealth. Power is employed and exercised through a net-like organisation. And not only do individuals circulate between its threads; they are always in the position of simultaneously undergoing and exercising this power.[5]

The view that power is never fixed in value, location, intensity, or direction is one of Foucault's true theoretical innovations. He resists a modern conception of power as that which only degrades and deforms, never produces and creates. Although Foucault's language of "subjection," "subjugated knowledge," "the historical knowledge of struggles," and "domination" can seem at times to support Wolin's negative characterization, Foucault took considerable pains to avoid being misunderstood on this point.

Foucault is fundamentally opposed to a view of power that casts it as merely repression. He states that

> it seems to me that the notion of repression is quite inadequate for capturing what is precisely the productive aspect of power. . . . Now I believe that this is a wholly negative, narrow, skeletal conception of power, one which has been curiously widespread. If power were never anything but repressive, if it never did anything but to say no, do you really think one would be brought to obey it? What makes power hold good, what makes it accepted, is simply the fact that it doesn't only weigh on us as a force that says no, but that it traverses and produces things, it induces pleasure, forms knowledge, produces discourse.[6]

Power for Foucault is clearly not the oppressive force that Wolin claims it is. Wolin also argues that "Foucault's conception [of power] is flawed by a narrow construction of state power as essentially negative and preventative . . . , parasitic rather than grounded . . ." (OT 182). He continues, insisting that "Foucault failed to grasp the positive role of the modern state in promoting the modernization of society. Although the state repressed . . . , it also created . . . the infrastructure of modernity, . . . in the form of modern science whose subsidization by the state for the past three centuries has made possible the phenomenal growth of scientific knowledge and its practical applications" (OT 182–83). It is equally untrue that Foucault banished all considerations of the state from his investigations of power, for he also believed that sovereignty was deeply implicated in the procedures and forms of governmentality.

Foucault's aversion to analyses of the state coincides with his wish to "conduct an ascending analysis of power, starting, that is, from its infinitesimal mechanisms . . . ," "concerned with power at its extremities, in its ultimate destinations, with those points where it becomes capillary, that is, in its more regional and local forms and institutions" (TL 99, 96). He understands this project to

> be the exact opposite of Hobbes' project in Leviathan. . . . [I]nsofar as he is a fabricated man, Leviathan is no other than the amalgamation of a certain number of separate individualities, who find themselves reunited by the com-

plex of elements that go to compose the State; but at the heart of the State, or rather, at its head, there exists something which constitutes it as such, and this is sovereignty, which Hobbes says is precisely the spirit of Leviathan. Well, rather than worry about the problem of the central spirit, I believe that we must attempt to study the myriad of bodies which are constituted as peripheral *subjects* as a result of the effects of power. [*TL* 97–98]

Traditional modern theoretical debates focused on the question of sovereignty and of how rights limit rule. The problem, as Foucault saw it, was that an analysis of "the way power was exercised—concretely and in detail—with its specificity, its techniques and tactics, was something that no one attempted to ascertain . . ." (*TP* 115–16). Foucault's focus on "capillary" forms of power, and investigations of power as it traverses bodies and effects subjects, lends some credence to the concern that Foucault ignores the state. Although Foucault deposes it from primacy in his formulation of power, he remarked in an interview: "I don't want to say that the State isn't important; what I want to say is that relations of power necessarily extend beyond the limits of the State. In two senses: first of all because the State, for all the omnipotence of its apparatuses, is far from being able to occupy the whole field of actual power relations, and further because the State can only operate on the basis of other, already existing power relations" (*TP* 122).[7] While Foucault's analyses do not explore state power at great length, the genealogical researches that follow in his wake need not avoid doing so. (In fact, further explication and elucidation of his thought and of power generally may demand it.) However, Wolin's hesitancy with Foucault's tentative treatment of the state has as much to do with its relevance for political theory as it has to do with its relevance for politics generally.

Foucault maintains that "we must eschew the model of Leviathan in the study of power" (*TL* 102), a sentiment mirrored in his claim that "we need to cut off the King's head: in political theory that has still to be done" (*TP* 121). For analysts interested in the study of power and for political theorists generally, these statements have two important implications. First, the field of investigation broadens dramatically once power is recognized to be no longer a property of the state. Acts, exchanges, identities, practices, and procedures that previously would have been ignored as irrelevant or of secondary importance now take on significant roles in analyses of power. Second, and more tellingly for Wolin, the phrase "cut off the King's head" suggests that political theory will no longer look the same because the theorist's position has been fundamentally altered and expanded.

Foucault frames his project in strict opposition to Hobbes, who, at the time of the publication of "Vocation," was the subject of Wolin's major explication of the epic political theorist.[8] Hobbes serves as the shining example of the heroic theorist who authors himself into history as an epic figure, displaying great feats in the affairs of the world by grappling with them textually. Foucault threatens to end the tradition of political theory whose exemplar is Hobbes with a regicidal decapitation. Ridding the state of its perceived monopoly on power, then, is related to unseating the political theorist from a traditional position of prestige. This is an important link between Wolin's reading of Foucauldian power and his view of Foucault's treatment of political theory as contradictory. If power is a richer, more nuanced concept for Foucault, then perhaps his dismissal of traditional political theory is more tactical than reactionary.

Wolin claims that for Foucault theory is "both dangerous and impotent" (*OT* 191). Foucault *is* wary of most theoretical projects because they require a coherence of thought and purpose that is often authoritarian in its demands. And he *did* think that much theorizing about politics, and particularly about power, was wasted effort that never grasped power at the level of exchange and so was politically ineffective. But a closer reading of his discussion of traditional political theorists suggests another, more revealing reason for distancing himself from what he termed "global totalitarian theories" that bears on the consideration here.

The risk of political theory for Foucault is not captured adequately in the dualism proposed by Wolin. A long quote from Foucault regarding his use of Jeremy Bentham in *Discipline and Punish* is helpful here:

> If I had wanted to describe "real life" in the prisons, I wouldn't indeed have gone to Bentham. But the fact that this real life isn't the same thing as the theoreticians' schemas doesn't entail that these schemas are therefore utopian, imaginary, etc. One could only think that if one had an impoverished notion of the real. . . . [T]hese programmes induce a whole series of effects in the real . . . : they crystallize into institutions, they inform individual behavior, they act as grids for the perception and valuation of things. . . . [I]f the prisons were seen to have failed, if criminals were perceived as incorrigible, and a whole new criminal "race" emerged into the field of vision of public opinion

and "justice," if the resistance of the prisoners and the pattern of recidivism took the forms we know they did, it's precisely because this type of programming didn't just remain a utopia in the heads of a few projectors.[9]

Theoretical works such as Bentham's Panopticon project are useful texts for Foucault and others because they harbor within them the dreams of society while they represent the danger of theory incompletely realized.

Theories do not enter into the world unmediated and become realized in the whole of their grand design. They need interlocutors, they meet resistances, and they are subject to alterations due to ideological conflict, communicative limitations, budgetary constraints, and the like. They come into the world incomplete but they leave it transformed. From Bentham's prison project sprung whole new categories of criminality, new versions of social justice, and new strategies for reform, while new typologies of behavior began to inform the carceral networks coming into place. Theory here is not so much "dangerous" for its totalitarian qualities or "impotent" for its lack of impact, but instead "risky" because its effects on the world are unpredictable. That is, theories are both powerful and weak; they create new categories of knowledge and modalities of existence while they depend upon translation, mediation, and interpretation in their move from text to reality.

Wolin's final criticism of Foucault is of his conflation of theory and practice, which Wolin takes to render the theorist's position untenable. We should be skeptical of this claim if for no other reason than that Foucault himself produced theoretical works and, as the analysis herein attests, Foucault had no reflexive aversion to theoretical knowledge. Recognizing the riskiness of political theory is not equivalent to dismissing it altogether. Foucault's stance on political theory reveals another opposition to Wolin's conception of the theorist's vocation. Wolin, as seen above, maintains that it is in the nature of action to fail to live up to theory, and it is the theorist's role to point out the discrepancy. Theorists need to have a spectator's view of political events for Wolin in order to evaluate a political regime, to see how well it lives up to its legitimating claims. As such, action's inability to meet the demands of theory serves to authorize the theorist's practice. For Foucault, theory's inability to become fully realized is doubly troubling. He recognizes the authoritarian impulses of the most ambitious theories (as does Wolin) and so distrusts them (as Wolin suggests), but Foucault also finds cause for alarm in the effects on the world of unrealized theory. As the above example of Bentham indicates, Foucault is wary of unified theories precisely because they introduce profound changes in subjectivity and other political formations even when they go unrealized. While Wolin sees moments of unrealized theory as opportunities for more theorizing, Foucault wonders if instead we need more critical examinations of what theory does to the world.

Theory falls from grace in Foucault, not principally for its authoritarian tendencies, but for one of the primary reasons for which Wolin esteems it: its unrealizability. To be sure, this should be taken to mean not that Foucault wants a realizable political theory, but rather that he notes a failing in theory precisely where Wolin finds its value for the world. In Wolin's formulation of the relationship between theory and action, the blame for the effects of unrealized theory lies in "the nature of action," not in the nature of theory. One could thus be led to imagine that Foucault somehow valorizes reality at the expense of theory. While Foucault does bring theory down from the heights, it is not to dispose of it but instead to transform it. Wolin fears that such a transformation will reduce theoretical knowledge to technical knowledge. But Foucault is not proposing a new pragmatism, with theory in the service of action, so much as a reevaluation of the relationship between theory and action. We need to return now to this relationship, forecast earlier in the discussion on Foucault and truth, in order to address Wolin's concerns about the meaning of Foucauldian knowledge in the political world.

Foucault's refusal to privilege theoretical knowledge over technical knowledge undermines the knowledge divide issued in "Vocation," but not in the way Wolin fears. Foucault is not proposing a reversal in Wolin's hierarchy but rather its removal. Wolin mistakes the products of Foucault's efforts for those of the reign of technical knowledge. Foucauldian power/knowledge, however, does not effect the replacement of theoretical concerns with practical and technical ones. It instead expands the theoretical project to include its own practices as objects of study while simultaneously opening up regimes of truth and practices of domination to theoretical examination. Foucault bridges the knowledge divide by expanding the theoretical position to include interrogations of technical, practical, procedural, *and* philosophical matters. The "cost" of this new understanding of theory—if one wants to revert to Wolinian language—comes in the form of a theoretical position invested with, not divested of, power. To measure this cost, we need to position power/knowledge against technical knowledge.

Foucauldian power/knowledge testifies to the inseparability of power and truth. "There can be no possible exercise of power," writes Foucault, "without a certain economy of discourses of truth which operates through and on the basis of this association. We are subjected to the production of truth through power and we cannot exercise power except through the production of truth" (*TL* 93). For Foucault, "truth isn't outside power, or lacking in power. . . . Truth is a thing of this world: it is produced only by virtue of its multiple forms of constraint. And it induces regular effects of power" (*TP* 131). Truth invests lived reality through the performance of discursive formations that circulate, distribute, modify, and enforce the coded valences of truth and falsity. Power/knowledge differs from traditional theoretical knowledge in that it takes no refuge in the notion of privileged or esoteric principles that exist only for the most diligent seekers. It differs from technical knowledge in that its concern with political technologies, tactics, and strategies is not fueled by a desire to solve the problem of "the political"—that is, to end political contestation in the name of progress, science, rationality, or security, a desire that would surely be as abhorrent to Foucault as it would be to Wolin—but is instead informed by a recognition of the manner in which practices are knowable only through an examination of the discursive strategies that allow us to think about and evaluate them. That is, power/knowledge cannot easily separate theoretical from technical concerns because theory has its own techniques, and techniques are invested with theoretical commitments.

While the implications of power/knowledge for the vocation of political theory are severe, there is little to suggest that theorists will become "technicians of power" as a result of Foucault's work. Wolin views Foucauldian power/knowledge suspiciously because "the tensions between theory and practice have disappeared" (*OT* 193). One interpretation of Wolin's phrase is that theorists become primarily concerned with proposing technical adjustments to rule, but that cannot be right. Foucault is frequently faulted by political theorists for his lack of a normative theory and model of rule, not for reducing the theorist to a technical advisor to power. Foucault is not concerned with *technē* as "know-how" but instead as a way to answer the question "How do we know?" While such epistemological questions have been within the purview of theorists from political theory's origins, Foucault changes the emphasis of the theoretical preoccupation by treating *technē* as technique, technology, and tactic as an answer to the question. Knowing does not become a technical question, and knowledge is not put at the service of "know-how," but research into what is called "know-how" is transformed into a key element in understanding the constitution of power/knowledge in a technological age. Our practices, strategies of domination, political tactics, and technologies of power are found not to detract from the *bios theoretikos* but to be constituent elements in the contemplation of traditional political theoretical concepts such as power, authority, rule, justice, and equality.

After Foucault, and with power/knowledge, the theoretical project enters a new territory through which one moves cautiously, taking careful notice of the way that concepts enter into the world, the way they are said to somehow "appear" there, and the events and procedures through and by which they are performed. "How do we know?" is in this way brought to meet "know-how," but the theorist does not become the technician's servant. The theorist learns to interrogate technical knowledge for what it can reveal about political concerns and possibilities, and therefore expands the theoretical project accordingly. Foucault can rightfully be seen not as escaping the tensions between theory and practice, as Wolin believes, but instead as putting them to use productively. If the tensions themselves are not investigated, they are likely to solidify into disciplinary norms and boundaries that come to seem naturally given. The tensions do not disappear for Foucault; on the contrary, they propel his analyses.

Foucault makes good on the unrealized promise of a historicized, "enriched" technical knowledge that "Vocation" suggests and yet cannot admit without subjecting political theory to the same critical gaze that method receives. I have argued that Wolin paints a uniformly underdeveloped picture of Foucault because of his anxiety about a threatened privileged theoretical perspective. Importantly, Wolin thinks that he is defending both the theorist and "decentered politics" from Foucault (*OT* 199). Wolin wants to preserve this ground so as to save a place both for theory and for political agency. The major question regarding what political theory needs to be "after Foucault" is whether or not theorists can do their work once implicated in networks of power in the way that Foucault suggests. Must there be theoretical positions untouched by power? Is this so only if one has an outmoded view of power that understands it only negatively as domination or repression? While Wolin charges Foucault with thinking as much, I hope my efforts to counter this claim have been successful. What remains interesting is that both Wolin and Foucault ultimately advance preferred theoretical positions that are local rather than global, partial rather than universal, resistant to state power rather than complicit in its machinations, and that give voice to desires for freedom without employing the language of liberalism. With these shared sympathies in mind, what follows is a rumination that tries to think simultaneously with Foucault *and* with Wolin, guided by my perception that Wolin's criticisms of Foucault are at odds with his deeper commitments about the role of political theory.

POLITICAL THEORY AS A PROVOCATION . . .

Critique doesn't have to be the premise of a deduction which concludes:
this then is what needs to be done. It should be an instrument for those
who fight, those who resist and refuse what is.
—Michel Foucault

Foucault makes a distinction between the "universal" and "specific" intellectual that bears importantly on a consideration of the role of the contemporary political theorist. The universal intellectual "was acknowledged the right of speaking in the capacity of master of truth and justice. He was heard, or purported to make himself heard, as the spokesman of the universal." Times have changed, however, and intellectuals have grown increasingly accustomed to working "within specific sectors, at the precise points where their own conditions of life or work situate them" (*TP* 126). The project for the intellectual, and by extension for the theorist, is no longer concerned primarily with the expression of universal values or eternal truths, but instead with speaking from his/her institutional positions of the tactics of domination and the discursive blocs that facilitate the smooth functioning of power. For the specific intellectual, "it's not a matter of emancipating truth from every system of power (which would be a chimera, for truth is already power) but of detaching the power of truth from the forms of hegemony, social, economic, and cultural, within which it operates at the present time" (*TP* 133). Political theorists are implicated in the production of truth and regimes of knowledge. Foucault asks such intellectuals to use their positions in the matrices of truth-production to contest the rule of knowledge (and so rule by experts or elites) by "seeing historically how effects of truth are produced within discourses which in themselves are neither true nor false" (*TP* 118). The specific intellectual is called to help "with the insurrection of knowledges that are opposed primarily not to the contents, methods or concepts of a science, but to the effects of the centralising powers which are linked to the institution and functioning of an organised scientific discourse within a society such as ours" (TL 84).

Foucault's injunctions to the specific intellectual function less as methods and more as gestures toward an unnamed and undeveloped project. Foucault's writing on the two kinds of intellectuals can be interpreted as a proposal for a method, but to do so would miss the point. Foucault is not interested in replacing one program with another; he intends to transform intellectual subjectivity by making an ongoing interrogation of one's theoretical practices a constitutive part of those practices. For "detaching the power of truth from the forms of hegemony, social, economic, and cultural, within which it operates at the present time" requires that the theorist's own social, economic, and cultural position come into question. This is not to be read as navel-gazing but instead, I think, as a call to approach one's "vocation" with trepidation, inquisitiveness, skepticism, and humility. The trappings of intellectual subjectivity deserve to be unpacked, analyzed for their impact on one's work, and constantly kept in mind lest one be tempted to inhabit the "universal" position.

Wolin suggests a theoretical project that complements such an attitude, as well. Wolin describes the future for the vocation of political theory in his critique of Foucault as "a return to a critical conception of theory, one that can intimate but not prescribe practice, [that] can preserve the means of thinking that can grasp state-centeredness and point to ways out of it" (OT 200). Wolin's theorist, like Foucault's specific intellectual, is meant to speak against the apparatuses of domination like the state without laying out a program for political action as the epic theorist did long ago. That time, like that of the universal intellectual, has passed for political theory. Wolin's description of the character of theory he proposes borrows the concept of "self-consuming theory" from Stanley Fish, emphasizing "the playful, self-derisive mien of theory [that does not] surrender . . . its potential to decentered politics" (OT 199). Although Wolin takes note of the concept of the specific intellectual from Foucault, he dismisses it because Foucault refuses to answer the question, "[W]hy should the specific intellectual employ his or her knowledge in political struggle and why should he side with the dominated?" (OT 196). This is a question that seems fair, but reveals a basic misunderstanding of Foucault.

Foucault did not prescribe a plan of action for theorists or citizens because for him the idea of a thinker prescribing such a plan resonated too closely with theory's more authoritarian tendencies. Providing a map to the political world or to the theorist's vocation would have been not only inconsistent for this thinker of discipline, risk, security, discontinuity, and the arbitrary; it would have been, in the deepest sense, nearly unthinkable. But Foucault does not abandon us so much as choreograph tactical moments for us to interject our unease with and objections to the world he describes and the practices he intimates. Using Foucault to think through "Political Theory as a Vocation" as it appeared thirty years ago and as it is read by us today means giving up a desire for final answers and grand schemes; it means looking instead for productive readings of the implications for our work in the thought of both thinkers.

In the same way that Foucault's analytics of power have at times been transformed into stark prohibitions against studying the state formation, "Vocation"'s knowledge divide has been used to cultivate a disciplinary tendency that discourages contact with empirical issues and events as a central part of theoretical enterprises. False and overly simplistic views of what is or is not political theory, what is or is not a theoretical text, what is or is not a theoretical project, have sprung out of a false dichotomy strategically issued by Wolin but subsequently reified through usage. Wolin's critique of Foucault revealed lingering attachments to a vision of the theoretical perspective rid of power relations and provided further evidence as to how the "vocation of the political theorist" relies on uncritical views of truth and power. And yet there are crucial commonalities in their thought, including the local character of the future of political theory, which sparked the original engagement of the two in this piece. I would like to end with an additional shared sentiment to suggest the replacement of Wolin's conception of a "vocation" for political theory with something along the lines of an "ethos."

. . . O R ,   A N   E T H O S   O F   P O L I T I C A L   T H E O R Y

In "Vocation," Wolin asks, "When we choose a theory or a method, are we choosing something momentous, like a self, or something innocuous, like an 'intellectual construct' or 'conceptual scheme'?" (V 1075). In answer to his own question, Wolin responds that "the adoption of a theory signifies a form of submission with serious consequences both for the adoptor and for those who imitate him. . . . *A certain sensibility is needed, qualities of thinking and feeling which are not readily formulable but pertain to a capacity for discriminative judgment*" (V 1076, italics added). He adds, "Perforce, a political theory is, among other things, a sum of judgments, shaped by the theorist's notion of what matters, and embodying a series of discriminations about where one province begins and another leaves off" (V 1076). Foucault, in "What Is Enlightenment?" suggests approaching "modernity rather as an attitude than as a period of history. And by 'attitude,' I mean a mode of relating to contemporary reality; a voluntary choice made by certain people; in the end, a way of thinking and feeling; a way, too, of acting and behaving that at one and the same time marks a relation of belonging and presents itself as a task. A bit, no doubt, like what the Greeks call an *ethos*." Foucault's point in that essay is to suggest that scholars, "rather than seeking to distinguish the 'modern era' from the 'premodern' or 'postmodern,' . . . try to find out how the attitude of modernity, ever since its formation, has found itself struggling with attitudes of 'countermodernity.'"[10] To borrow a phrase from Foucault, if the version of political theory that must resort to the knowledge divide to maintain its identity is theory's "modern" semblance, Wolin's sentiments concerning a theoretical sensibility contain the germ of a "countermodernity" for the vocation of political theory. The continued practice of political theory does require something akin to the "sensibility" of which Wolin speaks that is not "readily formulable" in the same way that Foucault's directives to the specific intellectual are at best gestural. Imagining political theory to demand something like a "sentiment" or "a sum of judgments" frees political theory from definitional exercises that are expressly concerned with attention to canonical matters and the policing of disciplinary boundaries.

My misgivings about "Vocation" stem in part from the unresolved tension that propels it and, just as strongly, from the way that it has been read to privilege some theoretical projects over others. The reason that the knowledge divide poses such a problem from my perspective is that I have always suspected that "Vocation"—incredibly rich, wonderfully frustrating—hid within it a counterproposal for the vocation of political theory. Although the counterproposal is less developed, it is also considerably less authoritative and prone to problematic applications. Speaking of political theory as a "sum of judgments" requiring "a capacity for discriminative judgment" provides a model for a political theory that will not create disciplinary harmony (our judgments are bound to conflict and our discriminations will surely not be the same) but that will disallow quick dismissals of theoretical projects simply because they do not conform to canonical imperatives or because they take as their targets material that is superficially deemed to be more empirical than theoretical. Works that traverse the knowledge divide are able, under an ethos of political theory, to receive a fair hearing as they appear before theorists who share more than an object of study, but "a way, too, of acting and behaving that at one and the same time marks a relation of belonging and presents itself as a task." What I have called "political theory as a provocation" could, I think, be better pursued as an ethos of political theory.

The alternative to cultivating a sensibility or ethos is hoping and working for the return of an ironclad, clearly defined, and strongly held vocational identity to unite us. Such efforts will be as misplaced as they will be counter-productive. Or, more accurately, they will be productive, but what they will produce is far from the confident, dedicated, and secure intellectual work-force promised. If we continue to search for a singular identity, vocation, and subject, we shall produce it with the same practices and the same effects as have been witnessed in the disciplines that Foucault and others have investigated: through a series of exclusions, disavowals, incitements, and prohibitions. As Foucault notes, "Power never ceases its interrogation, its inquisition, its registration of truth; it institutionalises, professionalises and rewards its pursuit" (TL 93). The disciplinary power of political theory can do the same. In opposition to this I am not putting my hopes behind pluralism but am instead advancing a rigorous commitment to multiplicity in our field in voice, method, identity, subject, and politics.

When I speak of "political theory as a provocation," it is in this sense: to refuse the docility offered by strict adherence to tradition, to invite disagreement among one another through the pursuit of discontinuous projects, to accept within ourselves the unease that accompanies such a state of affairs, and to incite ourselves and our students to continually attend to and revise the substance of the political world and its meanings. The movement from vocation to provocation is perilous, discomforting, and vertiginous, but no more so than the political world that brought us to our tasks and to these texts in the first place. While theory may not tack alongside politics perfectly moment for moment, that is no excuse to use the theoretical position as an opportunity to shield ourselves from the world's events or its gaze. Political theory can be provocative if it supplies a jolt to quotidian existence and serves to question the means by which we justify our injustices, our inequalities, our shackles, and our privileges. This entails adjusting our sights and expanding our scope to include researches and analyses that defy simple categorization as they provide unconventional results. It may even make speaking as a "we" or for an "us" or of "our" project provisionally impossible.

What political theory as a provocation takes for granted is that our silences speak as loudly, and should be read as closely, as our words. Much can be gleaned about the current state of affairs by interrogating our field's noticeable silences as they preserve, in the United States alone, liberal democracy's open cruelties such as, to name only a few, the carceral industrial complex, devolution's coercive expansion of the state apparatus, the elevation of medical care to the status of a luxury item, and the grossly diminished futures of those abandoned in the wake of welfare reform and of the repeal of affirmative action. If we refuse to interrogate these topics with the same zeal that we have displayed when examining Plato's cave or Hobbes's Leviathan, we shall have abandoned our duty as scholars and citizens and should end our mourning over the postmodern condition and its current politics. If we think that theoretical rumination and investigation truly offer more to the understanding of politics and its problems than do game theory, voting behavior, or opinion polling, let us display such beliefs in word *and* deed. None of this is to say that we are to take over the business of political science, routing out empiricists, behaviorists, methodologists, and the like. It is rather to say that most of us came to political theory not to escape historical and political events but because we believed that the theoretical practice offered rich and worthwhile insights for the political world.

NOTES

For their invaluable comments on earlier drafts of this essay, I want to thank Gastón Alonso Donate, Wendy Brown, Peter Euben, Jason Frank, Niko Kolodny, Bronwyn Leebaw, Masha Raskolnikov, Michael Rogin, and John Tambornino.

1. Mark Reinhardt, "Look Who's Talking," *Political Theory* 23, no. 4 (November 1995): 689.

2. Sheldon S. Wolin, "Political Theory as a Vocation," *American Political Science Review* 63 (1969): 1062–82, hereafter also referred to as "Vocation," cited in text as V, along with pertinent page numbers.

3. Ibid., 1073 (quoting Robert Dahl, *Modern Political Analysis* [Englewood Cliffs, N.J.: Prentice-Hall, 1963], 8.)

4. Sheldon S. Wolin, "On the Theory and Practice of Power," in *After Foucault*, ed. Jonathan Arac (New Brunswick, N.J.: Rutgers, The State University Press, 1988), 179; hereafter cited in text as *OT*, along with pertinent page numbers.

5. Michel Foucault, "Two Lectures," in *Power/Knowledge*, ed. Colin Gordon (New York: Pantheon, 1980), 98; hereafter cited in text as *TL*, along with pertinent page numbers.

6. Michel Foucault, "Truth and Power," in *Power/Knowledge*, 119; hereafter cited in text as *TP*, along with pertinent page numbers.

7. Foucault decenters the state from political analyses, but his directive to explore power at its extremities has been, admittedly, turned into a dogma by some adherents. See Wendy Brown's illuminating discussion of this concern in her *States of Injury* (Princeton: Princeton University Press, 1995), 16.

8. Sheldon S. Wolin, *Hobbes and the Epic Tradition of Political Theory* (Los Angeles: University of California Press, 1970).

9. Michel Foucault, "Questions of Method," in *The Foucault Effect*, ed. Graham Burchell, Colin Gordon, and Peter Miller (Chicago: University of Chicago Press, 1991), 81.

10. Michel Foucault, "What Is Enlightenment?" in *The Foucault Reader*, ed. Paul Rabinow (New York: Pantheon, 1984), 39. The idea of locating another of Foucault's contributions to political theory in the notion of an "ethos" comes from an excellent essay by Niko Kolodny issued as "a defense of Foucault's evasions." See Niko Kolodny, "The Ethics of Cryptonormativism," *Philosophy & Social Criticism* 22, no. 5 (London: Sage, 1996): 63–84.

SHANE GUNSTER

10 // GRAMSCI, ORGANIC INTELLECTUALS, AND CULTURAL STUDIES

Lessons for Political Theorists

The purpose of discussing cinema or teen-age culture in New Left Review *is not to show, in some modish way, that we are keeping up with the times. These are directly relevant to the imaginative resistances of the people who have to live within capitalist societies. . . . The task of socialism today is to meet people where they are, where they are touched, bitten, moved, frustrated, nauseated—to develop discontent and, at the same time, to give the socialist movement some* direct *sense of the times and ways in which we live.*[1]

In considering the vocation of political theory amid an academy whose critical faculties are both isolated and increasingly rationalized, Gramsci's organic intellectual remains a seductive analytic category for those drawn to the possibility of a more active and engaged politics than one currently finds in most universities. It recognizes the value of theory—the organized, reflective, and conceptual mediation of the real—at the same time as it promises relevance and effectivity insofar as these ideas might be "organically" connected with social groups united by the desire for progressive social change. An ideal type, perhaps, it nevertheless constantly serves to remind us of both the limitations and the possibilities of political theory. Few theoretical traditions have grappled with the contemporary significance of this concept as openly as cultural studies.[2] Although its own institutionalization proceeds rapidly and cultural studies is certainly no more "organic" than other academic disciplines, its tentative positioning vis-à-vis theory and "the real" can furnish some useful insights into the role that theory might play in an emancipatory political practice. In many respects, the division of academics into specialized fields of study leaves us ill-equipped to deal with the mélange that has become social life at the turn of the millennium. On their own, the discrete tools and traditions offered by both political theory and cultural studies offer limited resources either to make sense of our world or to participate in emancipatory struggles that might make it a better place to live. While political theory frequently appears condemned to nostalgic reflection, cultural studies often dulls its critical edge in the never-ending stampede to document the newest styles and counterstyles of the cultural marketplace. But insofar as one might preserve a *tension* between these two disciplines and use them to cross-fertilize each other, new possibilities may arise. In the pages that follow, I hope to show how the mediation of cultural studies through the prism of the organic intellectual can make available conceptual resources that might help political theorists respond to some of the challenges identified by Sheldon Wolin in the essay that opens this volume. The account of cultural studies that follows, then, is neither complete nor representative; rather, guided by the memory of a vocation that once insisted on the possibility that current forms of social organization might be "systematically mistaken,"[3] I have tried to extract those elements that might serve useful in breathing new life into a theoretical practice that is both critical *and* political.

GRAMSCI'S ORGANIC INTELLECTUAL

In *The Prison Notebooks,* one of Gramsci's principal concerns was to refute the primary organizing myth of modern intellectuals: that they are somehow independent from social forces and structures. Commenting upon how to distinguish intellectuals from others in society, he noted that

> the most widespread error of method seems to me that of having looked for this criterion of distinction in the intrinsic nature of intellectual activities, rather than in the ensemble of the system of relations in which these activities (and therefore the intellectual groups who personify them) have their place within the general complex of social relations.[4]

Gramsci used this broader perspective to show how all intellectuals actually occupy functional positions vis-à-vis "fundamental" social groups or classes. Those who persisted in defending their autonomy, an illusion assisted by the fact that the class to which they had once "belonged," the feudal aristocracy, had itself been superseded, Gramsci described as "traditional" intellectuals. While the general irrelevance of most Italian intellectuals to Italian social, cultural, and political life for the last two centuries is a constant theme in Gramsci's writings, he argued that these individuals were being slowly connected with the dominant class as an evolving capitalism bound state, civil society, and the economy into a tightly knit productive matrix. Those intellectuals who were tied directly and openly to a particular class formation, Gramsci labeled "organic." Their function was primarily organizational and connective: not only did they give their own class "homogeneity and an awareness of its own function"[5] in the economic, social, and political fields, but they also helped construct the hegemony of this class by exercising "moral and intellectual leadership" over subordinate groups, which included representing the interests of their class as the universal interests of all and monopolizing the technical knowledge required for the ongoing production and reproduction of society.

Of course, it is not the bourgeois, but rather the proletarian organic intellectual that has excited the imagination of critical theorists. Gramsci assigns to such individuals the task of systematizing and reorganizing the experience and cultural formations of subaltern groups. As a result of the many contradictions in their lives, their constant subjection to hegemonic culture, their inability to achieve a mediated relationship with their environment, and, one might add, the sheer physical exhaustion that characterizes their existence, "innovation cannot come from the mass, at least at the beginning, except through the mediation of an elite for whom the conception implicit in human activity has already become to a certain degree a coherent and systematic ever-present awareness and a precise and decisive will."[6] This "elite" needs to conduct "a criticism of 'common sense,' basing itself initially, however, on common sense in order to demonstrate that . . . it is not a question of introducing from scratch a scientific form of thought into everyone's individual life, but of renovating and making 'critical' an already existing activity."[7] Cultural forms that can express a radical critique of society will already exist, but they are "raw" and disorganized, incapable of generating anything more than spontaneous dissatisfaction. However, when they are linked together in particular ways, their effects can be multiplied and coordinated, laying the groundwork for the reception of more critical systems of thought. This reorganization is the task of the organic intellectual. One does not bring the philosophy of praxis to the masses by reading from *Capital*. Instead, guided by more advanced philosophical systems that have been worked out in more traditional scholarly fashion, one must assemble existing cultural forms that already have some resonance with subaltern groups in prosecuting an *imma-nent* critique of their environment. In a modern context, bourgeois ideals of liberty and equality can be used to draw attention to the failure of bourgeois society to extend these ideals to more than a few. Once a basic reception to critique has been established, one can move on to more sophisticated cultural and political projects. The formation of class consciousness is not synchronic, but diachronic: it is acquired historically as the cultural forms capable of giving it expression are diffused throughout subaltern groups. For Gramsci, then, the art of radical politics resides in grafting the compelling cultural expression of existing structural contradictions (manifested through human suffering *and* collective potential) to organizational mechanisms that can diffuse such expressions in the formation of a collective will.

CULTURAL STUDIES AND ORGANICITY

While cultural studies has many antecedents, it is fair to say that Gramsci's work on the relationship between culture and hegemony as inflected through the work of the Centre for Contemporary Cultural Studies (CCCS) in Birmingham has loosely served as its dominant problematic. In an oft-quoted phrase, Tony Bennett defines cultural studies as "a fairly dispersed array of theoretical and political positions which, however widely divergent they might be in other respects, share a commitment to examining cultural practices from the point of view of their intrication with, and within, relations of power."[8] In other words, it is not simply a question of studying culture in anthropological terms, but, more specifically, looking at how culture helps sustain the dominance of oppressive social, political, and economic structures as well as to furnish the resources for individuals and groups to resist (and possibly transform) these structures. Rather than undertake the task of trying to answer the question "What is cultural studies?"[9] I will sketch out five major themes—conjuncture, totality, affect, representation, and the university—through which cultural studies might help to better grasp the possibilities and limitations of political theorizing within the university. While such themes certainly do not exhaust the field (and by no means represent an adequate political practice), I will argue that they are the key points through which cultural studies has grappled with the lingering "shadow"[10] that Gramsci's ideal of organicity casts across all academic work.

CONJUNCTURE

A guiding imperative of cultural studies has been the need to engage with those events and practices that have contemporary importance in the world beyond the academy. It does not theorize for the sake of theorizing, but in response to particular social, material, and historical conditions. As Stuart Hall notes,

> in thrusting onto the attention of scholarly reflection and critical analysis the hurly-burly of a rapidly changing, discordant and disorderly world, in insisting that academics sometimes attend to the practical life, where everyday social change exists out there, cultural studies tries in its small way to insist on what I want to call the vocation of the intellectual life. That is to say, cultural studies insists on the necessity to address the central, urgent, and disturbing questions of a society and a culture in the most rigorous intellectual way we have available.[11]

In refusing the comfortable straitjacket of the narrowly exegetical style that seems typical of much academic theorizing (i.e., writing books about books), cultural studies tries to move beyond the walls of the university by focusing upon the specific and always shifting ways in which popular cultural practices are bound up in larger social formations.[12] Cognizant of the alarming tendency of critical theory to endlessly feed upon itself, cultural studies uses its conceptual apparatus to try and explain the historical significance of events and practices that it has not itself theoretically produced. By the same token, it does not propose a crude empiricism that slavishly bases itself upon a positivist conception of the "real world." Instead, as an intellectual practice it is constantly moving back and forth between theory and human practice, refining its theoretical tools through their application to the world of popular culture. Shifting between different levels of complexity and abstraction helps to keep theory off-balance and productive, preventing its degeneration into an ossified and self-contained irrelevance. Theory does not survive unscathed from these encounters with "the real"; instead, it too is continuously and productively modified as it engages with the world outside. Indeed, Paul Willis's characterization of ethnography as preserving the possibility of "*being surprised,* of reaching knowledge not prefigured in one's starting paradigms,"[13] is a tradition that cultural studies as a whole has tried to maintain.

One of the major reasons why Gramsci focused so heavily upon cultural practices is that they gave him a window into the thoughts and feelings of nonintellectuals: in a letter written just after his imprisonment, he explained that reading commercially successful novels was interesting "if one looked at them from the following angle: why are these books always the most read and the most frequently published? What needs do they satisfy and what aspirations do they fulfill? What emotions and attitudes emerge in this squalid literature, to have such wide appeal?"[14] By focusing upon the popular, intellectuals are effectively forced to engage with the cultural forms and practices through which people experience the social, political, and economic structures in which they live. Cultural studies is rooted in an understanding of culture as the fragmented and contradictory process through which human beings actively borrow from a hodgepodge of semiotic formations to individually and collectively give meaning to and understand their world. Thus, the analysis of culture helps us to take an inventory of the most important problems and issues *as experienced and expressed by the populace.*[15] Of course, one cannot be satisfied with an inventory. Instead, cultural analysis needs to actively investigate the contradictions within and between cultural practices, probing for weaknesses in the hegemonic formation, identifying ways of bringing these contradictions to consciousness and assembling the critical fragments into a more organized reflection on the exploitative foundations of the social formation as well as its emancipatory potential. Therefore, the conjuncturalism of cultural studies, its focus upon specific cultural practices, is part of laying the groundwork for a progressive politics that meets people where they actually are, addresses the issues that they think are important, and speaks to them in a language that connects with their experience.

TOTALITY

The concept of totality occupies an extremely tenuous position in contemporary political theory, thanks in large part to the poststructuralist theorizing of French intellectuals such as Derrida, Foucault, and Lyotard. In many respects, cultural studies is no exception: inspired by the continental tradition, its texts almost always include a modest refusal of universality and totality and an insistence upon the tentative specificity of one's own work. Nevertheless, I would argue that an underlying commitment to totality is required to give cultural studies much of its critical force. In this context, totality refers to the ongoing requirement that cultural practices, forms, and events should never be analyzed in isolation from their relations with the broader social formation. Raymond Williams, frequently venerated as one of the fathers of cultural studies, insisted that culture could not be effectively understood unless its linkages with other planes of social existence were fully investigated. What made culture an interesting area of inquiry for Williams was not the isolated qualities that inhered in any particular object, but rather how cultural forms were able to capture the "structure of feeling" of certain historical periods and express how a specific social formation was actually lived and experienced. While contemporary cultural studies has moved away from Williams's notion of culture as the expressive creation of autonomous, "humanist" subjects, it has preserved his belief that critical cultural analysis must be informed by an awareness of how culture is integrated with other social practices, activities, and structures. Indeed, the most interesting work in cultural studies does not take culture per se as its object, but rather attempts to trace out its multiple effects vis-à-vis the ongoing construction, maintenance, and undermining of hegemonic systems. In order to do this, one needs to have some operational conception of the social totality in which culture operates. The broadly heuristic character of such a conception is a far cry from the ontological permanence of some of Hegel's totalitarian musings: one must challenge the wilder (and, one often suspects, rhetorical) claims of French intellectuals that see a straight line from conceptual analysis of this sort to the Gulag. Instead, cultural studies insists upon a much more fluid conception of a differentiated, constantly shifting social whole that is nevertheless theoretically necessary to prevent the analysis of discrete events and processes from falling into a simplistic cultural pluralism.

One of the most celebrated theoretical and institutional tendencies of cultural studies has been its interdisciplinary approach. When one proposes to examine the relations of culture with the social totality, the traditional tools of aesthetics no longer suffice. Instead, it is necessary to selectively draw upon many academic disciplines, bringing them into a productive cross-fertilization. As Richard Johnson explains, different cultural practices will require different techniques of investigation: "cultural processes do not correspond to the contours of academic knowledges as they are. No one academic discipline grasps the full complexity (or seriousness) of the study." [16] While the cultural practices of the shop-floor, for example, may require a "dense" ethnography to fully grasp their close relations with the physical processes of industrial production, the more discrete mediums of film and television might be more susceptible to textual analysis. It is unrealistic to expect a single discipline to harbor sufficient expertise to adequately explore the specificity of each and every cultural formation. Instead, cultural studies, "designed as a series of raids on other disciplinary terrains,"[17] employs a kind of academic pragmatism, using whatever conceptual tools it can lay its hands on to better understand its object. Such interdisciplinary pragmatism is facilitated by an openness to collective academic work: individuals with different theoretical competencies can be assembled into teams to conduct research in particular areas. In the absence of this type of approach, the study of culture can only be conducted in fragments, leading to a dangerously incomplete and dispersed understanding of the effects of cultural processes. As a case in point, witness the pessimism with which the Frankfurt School regarded mass culture: while their analysis brilliantly highlighted certain tendencies within the cultural practices of late capitalism, it also entirely missed the means by which ordinary people often use these cultural resources to resist structures of exploitation and oppression. Conversely, the naïve (fatalistic?) optimism of many contemporary cultural critics who celebrate the seemingly endless diversity of postmodern cultural formations largely fails to analyze the complicity of such formations in the reproduction of inequality and subordination.

Arguably, the most potent theoretical tool developed by cultural studies in its analysis of the relations between culture and the social formation is the concept of articulation.

> Articulation is the production of identity on top of difference, of unities out of fragments, of structures across practices. Articulation links this practice to that effect, this text to that meaning, this meaning to that reality, this experience to those politics. And these links are themselves articulated into larger structures, etc.[18]

In simple terms, articulation recognizes that while cultural practices and ideological concepts do not have any *essential* identity (i.e., one cannot say in advance that "nationalism" is either a reactionary or a progressive concept), they are always linked together with specific social formations and have specific effects. Drawing upon Gramsci's conception of "historic bloc," it refers to the (temporary) fusion of ideological concepts, cultural practices, social identities, and organizational structures into relatively fixed political formations. It allows one to recognize the specificities of different pieces of a formation while at the same time insisting that, historically, these pieces are always joined together in particular ways. In the words of Fredric Jameson, articulation thereby serves as "a punctual and sometimes even ephemeral totalization."[19] The conceptual totalities constructed through articulation are predominantly spatial, not temporal: the emphasis is less upon their origins (and teleological paths) than on the libidinal and affective flows, somatic energies, and institutional matrices that hold them together from moment to historical moment. Thus, articulation theoretically reinforces the contingent totality of real historical social formations, allowing us to analyze the fluid relations between different elements while helping to avoid the dangers of a conceptual and identitarian totalitarianism that reifies a complex reality into a singular, functional theoretical system. Indeed, the critical energies that animate cultural studies grow out of the contradictions that it discerns within the social mass, their pressures endlessly cracking and breaking the smooth face that the hegemonic culture tries to present to the world. The different components of a political or cultural formation will always already be charged with certain ideological polarities (not logically, but *historically* produced) that will, to some extent, govern their combination with other elements. Indeed, the presence of such contradictions is what drives the potential for *immanent* critique that makes possible the project of the organic intellectual in the first place. The analysis of culture contributes to this goal by looking to how cultural forms and practices can either help bring these contradictions to consciousness, or render them nonantagonistic through their suppression and the (often pathological) dispersion of their effects throughout society.

AFFECT

Part of the magic of cultural practices is how they allow people to make affective investments in particular ideological formations or semiotic systems: they help to determine how these things come to *matter* to individuals and groups. Why and how are such powerful emotional, libidinal, and somatic connections forged between certain signs and concepts and people? How are these connections articulated and organized into political formations? To find the answer, cultural studies insists that we must expand our analytic gaze beyond the traditional categories of rationality, logic, and self-interest to the field of the popular, where many of these supra- and subcognitive connections are actually made. Lawrence Grossberg, whose work explores the multiple connections between affect[20] and politics, argues that

> [t]he most obvious and perhaps the most frightening thing about contemporary popular culture is that it matters so much to so many different people. The sources of its power, whatever it may seem to say, or whatever pleasures it may offer, can be identified with its place in people's affective lives, and its ability to place other practices affectively.[21]

Ideologies do not become effective simply through the dispersal of concepts, ideas, and signs that logically express the interests of certain segments of the social formation; rather, people must actively connect themselves to one or more sites that are bound together in an affective chain such that the energy invested through one cultural practice is organized, focused, and condensed in other sites on the chain. The effectivity of signification and discourse is located within a broader social matrix in which signs and concepts must be actively and continuously made to matter.[22] In this way, ideological formations that appear logically contrary to the rational self-interest of a particular group may be passionately adopted due to their placement in a particular affective chain: it is not so much a case of "false consciousness" as it is a recognition that political identities frequently evolve in tandem with cultural processes that largely bypass the acts of cognitive assessment and evaluation that have traditionally been associated with politics per se. While it may not be in one's self-interest to support a certain ideological perspective or party (and one may even know this), such support can satisfy certain affective needs and desires (however they are constructed). The physical and emotional energies invested in sporting activities, for example, are frequently connected to symbols of national identity, making some of these energies subsequently available for political deployment in situations that are entirely unconnected, in a logical sense, to the initial site in which the investments were actually made. Thus, culture is not only political insofar as its representation of the world tends to naturalize, valorize, and reinforce certain political, economic, and social structures and practices but also as it functions to affectively "charge" them. The grounds for identification between people and power are thereby expanded beyond rational self-interest and/or naked domination into the complex and immensely productive problematic of hegemony, where individuals and groups are linked and actively link themselves into the social formation in a variety of direct and indirect ways.

These insights not only apply to a critical analysis of existing hegemonic systems, but also can help inform an organic progressive politics. In discussing the nature of the connection that must be developed between intellectuals and ordinary people, Gramsci explains that

> [t]he intellectual's error consists in believing that one can know without understanding and even more without feeling and being impassioned (not only for knowledge in itself but also for the object of knowledge): in other words that the intellectual can be an intellectual (and not a pure pedant) if distinct and separate from the people-nation, that is, without feeling the elementary passions of the people, understanding them and therefore explaining and justifying them in the particular historical situation. . . .[23]

While cultural studies can make no claim to help one "feel" the "elementary passions" of the people, it does take these passions seriously, and this knowledge can be extremely useful in understanding how to connect critical thought with popular forces to produce critical action. In this sense, cultural studies does not itself constitute an organic politics, but its theoretical and empirical insights can contribute to the development of such a politics in other social locations. One hopes that it might persuade such a politics of the need for more than simply rational persuasion ("it is in your interest to do this"), of the need to exploit the contradictions between cultural practices and political formations to displace and break up existing affective chains, and of the need to construct its own "affective commonalities"[24] so that the energies of everyday cultural life can be deployed by a progressive politics. Gilles Deleuze and Felix Guattari insist that "Hitler got the fascists sexually aroused. Flags, nations, armies, banks get a lot of people aroused. A revolutionary machine is nothing if it does not acquire at least as much force as those coercive machines have for producing breaks and mobilizing flows [of affect]."[25] Finally, these insights need to be applied as much to academics as to any other social group. Just as we can recognize the futility of using rational argument alone to persuade an individual to adopt a progressive politics, we must similarly attend to the very real limitations that exist in using abstract arguments to convince academics to change their own practices. Such arguments need to be supplemented with suggestions as to how certain practices can be made more interesting, more fulfilling, and (dare one say it) more fun. Ethnography, interdisciplinarity, collective work, and accessible discourse, for example, are all potential contributors to a more organic intellectual practice: we need to ask what cultural and institutional supports have to evolve to create communities that facilitate affective as well as intellectual commitments to these activities.

REPRESENTATION

For a variety of historical reasons, including the anarchic struggles of the late 1960s in the West, the wide variety of decolonization movements in the Third World, and the rise of so-called "identity politics," the practice of representation stands in considerable disrepute on the Left. Many critical intellectuals have become extremely sensitive to both the (discursive) violence of representation and the capacity of subaltern groups to speak for themselves, as was perhaps most directly expressed in a 1972 conversation between Foucault and Deleuze:

> [In May 1968], the intellectual discovered that the masses no longer need him to gain knowledge: they *know* perfectly well, without illusion; they know far better than he and they are certainly capable of expressing themselves. . . . The intellectual's role is no longer to place himself "somewhat ahead and to the side" in order to express the stifled truth of the collectivity; rather, it is to struggle against the forms of power that transform him into its object and instrument in the sphere of "knowledge," "truth," "consciousness," and "discourse."[26]

While they would entirely disagree with the initial reasoning in this quote, members of the Frankfurt School similarly warn against attempts to construct any direct, representative relationship with "the masses."[27] In this sense, both Foucault and Adorno flip Gramsci's metaphor of organicity on its head: the main task of a critical thinker is actually to *avoid* becoming an organic intellectual "for the other side," where one's work (intentionally or otherwise) comes to actively reproduce structures of power and domination. These views have been subject to penetrating criticism from a number of quarters,[28] and I have no desire to rehearse those arguments here. Instead, I want to make one or two suggestions as to how cultural studies can help us to think a bit more critically about the question of representation.

In the first place, the possibility of an organic relationship between intellectuals and nonintellectuals problematizes the singular, totalitarian critique of representation that one often finds in contemporary theory. The metaphor of organicity introduces a historical dialectic into the relation of representation such that its success (and desirability) becomes predicated on the extent to which the people become more or less active in determining how they are represented and which issues are of greatest importance to them. In somewhat different terms, Gramsci argues that in "the formation of leaders, one premise is fundamental: is it the intention that there should always be rulers and ruled, or is the objective to create the conditions in which this division is no longer necessary?"[29] Not all kinds of authority are equally rigid and oppressive, nor do they all construct similar relations of dependence: instead, a critical theory of intellectuals needs to recognize how organic relations permit the construction of an authority that is fluid, tentative, and dialogic, but still preserves the mediation that is required for the intellectual to *critically* represent a particular constituency. In other words, we cannot so easily dismiss the privileges of our own social location and avoid the responsibility of using it to tactically amplify and translate the voices of those who have been silenced. Conversely, our institutional location gives us a rather unique vantage point with sufficient distance from the hurly-burly of the everyday to reflect upon and analyze the effectivity of oppositional practices and resistances vis-à-vis the larger social totality, its contradictions, and the ever-present possibilities for emancipation that lie within it.

Cultural studies can contribute to an organic representative practice in at least two specific ways. First, it can deploy a range of investigative tools, from ethnography to textual analysis, to help recover the experience of those subaltern groups that do not have adequate means to express themselves beyond their own communities.[30] The pioneering work of E. P. Thompson in *The Making of the English Working Class*[31] remains one of the best examples of how such work can not only rescue from mnemonic oblivion the physical history and cultural forms of oppressed groups, but also deploy this memory to break up the hegemony of dominant historical narratives, thereby helping to establish creative spaces in which to envision alternative trajectories. In this case, Thompson's history restores both the massive suffering that lies hidden at the origins of capitalism (shattering its mythic origins in mutually beneficial exchange and the peaceful drive for industrious efficiency) and the molecular agency that helped make a class. It shows how cultural studies can be a potent weapon in both the "insurrection of subjugated knowledges" [32] and the ongoing struggle of critical historical inquiry to "brush history against the grain." [33] The recovery of historical experience alone is clearly not an adequate form of representation, and yet it also seems clear that such efforts can and must be a part of any kind of organic relationship. Given the importance of culture in how individuals experience their world, cultural studies is uniquely placed to make these experiences available as a cultural resource not only to subaltern groups that may have had their past taken from them (or forgotten it themselves), but also to other individuals and groups that have been similarly embedded in structures of exploitation and oppression.

Second, and closely related to this last point, cultural studies can help translate subaltern experiences that are normally expressed in a particular, localized cultural medium into other cultural forms in order to promote linkages (cultural, social, and political) between different groups and individuals that might not otherwise be able to share their experiences. It is an open secret that the culture industries help sustain the hegemony of liberal democratic capitalism by bleaching out, displacing, and otherwise sublimating the subversive emotions and critical sentiments that are frequently generated by the physical, emotional, and cognitive experience of exploitation. Drawing upon the "raw materials" of the hegemonic culture, subaltern groups frequently develop creative and highly complex cultural subsystems to express, reflect upon, and often mythically resolve the painful contradictions of their everyday lives. Nevertheless, these critical subcultures remain isolated and marginalized insofar as the capacities for communication between them are neutralized. Cultural studies can use its unique institutional location and research tools to explore and translate the similarities between different groups that are embedded in broadly equivalent structures of domination and engaged in similar practices of resistance. As a host of critical theorists have pointed out, liberal capitalism functions in part by individualizing its subjects, isolating them from each other, and reconstituting them in groups, such as "the nation," that are hospitable to its own ends. Cultural studies can help fight this process, translating the experience of exploitation into common languages for widespread dissemination as well as into more specific cultural forms that will have resonance within particular communities, and thereby participate in the construction of networks of organized, united, and counterhegemonic resistances.

THE UNIVERSITY

At a 1990 conference titled "Cultural Studies Now and in the Future," Stuart Hall warned that the institutionalization of cultural studies within universities constituted a "moment of profound danger."[34] In recent years, many in the field have come to echo this sentiment, arguing that such integration dulls the critical edge of cultural studies: no longer "surprised" by the world outside the academy (indeed, rarely even venturing outside its walls), it has ossified into a disciplinary formation like all others, feeding upon itself at conferences and in specialized journals with a theoretical jargon incomprehensible to the uninitiated.[35] Leaving aside the self-disciplinary pleasures that always lurk behind such self-deprecation, there is clearly much truth in this diagnosis. But having alluded to it, my intention is not to wallow in this (ritualized) confession of theoretical decadence. Instead, I want to explore one or two suggestions offered up by cultural studies for how we might think about and respond to the problems of institutionalization.

One very simple suggestion offered by cultural studies to counteract the isolation of contemporary academia is to work collectively, and preferably within an interdisciplinary context. Rather than dividing intellectual work along traditional disciplinary boundaries, one might flexibly gather academics with complementary areas of expertise together into investigative teams that research specific issues and problems. Hall describes early efforts at the CCCS as an "attempt to make intellectual work more collective in the actual forms of practising: to constitute research and groups of projects and studies around working collectives rather than serial groups of competing intellectuals, carrying their very own thesis topics like batons in their knapsacks."[36] What such individuals would share is not necessarily a common methodology or set of skills, but a commitment to an emancipatory theoretical practice. In addition to their research benefits, such practices also have organizational consequences insofar as they facilitate the formation of broad critical subcultures within and between universities. These networks can anchor critical interventions into the public sphere; facilitate the exchange of information and analysis between different countries, intellectuals, activists, and social organizations (e.g., unions, social movements, etc.); and provide resources with which to resist the increasing corporatization, "rationalization," and downsizing of universities themselves. Such collective practices are particularly important at the graduate-student level: therapeutically, they would help to counteract the massive isolation in which most of us complete our research; patterns of conduct (i.e., interdisciplinarity, collective habits, etc.) and relationships established at this time might serve as a foundation for future intellectual work (and might help resist or deflect integrative pressures later in one's career); and the diverse backgrounds of many graduate students have the potential to make this an extremely productive exercise. I am not saying that we ought to do away with individual intellectual work, but that its supplementation with collective efforts is relatively easy to accomplish and might yield some important achievements vis-à-vis an emancipatory political practice.

Much of the original pressure for British cultural studies emerged out of the extramural adult education conducted by socialist intellectuals such as Thompson, Williams, and Richard Hoggart in postwar Britain. It is fair to say that cultural studies continues to devote more attention to the pedagogical relation than most other "critical" academic disciplines. Again, Hall's words frame the issue nicely:

> We talk about intellectual practice as if it is the practice of intellectuals in the library reading the right canonical texts or consulting other intellectuals at conferences or something like that. But the ongoing work of an intellectual practice for most of us, insofar as we get our material sustenance, our modes of reproduction, from doing our academic work, is indeed to teach.[37]

The most important contribution that cultural studies makes to pedagogy is its insistence that any kind of critical education must be rooted in the culture, experience, and knowledge that students bring to the classroom. This is not to call for a naïve celebration of popular cultural forms with students, nor to convert the educational process into a cathartic and empowering expression of "subaltern" emotions and thoughts that can find no outlet in mass culture. The classroom is *not* the place where the perfect democracy or ideal speech situation can be modeled: "Rather than empowering students to express their opinions, it seems more important to give them information and skills that allow them to gather information from disparate sources, analyze it, and formulate informed evaluations, since critical thought involves understanding where 'opinions' come from in the first place."[38] Critical pedagogy involves bringing to consciousness the contradictions that people experience in their everyday lives but do not necessarily understand as contradictions. It tries to use the frustrations and pleasures of everyday life in the hopes of motivating students to acquire some rudimentary critical skills with which to think differently about those parts of their world that matter to them. Finally, cultural studies does not understand the pedagogical relation as a linear, one-way exchange: instead, intellectuals also need to see their students as a resource for continually engaging with the shifting cultural terrain of the social formation, refining the accessibility and relevance of their own ideas, and evaluating the organicity of their own theoretical practice.

For Gramsci, a crucial component of organicity is the evaluation of intellectual activity based upon its effect, function, and relations with other social processes rather than simply on its intrinsic value. In short, it demands some kind of individual and collective self-reflexivity. Carol Stabile argues that "such agency as we have must be contextualized and understood within the limits imposed by the institution. *Agency begins only at the point at which we recognize and think critically about these limits.*"[39] Only by evaluating our own activity in this way—by considering its limits and its possibilities both within and beyond the university—can we begin to understand how it might be modified to better contribute to a broadly based emancipatory politics. In this sense, we do well to remind ourselves of the fears of Foucault and Adorno: the organic intellectual is not merely a normative ideal to strive for, but also a critical concept through which to diagnose our own complicity in domination as well as the reproduction of hegemonic patterns within our own institutions. What Foucault, Gramsci, and the Frankfurt School share is a rejection of Mannheim's "free-floating intellectuals" as an ideological category that simply passes over the contradictions between the possibilities for creative autonomy that linger within academic work and its continual integration and subordination within advanced capitalism. Despite its frequent one-sided deployment, Gramsci developed his concept of the organic intellectual as much to criticize the Crocean fantasies of autonomy used by traditional intellectuals to justify their self-isolation from political struggle as to articulate the need for a particular kind of relation between intellectuals and subaltern groups. While the self-reflexivity of cultural studies is most often no more than formulaic, this recognition at least opens the way for more substantive investigations into the effects of institutionalization. Moreover, the techniques that it has developed to analyze the effects of specific cultural formations and practices can easily be turned against itself to trace the connections between its own work and other structures.

Without question, the easiest target for anyone questioning the relevance of critical academic work is the raw incomprehensibility of most theoretical discourse. There cannot be many, even (or, perhaps, especially) among those who specialize in these fields, who have not felt their frustration boil up into anger at the monstrous discourse employed by many academics. This is not to say that there are not persuasive arguments to justify difficult and abstract language: Adorno, for example, defended a density that was both stylistic and substantive insofar as it should be truth, not communication as such, that should be the test of academic rigor; he also believed that such language, like the dissonant atonality of high modern art, helped resist the (mis)appropriation of such work by the identitarian, one-dimensional, and instrumentalized conceptual systems of late capitalism. But the somber call for "negative dialectics" rings a bit hollow in the face of the integration of critical theory into the bourgeois university, particularly when the comfortable lives of its (tenured) inhabitants contrast so vividly with the growing poverty, violence, and misery scattered outside. Instead, I think we need to take a different approach to accessibility, guided by the proposition that the effects of critical theorizing will be fatally circumscribed unless it somehow connects with those outside its own communities.[40] Admittedly, the complexities of contemporary theory offer unique ways of thinking about the world that simply cannot be reproduced in the often one-dimensional language of mass culture. However, I do think it is incumbent upon communities of critical intellectuals to try and translate some of their ideas into a form that can be more commonly understood. Moreover, such efforts will only succeed if they are instantiated within specific institutional practices: as noted above, interdisciplinary teams and seminars might be a good place to start trying to express one's theoretical work such that those from other disciplines are able to understand and use it; classroom situations, graduate and undergraduate, furnish different opportunities to communicate one's ideas in ways that make them both interesting and relevant for others; and workgroups dedicated to public writing and speaking, as well as formal structures for liaising with activists from other communities, can also help the dissemination of ideas beyond the academy. These are but a few suggestions for how we might start to cultivate an increasing accessibility to our own discursive products. Such processes do not only help disseminate critical theory, but, as I noted above, this shifting back and forth between different levels of complexity and abstraction can also help generate better theory. The incestuous, self-contained environment of academia weakens critical theory: frequent repetition of the same concepts, ideas, and conclusions in a context that never changes cannot but weaken the capacity for critical reflection. The dangers of instrumentalism notwithstanding, I think it does an academic good to have to explain terms like "deconstruction," "relative autonomy," "cultural formation," and "dialectic" to someone who does not already know what they mean. It helps reduce the conceptual slippage and logical sloppiness that can be so easily hidden in the dense thickets of theoretical discourse.

CONCLUDING THOUGHTS

"[W]e live in a utopia in which loss has been systematized," observes Sheldon Wolin, "a utopia whose existence depends symbiotically on the perpetuation of dystopia."[41] His artful shift from vocation to invocation strategically positions loss as a critical concept through which one might rethink how contemporary academia is both intertwined with such a dynamic and yet might also adapt so as to challenge it. At first glance, Wolin's call for invocation might sit rather uneasily with my own advocacy of cultural studies as offering a set of valuable resources to political theorists; few intellectual fields, for instance, offer more compelling evidence of the metamorphosis of critical into descriptive or normal theory. As I have tried to argue, however, the juxtaposition of Gramsci's organic intellectual with the tools of cultural studies opens up important new terrain to political theory. The systematization of loss that Wolin identifies is, to a great extent, presided over and managed by the cultural industries of liberal capitalism. Neither the utopia (though I use this term guardedly) nor the dystopias of which Wolin speaks are exclusively produced through cultural means, but their peculiar (and ongoing) fusion into a postmodern hegemony is a practice in which culture is a dominant participant. As the consequences of such a hegemonic formation spill over into politics, we, as theorists of the political, ignore the sphere of culture at our peril.

Moreover, it is not only as prophets of doom that our attention ought to be directed this way. The affective, somatic, and libidinal investments that give such strength to this hegemony simultaneously contain—if only as a shadowy absence—the desires, imagination, and creative resources that are the very lifeblood of political theory. If the dreams that once made "the political" their home have not entirely abandoned it, they have surely taken up residence elsewhere. Indeed, in the face of the disembodied, narcissistic self-indulgence that Wolin identifies as masquerading as politics these days,[42] it has perhaps never been more appropriate for political theorists to expand their gaze to other forms of social life. Finally, attending to the cultural forms and practices (hegemonic and otherwise) through which most people give expression to their hopes, fears, and dreams (or lack thereof) can help counteract our own self-positioning in the phantasmagoric world of "permanent revolution."[43] But it is not only cultural studies that has lessons for us to learn; rather, it is in the many points of contact between cultural studies and political theory that one constellation of the organic intellectual may be traced. Following Wolin, I would argue that political theorizing has the unique capacity (among secular disciplines) to conceptualize loss not simply as a ubiquitous and irrevocable element of human existence, but as inaugurating the potential for redemption, as "the gathering point of dystopia."[44] My point is not that we ought to lay down our tools as political theorists and exchange them for the shiny new toys that have been forged in yet another enclave of the university. Rather, it is that cultural studies makes available vital theoretical, analytical, and even empirical resources that serve us well in the pursuit of our own unique vocation.

NOTES

An earlier version of this paper was presented at the "Vocations of Political Theory" conference at Johns Hopkins University, February 27–28, 1998. I would like to thank John Tambornino, Jason Frank, and Sean Saraka for their helpful comments on earlier drafts. I would also like to acknowledge the generous financial support provided by the Social Sciences and Humanities Research Council of Canada.

1. Editorial Collective, "Editorial," *New Left Review* 1 (January–February 1960): 1, as cited in Tony Bennett, "The Politics of the 'Popular' and Popular Culture," in *Popular Culture and Social Relations,* ed. Tony Bennett, Colin Mercer, and Janet Woollacott (Philadelphia: Open University Press, 1986), 10.

2. In reflecting upon the origins of cultural studies at the Centre for Contemporary Cultural Studies in Birmingham, for example, Stuart Hall claimed that "there is no doubt in my mind that we were trying to find an institutional practice in cultural studies that might produce an organic intellectual." See Stuart Hall, "Cultural Studies and Its Theoretical Legacies," in *Cultural Studies,* ed. Lawrence Grossberg, Cary Nelson, and Paula Treichler (New York: Routledge, 1992), 281.

3. Sheldon Wolin, "Political Theory as a Vocation," *American Political Science Review* 63, no.4 (1969): 1080.

4. Antonio Gramsci, *Selections from the Prison Notebooks,* ed. and trans. Quintin Hoare and Geoffrey Nowell Smith (New York: International Publishers, 1971), 8.

5. Ibid., 5.

6. Ibid., 335.

7. Ibid., 330–31.

8. Tony Bennett, "Putting Policy in Cultural Studies," in *Cultural Studies,* ed. Lawrence Grossberg, Cary Nelson, and Paula Treichler (New York: Routledge, 1992), 23.

9. On this question, see Stuart Hall, "Cultural Studies and the Centre: Some Problematics and Problems," in *Culture, Media, Language,* ed. Stuart Hall, Dorothy Hobson, Andrew Lowe, and Paul Willis (New York: Routledge, 1980); Richard Johnson, "What Is Cultural Studies Anyway?" *Social Text* 16 (Winter 1987); and Ioan Davies, *Cultural Studies and Beyond* (New York: Routledge, 1995).

10. Hall, "Cultural Studies," 288.

11. Stuart Hall, "Race, Culture and Communications: Looking Backward and Forward at Cultural Studies," *Rethinking Marxism* 5, no. 1 (Spring 1992): 11.

12. On the tendencies of contemporary theory toward "overtheoretization," see Sheldon Wolin, "Political Theory: From Vocation to Invocation."

13. Cited in Rosalind Brunt, "Engaging with the Popular: Audiences for Mass Culture and What to Say about Them," in *Cultural Studies,* ed. Lawrence Grossberg, Cary Nelson, and Paula Treichler (New York: Routledge, 1992), 71.

14. Antonio Gramsci, *Selections from Cultural Writings,* ed. David Forgacs and Geoffrey Nowell-Smith, trans. William Boelhower (Cambridge: Harvard University Press, 1985), 342.

15. These remarks should not be taken to indicate a belief that culture somehow constitutes the pure and untrammeled desires of the population at large. Cultural studies has moved away from the expressive culturalist tradition (in which culture was understood as issuing forth from centered autonomous subjects or groups of subjects) to a recognition that cultural formations construct their subjects as much as they are constructed by them. Nevertheless, cultural studies does believe that human agents are capable of an active relationship with cultural formations and, consequently, these relations are among the best places to look in order to understand the various thoughts, emotions, sensibilities, and so forth of the people (or any of its various fragments) at any one time.

16. Johnson, "What Is Cultural Studies Anyway?" 42.

17. Stuart Hall, "The Emergence of Cultural Studies and the Crisis of the Humanities," *October* 53 (Summer 1990): 16.

18. Lawrence Grossberg, *We Gotta Get Out of This Place* (New York: Routledge, 1992), 54.

19. Frederic Jameson, "On Cultural Studies," *Social Text* 34 (1993): 32.

20. My discussion of affect is largely inspired by Larry Grossberg's work in this area.

21. Grossberg, *We Gotta Get Out of This Place,* 80.

22. Grossberg, for example, notes that "affect has a real power over difference, a power to invest difference and to make certain differences matter in different ways. If ideology (and even pleasure) constitute structures of difference, these structures are unrealized without their inflection through an affective economy. For it is affect which enables some differences (e.g., race, gender, etc.) to matter as markers of identity rather than others (e.g., foot length, angle of ears, eye color) in certain contexts." Ibid., 105.

23. Gramsci, *The Prison Notebooks,* 418.

24. Grossberg, *We Gotta Get Out of This Place,* 393.

25. Cited in ibid., 394.

26. "Intellectuals and Power: A Conversation between Michel Foucault and Gilles Deleuze," in *Language, Counter-memory, Practice,* ed. Donald Bouchard (Ithaca: Cornell University Press, 1977), 207–8.

27. For Adorno's most concise exploration of intellectual responsibility, see his "Commitment," in *The Essential Frankfurt School Reader,* ed. Andrew Arato and Eike Gebhardt (New York: Continuum, 1992).

28. On Foucault/Deleuze, see Gyatri Spivak, "Can the Subaltern Speak?" in *Marxism and the Interpretation of Culture,* ed. Cary Nelson and Lawrence Grossberg (Urbana: University of Illinois Press, 1988); on Adorno, see Ben Agger, *The Discourse of Domination: From the Frankfurt School to Postmodernism* (Evanston, Ill.: Northwestern University Press, 1992).

29. Gramsci, *The Prison Notebooks,* 144.

30. In part, this speaks to Wolin's discussion of "invocation." See Wolin, "Political Theory: From Vocation to Invocation."

31. E. P. Thompson, *The Making of the English Working Class* (New York: Penguin Books, 1991).

32. Michel Foucault, "Two Lectures," in *Power/Knowledge,* ed. Colin Gordon (New York: Routledge, 1980), 78.

33. Walter Benjamin, "Theses on the Philosophy of History," in *Illuminations,* ed. Hannah Arendt, trans. Harry Zohn (New York: Schocken Books, 1969), 257.

34. Hall, "Cultural Studies," 285.

35. The most famous critique of an overly jargonistic and academicized Left is Russell Jacoby's *The Last Intellectuals* (New York: Basic Books, 1987).

36. Hall, "Cultural Studies and the Centre," 44.

37. Hall, "Cultural Studies and Its Theoretical Legacies," 290.

38. Carol Stabile, "Politics, Pedagogy and Political Struggle," in *Class Issues: Pedagogy, Cultural Studies and the Public Sphere,* ed. Amitva Kumar (New York: New York University Press, 1997), 213.

39. Ibid., 211.

40. Ben Agger, "Theorizing the Decline of Discourse or the Decline of Theoretical Discourse?" in *Critical Theory Now,* ed. Philip Wexler (New York: Falmer Press, 1991).

41. Wolin, "Political Theory: From Vocation to Invocation," 16.

42. Ibid., 11.

43. Ibid., 20.

44. Ibid., 20.

PART VI

PRACTICING POLITICAL THEORY

11 // READING THE BODY

Hobbes, Body Politics, and the Vocation of Political Theory

In his remonstrances against those methods-oriented scholars who would "impoverish the past by making it appear like the present," Sheldon Wolin declares that "one reads past theories, not because they are familiar and therefore confirmative, but because they are strange and therefore provocative."[1] In the course of his eloquent and pointed portrayal of the call to political theory in "Political Theory as a Vocation," Wolin charges political theorists with the task of working against the conformism that attends the confinement of the political world within the boundaries of the familiar. He bids them to reject and position themselves against the accommodationist mentality that he believes is facilitated by the rising dominance of behaviorist methodologies in the study of politics. In his recounting, political theorists are animated by a sense of justice, by a sense that there is something "systematically mistaken" in current political relationships (Wolin, 1080). Their task is to unsettle received understandings of the right-orderedness of politics, to "reassemble the whole political world" in an unfamiliar way, and to do so through an imaginative engagement with the tradition of political theory (1078).

Wolin's portrait of political theorists as purveyors of the heterodox stands in tension with his own recognition of the importance of tacit political knowledge to the task of redescribing the political world. Tacit political knowledge, he argues, is a "complex framework of sensibilities built up unpremeditatedly" and upon which we draw in our reflective inquiries (1071). It comprises a broad tradition of understanding and "tells us what is appropriate to a subject and when a subject-matter is being violated or respected by a particular theory or hypothesis" (1071). Jacques Derrida appears to concur with Wolin in his suggestion that tacit political knowledge is crucial to the vocation of the political theorist. He points out that any interpretation of a political event or a text involves the production and affirmation of consensus.[2] Indeed, in Derrida's analysis, what makes a given interpretation recognizable to others as a commentary on a common text is a reliance upon a "minimal consensus" about what makes a text intelligible or comprehensible. What enables different interpretations to circulate in critical interchange is an implicit agreement that constitutes and stabilizes the "norms of minimal intelligibility" (Derrida, 147). Such norms establish what is to be taken as axiomatic by those engaged in interpretive practices; they serve as a common ground upon which exegesis, analysis, and criticism take place. Wolin's approbation of both the unfamiliar and the tacitly known suggests that if political theorists are to engage in what he calls "fundamental criticism" (Wolin, 1068) rather than merely rearrange the theoretical possibilities provided by extant political relationships, we must engage in a certain amount of self-reflection regarding the commonplaces that make our provocations comprehensible to others. If we are indeed to find unexpected resources in the tradition of political theory, if we are to find texts or figures strange and strangely useful in our critical endeavors, we must be willing to question the "connotative context" and the "supporting folklore," the "stock of ideas" and the "cultural resources" that together constitute the tacit background knowledge that enables us to engage with one another (1071, 1073).

Such tacit political knowledge, such norms of minimal intelligibility, are precisely what are at stake and reaffirmed in many interpretations of Thomas Hobbes's political theory. Hobbes forwards what Richard Flathman has termed a "metaphysical materialism."[3] The analytical starting point of his entire political philosophy is the axiom that "The World, (I mean not the Earth onely, that denominates the Lovers of it Worldly men, but the Universe, that is, the whole masse of all things that are) is Corporeall, that is to say, Body."[4] Everything that exists is matter: There is nothing else. This materialist metaphysics forms the basis of Hobbes's account of human nature, subjectivity, ethics, and politics. Indeed, in his view, it must, for "the principles of the politics consist in knowledge of the motions of the mind, and the knowledge of these motions from the knowledge of sense and imagination," which in turn require knowledge of "the first part of philosophy, namely, geometry and physics."[5] While Wolin castigates Hobbes for the scientism and despotism that he believes is inseparable from the latter's materialist account of human nature, the fact that Hobbes develops his theory of political subjectivity from the principles of his metaphysical materialism is not widely incorporated into our common understandings of his work.[6] Quite to the contrary: Many of Hobbes's interpreters disparage his illogic and philosophical impropriety in forwarding a metaphysical materialism, and deny that it has any relevance at all for his political thinking. What in Wolin's work takes the form of a politically inspired intervention in the name of critical reflection and political imagination is, in the work of many of his contemporaries, a dismissive excision undertaken for the sake of theoretical orthodoxy.

In the charged political context of the 1960s, Wolin protested against the increasingly popular presumption that behaviorism is the next step in a smoothly progressive tradition concerned with the attainment of political knowledge (Wolin, 1077). In the course of his disputation, he forwards an alternative to the impoverished accounts of politics issued by behaviorist political scientists. In doing so, he implicitly draws an "anti-behaviorist" picture of the political subject—an acculturated, self-reflective, engaged, and principled actor. However, in a peculiar twist of iteration and application, the original contestatory impetus that found expression in his words has taken on a more conservative tone. Wolin's counterstance to behaviorism has calcified into a broader consensus that defines the limits of intelligibility in theoretical interpretation and squelches the curious before it can be appreciated. That is, the political moment that marks his challenge to the growing influence of behaviorist accounts of politics has transformed, in the work of many of Hobbes's interpreters, into a set of theoretical truths that define and delimit what is appropriate for analysis. The characteristics of political subjectivity that Wolin counterposes to behaviorist versions have been abridged, deracinated, and more definitively rearticulated as simple, self-evident fact; they have become a commonplace in political theoretical interpretation, deposited in the domain of ontology, and invoked to domesticate Hobbes's materialist metaphysics. In short, academic politics have so affected the practice of political theory that political theorists are wary of any kind of metaphysical materialism: Because they find it difficult to conceive of a materialism that is not also a deterministic behaviorism, they react against Hobbes's metaphysical materialism and write it out of political existence.

BODY POLITICS

Hobbes's effort to develop an ethical and political theory by reasoning from physics and physiology does not sit well with many of his interpreters.[7] In fact, his metaphysical materialism has incited, among his critics, an extraordinary admixture of ad hominem attacks and charges of rash and bungling logic.[8] Many of these refusals to countenance what has been called Hobbes's "monstrous piece of metaphysics" center on what is considered his perverse mixing of categories (Peters and Tajfel, 180). "Reality," his critics charge, is characterized by clear distinctions between the mind and the body, and between the concepts and the language appropriate to talking about each: Since mind and body are ontologically distinct categories, they cannot correctly be conceived as equivalent. As one critic put his objection, "Structural features of one realm of reality cannot be derived by deducing them from the characteristic features of another realm."[9] Mind and body, psychology and physiology, are simply different features of reality: The substance and activity of the mind cannot be derived from the workings of the body because they are logically and phenomenologically distinct.[10] To accept this is to accept an incontrovertible fact. To assert anything to the contrary is absurdity.[11] And so, in what is deemed his "dubious or trivial" application of scientific terms to human behavior, Hobbes is charged with failing "to see what later generations have called 'philosophical problems' in moving from physiology to psychology" (Peters, 94–95).

The hyperbole inspired by what is seen as Hobbes's improper commingling of metaphysical categories suggests that his materialism, and more specifically the account of subjectivity that he derives from it, represents a crisis that must somehow be contained or overcome if his political theory is to be recognized as making sense. Indeed, the problem posed by Hobbes's metaphysics is so dire that his readers are compelled to correct or rehabilitate his political theory, to act as if Hobbes meant to leave the "erroneous," materialist parts out—or, more accurately, to perform that omission in his stead. So, for example, Watkins attributes to Hobbes a desire for logical rigor, points out the utter impossibility of talking about physiology and psychology in the same breath, and surmises, generously, that "Hobbes must have made a fresh start when he turned from nature to psychology" (Watkins, 238). What is at stake in such interpretations? In their appeal to the brute reality of the distinction between the mind and the body, Hobbes's critics attempt to dispel the specter of behaviorism that is raised by his metaphysical materialism. It is a behaviorist threat to a "commonsense" notion of political subjectivity that they effectively head off in their efforts to make better sense of his theory of politics.

Many objections to Hobbes's materialist metaphysics are formulated around the conviction that the only theory of subjectivity he could derive from it would deprive individuals of political agency. According to his wary readers, voluntary action is action that is self-consciously directed toward a particular goal; it is action with an intention and purpose informed by desire and belief. As Bernard Gert contends, "To have a motive for doing an action entails both that one have some belief and that he regard this belief as his reason for doing that action."[12] But if, as they see it, Hobbes insists that mind is really body and therefore not mind at all, his subject cannot be understood as possessing a mind, cannot be conceived as having beliefs, and consequently cannot be imagined as having motives for action.[13] Indeed, the kind of subject ostensibly implied by Hobbes's materialist metaphysics cannot be self-directing, cannot self-consciously or deliberately initiate action.[14] In these worried accounts of Hobbes's work, all that such subjects would be capable of is reacting to the stimuli around them (Peters and Tajfel, 182). In other words, to grant Hobbes's materialism would also be to grant that human action is determined by forces external to the subject (Peters, 168). What underlies the repudiation of Hobbes's metaphysical materialism by political theorists is the sense that he makes it impossible to conceive of individuals as the origin of their own action. The political concern cloaked in the rigors of logic and ontology is the fear that Hobbes might condemn us to a crude stimulus-response model of politics.

Ostensibly in defense of the self-evidence of the categorical distinctions he purportedly violates, Hobbes's critics engage in what amounts to a collective rewriting of his political theory. By variously excising or correcting for his materialist metaphysics, Hobbes's critics read the distinction between the mind and the body into his philosophy and amend his account of the subject. By making recourse to reportedly unassailable philosophical principle, they reconstitute and reconfirm an implicit consensus about what political subjects are and what constitutes the parameters of political action. What emerges from these wrangles with Hobbes's materialism is the iconographic "Hobbesian subject *qua* rational actor," the self-interested, instrumentally oriented egoist who springs to mind with the invocation of Hobbes's name. As one commentator describes this familiar figure, "All that is postulated" by Hobbes "is a reasoning being having a number of objectives and in a context with similar beings" (McNeilly, 165). Although scholarly tracts differ in their elaboration of what happens to such individuals in Hobbes's political theory, this figure of the rational actor serves as a commonplace in our theoretical imaginations, provoking knowing nods of recognition in academic and even in popular discourse. And of course, what is important about such Hobbesian individuals is that they make a *decision* to enter into a political compact with one another: They recognize the danger in the anticipatory violence in which they each engage in order to forestall the attacks that any reasonable person can assume will transpire.[15] They comprehend that danger, and in order to ameliorate it, each makes a rational decision to participate in a political covenant with everyone else, each voluntarily submits to a sovereign who will ensure their mutual compliance to the rule of law.[16] A rational political actor; a rationalist account of the constitution of political order.

What is so distinctive and problematic about such readings of Hobbes is the conceptualization of the cognitive processes involved in social and political interaction. Within such rationalist interpretations of Hobbes, each individual is construed as a statistically inclined political strategist who confronts a field of possibilities and mentally tests the advantages and disadvantages of different courses of action.[17] The decision whether to engage with others is a deliberate, intellectual one, and in some interpretations is described as the result of mathematical operations involving the presumed intentions of all the so-called players.[18] The decision to covenant is a thoughtful, meditative resolution that individuals make prior to political engagement, and therefore abstracted from a particular social and political context. In short, the account of political action proffered by such interpretations entails modeling imaginary antagonists who have no social ties or affective histories and whose social interactions are guided solely by self-reflective and rational considerations informed by conscious desires.[19] So, while many rationalist readings of Hobbes's political theory may represent a political achievement in the face of the pretensions of behaviorist political scientists, they are also somewhat bothersome: When Hobbes's critics contrive to make his political theory logical and coherent within the terms of their engagement, when their rationalist readings reference and sustain such a "commonsense" notion of political subjectivity, they consolidate an understanding of politics as instrumental action undertaken by socially disaffected individuals. By extension, and quite against the political impetus originally behind such theoretical interventions, they promote a cynical apathy vis-à-vis the political status quo. That is to say, in making the political world and Hobbes's political theory conform to the requirements of intelligibility that attend a rationalist conception of the subject, they end up defending a vision of politics that works against their apparent commitment to ethical and deliberative political action. Indeed, and perhaps ironically, the logic in such rationalist renditions of political action has been condensed and extended to develop a theoretical methodism that has displaced behaviorism as the veritable science of political behavior: [20] The "Hobbesian subject *qua* rational actor" has been a pivotal figure in the rational-choice and game-theoretic approaches to the study of politics, approaches that have reduced politics to action that can be quantified, rendered in formulas, and illustrated in mathematical graphs.

Contrary to what has become a commonplace in our political theoretical imaginations, Hobbes does not forward a rationalist account of political subjectivity or politics. Neither does he propound a variant of the Cartesian dualism whose suppositions undergird the rationalist readings of his work. In fact, Hobbes positions himself against the "gross errors" of metaphysicians who, "because they can conceive of thought without the consideration of body, . . . infer there is no need of a thinking-body" (DCP, 3, 34).[21] He rails against what Michael Oakeshott describes as the hypostatization of the activity of thinking, arguing that it is wrong to promote belief in "Abstract Essences, and Substantiall Formes" (L, 46, 689).[22] Indeed, in a protestation that is obviously directed against Cartesian, religious, and Aristotelian conceptions of thought, Hobbes exclaims that many people, "not knowing what Imagination, or the Senses are," perpetuate errors in their teaching:

> Some saying, that Imaginations rise of themselves, and have no cause: Others that they rise most commonly from the Will; and that Good thoughts are blown (inspired) into a man, by God; and Evill thoughts by the Divell; or that Good thoughts are powred (infused) into a man, by God, and Evill ones by the Divell. Some say the Senses receive Species of things, and deliver them to the Common-sense; and the Common Sense delivers them over to the Fancy, and the Fancy to the Memory, and the Memory to the Judgement, like the handing of things from one to another, with many words making nothing understood [L, 2, 93].

For Hobbes, thought is neither autogenetic, a whispered inspiration from God, nor an infusion from the devil. Thoughts are not "species of things" or entities that can be transferred and bandied about. In his account, "the Original" of all thoughts "is that which we call Sense; (For there is no conception in a mans mind, which hath not at first, totally, or by parts, been begotten upon the organs of Sense)" (L, 1, 85). In a claim that confounds a tidy distinction between mind and body, Hobbes declares that perception and thought are an operation of physical movement. Thoughts spring from the active impression of objects upon an individual's physical organs of sense: Sense, he explains, "is nothing els but originall fancy, caused by the pressure, that is, by the motions, of externall things upon our Eyes, Eares, and other organs thereunto ordained" (L, 1, 86).[23] In Hobbes's account, thoughts and "imaginations" are corporeal or physical motions, and because they are corporeal they cannot properly be considered apart from or in contradistinction to bodies. Thoughts and motions internal to the individual are not qualitatively different phenomena; the mind cannot be conceived as an entity separate from or independent of the body.[24] In short, Hobbes conceptualizes the subject as an animate body with the capacity to think: a thinking-body.

And it is a specifically *thinking*-body rather than, as Hobbes's rationalist critics fear, a merely unthinking, reactive machine-body whose actions are determined by external stimuli. In Hobbes's recounting, the motions that occasion an idea are retained in the thinking-body in the form of memory; these memories enable "former and later phantasms [to] be compared together, and distinguished from one another" (DCP, 25, 393). Such memories, or remembered thoughts, are the basis for the comparisons that constitute the processes of reasoning and judgment—whether construed as prudence or as science—and reason and judgment are integral to any activity undertaken by the subject (L, 5, 111). Action always depends, Hobbes avers, "upon a precedent thought of *whither, which way,* and *what*" (L, 6, 118). Since answers to such questions require opinion, reason, and judgment, and these in turn require imagination, "the Imagination," he contends, "is the first internall beginning of all Voluntary Motion" (118).

At the same time that we appreciate the thinking capacity of Hobbes's subject, a capacity that challenges the idea that Hobbes's is a deterministic materialism, we must remain cognizant of the fact that it is also a corporeal subject, a thinking-*body*. Hobbes believes that, as peculiar incarnations of matter, individuals are subject to two sorts of motion, one "Vitall," the other "Animall, . . . otherwise called Voluntary" (L, 6, 118). The first of these, "Vitall Motion," defines a particular body as a living body. It is the movement of life itself, "begun in generation, and continued without interruption through their whole life; such as are the course of the Bloud, the Pulse, the Breathing, the Concoction, Nutrition, Excretion, &c" (118). Vital motion is the spontaneous functioning of the body, and since it is a reflexive or physically compulsory motive force, it "needs no help of Imagination" (118). However, even though vital motion needs no conscious inducement, it is modified to varying degrees by individuals' interactions with other animate and inanimate objects in the world. This alteration takes the form of either corroboration or debilitation, or what Hobbes calls, respectively, appetite and aversion, or desire and fear.[25] As he explains, "The original of life being in the heart, that motion in the sentient, which is propagated to the heart, must necessarily make some alteration or diversion of vital motion, namely, by quickening or slackening, helping or hindering the same" (DCP, 25, 406). Appetite and aversion, desire and fear, are idioms of vital motion, the movement toward that which an individual believes will be pleasurable or away from that which is perceived as the cause of pain. Importantly, as Hobbes elaborates his account of desire and fear, he reveals what he understands to be the relationship between perception, affect, and cognition: The processes of sense perception that Hobbes believes are the origin of thought are the same processes that constitute desire and fear (L, 6, 121). The way we perceive the world is overlaid with what we know and feel; the way we react to the world is shaped by our opinions and judgments about what we perceive.

The imbrication of perception, affect, and cognition in Hobbes's account of subjectivity suggests that the rationalist reconstructions of social interaction—or, more properly speaking, of antisocial interaction—are wrong.[26] Far from being characterized by quick reasoning followed by violent action, Hobbesian social encounters take place on affective, gestural, and symbolic as well as cognitive planes. In his rich discussions of honor and power, Hobbes explains that individuals express and take cognizance of their opinions and evaluations of one another through gesture, countenance, bearing, and action.[27] To ask advice, to give way, to show love or fear, or to imitate is to demonstrate that one values another person, that one thinks highly of another, that one appreciates or respects his or her power or talents. To mock or to pity, to be obscene, rash, or impudent, to ignore, to dissent, or to distrust is to indicate one's low estimation of another, to give an unfavorable evaluation of someone's ability or standing, to convey one's disrespect. To signal any such appraisals of another affects that other's and everybody else's sense of self and social standing, for each individual's self- and public worth is dependent upon and constituted through mutual comparison (L, 10, 152). Hobbes specifies the evaluative meaning or the significance of such actions and gestures in his discussion of the passions. The passions, he contends, are sometimes simple, sometimes elaborate articulations of desire and fear. For example, when desire for an object coincides with an opinion of success, it is what we call hope; "Constant Hope" is "Confidence in our selves" (L, 6, 123). So, in Hobbes's recounting, when one acts confidently, one signals to others one's sense of capability, of potential success, one's sense of power. Our countenance and bearing, many of our gestures and actions, convey our attitudes and our dispositions—our passions—as they are modulated by anticipation, fancy, expectation, and memory.

Of course, interacting with others is not a matter of simply "reading" other people's actions, gestures, or countenance—would that it were so simple. Hobbes concedes that the diversity of experiences, tempers, and objects of desire among individuals makes such reading an extremely difficult task; that individuals are, for the most part, inscrutable.[28] In fact, he contends that if this reading is done with a view to what is necessary for individuals to be able to constitute political order, as he intends to do, it is "harder than to learn any Language, or Science" (L, Intro., 83). As I suggest below, in order for individuals to be able to "read" one another, they must participate in the ethical and political practices that Hobbes lays out in his political theory. The point here, however, is twofold: First, in Hobbes's view, social interaction is incredibly complex for those individuals it involves. To be sure, people may exercise their capacity for reason when they interact with one another, but interpretations that focus on this hardly capture the whole of it: Hobbes's thinking-bodies also engage in a whole host of practices of appraisal, estimation, acknowledgment, and recognition that derive from sensual, affective, and perceptual processes. Second, when Hobbes extends his analysis of perception, sense, thought, and desire to the social and political world, he gives no reason for us to believe that he thinks individuals are isolated "atoms" or, as Wolin disparagingly puts it, "dehistoricized bits of matter in motion."[29] The theories of epistemology, psychology, and intersubjectivity that derive from his account of subjects as thinking-bodies underscore the ineluctable embeddedness of Hobbesian individuals in the social and political environments in which they act. Hobbes suggests that individuals' desires, their sense of possibility, and their will to action both shape and are shaped by their perceptions of and their relations with other people with whom they interact.

READING THE BODY

Hobbes's metaphysical materialism, and more particularly his conceptualization of subjects as thinking-bodies, has important implications for contemporary and feminist political theorists, particularly those who are interested in the materiality of the subject. To get to these implications, however, we must challenge the assumption that for Hobbes, the body is, figuratively speaking, always female. Unfortunately, the feminist political insight that women are frequently associated with and reduced to the body has bound many feminist political theorists to an equivalent theoretical presumption in their critical interpretive work. Both Carole Pateman and Christine Di-Stefano, for example, rely on the assumption that "woman" is "body" in their effort to produce readings of Hobbes that expose the sexist or masculinist underpinnings of his thinking. Their political commitment to feminist theoretical assumptions about the femininity of the body circumscribes their engagement with Hobbes's political theory, with the effect not only that they find in Hobbes what they thought they would—the familiar equation of woman with body—but also that they reaffirm the very associations they ostensibly seek to challenge.[30]

Pateman and DiStefano argue that in Hobbes's political theory, as in the historical legacy that justifies and veils the subordination of women by appeals to nature, women's bodies function as the linchpins of their social and political subordination. More specifically, they contend that in Hobbes's theoretical imagination, women *cum* bodies are necessarily excluded or expelled from the scene of politics. For example, in her probing analysis of the sexual silences in the logic of social contract theory, Pateman asserts that for Hobbes, as for other social contract theorists, women are unable to "create and maintain political right" because of their bodies.[31] She explains, "The body of the 'individual' is very different from women's bodies. His is tightly enclosed within boundaries, but women's bodies are permeable, their contours change shape and they are subject to cyclical processes" (Pateman, 96). She suggests that for Hobbes, the changeable or inconstant character of women's bodies—marked by their capacity for reproduction—disqualifies them from political participation. Yet variability of the body is not something that Hobbes identifies as peculiar to women or as an impediment to political action. In fact, he argues that "the constitution of a mans Body, is in continuall mutation," a mutability that leads, in his account, to a politically challenging diversity of interests and objects of desire (L, 6, 120). All people's bodies are always changing—even the processes of perception and cognition involve change. DiStefano reaches a conclusion that is similar to Pateman's.[32] She claims that women's absence from Hobbes's political theory can be traced, in part, to his rejection of the body. In her analysis, because women figuratively are the maternal body, all bodies and all women must be ejected from the sphere of politics so that Hobbes's masculine individual can achieve political subjecthood. So, even in the face of Hobbes's overt attention to embodiedness and its ethical and political significance, DiStefano declares that "the body, that physical locus of dependence on the (m)other, is eliminated from his achieved versions of self-hood" (DiStefano, 50).

I believe Pateman and DiStefano misread the body in Hobbes. Which is to say that in their effort to locate political exclusion in Hobbes's political theory in the sexually differentiated body, or more specifically in the maternal body, they import modern understandings of sexual difference into a context in which it does not make sense to do so and effectively produce the body as female in their interpretive practice. To make this criticism is not to suggest that Hobbes posits a "generic" subject; far from it. But as Thomas Laqueur points out, it was not until around the eighteenth century that, in Europe, the biological body was conceived as the locus of sexual difference.[33] Before that period, sexual identity was measured much more in terms of one's place in the order of things: Biology was seen as merely a reflection or illustration of larger cosmological truths. For instance, in the Jacobean pamphlet wars about cross-dressers and Parisian gender-bending fashions in England in the late sixteenth and early seventeenth centuries, the focus of controversy is the muddling of social order and the roles necessary to sustain that order, and not the perversion of nature, or the naturally sexed body, per se.[34] In Laqueur's recounting, it was only when the organizing power of such cosmologies became so fragile as to be ineffective that reproductive physiology was positioned as the origin or natural foundation of sexual difference. Consequently, when Pateman and DiStefano argue that Hobbes excludes women qua bodies or bodies qua women from politics and political consideration, they reconfirm a commonplace in contemporary feminist political theory at the same time that they overlook the possibility that Hobbes gives an unfamiliar and potentially insightful analysis of the relationship between difference, inequality, and political order.

And indeed, Hobbes appears to subscribe to a position that would see sexual identity as derived from social and political interrelationship. As Richard Flathman has pointed out, Hobbes's skepticism and nominalism push him to recognize that there is no natural meaning to the world and that social hierarchy and political order are matters only of convention.[35] Such epistemological and theoretical insights have been central to feminist efforts to define women's oppression as an issue of politics rather than one of natural subordination. In fact, as feminist theorists have refined and expanded the scope of what Linda Zerilli has termed "gender skepticism," not only has the givenness of the gendered organization of social and political life been challenged.[36] The natural self-evidence of the "sex" and "race" of material bodies has also been called into question.[37] Hobbes's account of social interaction among thinking-bodies suggests that his political theory might be an important resource for such theorists of the body: In his analyses of the place of the body in the constitution of social hierarchy and political order, he not only presumes that social order is a matter of human artifice. He also suggests that politically significant natural difference—conceived here as an inherent attribute of the body—is a perceptual and material effect of social and political practices.

Hobbes writes at a period in which those cosmologies that have seemed to organize the social and political world have been called into question.[38] In his view, there is no rational, divine, or cosmological order; there is no essential bodily difference, regal or sexual, that can direct or found social order. Indeed, he builds upon his recognition that "the Principles of naturall Science, . . . cannot teach us our own nature, nor the nature of the smallest living creature" (L, 31, 404) to give an acerbic critique of Aristotle and other like scholars who make recourse to nature to explain political status and hierarchy (L, 15, 211). Hobbes believes that since the names that we give to things signify only "what we *imagine* of their nature," they must be considered in light of "the nature, disposition, and interest of the speaker" (L, 4, 109, italics mine). To put forth arguments about natural inequality, natural political wisdom, or natural political ineptitude is to give poorly veiled justifications for social and political relations that are conventional in character. Aristotle, he claims, fell prey to a "vain conceipt" of his own wisdom, as many people do, and formulated his theory of politics accordingly (L, 13, 183). Hobbes's skepticism and nominalism entail the recognition that there is nothing natural to political order. In a move that resembles those made by feminists in their analyses of the political constitution of "the natural," he argues that the social and political hierarchies that organize society and politics are the effect of social and political relationships: If we consider people in their "natural condition," that is, as they might be if we could subtract the social rules and political practices that make us who we are, the "question who is the better man, has no place" (L, 15, 211).

In his analysis of the processes by which the titular aristocratic class is produced as socially and politically superior, Hobbes suggests that seemingly natural differences are in fact the effect of political relationships of inequality. If we draw on his contention that people's senses of themselves and of one another derive from complex processes of mutual appraisal, we can see that, in his view, politically significant differences are constituted through visible bodily practices that sort people and mark social and political standing. According to the account of social interaction that Hobbes develops from his metaphysical materialism, thinking-bodies function as signs for one another: One's self-evaluation in comparison with others can be observed in one's gestures, countenance, and actions. Such mutual appraisals constitute a series of acknowledgments of greater and lesser power, and are accompanied by varying levels of privilege, respect, and social allegiance. They are effectively a negotiation of relative social placement, and they position individuals in relationship to one another. Importantly, then, social hierarchies are the product of opinions that are produced, at least in part, through active and bodily signifying practices. In Hobbes's telling, when people agree in their recognition of a particular person or group of persons as most powerful, that is, when they constitute a common power over them as sovereign, that sovereign consolidates the extant social and political relationships and hierarchies by granting titles of honor, titles that "signify . . . the value set upon them by the Soveraigne Power of the Common-wealth" (L, 10, 158). Importantly, in distributing such honors, the sovereign stipulates "what signes of respect, in publique or private meetings, they shall give to one another" (L, 18, 236). In other words, the sovereign determines what sorts of gestures, actions, and modes of conduct are to be followed by the people to convey their recognition of the superior power and honor of the titled. Of course, as Hobbes admits, over time the active offices conferred by such titles became defunct, which leaves the gentry with titles that "serv[e] for the most part, to distinguish the precedence, place, and order of subjects in the Common-wealth" (159). What results from this process is a social and political order whose constitutive hierarchy is made visible, consolidated, and sustained through the bodily gestures, manners, and actions of the general population. That is, the political inequality that instantiates order is manifested through the body, located *in* the body as a marked, politically significant difference.

Hobbes's insights in this regard may be applicable to other sorts of "difference," such as gender and race, that concern contemporary and feminist political theorists. Indeed, drawing on Hobbes's objection to the claim that gender hierarchies derive from the fact that men are naturally "the more excellent Sex" (L, 20, 253), Gabriela Slomp has suggested that relations of subordination and superordination "become" gender difference through "custom not contradicted."[39] What is important to recognize, then, is that in Hobbes's recounting, the production of differences, and of the hierarchies from which they derive, is integral to the constitution of order. The significance of bodies, or, more properly put, the signifying function of bodies, is central to the production and reproduction of power and political order.

Given the understanding of the relationship between bodies, difference, and order that Hobbes derives from his metaphysical materialism, a crucial question is how the significance of bodily gestures is generated: How do people's bodies and actions come to be meaningful and meaningfully read in social and political intercourse? This is the question to which Hobbes addresses himself in his political theoretical work. In his introduction to *Leviathan*, Hobbes describes his theoretical task as a lexicographical one: He proposes to provide a lexicon that will enable individuals to "learn truly to read one another, if they would take the pains" (L, Intro., 82). In elaborating upon his project, he explains that the popular but frequently misunderstood enjoinder, "*Nosce teipsum,* Read thy self," is meant

> to teach us, that for the similitude of the thoughts, and Passions of one man, to the thoughts, and Passions of another, whosoever looketh into himself, and considereth what he doth, when he does *think, opine, reason, hope, fear, &c,* and upon what grounds; he shall thereby read and know, what are the thoughts, and Passions of all other men, upon the like occasions [82].

Hobbes suggests that if individuals reflect upon the actions they take when they have certain passions and opinions, if they consider carefully the thoughts and dispositions that prompt what they do, they will be able to "read" one another.[40] He concedes that "the constitution individuall, and particular education do so vary" that such reading is a difficult task, that "the characters of mans heart" may be "blotted and confounded" with "dissembling, lying, counterfeiting, and erroneous doctrines" (83). However, the difficulty of the exercise makes it no less necessary for the political moment, and Hobbes undertakes to perform such a reading himself, explaining, "When I shall have set down my own reading orderly, and perspicuously, the pains left another, will be onely to consider, if he also find the same in himself" (83). Hobbes's political theory represents an effort to explain how individuals must read one another and contrive to be read for the purposes of creating civil society. It is a metaphysical, ethical, and political project that outlines the principles and practices necessary to generate and sustain the mutual intelligibility that he believes is integral to the art of constituting political order.

CONCLUSION

Given the clarity with which Hobbes articulates his intent to build his political theory upon the assumptions and insights of his materialist metaphysics, and the wealth of text he devotes to the analysis of the body, the passions, the complex texture of social relationship, and the symbolic requirements of power, it is interesting to trace how the rationalist Hobbesian subject has become such a definitive feature of our political imaginations. Our political and theoretical commitments inevitably frame our interventions into the canon; they subtend our recognition of what Wolin, citing Adorno, refers to as the "cross-grained."[41] When a critical political sensibility achieves something of a consensus, as Wolin's intervention has for many political theorists and as the recognition that gender is an organizing category of difference has for feminist political theorists, its constitutive understandings become tacit norms of intelligibility. As we have seen in the case of Hobbes, while such tacitly held norms are politically useful, they also perform a disciplinary function, sorting and demarcating what is appropriate to and possible in a political theoretical analysis. Our political presumptions can bind us to theoretical presumptions whose status as *presumptions,* as what is given or taken for granted at the outset, may serve to undermine the very political projects to which we are committed. It may not be possible to identify the processes by which a theoretical intervention into politics is transformed into an analysis driven by the imperatives of a particular discourse. We may not be able to discern at what remove from the social context of a debate a political conviction takes on the tenor of a quest for philosophical or theoretical rectitude. However, it is clear that there is more to the task of political theory than preventing the confinement of our theoretical imaginations within prevailing political sense. If we are to advance what is best in our aspirations toward justice, we must be wary of defining the political via reference to theoretical orthodoxy and hold up for question even our most valued theoretical truths.

NOTES

For their tremendously useful comments and suggestions, many thanks to Wendy Brown, Peter Euben, Richard Flathman, Debra Liebowitz, Anne Manuel, Melissa Orlie, and Linda Zerilli. I am also grateful to the participants of the "Vocations" conference and the editors of this volume for their helpful questions and responses.

1. Sheldon Wolin, "Political Theory as a Vocation," *American Political Science Review* 63, no. 4 (1969): 1077.

2. Jacques Derrida, *Limited, Inc.,* trans. Samuel Weber (Evanston, Ill.: Northwestern University Press, 1977), 147.

3. Richard Flathman, *Thomas Hobbes: Skepticism, Individuality and Chastened Politics* (Newbury Park, Calif.: Sage Publications, Inc.), 4.

4. Thomas Hobbes, *Leviathan,* ed. C. B. Macpherson (London: Penguin Books, 1968), chap. 46, 689. Hereafter cited in text as L, along with chapter and page numbers. Hobbes continues this declaration with the contention that "every part of Body, is likewise Body, and hath the like dimensions; and consequently every part of the Universe, is Body, and that which is not Body, is Nothing; and consequently no where" (L, 46, 689).

5. Thomas Hobbes, *De Corpore,* in *The English Works of Thomas Hobbes of Malmesbury,* ed. Sir William Molesworth (London: J. Bohn, 1839), chap. 3, 34. Hereafter cited in the text as DCP, along with chapter and page numbers. Earlier in *De Corpore,* Hobbes gives a similar but longer statement of his project, claiming, "seeing that, for the knowledge of the properties of a commonwealth, it is necessary first to know the dispositions, affections, and manners of men, civil philosophy is . . . commonly divided into two parts, whereof one, which treats of men's dispositions and manners, is called *ethics;* and the other, which takes cognizance of their civil duties, is called politics, or simply *civil philosophy.* In the first place, therefore, . . . I will discourse of *bodies natural;* in the second, of the *dispositions and manners of men;* and in the third, of the *civil duties of subjects*" (DCP, 1, 11–12, italics in the original).

6. Sheldon Wolin, "Hobbes and the Culture of Despotism," in *Thomas Hobbes and Political Theory,* ed. Mary Dietz (Lawrence: University Press of Kansas, 1990), 31 and passim. For an earlier and slightly less condemnatory analysis of the scientism

in Hobbes's political theory, see Wolin, *Hobbes and the Epic Tradition of Political Theory* (Los Angeles: University of California, 1970).

7. The analysis that follows is indebted to Tommy Lott's provocative essay "Hobbes's Mechanistic Psychology," in *Thomas Hobbes: His View of Man*, ed. J. G. van der Bend (Amsterdam: Rodopi, 1982).

8. Richard Peters and Henri Tajfel, for example, exclaim that "[t]here is something almost incredibly hard-headed and naïve about Hobbes' gross materialism." See Peters and Tajfel, "Hobbes and Hull: Metaphysicians of Behaviour," in *Hobbes and Rousseau: A Collection of Critical Essays*, ed. Maurice Cranston and Richard Peters (Garden City, N.Y.: Anchor Books, 1972), 180. In a separate discussion, Peters suggests that Hobbes was "curiously" unaware of the "logical mistakes" he committed. See Peters, *Hobbes*, 2d ed. (Harmondsworth: Penguin, 1967), 159. J. W. N. Watkins proposes that Hobbes was afflicted by self-deception in his effort to develop an account of subjectivity from his materialist metaphysics. See Watkins, "Philosophy and Politics in Hobbes," in *Hobbes Studies*, ed. Keith Brown (Oxford: Blackwell, 1965), 251.

9. Thomas Spragens, Jr., *The Politics of Motion: The World of Thomas Hobbes* (Lexington: University Press of Kentucky, 1973), 165.

10. Watkins states his objection quite clearly when he declares that "[p]sychological conclusions about thoughts, feelings, and wants cannot be deduced from materialistic premises about bodily movements" (Watkins, 238). See also Watkins, *Hobbes's System of Ideas: A Study in the Political Significance of Philosophical Theories* (London: Hutchinson University Library, 1965).

11. For example, Richard Peters describes Hobbes as having "produced a description of what we already know in rather bizarre terminology or descriptions which seem absurd because of the inapplicability of mechanical concepts" (Peters, 94).

12. Bernard Gert, "Hobbes, Mechanism, and Egoism," *Philosophical Quarterly* 15, no. 4 (1965): 341.

13. F. S. McNeilly, "Egoism in Hobbes," in *Ethics*, vol. 2 of *Thomas Hobbes: Critical Assessments*, ed. Preston King (New York: Routledge, 1993), 164.

14. Gert contends that Hobbes's claim that the subjects he describes can imagine or have thoughts is tantamount to "illegitimately" attributing beliefs to a machine (Gert, 347). Elsewhere, he complains that Hobbes "makes deliberation sound more like a succession of emotional states than a consideration of the consequences of various courses of action." See Gert, "Hobbes's Psychology," in *The Cambridge Companion to Hobbes*, ed. Tom Sorrel (Cambridge: Cambridge University Press, 1996), 162.

15. Francois Tricaud describes this dynamic as follows: "A may reckon that B may be reckoning that it is profitable for him (i.e., B) to kill A; and A will conclude that it is wiser for him (i.e., A) to kill B first. Of course, at the same moment, B is going through a similar reasoning: the faster reckoner will be the first striker." See Tricaud, "Hobbes's Conception of the State of Nature from 1640–1651: Evolution and Ambiguities," in *Perspectives on Thomas Hobbes*, ed. G. A. J. Rogers and Alan Ryan (Oxford: Clarendon Press, 1988), 122.

16. There is a huge number of theorists I could cite for examples. See, for a few instances, Peters, *Hobbes*, 157–59; Leo Strauss, *The Political Philosophy of Thomas Hobbes*, trans. Elsa Sinclair (Chicago: University of Chicago Press, 1952), 132 and passim; A. E. Taylor, "The Ethical Doctrine of Hobbes," in *Ethics*, vol. 2 of *Thomas Hobbes: Critical Assessments*.

17. The avid commitment to the idea that individuals are self-reflective, rational actors is startlingly obvious in Peters and Tajfel's assertion that "there is a manifest difference between compulsive and rational behaviour. A person who deliberates rationally about a means to an end will be influenced by logically relevant considerations. For him there is a difference between good and bad reasons for a course of action. But for a compulsive [who is presumably to be likened to the rejected materialist version of Hobbes's subject] there is no such similar distinction. No reasons make any difference to what he does. Like a man under post-hypnotic suggestion he will only 'reason' to find excuses for what he is going to do anyway" (Peters and Tajfel, 182).

18. See, for example, David Gauthier, *The Logic of Leviathan: The Moral and Political Theory of Thomas Hobbes* (Oxford: Clarendon Press, 1969); Gauthier, "Hobbes's Social Contract," in G. A. J. Rogers and Alan Ryan, eds., *Perspectives on Thomas Hobbes*; G. S. Kavka, *Hobbesian Moral and Political Theory* (Princeton: Princeton University Press, 1986).

19. In his push against determinist accounts of politics, Peters states that "[i]n ethics and politics, actions are only interesting in so far as they are consciously directed towards their goals" (Peters, 145).

20. For a lively discussion of the explanatory power of rational-choice theory and the question of whether explanatory power is a standard according to which the success of rational-choice theory should be measured, see Donald Green and Ian Shapiro, *Pathologies of Rational Choice Theory* (New Haven: Yale University Press, 1994), and their respondents in *The Rational Choice Controversy: Economic Models of Politics Reconsidered*, ed. Jeffrey Friedman (New Haven: Yale University Press, 1996).

21. Tom Foster Digby is one of the few theorists I have found who also takes up Hobbes's notion of the "thinking-body." See Digby, "Bodies and More Bodies: Hobbes's Ascriptive Individualism," *Metaphilosophy* 22, no. 4 (October 1991).

22. Michael Oakeshott states that there is a notion that "there is something called 'the mind,' that this mind acquires beliefs, knowledge, prejudices in short, a filling which remain nevertheless a mere appendage to it, that it causes bodily activities, and that it works best when it is unencumbered by an acquired disposition of any sort. Now, this mind I believe to be a fiction; it is nothing more than an hypostatized activity. Mind as we know it is the offspring of knowledge and activity; it is composed entirely of thoughts. . . . The whole notion of the mind as an apparatus for thinking is, I believe, an error." See Oakeshott, *Rationalism in Politics and Other Essays* (Indianapolis: Liberty Press, 1991), 109.

23. According to Hobbes, "The cause of Sense, is the External Body, or Object, which presseth the organ proper to each Sense, either immediately . . . or mediately" (L, 1, 85). He illustrates nicely the effect of such impressions by explaining that "as

pressing, rubbing, or striking the Eyes, makes us fancy a light; and pressing the Eare, produceth a dinne; so do the bodies also we see, or hear, produce the same by their strong, though unobserved action" (86).

24. Hobbes makes a similar argument against seeing the soul as separate from the body, explaining that "[t]he *Soule* in Scripture, signifieth alwaies, either the Life, or the Living Creature; and the Body and Soule jointly, the *Body alive*" (L, 44, 637–38). This point was brought to my attention in Tracy Strong, "How to Write Scripture: Words, Authority, and Politics in Thomas Hobbes," *Critical Inquiry* 20 (Autumn 1993): 152.

25. Hobbes describes appetite as "a corroboration of Vitall motion, and a help there unto"; it is a movement toward an object whose motion helps or fortifies an individual's vital motion (L, 6, 121–22). Similarly, aversion is a "retiring" motion or movement away from things "which we know have hurt us; [and] also that we do not know whether they will hurt us or not" (119–20). An object inspires aversion when it is deemed offensive "from hindering, and troubling the motion vitall" (122).

26. For a fairly typical example, see Francois Tricaud, "Hobbes's Conception of the State of Nature," passim.

27. See, in particular, *Leviathan*, chap. 10.

28. Richard Flathman makes this inscrutability or opacity of Hobbes's subject a central feature of his argument that respect for and protection of individuality lies at the heart of Hobbes's politics. See Flathman, *Thomas Hobbes*.

29. Wolin, "Hobbes and the Culture of Despotism," 25.

30. For variants of such critiques of feminist political theory, see Christina Crosby, "Dealing with Differences," in *Feminists Theorize the Political,* ed. Judith Butler and Joan W. Scott (New York: Routledge, 1992); Linda Zerilli, *Signifying Woman: Culture and Chaos in Rousseau, Mill and Burke* (Ithaca, N.Y.: Cornell University Press, 1994).

31. Carole Pateman, *The Sexual Contract,* (Stanford, Calif.: Stanford University Press, 1988), 96.

32. Christine DiStefano, *Configurations of Masculinity: A Feminist Perspective on Modern Political Theory* (Ithaca, N.Y.: Cornell University Press, 1991).

33. Thomas Laqueur, *Making Sex: Body and Gender from the Greeks to Freud* (Cambridge, Mass.: Harvard University Press, 1990), 5 and passim.

34. *Three Pamphlets on the Jacobean Antifeminist Controversy,* with an introduction by Barbara J. Baines (Delmar, N.Y.: Scholars' Facsimiles and Reprints, 1978).

35. Flathman, *Thomas Hobbes*.

36. See Linda M. G. Zerilli, "Doing without Knowing: Feminism's Politics of the Ordinary," *Political Theory* 26, no. 4 (August 1998): 435–58.

37. There is a huge range of work that examines the social and political constitution of the "natural" body. See, for example, Judith Butler, *Bodies that Matter: On the Discursive Limits of "Sex"* (New York: Routledge, 1993); Londa Schiebinger, *Nature's Body: Gender in the Making of Modern Science* (Boston: Beacon Press, 1993); K. Anthony Appiah and Henry Louis Gates, Jr., eds., *Identities* (Chicago: University

of Chicago Press, 1995); David Hillman and Carla Mazzio, eds., *The Body in Parts: Fantasies of Corporeality in Early Modern Europe* (New York: Routledge, 1997); Alan Hyde, *Bodies of Law* (Princeton: Princeton University Press, 1997).

38. See, for example, Ernst Kantorowicz, *The King's Two Bodies: A Study in Mediaeval Political Theology* (Princeton: Princeton University Press, 1957); Christopher Hill, *The World Turned Upside Down*. . . . (New York: Penguin, 1972); Keith Thomas, "The Social Origins of Hobbes's Political Thought," in *Hobbes Studies,* ed. Keith Brown (London: Routledge, 1965); Michael Walzer, "On the Role of Symbolism in Political Thought," *Political Science Quarterly* 8, no. 2 (June 1967).

39. Gabriela Slomp, "Hobbes and the Equality of Women," *Political Studies* 42 (1994): 449.

40. With an attention to issues of conscience that distinguishes his reading from mine, Tracy Strong argues that the language of legibility that Hobbes invokes in this injunction to look inward bespeaks an attempt to model political authority along the lines of scriptural authority in Protestantism. See Tracy Strong, "How to Write Scripture: Words, Authority, and Politics in Thomas Hobbes," 143 and passim.

41. See Sheldon Wolin, "Political Theory: From Vocation to Invocation," this volume, quoting Theodor Adorno, *Minima Moralia: Reflections from Damaged Life,* trans. E. F. N. Jephcott (London: New Left Books, 1974 [1951]), 151.

12 // WORK, SHAME, AND THE CHAIN GANG

The New Civic Education

Thus the convict pays twice; by the labour he provides and by the signs that he produces. At the heart of society, on the public squares or highways, the convict is a focus of profit and signification. Visibly, he is serving everyone; but, at the same time, he lets slip into the minds of all the crime-punishment sign: a second, purely moral, but much more real utility.[1]

OPERATION HUMILIATION

During his gubernatorial campaign, Fob James Jr., suggested on a public talk show that Alabama should bring back chain gangs. Instead of "lifting weights or watching cable t.v.," Alabama prisoners would be "out working," where passersby could see them toil.[2] What the talk-show host dubbed "Operation Humiliation" would become public policy in 1995, shortly after James's inauguration.[3]

Florida Senator Charlie Crist introduced chain-gang legislation as well. Recalling chain gangs alongside highways as a young man, Crist was impressed by Florida's commitment to hard work and respect for the law. Now, he insists, "That's the image Florida needs today—instead of one of innocent citizens and tourists being robbed and raped every day."[4]

"America's Toughest Sheriff," Maricopa County Sheriff Joe Arpaio, brought chain-gang labor to Arizona in 1995, too.[5] Forcing both women and men on the chain gang to wear pink underwear, eat green, moldy bologna, and live in "tent cities," Arpaio now boasts of the largest tent compound in the country, with 1,600 men and women under canvas roofs.[6] At the helm of the "first female chain gang in the world," Arpaio prides himself as an "equal-opportunity incarcerator."[7]

Together, James, Crist, and Arpaio register a faith that hard work and humiliation will instruct not just convicts, but passersby, about the importance of controlling crime and respecting the law. By punishing through humiliation, James, Crist, and Arpaio hope that passersby will read such messages on the laborers themselves. Details of their individual programs differ. But one consensus has emerged—convict labor must be performed in public view. Visibility—or publicity—undergirds the chain gang's appeal.

As chain gangs reemerge in states ranging from Arizona to Massachusetts, I want to examine this phenomenon in terms of the implications of past practices and the narratives that authorize their return.[8] To this end, I rely upon Alex Lichtenstein, Matthew Mancini, and David Oshinsky's research to demonstrate how nineteenth- and early-twentieth-century-American convict leasing and chain gangs brutally conscripted African-American labor in the service of Southern modernization. I also draw upon the eighteenth- and early-nineteenth-century French and American accounts of Michel Foucault and Michael Meranze, which suggest that visibility may establish a relationship of *sympathy* between convicts and passersby. Finally, through the works of Judith Butler and Wendy Brown, I argue that the violent, racialized history of American convict labor and the increasing scope of the late modern state render today's chain gang ill equipped for the kinds of resignification witnessed in the eighteenth and early nineteenth century.

WORKHORSES AND MALINGERERS

Prior to the Progressive-era chain gang, but after the abolition of slavery, convict labor was bartered through private leases. As part and parcel of Reconstruction, convict leasing emerged as a way for landowners and business people to hold laborers for extended periods of time, typically twenty years, allowing the South to sidestep physical incarceration altogether. Matthew Mancini explains, "For half a century following the Civil War, the Southern states had no prisons to speak of. . . . Instead, persons convicted of criminal offenses were . . . leased—literally contracted out—to businessmen, planters, and corporations in one of the harshest and most exploitative labor systems known in American history."[9]

As black convicts were rendered the cheapest solution to the loss of slave labor, a way to generate profits and "spur industrial development," the convict lease became brutal and convenient.[10] David Oshinsky describes how "prisoners were tortured for minor infractions of the rules. Some were whipped to death; others, strung up with their thumbs. . . . By the time the job ended, the land alongside the tracks was dotted with graves."[11] Roughly two-thirds of the convicts did not return. These details recount the 1876 case of Live Oak, Florida, although they apply to many others. Convict leasing was often more brutal than slavery. In a slave economy, landowners were responsible for the care—however poor—of their slaves. But lessees worked their convicts to death. One Southern employer explained the "benefits" as follows: "Before the war we owned the negroes. . . . But these convicts: we don't own 'em. One dies, get another."[12] As convicts died off from violence, malnutrition, and disease, lessors simply provided new workers as part of the contract. A "human bridge between the Old South and the New," the convict lease allowed white supremacy to retain its antebellum status, while offering economic benefits to a devastated region.[13] Firms brokering convicts, and the farms and businesses relying upon them, reaped huge profits in this "functional replacement for slavery."[14]

The Progressive belief that "the greed of the convict lessees would be supplanted by the reformatory power of the state" shifted convict labor from the hands of private individuals to state and county programs.[15] The state, however, did not improve public attitudes toward convicts or the conditions in which they lived. This public form of labor, used for road-building efforts, became known as the road gang or chain gang. According to Lichtenstein, Progressives "promoted this reform as the embodiment of penal humanitarianism, state-sponsored economic modernization and efficiency, and racial moderation."[16] Regrettably, working for the public roads project was no improvement from the cruelty of the private lease. Progressives appealed to the "reformatory" power of the state, but continued to exploit the economic advantages of the convict lease. In the end, the racial economy of slavery provided social and economic capital for Southern modernization.[17]

Ultimately, chain gangs fell out of favor for two reasons: the increased visibility of white prisoners on the gang, and the changing demands of the South's economy. When I Am a Fugitive from the Georgia Chain Gang!, Robert Elliott Burns's book and movie, revealed the brutal conditions under which Georgia's chain gangs lived, it publicized an important shift in chain-gang composition: "Black and white convicts [now] worked the roads together, chained to one another in full view of the public."[18] Lichtenstein explains, "The resulting increased *visibility* of white prisoners began to erode the public faith in the benefits and justice of penal labor. The national horror which greeted Burns's tale cannot be divorced from the fact that this particular victim of the chain gang had white skin."[19] As convict labor whitened, its brutality was brought into sharp relief. Hard time, accompanied by the humiliation and brutality of the chain gang, was a form of justice acceptable for black men only. Proper criminality was inextricably tied to the condition of blackness. One road commissioner portrayed the dilemma as follows: "While a sentence [on the chain gang] would forever ruin a white man previously respectable, it had no such effect on a respectable Negro."[20] Reforming character and contributing to postbellum progress, chain gangs were to be comprised of black men.[21]

Today, the majority of the men on the chain gang are black, and even where white men stand in for them, the resonance of convict leasing and early chain gangs is inescapable.[22] If Progressives saw black men as workhorses, suitable for their road-building efforts, today's reformers see black men as lazy and shiftless. One guard explains: "These kind of people aren't constituted for work. We get 'em out here and show 'em how to work."[23] Laziness, deviance, and blackness appear as a carefully packaged metonymy, crafted for the benefit of passersby.

By way of programs like "Operation Humiliation," today's chain gangs are forced to be the objects of shame.[24] One convict explains, "We were doing the same work as before, only now they chain us up like animals so that the Governor *can make it look like* he's doing something about crime."[25] Sometimes they aren't doing any "work" at all. As part of his "character building" scheme, Alabama Prison Commissioner Ron Jones devised a plan for "men on the chain gang [to] spend their days breaking large boulders into small rocks with sledgehammers and pickaxes. Neither the prison nor the state highway department [had] any need for the crushed rock."[26] Championed for the penalty of hard work and the humiliation it brings the convict, today's chain gang is justified not by an appeal to convicts as workhorses, but their status as unproductive citizens who deserve such treatment.

The chain gang is staged to pose a threat of slipping into an abyss signified by black masculinity. At the same time, it allows passersby to constitute themselves as wholly different from the workers on the gang. Yet because of the instability of the boundary between the "subject" watching and the "object" being watched, the message reformers convey is never complete. Indeed, it derives its salience from this fragility. After all, the men on the chain gang are not the most severe offenders. In Arizona, inmates on the chain gang are "either awaiting trial or [have] received a sentence of a year or less, and probation violators are rampant."[27] Their relative docility qualifies them for chain-gang labor in the first place.

PUBLICITY AND ILLEGIBILITY

Given the history of convict labor in the United States, there are a number of ways to think about its reemergence. The most obvious interpretation is an extension of the arguments made by Mancini, Lichtenstein, and Oshinsky, which suggest that penal practice and convict labor, specifically, represent the views a nation holds on the value of work, the status of race relations, and economic imperatives. In simpler terms, racist countries, or racist regions, support racist policies. Therefore, it should come as no surprise that in spite of Progressive efforts to usher the South into a new wave of race relations, part of which turned on greater dignity for African-Americans, "true" Southern values ultimately prevailed in their policies and practices.

This historical account suggests that the chain gang's meaning can be tied to the values and commitments of the region or country it represents. Speaking of *today's* chain gang, Lichtenstein argues that it provides an "image of black men working in chains [that] reminds the crowd . . . of a world they think they have lost, a world where tough laws punished crime swiftly and severely, where prisoners paid their 'debt to society' in the coin of hard labor, and where the members of the underclass, African-Americans in particular, knew their place." [28] Without question, he affirms, "this is what the chain gang is all about." [29] The United States, *true to its racist origins,* invokes one of its most hideous narratives, this time to perform only symbolic work.

In order to complicate the view that collective values transparently manifest themselves in public punishment, specifically convict labor, I turn to Michel Foucault's and Michael Meranze's accounts of eighteenth- and early-nineteenth-century France and America, respectively. In each of these cases, convict labor and other forms of public punishment provide curious opportunities for convicts and passersby to build a form of solidarity. The French and American reformers remained committed to making punishment visible, but their efforts to control through punishment and humiliation often backfired in the form of resistance.

Foucault reveals the peculiar ways in which punishments that represented the brute force of a monarch, like public executions, unwittingly conferred opportunities for people to rally together against the regime. In the French case, the physical demonstration of the "horror of the crime and the invincibility of power" at the execution fostered an uncanny bond among those who witnessed its effects. [30] In fact, as Foucault explains, "the ceremony of the public execution" did not aggrandize the power of the sovereign, but produced cohesion among the people.[31] The public execution was finally abandoned by the reformers of the eighteenth century for two reasons: To dilute the solidarity it fostered among witnesses, and to model a sovereign that would not expose its brutality to the people.

A series of French reforms grew out the public execution. A kinder, gentler, form of punishment emerged. Toward the end of the eighteenth century, the body of the condemned man would no longer be the property of the sovereign, but "the property of society, the object of a collective and useful appropriation."[32] Naked, sovereign power would become clothed in a language of decency. In what Foucault names the "punitive city," punishment operated in a "new 'economy' of the power to punish," which would be "distributed in homogeneous circuits capable of operating everywhere . . . down to the finest grain of the social body."[33] If public executions turned punishment into a festival, reformers would replace the festival with a "school."[34]

The chain gang occupied a peculiar status in France's progression from public executions to incarceration. Unlike its festival-style counterpart, the public execution, the chain gang survived until 1837. Although the chain gang was part of the "great tradition of the public execution," it accommodated the "gentle way of punishment," and reformers hoped it might hold some capacity for education. However, it spurred much of the mayhem of public executions. As a "saturnalia of punishment, a penalty turned into a privilege," the chain gang actually galvanized support for convicts, and, most significantly, mocked the power of the authority that bequeathed the punishment in the first place.[35] When the chain gang traveled through town, passersby could see "ribbons, braided straw, flowers or precious stuff" that convicts attached to their collars and chains.[36] Ultimately, reformers could no longer bear such a troubling "affirmation of the crime" and "black heroization."[37] Worse, the chain gang performed no public service and, in the words of its opponents, "[taught] the population nothing."[38]

Public works, however, were another story. In both eighteenth- and early-nineteenth-century France and America, they played a central role in punishment reforms. Securing a common interest in order, the image of convict labor offered a verifiable representation of collective values. Thus, public works had a dual appeal. In Foucault's words, "the convict pays twice; by the labour he provides and by the signs that he produces. At the heart of society, on the public squares or highways, the convict is a focus of profit and signification. Visibly, he is serving everyone; but, at the same time, he [serves] . . . a secondary, purely moral, but much more real utility."[39] An eighteenth-century American reformer applauded public works because "[u]nlike brief public punishments, the continuing presence of convicts [laboring] would make a lasting impression on the citizenry."[40] Capitalizing on similar hopes, Senator Crist, Sheriff Arpaio, and Governor James work to transmit their image of how America ought to be.

Surprisingly, the careful reforms in both France and America were open to the same kind of resignification evident in the public execution and chain gang. In the hands of a fired-up crowd, reforms committed to transmitting virtue assumed new—and unforeseen—meaning. The body of the offender did not provide a form of moral and civic education. Rather, it became conscripted by forces anathema to reform. The tenacity of the commitment to public reform ultimately revealed an underlying anxiety about the certainty of the messages punishment would convey.

These fears were not misguided. In America, as Meranze explains, efforts to deploy convict labor as an "orderly progression of silent, repentant convicts . . . [who] would make criminal justice manifest" resulted in an "actual experience of public labor [that] . . . belied these expectations. . . . Rather than a theater of tragic sobriety and submission, public labor appeared a black comedy, subverting the very distinctions of vice and virtue. The presence of the subjects of penal labor seemed to corrupt the city's already precarious social virtue."[41] The effect was hardly that of producing proper citizens: "Criminals in the streets appeared to be actively seducing the community away from virtue."[42] Together, Foucault and Meranze suggest that publicity, even when orchestrated in "tiny theatres of punishment," guarantees neither instruction for passersby nor humiliation of convicts on display.[43]

OBJECTING TO ABJECTION

If the historical accounts of public punishment suggest it reflects *and* produces public values, a subsequent question comes forth: Does this instability leave today's chain gang open to resignification? Given that contemporary American values are plural, contested, and fragmented, how might we understand the meaning of visible punishment today? Might its return provide new opportunities for resistance?

In *Bodies That Matter,* Judith Butler assists this inquiry in three ways. First, she offers a tool, through Althusser, to consider how subjects are brought into being through interpellations of abjection, and the role abjection plays in providing social bonds. Second, she recognizes that simply identifying the fact that a sign has no secure referent does not render its meaning wholly unstable. Finally, Butler provides critical frameworks for imagining a potentially radical politics of resignification.

In order to make inroads into the heterosexual matrix of power, Butler appropriates Althusser's concept of "interpellation," or the process by which subjects are "hailed" into being. Providing a form of social cohesion, a "*shaming* interpellation" marks certain individuals as deviant, and in so doing underwrites the community of people whose subjectivity is constituted against them. As it constitutes "queer," Butler explains: "The term 'queer' has operated as one linguistic practice whose purpose has been the shaming of the subject it names or, rather, the producing of a subject *through* that shaming interpellation."[44] In other words, the act of naming simultaneously produces a subject and marks him or her as not only aberrant from the norm, but a threat to it.

The process of a "shaming interpellation" can be expanded to include other actions through which individuals are constituted as deviant. In the context of today's chain gang, the process of interpellation is manifold. At the very least, it comes from the state and/or county program and from passersby who "honk, yell, and howl" at the men on the gang.[45] Thus, just as "a social bond among homophobic communities is formed through time," as "queers" are hailed as "queers," chain gangs provide a social bond for Americans who are anxious about American identity, especially along the lines of race relations, crime, and the status of work.[46]

However, as Butler warns, the act of bringing some*body* into being is never complete. Moreover, its failure may provide political opportunities for resistance to the very regime that hailed the subject itself. Just as the French "school" of punishment was meant to educate but often became a site of subversion, hailing somebody into being does not ward against disobedience. I quote Butler at length to explain the significance of failure in the act of interpellation:

[Althusser] does not consider the range of *disobedience* that such an interpellating law might produce. The law might not only be refused, but it might also be ruptured, forced into a rearticulation that calls into question . . . its own unilateral operation. . . . *Here the performative, the call by the law which seeks to produce a lawful subject, produces a set of consequences that exceed and confound what appears to be the disciplining intention motivating the law.* Interpellation . . . creates more than it ever meant to, signifying in excess of any intended referent. It is this constitutive failure of the performative, this slippage between discursive command and its appropriated effect, which provides the linguistic occasion and index for a consequential disobedience.[47]

Butler criticizes Althusser's interpellation because it operates as a *formative* call, which, unlike a *performative* call, does not presume the possibility of failure and resistance.[48] Moreover, performative calls, because they are incomplete, produce fissures in the identity of the subject they hail, *and in the social bond itself.*

Accordingly, the community that is constituted against the deviance of "queers" or chain gangs is fragile. Not everyone in the "normal" community exists in the same relation to the abject population from which it derives its grounding. Recalling Lichtenstein's indictment of the contemporary chain gang that "reminds the crowd . . . of a world they think they have lost," Butler provides another reminder: All who pass by, all in the crowd, might not "read" the chain gang in the same way. For many, the resurgence of chain gangs surely brings reminders of a world *they are glad to have lost,* and the visible threat of its return.

If, then, every performative, or "call by the law which seeks to produce a lawful subject," fails, whether hailing someone as "queer" or as criminal, does every performance become politically up for grabs? Butler's work suggests an emphatic "no," and yet she struggles to elucidate terms and conditions under which resignification is *impossible.* Speaking of queer politics, Butler asks how "a term that signaled degradation has been turned . . . to signify a new and affirmative set of meanings . . . ? Is this a reversal that retains and reiterates the abjected history of the term . . . ? If the term is now subject to a reappropriation, what are the conditions and limits of that significant reversal?"[49] Butler suggests that some terms resignify better than others. In her words,

When and how does a term like "queer" become subject to an affirmative resignification for some when a term like "nigger," despite some recent efforts at reclamation, appears capable of only reinscribing its pain? How and where does discourse reiterate injury such that the various efforts to recontextualize and resignify a given term meet their limit in this other, more brutal, and relentless form of repetition?[50]

How *does* resignification become a political possibility rather than a form of brutal repetition? In part, the "truth" of the performance is secured as the constitutive conventions that mobilize the interpellation cannot be seen as performance at all. For the chain gang to be open to meaningful resignification, the "shaming interpellation" must reveal a space where cracks and fissures in the interpellation become manifest.

Butler's politics suggest that the fears of eighteenth- and nineteenth-century reformers may be correct. The chain gang *can* unleash a whole set of significations wholly out of the control of the people who put them there. When coupled with the anxiety of the reformers Foucault and Meranze describe, Butler's work invites an important question about opportunities for "being addressed and constituted by the law, ways of being occupied and occupying the law, that disarticulate the power of punishment from the power of recognition."[51] If a "shaming interpellation" can become a site of queer pride, could the chain gang acquire new significance, if not by the disruptive actions of the men and women themselves, then *through interaction with passersby*?

In part, Butler answers this question herself. While history does not render a change in meaning impossible, the tenacity of repetitive citation over time wards against it. Although Butler insists that every successful performance "is always and only provisional," she also warns that when an "action echoes prior actions, . . . [it] *accumulates the force of authority through the repetition or citation of a prior, authoritative set of practices*."[52] The performative call of today's chain gang does not perfectly replicate the past injury. However, its discourse has a history that "*not only precedes but conditions* its contemporary usages."[53] No invocation of the chain gang mirrors the antebellum slave economy, the convict lease, or the Progressive-era road gang, but their historical force invariably shapes today's political effects.

THE SELF-EFFACING STATE

In addition to the limitations a violent history brings to shifting the meaning of chain gangs, the late modern state poses its own set of obstacles. Butler, cautious in her argument about the possibilities for resignifying abject bodies, accounts for "'ever old' . . . relations of social power" that make the "utopics of radical resignification" difficult, if not impossible.[54] However, she does not consider the extent to which an increasingly bureaucratic mode of governance limits the kind of public spaces in which resignification might occur.

In the case of today's chain gang, Wendy Brown's account of the increasing scope and power of the late modern state suggests that the transformation of eighteenth-century convict punishment is unlikely. The diffuse nature of the state Brown describes renders the face-to-face confrontation of the subjects and sovereign that marked the public execution impossible. Likewise, there are few communities conducive to staging "tiny theatres of punishment." Moreover, as convicts are chained to themselves or to each other with gun-toting sentries on post, the "public" of the chain gang is wholly restricted. As for passersby, the contemporary United States is hardly a world in which common public spaces exist for individuals to pursue political action.[55] In other words, the politics of the chain gang lacks the space for the kinds of transformation Butler hopes queers might enjoy.

Brown approaches the state to determine its suitability as an "instrument or arena of *feminist* political change," rather than analyze the politics of punishment, but her insistence on the ubiquity of the late modern state applies here, as well.[56] Moreover, Brown's work aptly illustrates the case of chain gangs, precisely because they, like other modalities of the state she interrogates, are simultaneously everywhere and nowhere at all. In some states, chain-gang policies have been introduced in the form of legislation; in others, under gubernatorial decree. They are not implemented by the U.S. Department of Justice, but by local sheriffs, state prison commissioners, and prison wardens. Increasingly tied to the marketplace and state and local governments, chain gangs claim an interest in profits, but also justify themselves by appeals to public goods in safety and welfare.

According to Brown, this omnipotent downsizing remains "the central paradox of the late modern state,"[57] whose domain of power has increased exponentially, even as it appears obsessed with its own symbolic destruction. From local campaign speeches to the State of the Union address, politicians at every level claim an interest in returning power to state and local government—and, by association, to the people. Brown elaborates, "the late modern state . . . represents itself as pervasively hamstrung, quasi-impotent, unable to come through on many of its commitments, because it is decentralizing (decentering) itself, because 'it is no longer the solution to social problems,' . . . because it has forgone much of its power in order to become 'kinder, gentler.'"[58] As it disavows its own strength and capacity to affect social policy, it becomes more and more powerful through increasingly diffuse "sites and operations of control."[59]

The chain gang corresponds with these gestures. Pleas ranging from giving convicts a chance to stay fit, allowing counties and states to develop their own prison programs, providing a public service, and instructing and educating passersby, authorize chain-gang labor today. The chain gang neither aggrandizes a centralized state nor represents a ruling bloc modeling prison policy across the country.

The Progressive state did not protect against the horrors of the private lease system. The late modern state maintains its strength as it claims to open up new loci of control. Because the "contemporary U.S. state is both modern and postmodern, highly concrete and an elaborate fiction, powerful and intangible, rigid and protean, potent and without boundaries, decentered and centralizing, without agency, yet capable of tremendous . . . effects," it is neither the "carceral city" of Foucault's nightmare, nor a space suited for the resignification of which Butler dreams.[60]

GENDER TROUBLE AND CHAIN-GANG DRAG

Importantly, as Butler and Brown suggest, the incomplete nature of performances and the ubiquity of the late modern state can foster opportunities for resistance. Often, acts of resistance further instantiate a regime of power. At other times, they assume unruly forms. Such has been the case in the resistance to chain gangs in the contemporary United States. Lawsuits, parody, debates over the suitability of women for chain gangs, and criticism of punishment by humiliation have all emerged to trouble their straightforward implementation.[61] The chain gang has by no means become a neatly sealed representation of antebellum values.

The operations in Alabama and Florida have faced challenges. In 1996, after a prison guard fatally shot Abraham Israel McCord, who was shackled to four other convicts in the typical Alabama style, the "cruel and unusual" aspects of chaining men to each other were brought into sharp relief. In what was hailed as a victory for prisoners' rights, the state of Alabama and the prisoners reached a settlement that would end the practice of chaining inmates *to each other,* but still allow prisoners to labor in single shackles, wearing chains connected at their ankles. The Florida program of Senator Crist's dreams was passed in 1995, but has been bottlenecked by the officials at the Department of Corrections, who view chain gangs as "costly and inefficient." In a strange twist of poetic justice, Florida gangs work *inside* prisons, prohibiting them from teaching the lessons of Crist's boyhood memory.[62]

In an extraordinary plea for equality, the Southern Poverty Law Center not only brought "cruel and unusual" charges on behalf of the inmates, but also objected to the exclusion of women from Alabama gangs. In response to the latter challenge, Prison Commissioner Ron Jones, the mastermind behind James's gubernatorial chain-gang promise, agreed to put "ladies in leg irons." In so doing, he lost his job when Governor James insisted that "[t]here will be no women on any chain gang in the state of Alabama today, tomorrow, or any time under my watch," and demanded Jones's resignation.[63] For the same reason that Sheriff Arpaio, unconstrained by Alabama-style chivalry, runs the risk of emasculating men and masculinizing women as he marshals the uncanny combination of hard physical labor in pink underwear, Governor James denied female chain gangs in Alabama. Watching women toil on the chain gang, day in and day out, might ultimately fracture "Southern womanhood."[64]

More bizarre, in the immediate aftermath of Alabama's chain-gang revival, Alabama witnessed a perverse inversion of the shame Governor James hoped to bring to the men on the chain gang. Attracted to the public spectacle, "dozens of people" called the Alabama Department of Corrections to inquire about buying chain-gang apparel. The interest became so great that a local businessman responded to the popularity by creating "Chain Gang Apparel, Inc."[65]

Others fear the chain gang will result in a celebration of crime. This line of reasoning confronts the new Massachusetts program. One *Boston Herald* op-ed contributor worried that chain gangs in Bristol County run a "palpable risk [of] . . . backfire by making folk heroes—veritable Cool Hand Lukes—out of prisoners."[66]

In spite of these trends, it is too soon to tell if the chain gang, like other efforts to educate the public via convict labor, will produce new ruptures, new lacunae of political opportunity. The appeal of "chain-gang apparel" evinces the most convincing inversion of vice and virtue. However, its significance should not be overstated. As Butler argues in her discussion of the potential and limitations of drag performances, "There is no necessary relation between drag and subversion, and . . . drag may well be used in the service of both the denaturalization and reidealization of hyperbolic heterosexual gender norms. At best, . . . drag is a site of a certain ambivalence."[67] While I may overstate the relationship between drag as subversion and chain-gang apparel as a resignification of the chain gang from a site of shame to a site of pride, Butler's warning is right on the mark. The simple *act* of non-criminals wearing chain-gang apparel does not denaturalize the chain gang itself.

CRUEL, UNUSUAL, AND MUNDANE

For the most part, attitudes toward punishment in Alabama are business as usual. After the Alabama settlement, the media reported that "Alabama Backtracks on Its Chain Gangs," "Chain Gangs Are Halted in Alabama," and "Alabama Agrees to Abolish Chain Gang Shackles."[68] Yet prison officials knew better. Writing to dispel this representation of Alabama corrections, Alice Ann Byrne, Assistant General Counsel of the Alabama Department of Corrections, wrote a letter to *Newsweek* to reassert their presence. She writes, "Your article stated that Alabama has discontinued the use of chain gangs. Not only is this incorrect, but just the opposite is true. As individual chains have proved to be more efficient, Alabama is increasing the number of inmates on its chain gangs by at least 10 percent."[69] The rise in Alabama chain gangs has presented a few logistical problems, but humanitarian objections have dwindled since the settlement. As this book went to press, the Alabama Department of Corrections faced a guard shortage created by its penchant for chain-gang labor. "Out of a need for more guards *in* prison," Alabama's Limestone Correctional Facility reluctantly brought its chain gangs to a "quiet end"—at least for now.[70] Florida and Arizona initiated their programs with single chains in place.[71] And Arizona continues to have both men and women on its chain gangs without legal opposition.

The shock and outrage that swept the nation in the summer of 1995 have waned considerably. In November 1999, Sheriff Arpaio put up "pup tents" to expand his program to include juveniles.[72] He is under investigation to determine whether his "detention officers crossed the line when they subdued an inmate, killed him and then allegedly tried to cover it up," but the symbolic war over implementing chain gangs appears to be over.[73] Without much resistance, a prison in Fort Madison, Iowa, introduced chain gangs in 1999.[74] In Bristol County, Massachusetts, where Sheriff Thomas Hodgson planned chain gangs for the first time in the state's history, convicts are chained together, five to a gang.[75]

In truth, there is no reason to hope or worry that the late modern state will become a place where passersby participate in a festival of punishment, or reside in "punitive cities" where "the presence of the people . . . [will] bring down shame upon the heads of the guilty; and the presence of the guilty person in the pitiful state to which his crime has reduced him must bring useful instruction to the souls of the people."[76] Even with existing resistance and a fragmented consensus on their desirability, chain gangs will not trouble gender or provide an opportunity for the people to feel "closer to those who paid the penalty."[77] I am less convinced that they might invigorate a deracinated public.

People passing along the highway in their private automobiles will not be able to look in the eye of the convict toiling along the side. More likely, they will simply see the image of a sentry standing watch over laboring convicts; "at best, passersby will be able to gauge the age and race of the men they see, characteristics that could bolster unfounded fears regarding the 'dangerous' proclivities of African-Americans and young men."[78]

The response to chain gangs should not be a reluctant endorsement of strict incarceration or another lawsuit marshaling the Eighth Amendment. The chain gang, in spite of its appeals to language of anti-incarceration, is still wrapped up in the American obsession with imprisonment. As Deborah Rhode explains in her account of the Alabama lawsuit, "Other nations offer much more humane and less expensive alternatives for nonviolent offenders. We could profit by experimenting, not by resurrecting our own failed methods of prison labor."[79] Similarly, retooling Eighth Amendment jurisprudence in order to determine, once and for all, whether chain gangs are "cruel and unusual" may further instantiate the condition of chain gangs.[80] As the Alabama settlement evidenced, judging the practice of shackling inmates *together* as "cruel and unusual," simply left room to amend the program to single-chain gangs. Worse, the juridical rendering left the impression that a simple change in technology had solved the problem of brutality.

As more states introduce chain gangs for their "added penalty of hard work and public shame for criminals, as well as a powerful deterrent for passersby," and fewer and fewer are met with significant opposition, chain gangs appear less cruel and unusual, and more mundane.[81] Their message may not be fully legible. For some passersby, chain gangs register hope in a form of moral and political progress. For others, they may incite rage, or convey an impression of Arizona or Massachusetts as a racist state. Still others will barely notice them toiling along the side of the road. With other performances that are repeated day in and day out, year after year, the chain gang may eventually become both more and less than a social construction. Like any *process of materialization that stabilizes over time to produce the effect of boundary, fixity, and surface we call matter,"* chain gangs may recoil into the woodwork of America.[82] As with rest areas, toll plazas, and exit signs, convicts dolled up in black and white stripes with "chain gang" emblazoned on their backs may become wholly unremarkable.

The constitutive nature of chain gangs does not make them weightless. Their history may not be univocal. But in the United States, they do more than evoke a horrendous, racist history of penal brutality. Over time, they normalize this history, and render chain gangs a "given" solution to rising crime and strained race relations. In this process of normalization, we risk forgetting the similarities between the stories that authorize chain gangs today and those of an emerging South. While it cheapens both eras to speak of the conditions in the same way, we would be unwise, to put it mildly, to believe the proud reforms of the years since the Civil War render the United States "safe" for chain-gang labor again.

NOTES

I would like to thank Eric Vrooman, Karen Zivi, and especially Jason Frank and John Tambornino for their thoughtful comments and suggestions on this essay.

1. Michel Foucault, *Discipline and Punish: The Birth of the Prison* (New York: Vintage, 1979), 109.

2. Editorial, Fob James, Jr., "Prison Is for Punishment," *USA Today,* August 28, 1995: 14A.

3. Mark Schone, "Alabama Bound," *Spin,* October 1995, cited in Lynn M. Burley, "History Repeats Itself in the Resurrection of Prisoner Chain Gangs: Alabama's Experience Raises Eighth Amendment Concerns," *Law and Inequality* (Winter 1997), available in LEXIS-NEXIS Academic Universe.

4. John Barry, "Return of the Florida Chain Gang: New Justice or Old Cruelty?"

Miami Herald, May 30, 1995, at 1A, 8A, in "Recent Legislation: Criminal Law—Prison Labor—Florida Reintroduces Chain Gangs.—Act of June 15, 1995, ch. 283, 1995 Fla. Sess. Law Serv. 2080, 2081 (West)," *Harvard Law Review,* February 1996, 109 Harv. L. Rev. 876, p. 879n16, available in LEXIS-NEXIS Academic Universe. Hereafter referred to as "Recent Legislation."

5. This title was bestowed on Sheriff Arpaio by a tabloid magazine after his 1992 election. See Jerry Nachtigal, "Toughest U.S. Sheriff under Fire," Associated Press, February 16, 1999. Available in LEXIS-NEXIS Requester. Importantly, the attacks on Arpaio documented in this article are not criticisms of chain gangs per se, but rather of an investigation of whether "detention officers crossed the line when they subdued an inmate, killed him and then allegedly tried to cover it up."

6. See Sheriff Joe Arpaio's home page: http://www.primenet.com/~arpaio/main.html.

7. Sue Anne Pressley, "Sheriff's Specialty: Making Jail Miserable; Arizona Lawman Draws Spotlight, Scrutiny with Tent City, Chain Gangs and Posse," *Washington Post,* August 25, 1997: A1.

8. Chain-gang programs have been proposed in varying degrees in Massachusetts, Indiana, Georgia, Wisconsin, Colorado, Kentucky, Maryland, California, Texas, Illinois, Colorado, and Kansas. See LEXIS-NEXIS Academic Universe.

9. Michael Mancini, *One Dies, Get Another: Convict Leasing in the American South, 1866–1928* (Charleston: University of South Carolina Press, 1996): 1–2.

10. David Oshinsky, *Worse than Slavery: Parchman Farm and the Ordeal of Jim Crow Justice* (New York: Free Press, 1996), 56.

11. Ibid.

12. A Southern employer explaining the benefits of convict leasing to reformer George Washington Cable in 1883. Ibid., 55.

13. Ibid., 57.

14. Ibid.

15. Alex Lichtenstein, "Good Roads and Chain Gangs in the Progressive South: The Negro Convict Is a Slave," *Journal of Southern History* 59, no. 1 (February 1993): 90. Hereafter referred to as "Good Roads." There are important exceptions to this characterization of Progressivism. For a thoughtful account of the participatory, and less state-centered, aspects of Progressivism that died during World War I, see Kevin Mattson, *Creating a Democratic Public: The Struggle for Urban Participatory Democracy during the Progressive Era* (University Park: Pennsylvania State University Press, 1998).

16. Alex Lichtenstein, *Twice the Work of Free Labor: The Political Economy of Convict Labor in the New South* (London and New York: Verso, 1996), 160. Hereafter referred to as *Twice the Work.* On this topic, see also Mancini, 20.

17. Lichtenstein, *Twice the Work,* xvi.

18. Ibid., 189–90.

19. Ibid., 190. Lichtenstein continues, "Indeed in 1931 and 1932, an almost identical but far less celebrated case of suffering, desperate escape, and fugitive life was

recounted by a black Georgian, Jesse Crawford, who with the help of the National Association for the Advancement of Colored People successfully defeated Georgia's attempts to extradite him from Michigan, whence he had fled." My emphasis.

20. Mark Peters, "Back on the Chain Gang: A Modern-Day Meltdown of Eighth Amendment Ideals," unpublished paper, provided by the Southern Poverty Law Center, Birmingham, Alabama: 10, 44f. This proposition is disputed, however. A 1925 study of chain-gang labor in North Carolina asserts that "the motive underlying the establishment and the continuance of the county chain gang is primarily economic. [But], another factor which may influence the judge in passing sentence is the general feeling that commitment to the county chain gang is more disgraceful and humiliating than a sentence to the state prison." Jesse F. Steiner and Roy M. Brown, *The North Carolina Chain Gang: A Study of County Convict Road Work* (Montclair: Patterson Smith, 1969 [1927]), 7.

21. These observations temper the conventional views that chain gangs were abolished because of the humiliation they brought to the South. Writing in the 1970s, historian Fletcher Green argued, with others, that "numerous reforms, and ultimately abolition," came about through the hard work of "those people who did see the degradation and feel shame." But the current work is more sobering. Chain gangs, like the convict lease, "eventually began to succumb to economic and social forces which redefined the place of penal labor in the South's political economy, rather than to the renewed clamor for humanitarian penal reform." As Lichtenstein, Mancini, and Oshinsky argue; chain gangs faded away because of economic incentives, and where indignation surfaced, it was racially motivated. See Mancini, 216; Lichtenstein, *Twice the Work,* 190.

22. Ibid., 47; Peters, 10.

23. Corsentino, 47.

24. While I use shame in this context to speak of a property affixed to a particular subject, Bernard Williams convincingly argues that unlike moral guilt, shame may function as a fluid, forgiving *ethic* suitable for postmetaphysical dilemmas. This debate lies beyond the scope of this essay. Whether the chain gang really extols guilt rather than shame is beside my point; the language of shame is present in the chain-gang debates, and it does assume the meaning of more conventional notions of morality. See Bernard Williams, *Shame and Necessity* (Berkeley: University of California Press, 1993). From a very different orientation, Jean Bethke Elshtain has also emerged as a defender of an ethic of shame. Borrowing liberally from Hannah Arendt, Elshtain insists that democracy needs shame in order to salvage the common world. She elaborates, "Shame—or its felt experiences as it surrounds our body's functions, passions, and desires—requires veils of civility that conceal some activities for all to see." See *Democracy on Trial* (New York: Basic Books, 1995), 55. Because Elshtain's notion of shame turns on the question of veiling and what ought to be hidden, rather than what should be exposed, I omit her from this essay, and discuss her politics at length in "Hiding for Whom? Obscurity, Dignity, and the Politics of Truth," *Theory & Event,* issue 3.3 (Fall 1999).

25. Michael Corsentino, "Back on the Chain Gang," *Prison Life* (Summer 1996): 53. My emphasis.

26. Ibid., 55.

27. Pressley, A10.

28. Alex Lichtenstein, "Chain Gang Blues," *Dissent* 43, no. 4. (Fall 1996): 10.

29. Ibid.

30. Michel Foucault, *Discipline and Punish: The Birth of the Prison* (New York: Random House, 1979 [1975]), 63.

31. Ibid.

32. Ibid., 109.

33. Ibid., 80.

34. Ibid., 111.

35. Ibid., 261.

36. Ibid.

37. Ibid.

38. Ibid., 263.

39. Ibid., 109.

40. Michael Meranze, *Laboratories of Virtue: Punishment, Revolution, and Authority in Philadelphia, 1760–1835* (Chapel Hill and London: University of North Carolina Press, 1996), 71. I thank Jason Frank for bringing this very helpful book to my attention.

41. Ibid., 87.

42. Ibid., 89.

43. Foucault, 113.

44. Judith Butler, *Bodies That Matter: On the Discursive Limits of "Sex"* (New York: Routledge, 1993), 226.

45. Corsentino, 51. Importantly for Butler, the passersby, sheriffs, and so on are also always already interpellated themselves. She explains in the case of judges citing the law: "Hence, the judge who authorizes and installs the situation he names invariably *cites* the law that he applies, and it is the power of this citation that gives the performative its binding or conferring power. And though it may appear that the binding power of his words is derived from the force of his will or from a prior authority, the opposite is more true: it is *through* the citation of the law that the figure of the judge's 'will' is produced and that the 'priority' of textual authority is established." See Butler, 225, and 224–26, more generally.

46. Butler, 226.

47. Ibid., 122. First emphasis in original; second emphasis mine.

48. Ibid., 121.

49. Ibid., 223.

50. Ibid.

51. Ibid., 122.

52. Ibid., 226–27.

53. Ibid., 227. My emphasis.

54. Ibid., 224.

55. I take this characterization of the political—and its absence—from Hannah Arendt's notion of the "common world." Regrettably, I cannot discuss this text at length here, although I do want to invoke Arendt's image of politics as a place where the kind of resignification that Butler wants to think about might actually occur. See Hannah Arendt, *The Human Condition* (Chicago: University of Chicago Press, 1958).

56. Wendy Brown, *States of Injury: Power and Freedom in Late Modernity* (Princeton: Princeton University Press), 169.

57. Ibid., 194.

58. Ibid.

59. Ibid.

60. Ibid., 174.

61. For debates in favor of and opposed to shame punishments, more broadly, see James Q. Whitman, "What's Wrong with Inflicting Shame Sanctions?" *Yale Law Journal* 107, no. 4 (January 1998); Stephen P. Garvey, "Can Shaming Punishments Educate?" *University of Chicago Law Review* (Summer 1998); Toni M. Massaro, "Shame, Culture, and American Criminal Law," *Michigan Law Review* (June 1991); Dan M. Kahan, "What Do Alternative Sanctions Mean?" *University of Chicago Law Review* (Spring 1996); Aron S. Bork, "Shame on You: An Analysis of Modern Shame Punishment as an Alternative to Incarceration," *William and Mary Law Review* 40, no. 2 (February 1999).

62. T. Christian Miller, "Senator's Chain Gang Plan Won't Be Heard," *St. Petersburg Times*, May 1, 1997: 5B.

63. Deborah L. Rhode, "Is There Sexual Parity for Prisoners?" *National Law Journal*, July 8, 1996, A19.

64. Ibid.

65. Tom Whitfield, "Chain Gang Chic May Be Fashion Fad," *Atlanta Constitution*, December 21, 1995, D 9: 3.

66. Wayne Woodlief, "Sheriff Shackles Himself to Silly Idea," *Boston Herald*, May 25, 1999, 27. Available in LEXIS-NEXIS Academic Universe.

67. Butler, 125.

68. Burley, n. 4, n. 5.

69. Tessa Gorman, "Back on the Chain Gang: Why the Eighth Amendment and the History of Slavery Proscribe the Resurgence of Chain Gangs," *California Law Review* (March 1997): 458n143.

70. "Revival of Chain Gangs Ended by Shortage of Corrections Officers," Associated Press State and Local Wire, October 25, 1999. Available in LEXIS-NEXIS Academic Universe. My emphasis.

71. The distinction between single chains and group chains has figured considerably in Eighth Amendment debates about chain gangs. In terms of physical cruelty, it may be apposite. However, for the argument about the psychological cruelty of invoking a trope of slavery, it is irrelevant. Many of the chain gangs during the early twentieth century used single chains. See photos of the Georgia road gangs in

Rockwell County and Brunswick, Georgia, shortly after the abolition of convict leasing in Georgia, in Lichtenstein, *Twice the Work*, 108b–c.

72. Suzie Steckner, "'Pup Tent' Jail Opens: Facility Designed for Juveniles Doing Time for Violent Offenses," *Arizona Republic* (November 10, 1998): B1. Available in LEXIS-NEXIS Requester.

73. Nachtigal.

74. "Prison Will Bring Back Chain Gangs," Associated Press State and Local wire, March 19, 1999. Available in LEXIS-NEXIS Requester.

75. Judy Rakowsky, "Some Officials Repelled by Chain Gang Idea; Westport Selectmen Say Shackles Convey Bad Image," *Boston Globe* (May 27, 1999): B3.

76. *Le Peletier de Saint-Fargeau*, Arch. Parl., XXVI, 3 June 1791: 322, cited in Foucault, *Discipline and Punish*, 112.

77. Foucault, *Discipline and Punish*, 63. Public opinion on chain gangs is divided. Initial polls revealed that "73 percent of Alabama residents supported the idea [of chain gangs]," but support differs considerably between blacks and whites. In Alabama, 77 percent of whites support the idea of chain gangs, and 53 percent of blacks do not. See Linnett Myers, "Alabama Puts Chain Gangs Back into Use," *Seattle Times* (May 4, 1995), cited in Peters, 23, 121f.

78. "Recent Legislation," 880–81.

79. Rhode, A19.

80. As examples of this effort, see Tessa Gorman; Lynn Burley; Yale Glazer, "Chains May Be Heavy But Not Cruel and Unusual," *Hofstra Law Review* (Summer 1996); Emily S. Sanford, "The Propriety and Constitutionality of Chain Gangs," *Georgia State University Law Review* (July 1997); Nancy A. Ozimek, "Reinstitution of the Chain Gang: A Historical and Constitutional Analysis," *Boston Public Interest Law Journal* (Spring 1997).

81. Amy Argetsinger, "Maryland County Plans to Use Chain Gangs: Inmates to Work Roads Shackled by the Legs," *Washington Post* (February 14, 1997): C1, C6.

82. Butler, 9.

13 // THE NOBILITY OF DEMOCRACY

NIETZSCHE AND DEMOCRACY

Democracy wants to create and guarantee as much independence *as possible: independence of opinion, of mode of life and of employment. To that end it needs to deprive of the right to vote both those who possess no property and the genuinely rich: for these are the two impermissible classes of men at whose abolition it must work continually, since they continually call its task into question. It must likewise prevent everything that seems to have for its objective the organization of parties. For the three great enemies of independence . . . are the indigent, the rich and the parties.—I am speaking of democracy as something yet to come.*[1]

This is one of the rare times Nietzsche, the author of these words, speaks favorably about democracy. Here Nietzsche speaks of democracy not as something that is but as something to come. This formulation fits a persistent theme in Nietzsche: that life is most vibrant when critical tension is maintained between, on the one hand, being, the herd, language as equalization, and the weight of tradition, and, on the other, becoming, genius, the unequal, and creativity. If democracy maintained *that* tension, it would make a powerful claim on Nietzsche. But he eventually decides that it never does. Nietzsche concludes that the modern institutions and sensibilities that render aristocracy impossible also render democratic mediocrity probable. So, in the main and for the most part, Nietzsche turns to the task of inspiring a new mode of nobility in a few free spirits here and there, treating modern democratic institutions and Christian sentiments (as he understands both) as impediments to that agenda. Why, then, do so many contemporary intellectuals draw selective sustenance from this untimely aristocrat in rethinking democracy? And why do so many others keep telling us—as if they were bringing news—that Nietzsche opposes our project?

The answer to the first question is that we think the ideal of democracy bequeathed to us (variously) by Rousseau, Tocqueville, Mill, Dewey, Rawls, and Habermas has to be reconfigured along several dimensions. Nietzsche, at the same time that he excoriates actually existing democracy, is distinctive in the nineteenth century in opening up the channels of reflection needed. We therefore find ourselves criticizing several aspects of Nietzscheanism even as we distill crucial themes from Nietzsche. Our relation to Nietzsche invites comparison to Marx's relation to Hegel, Rawls's relation to Kant, Arendt's relation to Heidegger, and Wolin's relation to Arendt. But what about those who reduce attempts to rework Nietzschean themes on behalf of democracy to a series of misunderstandings of him? Some, let us call them Straussians and conservative communitarians, themselves treat democracy as a second-best model of social life. They identify far more with aristocratic society than we do, even as they tell *us* how critical Nietzsche is of civic equality, social benevolence, and collective welfare. Others, let us call them Rawlsian liberals, Habermasian democrats, and Madisonian pluralists, think that the democracy is fine as it stands. The conceptions of freedom, equality, morality, and benevolence they pursue encourage them to read Nietzsche's accounts of the "unequal," "immorality," "freedom," and "hardness" reductively.

Let's suppose, for the fun of it, that this reductive reading of those who would save democracy from Nietzschean infusions is correct. That still does not address the enigma of Nietzsche. How does this protean thinker contribute distinctive elements to the nobility of democracy while he himself, after *Human All Too Human*, disparages it? Several things seem to be involved. Nietzsche, still bedazzled by an aristocratic imaginary he no longer endorses as possible, could not take his eye off the element of mediocrity and normalization in democracy long enough to explore its positive relation to possibilities he does admire. His taste was too rarefied to dip into the soup of democratic culture to feel, taste, and smell its delightful nuances. Finally, this protean thinker, prophetic in many ways, was not infinitely so. He overlooked a truth that many coming after him are better able to see: that some of the most noble elements in his vision have more chance of finding expression in a democratic culture in the late-modern age than in any other type of political culture. The paradox of Nietzsche is that the distinctive sensibility through which he opens the door to an ennobling of democracy is also one that inhibits him from walking through it.

Nietzsche makes his most promising contributions to democracy in exploring the effects that changes in pace and tempo have on the shape and weight of culture, in rethinking the ideas of inequality and difference, in plumbing how much of what goes on in moral judgment and reactive emotions proceeds below consciousness and language, in pursuing an ethic of cultivation that works upon corporeal judgments operating below the threshold of consciousness, in criticizing the image of the nation in which the democratic imagination is so often set, and in pursuing a pathos of connection across multiple lines of cultural distance and difference. Of course, each of these Nietzschean themes must be modified and reworked to fit it into a democratic problematic. But that is not such a big deal.

TEMPO AND IDENTITY

What makes it so unlikely, for Nietzsche, that a hierarchical, ordered culture of nobility could be rebuilt in the modern age? Several developments are important. But one that Nietzsche returns to often is the effect the acceleration of pace has on the experience of life. The connection between the acceleration of pace and the loss of aristocratic possibility is palpable in this statement from *Twilight of the Idols*.

> Democracy has always been the declining form of the power to organize. . . . For institutions to exist there must exist the kind of will, instinct, imperative which is anti-liberal to the point of malice: the will to tradition, to authority, to centuries long responsibility, to *solidarity* between succeeding generations backwards and forwards *ad infinitum*. . . . The entire West has lost those instincts out of which institutions grow, out of which the *future* grows; perhaps nothing goes so much against the grain of its "modern spirit." One lives for today, one lives very fast—one lives very irresponsibly: it is precisely this which one calls "freedom."[2]

Lurking within this lamentation is a theme important to things Nietzsche prizes positively. For the acceleration of pace, up to a point, enables us to come to terms with how unfinished and full of "gaps" nature is, to apply a certain experimentalism to ourselves, and even to cultivate a "spiritualization of enmity" between different types of faith. Acceleration of the pace of life, inscribed today in public media, military weaponry, Internet communications, technological development, air travel, population mobility, and cultural exchange, is indispensable to enactment of a generous, diverse democracy. So let's pull out the element of lamentation in Nietzsche's characterization. We will not forget the limits, dangers, and risks, merely set them aside for a moment.[3] Nietzsche paves the way himself in nodule #356 of *The Gay Science,* a book written before his equation between democracy and "nursemaid" community had hardened. In "How Things Will Become Ever More 'Artistic,'" Nietzsche says that in the "Old Europe" of, say, between 500 and 1000, the ponderous pace of events encouraged people to sink deeply into their roles. They readily forgot how "accidents, moods and caprice disposed of them . . ."

> But there are opposite ages, really democratic, where people give up this faith, and a certain cocky faith and opposite point of view advance more and more into the foreground. The individual becomes convinced that he can do just about everything and *can manage almost any role,* and everybody experiments with himself, improvises, makes new experiments, enjoys his experiments; and all nature ceases and becomes art.[4]

When the pace of life accelerates, nature ceases and becomes art. Inside this exaggeration is an insight. In an up-tempo world people become more alert to elements of historical contingency, accident, and power in the identities that occupy them. They can now see and feel how the habits and faiths they embody in, say, religion, gender, sexuality, ethnicity, and work could be otherwise, and they may even become more attuned to fugitive currents in themselves flowing in different directions. And this awareness opens up the possibility of work on ourselves, politically and individually. Perhaps you now work to modify one or more of your relational identities, seeking to squeeze *ressentiment* out of it. Or perhaps a new social movement arises that calls the certainty or civilizational necessity of your religious faith or sensual affiliation into question. It now takes *more work* to pretend that what you are in each domain of life conforms to a universal model commanded by a god or decreed by nature. Or, at least, you are now under more pressure to acknowledge how contestable such an assumption is, and to admit that it might be reasonable for others to actually contest it.

The acceleration of tempo and the corollary rise of social movements accentuates the experience of ourselves as "actors" who might "manage almost any role." Even nature is experienced less as a set of fixed forms and more as a set of forces marked by "gaps" (as Nietzsche puts it), mutations, and mobilities. Under these conditions what I will call the politics of becoming is now in a better position to compete with the politics of recognition. The cultural logic of recognition purports to *recall* things that are there intrinsically but have been forgotten, occluded, repressed, or oppressed, while the groan of becoming is that uncertain process by which new things reconfigure the old as they are ushered into being.

Losses and dangers accompany these developments. The biggest loss, to Nietzsche at least, is forfeiture of the ability to build a society of the old sort, the kind of society in which the old nobility could flourish.

> For what is dying out is the fundamental faith that would enable us to calculate, to promise, to anticipate the future . . . namely, the faith that man has meaning only insofar as he is a *stone in a great* edifice. What will not be built anymore henceforth, and *cannot* be built anymore is . . . a society in the old sense of that word; to build that everything is lacking. Above all the material. *All of us are no longer material for a society:* this is a truth for which the time has come.

The most ominous danger in a world in which "all of us are no longer material for a society" is that many who resent this experience of uncertainty and mobility in what they are will press insistently to return to a stonelike condition. An instinct to exercise unquestioned authority or, perhaps, to practice blind obedience will propel them in that direction. The problem is that you cannot *be* a stone unless those around you, whose relational identities help to specify what you are, make up an edifice in which you are set. So the defining conditions of democratic experimentalism can also inspire the reactive energies of democratic fundamentalism. Nietzsche associates the drive to return to society in the old sense with the anarchists and socialists of his day. Others might select different candidates for that honor today, such as the Christian Right. Whoever your favorite candidates are, listen to Nietzsche's account of what they yearn to become:

> It is a matter of indifference to me that at present the most myopic, perhaps most honest, but at any rate noisiest human type that we have today, our good socialists, believe, hope, dream, and above all shout and write almost the opposite. Even now one reads their slogan for the future, "free society." Free

society? Yes, yes! But surely you know, gentlemen, what is required for building that? Wooden iron! The well-known wooden iron. And it must not even be wooden.

"Wooden iron" is an old German expression for an unbreakable contradiction. Those who seek a democracy in which life is slow would for that reason crush the highest form of freedom to which democracy is connected. They implicitly imagine a world in which people are divided into peasants and nobles. In the interests of self-assurance and role-identification they would destroy the actor in the self and expunge artistry from the actor. They become the advocates of surveillance, regulation, and normalization in life.

Let's tarry over the positive possibilities for a moment longer. In a fast-paced democracy, where people become more like actors, it also becomes more possible to work on ourselves to modify, adjust, or sublimate destructive orientations to difference in ourselves and from ourselves entrenched in our identities, instincts, and moral codes. *Everything noble about democracy is connected somehow or other to this ability to become a little more artistic in relations with others and parts of ourselves.*

I have been appropriating Nietzsche's thought selectively, as promised. Let's turn to his new conception of nobility to see how it can be picked over. Nietzsche divides the new ideal of nobility into dissonant and interdependent parts. Those who are noble in the Nietzschean sense, first, work on themselves to overcome resentment against the lack of intrinsic meaning in life and the speed of modern life. "We ourselves wish to be our own experiments and guinea pigs,"[5] Nietzsche says. To be noble, then, is to "become what you are," even as you realize that modesty in method and objective is appropriate to becoming. But, second, the noble cultivate a grace and ease of conduct that is best accomplished through long practice and steady institutional support. To be noble is both to be one's own guinea pig and to cultivate grace of the self. The first is a condition of the second, but final harmony between these two dissonant components cannot be attained, particularly in a world of rapid pace and more than one nobility. And Nietzsche also insists that for nobility to be, there must be more than one type of nobility. It takes a plurality of noble types for any one type to be noble. And, I will add, this dissonant interdependence between the three elements of nobility—experimentalism, grace, and plurality—is precisely the condition of being appropriate to modern democratic life. Those academics and publicists who recoil from speed, ambiguity, and plurality align themselves more closely than they may realize to the nostalgia for slow, hierarchical culture. They pose barriers to democracy even as they seek to support it. For, as Nietzsche understood, democracy, speed, and plurality go together. Up to a point.

AN ETHIC OF CULTIVATION

But if the noble actor becomes a modest artist of itself, what part acts and what is acted upon? The revolution in brain research over the last few decades goes some distance toward answering that question. Experimental studies of the complex circuitry connecting the eight or so brains within each human, and of the numerous links between these brains and other somatic centers, generate a picture of thought, judgment, and feeling in which most of the action occurs below the level of consciousness and linguistic availability. "The bandwidth of consciousness is far more narrow than the bandwidth of our sensory perceptors."[6] There is a "half-second delay" between the reception of sensory material and conscious experience, during which time the wide band of sensory material is crunched down into a narrow band of perception, feeling, and judgment available for conscious inspection and decision. *Consciousness recognizes itself to be unmediated,* but in fact, as Nietzsche already insisted over and over, the slow, secondary medium of consciousness depends upon fast, complex circuits of simplification that precede and enable it. In a related image, we sometimes treat consciousness as an agent of repression that pushes painful memories and desires below the threshold of its own availability. But the logic of repression, while pertinent, is radically insufficient to the unconscious processes now under review. Without these crunching operations before and below consciousness, consciousness itself would be impossible. With it, seven-eighths of perception, thought, judgment, and feeling are organized before and below conscious surveillance. A leading brain researcher, Joseph LeDoux, applies this general point to the specific relation between conscious feeling and unconscious intensities of thought.

> . . . [C]onsciousness is neither the prerequisite to nor the same thing as the capacity to think and reason. An animal can solve lots of problems without being overtly conscious of what it is doing and why it is doing it. Obviously consciousness elevates thinking to a new level, but it isn't the same thing as

thinking. . . . Any organism that has consciousness also has feelings. However, feelings will be different in a brain that can classify the world linguistically and categorize experiences in words. . . . The difference between fear, anxiety, terror, apprehension, and the like would not be possible without language. At the same time, none of these words would have any point if it were not for the existence of an underlying emotion system that generates the brain states. . . . The brain states and bodily response are the fundamental facts of an emotion, and the conscious feelings are the frills that have added icing to the emotional cake.[7]

The difference between the rapid crunching operations before consciousness and the slow experience available to it does not correspond either to that between nature and culture or that between mind and body. LeDoux agrees that a dense network of linguistic contrasts is necessary to the refined differences of experience between, say, fear, anger, resentment, anxiety, and indignation. And a lot of culture gets "mixed into" the organization of thought-imbued intensities below consciousness. "The chamber of consciousness is small" (in Nietzsche's language), but the entire mind *is* a wide, interacting, multilayered corporeal complex with each layer containing distinctive capacities of cultural reception, intersection, and generation.

The fleeting experience of that which is prior to consciousness occurs repeatedly in everyday life. It arises when a shot rings out and you leap just before feeling a lump of terror in your stomach; in the experience of having been typing easily and efficiently at a rapid speed until you attended to *how* you were doing so and *where* the right keys were; in the experience of a violinist who escapes the clumsiness and slowness of consciousness by getting lost in the imperatives of performance; and in the performance of a point guard clearing his mind of clutter as he dribbles down the middle of the court so the ball can be delivered to a shooter at the right instant with exactly the right bounce in a movement too fast and precise to be entrusted to the slow time of consciousness. In each of these cases the sense of humor, shame, relief, or ebullience after the fact signifies both a fugitive experience of unconscious performance and how little credit or blame the conscious self can take for the event. The last three examples also suggest how much training and effort are needed to achieve a virtuoso performance.

The half-second delay. In the history of Western philosophy, Plato, Lucretius, Augustine, Spinoza, Kant, Nietzsche, Freud, and Deleuze all register this temporal difference between conscious and unconscious processes. In Augustine, it finds expression in that dense fund of memory below consciousness, in the cultural inheritance of original sin, and in a divine grace that can be received but not chosen and given but not known. Augustine's confessions work on the visceral register of subjectivity and intersubjectivity, cultivating tacit dispositions and sensibilities that prepare confessors to receive the will of God. In Kant, the supersensible register is unavailable to the crude concepts of speculative reason. It is *virtual,* in being real, efficacious, fixed, and eternal without being available to conscious articulation. But the imperatives of the "inscrutable" supersensible realm are also said to be *implicitly recognized* in the moral judgments of practical reason, *expressed spontaneously below the level of conceptual organization* in aesthetic judgment, and *subjectively presupposed* in teleological judgment. In their respective versions of a two-world metaphysic, then, Augustine and Kant invest moral and aesthetic authority in the half-second delay. The virtual, that is, the half-second delay, is figured as an authoritative, transcendental field that is not itself an object to be acted upon.

Lucretius, Nietzsche, and Deleuze, by contrast, set the half-second delay in a one-world metaphysic of immanent naturalism. They are *naturalists* in that they do not postulate a god as author of the immanent field. They are *immanent* naturalists in treating this field to be too fast and coarse to be available to clean representation or articulation without remainders. To represent this field is also to leave remainders that exert effects on the intensity of being. The difference between the two- and one-world metaphysics means that Augustine and Kant ground their moralities in commands emanating from a transcendental source, while Lucretius, Nietzsche, and Deleuze ground their ethics in a nontheistic gratitude for being that can be cultivated but not commanded into being. The latter three pursue an ethic of cultivation rather than a morality of command. Each therefore understands obligation, recognition, responsibility, and justice to be secondary effects of a generous sensibility that, they hope, is already there to some degree much of the time in most people. (Nietzsche calls this faith his "injustice.") Each then works experimentally upon those virtual implantations that exceed the reach of direct conscious control. These three thereby reject the "Western" conceit that you cannot be ethical unless you honor a two-world metaphysic and a command model of morality. The latter two agree that many citizens would not in fact be moral unless they projected the force of some commanding authority into the half-second delay. But they contend that this transcendentalization of the virtual field places too many crude and destructive cultural dispositions above the threshold of ethical review and artistic work. They cultivate arts and techniques to educate the virtual register itself.

Nietzsche's articulation of an immanent naturalism of several levels and speeds resonates with themes advanced by LeDoux.

> For to say it once more: Man, like every living being, thinks continually without knowing it: the thinking that rises to consciousness is only the smallest part of all this—the most superficial and worst—for only this conscious thinking *takes the form of words, which is to say signs of communication. . . .* The emergence of our sense impressions into our consciousness, the ability to fix them, and, as it were, exhibit them externally, increased proportionally with the need to communicate them to others by means of signs.[8]

In the nodule from which this statement is pulled Nietzsche tends to equate the difference between conscious and unconscious thinking to that between general cultural orientations and intensities unique to each individual. At other times, he sees how cultural intersubjectivity is itself mixed into the "instincts" through affectional ties, repetition, and punishment. We now encounter formulations such as "States of consciousness, beliefs of any kind, holding something to be true, for example—every psychologist knows this—are a matter of complete indifference and fifth rank compared to the value of the instincts"; and "Our true experiences are not garrulous . . ."; and "Our invisible moral qualities follow their own course—probably a whole different course; and they might give pleasure to a god with a divine microscope."[9]

Both noble arts of the self and negotiation of an ethos of agonistic respect between diverse constituencies depend upon distinctive implantations in those "concealed plantings and gardens" that precede and affect consciousness. Seldom can the effects desired be achieved simply by acts of will alone, nor is argument or deliberation *sufficient* to them. The self, rather, modifies to some extent the visceral organization of its own thinking, perception, feeling, and judgment by artful means.

To take an example, if you experience an intense but cognitively vague feeling of panic when the question of same-sex marriage comes up, another part of you may feel shame or doubt about this very response. You may suspect that your visceral response is grounded in an unstated demand to monopolize the field of normal sexuality while another part of you doubts the cultural necessity and justice of that monopolistic temper. Now you might authorize one part of yourself to work on other parts, applying gentle arts to those preconscious dispositions that fomented the anxiety. The arts available are multiple and, often enough, banal. You reenact modest variations of the engagements through which your current sensibility became installed. You might watch films in which stories of homosexual affection are highlighted; you might join gay-rights marches and educational events, monitoring the uneasiness you feel along with the now palpable awareness that the anxiety of public humiliation itself is one of the assaults gays face. You thus participate repetitively and strategically in activities that impinge upon the self at multiple levels, allowing heretofore disturbing images, gestures, rhythms, and timing to exert gentle effects upon you. You do so in order to recode modestly the register through which your sensual subjectivity is organized. As your anxiety diminishes, more generous thoughts, images, feelings, and judgments might become available, emerging as if from nowhere. Some of these may filter into your dream life, allowing work to proceed on new layers of your subjectivity. In Nietzsche's more grand language, those who "give style" to their character "survey all the strengths and weaknesses of their nature and then fit them into an artistic plan until every one of them appears as art and reason. . . . Here a large mass of second nature has been added; there a piece of original nature has been removed—both times through long practice and daily work at it."[10]

What is the relation between self-artistry and intersubjective ethics for Nietzsche? "Most of us," Nietzsche says, "are our whole lives long the fools of the way we acquired in childhood of judging our neighbors (their minds, rank, morality . . .) and of finding it necessary to pay homage to their evaluations." The transcendentalization of childhood judgments by priests, parents, politicians, political theorists, and philosophers further insulates these codes from ethical work. Ethics, as Nietzsche understands it, is intimately bound up with the work adults do on themselves to reconfigure the childhood code of morality and to reconsider the sanctity of the sources from which it was drawn. Nietzsche contends that we "have to *learn to think differently*—in order at last, perhaps, very late on, to attain even more: *to feel differently*."[11]

Nietzsche thinks that democracy encourages people to impose narrow restraints on others and their own potential selves that sanctify the gender, sensual, religious, and ethnic imperatives already installed in them. There is ample evidence to support that judgment. But there are also things that push against it. Changes in the pace and scope of public culture expose more people to more experiences of contingency in themselves today than even Nietzsche anticipated. Moreover, a larger minority of democrats cultivate more generous dispositions today than Nietzsche expected. Most important, in contemporary life, when time moves faster than heretofore, the noble mode of generosity Nietzsche admired will find expression in a democratic culture if it does so anywhere.

INEQUALITY AND DIFFERENCE

Within the contemporary American democratic left—small as it is—a debate rages over whether the politics of difference is compatible with a significant reduction of economic inequality. Those who support "the politics of difference" are said to sacrifice economic egalitarianism to hyperpluralism. In my judgment, however, the ethos of engagement needed to support a pluralization of culture is the same as that needed to generate support for reduction of economic inequality.[12] The two objectives complement and even depend upon one another. The specter of Nietzsche hovers in the background of these debates: defenders of the "politics of difference" often draw inspiration from him, while their critics assume that Nietzsche himself offers little support for cultural diversity and none for the reduction of economic inequality. Nietzsche indeed offers little support for the latter, but he does provide insights important to rethinking other dimensions of inequality with which it is institutionally associated.

One theme running through Nietzsche is that of a pathos of distance between constituencies who honor different moral sources and tastes. There is distance, marked by differences in being, punctuated by a pathos of connection and self-restraint across difference. Such a moral pluralism, however, "so far" has been attained only in an "aristocratic society" that has a "long ladder of an order of rank and differences in value between man and man, and that needs slavery in some sense or other."[13] Nietzsche's aristocratic vision issues in a moral pluralism more radical along one dimension than most democratic models of pluralism: It replaces the politics of "recognition" among diverse constituencies honoring the same basic source of morality with a pathos of distance between different castes honoring different moral sources. The hierarchy he praises is incompatible with democracy, while the pluralist element circulating through it may be more pertinent to the nobility of democracy than those national models of pluralism peddled by Tocqueville, Mill, Walzer, Habermas, and Rawls.[14]

Is it possible to pull Nietzsche's pluralism of moral types and sources out of the order of rank in which it is set? "Truth is hard," as Nietzsche asserts in the same nodule. But some considerations speak in favor of such a possibility. Nietzsche himself, as we have already seen, thinks the old nobility cannot be renewed in the modern age. And unlike most previous advocates of nobility, Nietzsche acknowledges that the gratitude for life *he* cultivates as an ethical source is grounded in a contestable reading of the fundaments of being. That's why he and Zarathustra talk about the indispensable place of "conjecture" in noble thought and why he treats "will to power" and "eternal return" as contestable "suppositions" to guide his thinking rather than as solid foundations that establish its certainty. If and as the questionable standing of our respective faiths became reciprocally affirmed in this way, the Nietzschean plurality of moral sources could be released from the fixed hierarchy in which it has "so far" been set. What is superior in the eyes of one constituency would no longer be treated as the transcendental source to which all others must accede. You would surpass both secular pluralism, where people leave their fundamental faiths in the private realm while hoping to resolve their differences by procedural means alone, and monotheistic nationalism, which professes the same general faith, such as Christianity or the "Judeo-Christian tradition." A huge step would be taken toward translating the vertical "pathos of distance" into a horizontal pathos of pluralism in which a variety of constituencies practice (what I call) agonistic respect toward one another. Each would bring its faith into the public realm where pertinent but would also acknowledge without rancor how contestable it is in the eyes of others. A positive ethos of engagement could now begin to grow out of reciprocal modesty. By turning one part of Nietzsche's thought against another we begin to sketch the distinctive ethos appropriate to pluralist democracy in the contemporary age.

A chronicler of my misuses of Nietzsche quotes the following statement to show that Nietzsche is inegalitarian in a way that makes him hopelessly at odds with democratic sentiments.

"Equality for equals, inequality for unequals"—*that* would be the true voice of justice: and what follows from it, "Never make equal what is unequal."[15]

How, though, does Nietzsche use the words "equal" and "unequal"? Is the philosopher of polytheism as infinitely preferable to monotheism likely to reduce the word "unequal" *entirely* to the idea of "inequality" within a single order of rank?

Consider the difference between Kant and Nietzsche on the judgment of beauty. Kant contends that the faculties of the "ordinary man" converge upon the same (equal) and unconditional judgment, while the self in which this "spontaneous" accord occurs lacks the capacity to translate that correct judgment into conceptual language. Kant treats aesthetic judgment, then, as a species of *general recognition*. Our judgments of beauty are *equal* because they spontaneously express the universal authority of the supersensible. Nietzsche contests such a reading.

> Nothing is so conditional, let us say *circumscribed,* as our feeling for the beautiful. Anyone who tried to divorce it from man's pleasure in man would at once find the ground give way beneath him. The "beautiful in itself" is not even a concept, merely a phrase. . . . Man has *humanized* the world: that is all. But there is nothing, absolutely nothing, to guarantee to us that *man* constitutes the model for the beautiful. Who knows what figure he would cut in the eyes of a higher arbiter of taste? [16]

When you place this statement about the conditional judgment of beauty into the context of other discussions in *Twilight of the Idols* about the unequal, the sensual character of philosophy, the relation between Greek philosophy and the philosopher's attraction to adolescent boys, and Nietzsche's own appreciation of Emerson, it may be plausible to conjecture that this devotee of Greek philosophy is signaling how adolescent boys are even more beautiful to him than, say, well-formed women.[17] The difference between Nietzsche's conditional, heterodox experience of beauty and those conditional, orthodox judgments misrecognized as unconditional by the community at large constitutes a power relation in which inadvertent injustice is enacted. For it is implicitly assumed that to treat all men equally is to treat them *as if* all were governed by a heterosexual model of feminine beauty. In the name of equality, considerable suffering is imposed upon one constituency. To the extent that those moved by heterodox desires are subjected by the community to the Kantian model, they are caught in a bind: they must either nullify themselves and pretend to participate in the orthodox model or confess to a difference that renders them perverse in the eyes of the community. And the "community"? Its reading of Nietzsche on the equal and the unequal shows how deaf it can be to its own injustice. For it is unjust to "make equal what is unequal. . . ." That is, it is unjust to treat difference as if it were the same.

A prephilosophical motivation is built into the dominant philosophical meanings bestowed upon the words "equal" and "unequal," then. It is the immoral desire to transcendentalize the conditional experience of one segment of the populace. To expose these motivations is to intimate the conditional character of beauty, to uncover an element of immorality in universal morality, and to inspire receptive readers *to engage the unequal as an field of differences not arrayed under a single standard.* The "unequal" now slips out of its transcendental straitjacket. And moral pluralism now begins to glow more brightly.

Above all else, Nietzsche contests the idea—inscribed in the texts and subtexts of many Christian and secular philosophies—that there is a single model of intrinsic identity against which good and bad copies are to be measured. The "spiritualization of enmity" between different sensualities begins when a large number of partisans mutually acknowledge the comparative contestability of their respective claims to embody the best copy of an intrinsic model. It acquires nobility when they become "spiritual," "prudent," "forbearing," and "thoughtful" in their relations.[18] Sensuality is a protean force before it is organized in one particular way or another. And "radical hostility, mortal hostility towards sensuality is always a thought-provoking symptom: it justifies making certain conjectures as to the general condition of one who is excessive in this respect."[19] Nietzsche's conjecture is that such excessiveness reflects the inability to bear life unless what you are or aspire to be is treated as the true copy of an intrinsic identity to which everyone else must conform. This theme is already put to work in the first section of *Twilight of the Idols,* when Nietzsche prepares later discussions of the unequal, the conditional nature of beauty, Greek philosophy, Greek youths, Emerson, justice, and the injustice of treating difference as if it were really or properly the same. It assumes the form of a question: "Are you genuine? Or only an actor? A representative? Or that which is represented? Finally, you are no more than an imitation of an actor. . . ."[20]

DEMOCRATIC NOBILITY

There is a profound difference between those who anchor democracy in the logic of recognition, variously configured, and those who situate it in an active tension between the politics of recognition and the politics of becoming. Kant and Nietzsche are the pivotal philosophers here, even though neither was himself committed to democracy. To *re-cognize* something, in the highest sense, is neither to acquire new knowledge of it nor to affirm it as an artifice worthy of endorsement: It is to experience as apodictic and authoritative something that has somehow been met before. That's why the logic of recognition is most at home with itself when it is set in a two-world metaphysic. We have already seen how the logic of recognition functions in Kantian aesthetics. Listen to its place in Kantian morality:

> For whatever needs to draw the evidence of its reality from experience must depend for the ground of its possibility on principles of experience . . . ; however, pure yet practical reason cannot be held to be dependent in this way. *Moreover, the moral law is given, as an apodictically certain fact, as it were, of pure reason, a fact of which we are a priori conscious.* . . . Thus the objective reality of the moral law can be proved through no deduction, through no exertion of the theoretical, speculative, or empirically supported reason. . . . Nevertheless it is firmly established of itself.[21]

To pull the slender thread of apodictic recognition out of his system would translate Kantian morality into a contestable doctrine unable to secure its own transcendental arguments. But what gives authority to apodictic recognition? Nothing, except institutional faith in recognition itself. Hegel, appreciating this embarrassment, folds a historical dimension into the promise of recognition. Recognition *is* conflictual and alienated in its early expressions, but its dialectical advance is informed by the promise of future redemption implicit in it. Nietzsche makes a more fundamental break. Refusing to kneel before such an inscrutable authority, he contests every philosophy at that distinctive point where it says "Everybody (who is ordinary, normal, rational, sane, civilized, or religious) recognizes this to be the essence of morality (or thinking, judgment, knowledge, consciousness, beauty, or identity)." Nietzsche construes recognition to be a secondary phenomenon lodged in a consciousness unalert to its dependence on the crunch of culture during the half-second delay. Gilles Deleuze continues Nietzsche's challenge to the metaphysical tradition of recognition when he says,

> Nietzsche's distinction between the creation of new values and the recognition of established values should not be understood in a historically relative manner. . . . The new, with its power of beginning and beginning again, remains forever new, just as the established was always established from the outset. . . . For the new—in other words difference—calls forth forces in

thought which are not the forces of recognition, today or tomorrow, but the powers of a completely other model, from an unrecognized and unrecognizable *terra incognita*.[22]

Nietzsche and Deleuze challenge the metaphysic of apodictic recognition with a countermetaphysic of immanent naturalism in a multilayered world, as they conjecture it, that thrives without a supersensible realm or divine order. A metaphysic of immanent naturalism builds the expectation of new, surprising events into its fundamental interpretation of the world. Its practitioners *expect* to be enchanted, frightened, or repulsed from time to time, as new events and identities are propelled into being. As mutations and experiments introduce new viruses and species into being. As new social movements, emerging out of intensive energies of difference and injury, propel novel constituencies into being to jostle established patterns of recognition, common sense, and justice. As minor cultural changes—here in deforestation, there in increased use of the automobile—accumulate slowly to produce rapid, massive shifts in the world's climate. As the collapse of an old empire transforms the previous structure of global relations. Or as a new religion bursts into the world to contest the array of faiths already there. According to immanent naturalism, the new, for better and for worse, periodically *becomes* out of disparate and virtual forces too separate, fast, and small to be captured entirely by our slow, derivative capacities of recognition or our coarse, ponderous categories of explanation.

The *politics of becoming* is that paradoxical movement by which new cultural identities are formed out of obscure or devalued energies and differences. A movement in the politics of becoming might seek a new line of flight to escape constraints that have become intolerable. Sometimes, as in the examples of Judaism, Christianity, and secularism in the past, and gay rights, the right to die, and atheism in the precarious present, the movement eventually places a new member on the legitimate register of civilizational identities. When that happens the new entry is apt both to exceed the purposes that propelled it into being and to alter those practices of identity, justice, and civilizational normality previously in place. Recognition of it is *a belated appreciation offered by those who have themselves been changed by its emergence as they come to feel more aspects of their own identities open to interrogation, contestation, or modification.* In a world of being and becoming, the most noble questions of ethics are not whether to give or withhold recognition of something already there "implicitly"; they are how to negotiate relations with newly emerging rights and constituencies in ways that enable a plurality of nobilities to be, and how to manage or contain those products of the politics of becoming that threaten to erase plurality and generosity.

Over the last twelve years or so, as I now see it, I have sought to challenge the hegemony of the politics of recognition in democratic theory by articulating a more actively ambivalent vision of democracy from the perspective of immanent naturalism. The goal is not to copy Christianity and secularism by seeking to make immanent naturalism the underlying philosophy of everyone. It is to contest the drive of each of these contenders for hegemony by placing another candidate into more active competition with them. It is to pursue a deep plurality of democratic life. The themes of an ethic of cultivation, the politics of becoming, agonistic respect, critical responsiveness, studied indifference, rhizomatic pluralism, and an ethos of engagement through which this effort has been articulated speak to a fast-paced world in which care for life already has an existential foothold and no transcendental source of morality is susceptible to universal recognition. The idea is to negotiate an intracultural ethos capable of sustaining democratic governance between a diversity of partisans honoring different moral sources. These themes express appreciation of the indispensability and fragility of a generous ethos to democratic politics. Each idea, in turn, draws part of its inspiration from a theme in Nietzsche. His presentations of a pathos of distance, nobility as multiple nobilities, the unequal, the immorality of morality, ethics as artistry, and the spiritualization of enmity provide fertile ground for plagiarization and transfiguration by democrats who respect the politics of becoming. It can be left to the academic police to decide whether these transfigurations depart too radically from the figure of Nietzsche. It remains an open question whether they can stand on their own as a network of ideas and practices appropriate to democratic culture.

But the question still might be pressed: What stance can democrats who cultivate critical responsiveness to the politics of becoming adopt toward devotees of the logic of recognition also committed to democracy? One temptation of the devotees of the politics of recognition, it seems, is either to absorb us into the matrix of recognition or, failing that, to excoriate us as "postmodernists," "nihilists," "hyperpluralists," or "half-baked neo-Nietzscheans." But that ice has begun to break. Some noble defenders of the logic of recognition now acknowledge the fundamental contestability of the faith they endorse.[23] And most democrats indebted to Nietzsche already affirm the comparative contestability of the themes they honor. Included in immanent naturalism itself is the conviction that neither we nor our adversaries can articulate the fundamental character of the world in a way that must become authoritative to all reasonable parties. And unlike most secularists, we welcome a plurality of fundamental perspectives into the public realm. You democratize deep plurality by negotiating a generous ethos of engagement among those who bring pertinent aspects of their private faiths into the public realm.

Zarathustra summons an ideal of agonistic reciprocity between interdependent partisans of differential power who find themselves respectively unable to pour their final vocabularies into the sink of certainty: "For many who are noble are needed, and noble men of many kinds, that there may be a nobility. Or as I said once in a parable: 'Precisely this is godlike, that there are gods, but no God.'"[24] In a democratic ethos, interdependent partisans, contending on behalf of different gods, bestow agonistic respect upon each other when they are noble enough to acknowledge that none is in a position to vindicate finally its own experience of recognition, divine faith, or immanent naturalism. Such an ethos is hard to negotiate and difficult to maintain. But democracy itself was woefully unrealistic at its inception. And even though it is not yet well represented in democratic theory, such an ethos already exerts real force in actually existing democracies. It turns out, upon inspection, that the basic question is not whether such a possibility is realistic but whether the pace of contemporary life makes it an imperative to pursue for democrats.

A democratic regime embodying a noble ethos of engagement does not escape restraint and limits. It sometimes becomes necessary, for instance, to constrain the reach of constituencies who insist that civilization cannot survive unless the particular identities they embody in religion, sensuality, reason, ethnicity, or nationality provide the authoritative model of being to which everyone must conform.

The nobility of democracy resides in a generous ethos of engagement between interdependent partisans. The nobility of political theory resides in the enactment of democratic nobility between diverse practitioners.

NOTES

1. Friedrich Nietzsche, *Human All Too Human*, trans. R. J. Hollingdale (Cambridge: Cambridge University Press, 1986), 383.

2. *Twilight of the Idols,* trans. R. J. Hollingdale (New York: Penguin Books, 1969), 93–94.

3. In a very thoughtful piece, Sheldon Wolin explores the way multiple "zones of temporality" in modern life render democracy, as he understands it, more difficult and precarious. See "What Time Is It?" *Theory & Event* 1, no. 1 (January 1997): 1; http://muse.jhu.edu/journals/theory_&_event/v001/1.1. I want to suggest that Nietzsche is closer to the mark on this question: a slow pace of life is more compatible with traditionalism, hierarchy, and aristocratism than with democracy. And Wolin's concern about speed draws him closer to Nietzsche's aristocratism than he may wish to be. That is not to say, however, that there are no risks and limits here. When speed accelerates too much the possibilities for deliberation and agreement are squeezed out. But speed, up to a point, is indispensable to the multilayered model of democracy supported here.

4. Nietzsche, *The Gay Science,* trans. Walter Kaufmann (New York: Vintage Books, 1974), 303. The quotations to follow all come from #356, 302–4.

5. Ibid., #319, 253.

6. Tor Norretranders, *The User Illusion: Cutting Consciousness Down to Size,* trans. Jonathan Sydenham (New York: Viking Press, 1998), 126.

7. Joseph LeDoux, *The Emotional Brain* (New York: Simon and Schuster, 1996), 302. For studies that reinforce this picture, see Antonio Damasio, *Descartes' Error: Emotion, Reason, and the Human Brain* (New York: Avon Books, 1994), and the Norretrander text cited above. An excellent essay exploring the implications of such research for ethics and politics is "The Autonomy of Affect," by Brian Massumi, in Paul Patton, ed., *Deleuze: A Critical Reader* (Oxford: Blackwell, 1996), 217–40. I explore some of these connections in chaps. 1 and 7 of *Refashioning the Secular* (Minneapolis: University of Minnesota Press, 1999).

8. Nietzsche, *The Gay Science,* #354, 298–99.

9. These formulations are found, respectively, in *The AntiChrist,* trans. R. J. Hollingdale (New York: Vintage Press, 1968), 151; *Twilight of the Idols,* 82, and *The Gay Science,* 274.

10. Nietzsche, *The Gay Science,* #290, 232. The relation between self-artistry and responsiveness to difference is not developed in this nodule. In this note, Nietzsche announces that "whether this taste was good or bad is less important than one might suppose." But what is particularly important in this note is cultivation of a self that overcomes the drive to revenge against the world for not providing a natural or transcendental *model* of what every self must be. It is ethically important to attain satisfaction with yourself without imposing your identity as the standard to which everyone must conform. "Whoever is dissatisfied with himself is continually ready for revenge, and we others will be his victims" (233).

11. Nietzsche, *Daybreak: Thoughts on the Prejudices of Morality,* trans. R. J. Hollingdale (Cambridge: Cambridge University Press, 1982), #103, 60.

12. For a symposium dealing with these issues, see "Left Conservatism," *Theory & Event* (Spring and Summer Issues, 1998) http://muse.jhu.edu/journals/theory_

&_event/voow/2.2. I argue that the politics of becoming and the reduction of economic inequality depend upon each other in *The Ethos of Pluralization* (Minneapolis: University of Minnesota Press, 1995), chap. 3.

13. *Beyond Good and Evil*, trans. Walter Kaufmann (New York: Vintage Books, 1966), #257, 201.

14. I discuss Tocqueville and Walzer on this question in *The Ethos of Pluralization*, chaps. 5 and 6, and Mill, Habermas, and Rawls in *Refashioning the Secular* (Minneapolis: University of Minnesota Press, 1999), chaps. 1, 2, and 3.

15. See Mark Redhead, "Nietzsche and Liberal Democracy: A Relationship of Antagonistic Indebtedness?" and my reply, *Journal of Political Philosophy* (June 1997): 183–202.

16. *Twilight of the Idols*, #19, 78.

17. I am not saying that Nietzsche was "homosexual." For a fascinating, comparative reading of the complexity of desire in Nietzsche and Oscar Wilde, see Eve Kosofsky Sedgwick, *Epistemology of the Closet* (Berkeley: University of California Press, 1990), 132–81.

18. *Twilight of the Idols*, "Morality as Anti-Nature," #3, 43. My sentence actually grafts what Nietzsche says about the spiritualization of sensuality in that paragraph to what he says about the spiritualization of enmity in the next. I find the two closely enough connected to justify this stitching. But if others don't, I am happy to defend the combination in my own voice.

19. Ibid., #2, 43.

20. Ibid., "Maxims and Arrows," #38, 26–27.

21. Kant, *The Critique of Practical Reason*, trans. Lewis White Beck (New York: Macmillan, 1993), 48–49.

22. Gilles Deleuze, *Difference and Repetition*, trans. Paul Patton (New York: Columbia University Press, 1994), 136.

23. There are welcome signs of this movement by Charles Taylor in Amy Guttmann, ed., *Multiculturalism and "The Politics of Recognition": An Essay by Charles Taylor with Commentaries* (Princeton: Princeton University Press, 1993), 36. I engage Taylor on this question in "Pluralism, Multiculturalism and the Nation-State: Rethinking the Connections," *Journal of Political Ideologies* (February 1996): 53–73. In *Strange Multiplicity: Constitutionalism in an Age of Diversity* (Cambridge: Cambridge University Press, 1995), James Tully presses the logic of recognition so far, in the interests of opening up space for aboriginal peoples, that it slides close to the politics of becoming.

24. Nietzsche, *Thus Spoke Zarathustra*, trans. Walter Kaufmann (New York: Penguin, 1978), 203.

CONTRIBUTORS

MARK B. BROWN is a Ph.D. candidate in the Department of Political Science at Rutgers University. His dissertation explores different modes of relating science and politics in light of their implications for democratic theory and environmental policymaking. His work has appeared in *Organization and Environment* and *Public Productivity and Management Review.*

WENDY BROWN is professor of political science and women's studies at the University of California, Berkeley. She is the author, most recently, of *States of Injury: Power and Freedom in Late Modernity.* Her *Liberalism Out of History* is forthcoming with Princeton University Press.

WILLIAM E. CONNOLLY is professor of political science at The Johns Hopkins University. His recent books include *Why I Am Not a Secularist* (Minnesota, 1999), *The Ethos of Pluralization* (Minnesota, 1995), *Political Theory and Modernity,* and *Identity\Difference: Democratic Negotiations of Political Paradox.* *The Terms of Political Discourse* recently won the Lippincott Award for "a work of exceptional quality that is still considered significant after a time span of at least fifteen years."

THOMAS L. DUMM is professor of political science at Amherst College and coeditor of *Theory & Event.* Among his recent books are *A Politics of the Ordinary, Michel Foucault and the Politics of Freedom,* and *united states.*

J. PETER EUBEN is professor of politics at the University of California, Santa Cruz, and review editor at *Political Theory.* He is the author of *The Tragedy of Political Theory: The Road Not Taken; Corrupting Youth: Political Education, Democratic Culture, and Political Theory;* and *Platonic Noise.*

RUSSELL ARBEN FOX is a Ph.D. candidate at the Catholic University of America. His dissertation examines Romantic and religious themes of community in the political philosophy of J. G. Herder and Charles Taylor. He has written articles for *Polity* and the *Review of Politics*.

JASON A. FRANK is a Ph.D. candidate in the Department of Political Science at The Johns Hopkins University. His dissertation is titled "The Government of Words: Institution and Representation in Postrevolutionary America."

SAMANTHA FROST received a Ph.D. from the Department of Political Science at Rutgers University and is visiting assistant professor of women's studies at the University of California, Santa Cruz. Her dissertation is titled "Acting to Order: Thinking-Bodies and Civil Subjection in Hobbes's Theory of Politics."

SHANE GUNSTER is a Ph.D. candidate in political science at York University. His dissertation, "Between Frankfurt and Birmingham: Commodification, Culture, Hegemony," draws upon critical theory and cultural studies to explore how the fusion of the commodity form with culture binds individuals to the structures of liberal capitalism.

JILL LOCKE is assistant professor of political theory and public law at Gustavus Adolphus College in St. Peter, Minnesota. She received a 1999–2000 Charlotte W. Newcombe Dissertation Fellowship for her dissertation, "Virtue and the Politics of Shame." Her work has appeared in *Theory & Event*.

DAVID PAUL MANDELL received his Ph.D. from the Department of Political Science at the University of Chicago and is now visiting assistant professor of political science at Reed College. His dissertation, "The Pluralist Imagination: Pragmatism, Pluralism, and Political Order," argues that the neglected language of "pragmatist pluralism" offers much-needed resources to challenge the inherited binaries governing contemporary political thought.

JOHN TAMBORNINO received his Ph.D. from the Department of Political Science at The Johns Hopkins University, where he was a James Hart Fellow and is now Visiting Lecturer. His dissertation is titled "The Corporeal Turn: Affect, Embodiment and Necessity in Political Theory," and his essays have appeared in *Polity* and the *Journal of Political Philosophy*.

LON TROYER is a Ph.D. candidate in the Department of Political Science at the University of California, Berkeley. His dissertation is titled "The Location of Terrorism: State Violence, American Politics, and the Docile Citizen."

SHELDON S. WOLIN has been professor at Princeton University and at the University of California, Berkeley. He was founding editor of *Democracy*, and among his many publications are *The Presence of the Past: Essays on the State and the Constitution* and the classic *Politics and Vision: Continuity and Innovation in Western Political Thought*.

LINDA M. G. ZERILLI is professor of political science at Northwestern University. Her publications include *Signifying Woman: Culture and Chaos in Rousseau, Burke, and Mill*.

INDEX

DATE DUE

			Printed in USA

HIGHSMITH #45230